GROWN UP ALL WRONG

Grown Up All
WRONG

Great Rock and Pop Artists from Vaudeville to Techno

ROBERT CHRISTGAU

Harvard University Press
Cambridge, Massachusetts
London, England
1998

Pages 477–478 constitute an extension of the copyright page.

Library of Congress Cataloging-in-Publication Data

Christgau, Robert.
    Grown up all wrong : 75 great rock and pop artists from vaudeville
to techno / Robert Christgau.
       p.   cm.
    Includes index.
    ISBN 0-674-44318-7 (cloth : alk. paper)
    1. Rock music—History and criticism.
    2. Rock musicians.
    3. Rock groups.
    I. Title.
ML3534.C49   1998
781.66′092′2—DC21   98-25779

In loving memory of my grandfather
Thomas Vincent Snyder, 1888–1971,
the first person I knew to own a forty-five-rpm record player
and to my parents,
George and Virginia Christgau,
for "Swinging on a Star," *South Pacific,*
and "One Meat Ball"

ACKNOWLEDGMENTS

A glance at the index, where his citations greatly outnumber any other critic's, is ample evidence of how much my old friend and colleague Greil Marcus remained in my thoughts as our ideas, tastes, and methods diverged. This book came to be because Greil suggested I consult Lindsay Waters at Harvard University Press about publishing a collection of my work. Lindsay has been enthusiastic, thought-provoking, and conceptually rigorous from the start. I am especially grateful that he understood how constricting it would be to stick to the canon, however that might be defined.

At *The Village Voice* and elsewhere, I've owed much to my editors Doug Simmons, M. Mark, Ann Powers, Eric Weisbard, Kit Rachlis, Greil Marcus, Joe Koenenn, Jim Miller, Lisa Kennedy, Craig Marks, Evelyn McDonnell, Richard Goldstein, Sue Cummings, Jonathan Cott, Vince Aletti, and Joy Press. But my warmest thanks are reserved for the endlessly supportive Joe Levy, who helped conceive the Rock & Roll & column where most of the nineties material first appeared, and who out of simple friendship offered invaluable advice on the shape and specifics of this book.

I do love to jaw about music, and so the friends, colleagues, and publicists who have contributed to this work are as innumerable as ever. But several fellow professionals, usually writers whose stock in trade is the ideas and information they shared with me, have proffered extraordinary aid: John Graziano (Emmett Miller), Lenny Kaye (New York Dolls), Robert Palmer (Chuck Berry, Master Musicians of Jajouka), Brian Cullman (Khaled, Lucinda Williams), Tom Gogola (Jimi Hendrix), Greil Marcus (Liliput), Leyla Turkkan (KRS-One), Rob Sheffield and Ira Robbins (Pavement), Gary Giddins (Nat King Cole, Emmett Miller), and Will

Friedwald (Nat King Cole). I presume that most of these citations are recent because I've forgotten others, and I apologize to anyone I've overlooked. Although he's cited in the text, I should also mention John Piccarella, whose collaboration on the John Lennon essay was strictly fifty-fifty.

Carola Dibbell is also cited in the text—when my Marshall Crenshaw piece seemed scant, I thought it only fair to crib chunks of hers, since she's the main reason I wrote it, and listened so hard to Crenshaw in the first place. Carola Dibbell is my wife and partner. She is also sometimes my ears. And without her sense of language enriching my life, I would not be the writer I am. Please don't blame her—the stuff you don't like is my fault. But if I ever make you smile, she was probably in there pushing.

Nina Dibbell Christgau is my daughter. She loves music as much as I do, and has been known to hear it better. As I continue to engage with rock and roll, which is fundamentally an art of becoming, she has been and will remain an example and an inspiration.

CONTENTS

GROWN UP ALL WRONG

Introduction: My Favorite Waste of Time

In 1971, while making the rent as a professor of rock and roll at the newborn California Institute of the Arts and pursuing my muse as a scantily paid *Village Voice* music columnist, I was treated to a backhanded compliment by a slightly younger Cal Arts colleague, a Marcuse translator just out of grad school. In the course of a disagreement about a movie, or film, she declared, "You're really very intelligent." Then she added: "Why do you waste your time on rock?" I'm just lucky that, refined as she was, she didn't continue, "Grow up, willya?" After all, I was pushing twenty-nine. But I already had grown up. The trouble was, as the Rolling Stones had put it before I or any of them was twenty-five—in a different context, but recontextualization is a way of life in this music—that I'd grown up wrong. I'd been easy to fool when I was in school. But I'd grown up all wrong.

That June an experimental CUNY program brought me back to New York, where in 1972 *Newsday* proffered a gig and in 1974 the *Voice* hired me as music editor. Except as a lecturer or adjunct, I was out of academia and glad enough of it. But though my colleague soon changed careers too, applying her intellect to first cocounseling and then real estate, her interrogation obviously stuck with me. So I admit I find it comforting that the idea of a professor of rock and roll is no longer an affront to the academic weal. Inexorably, academia moves to contain what it cannot ignore, and while its mandarin cultural studies sects and middlebrow popular culture programs still anger conservatives, both exist because the early rock critics were onto something.

For starters, we were one vanguard in what now seems to be called the culture wars—prepostmodern multieverythingists. Inspired by Andy Warhol, Ellen Willis, baseball, a literalistic notion of democracy, and above all rock itself, I worked from a "theory" of pop that was more an elaborate hunch. In essence it asserted the aesthetic and political equality of not just "folk," not just "popular," but crass and abject "mass" culture. Naive, defensive, and/or self-evident though the point may now seem, it felt essential in a reflexively hierarchical cultural environment to argue that rock and roll was "art" every bit as worthy as the English lit of my baccalaureate and the jazz, classical, and folk to which it was invidiously compared. In a left environment where Frankfurt School elitism informed the Freudian Marxism of the guru Marcuse himself, it seemed equally important to insist (as he vaguely and belatedly allowed) that this particular form of "mass culture" liberated far more than it oppressed—and that its most uneducated consumers understood things that Marcuse didn't.

But beyond these ideals, I had another reason for wasting my time: I was a writer, and rock was my subject. My theory of pop extended to myself, wordslinger for hire in a world half bohemia and half media—Grub Street, twentieth-century style. Like the musicians whose juice and oomph and smarts and value I proclaimed, I put a lot into what I did. While celebrating a moment highbrows assumed was disposable, I was also craftsman enough to intend that what I wrote would repay rereading down the line. Like literature, right—but also like the collected journalism of Pauline Kael, Tom Wolfe, Dwight Macdonald, Murray Kempton, Gay Talese, Jimmy Breslin, and A. J. Liebling, who included in his boxing book *The Sweet Science* an account of the 1955 Moore-Marciano fight so rich it convinced me that the fictional imagination I didn't have enjoyed no decisive aesthetic advantage over the reportorial eye I might yet develop. About criticism itself I was more ambivalent. Criticism was what you learned to do in graduate school, whose blandishments I had forsworn primarily because the evidence suggested they were hell on good writing. But my sense of pop-political mission eased my misgivings, and so did my love of language. Like most of my contemporaries, I'd learned to write by reading everything from the canon to the cereal box. But I was well aware that rock and roll had beefed up my propensity for the irreverent, the demotic, the neologistic, the slangy, the dirty, and the downright screwball, and I thought my literary quality the better for it.

In journalism as in rock and roll, the idea was to add aesthetic tension and social dimension to one's piddling self-expression by turning a received, commercially delimited form to one's own creative ends. But though I began Grub Streeting at Talese and Macdonald's *Esquire* and got my mainstream break from the eventual home of Kempton and Breslin, I didn't have what it took for the slicks or the dailies—in part because my gifts lay elsewhere, but in part because traditional havens of writerly journalism had been supplemented if not superceded. With all respect to such predecessors as Pauline Kael and her nemesis Andrew Sarris (as well as Gilbert Seldes, who championed "the seven lively arts" in the twenties), rock critics weren't just movie reviewers who processed records instead. In addition to making the world safe for the devotional fellatio and semiconsensual s&m popular music "coverage" turned into, we were also exceptionally well-situated to penetrate, exploit, and (if we kept our wits about us) rise above the hypocrisies and illusions of the so-called alternative press. That for all my pop bias the alternative press was where I felt at home is the paradox at the heart of all my criticism only if it's a paradox at all.

I mean, to me my situation seemed sensible enough. From early on I saw pop as class warfare in which paying customers thumbed their noses at cultural panjandrums and impelled entrepreneurs to give them what they wanted. I believed the mass bohemia of the sixties brought to fruition a selective consumption in which the young, freed of their parents' depression-instilled caution by an expanding economy, bought only what they needed and/or enjoyed, untempted by the twin evils of conspicuous consumption and delayed gratification. Admittedly, it was a little harder to figure out how to proceed from there to good politics, by which I meant and mean left politics—politics that attacked privilege. I told myself that because it was antihierarchical, pop was not merely antiauthoritarian—a reasonable notion that turns out to be true only insofar as fans maintain some critical distance from stars—but also democratic, communitarian, and even (propelled by that big beat) militant. These are progressively more dubious propositions. I didn't figure that the economy would stop expanding quite so soon, or that people's needs and, if they're lucky, pleasures burgeon as they get older; nor did I yet know enough about bohemia to understand how damnably idiosyncratic its politics can be. But I saw nothing inappropriate in examining the pop music of a left-identified mass/youth counterculture for a newspaper that predicated its exorbitant profitability on the imbrications of bohemians, students, artists, information professionals, and discretionary income.

Not that there was any lack of what my Marxist friends called contradictions. I just wasn't panicked by them. I've spent my life making fun of how nervously and self-righteously my chosen community resists the axiom that both pop music and newspapers are entangled with capitalism, and anybody who claims that that means I like capitalism is cruising for a bruising. A fireman's son who got off the status ladder willingly if abruptly after earning a scholarship-supported Ivy League diploma, I was convinced of the reality of class, and far readier to fight the rich than my genteelly aspiring, politically centrist parents. Taught to respect my own intelligence at home and love my neighbor in church, I hit the sixties full of beans and drew my own conclusions. Among these was a gut opposition to the Vietnam War as well as the systemic racism that was its domestic doppelganger. But in my disdain for a cultural privilege I have always seen as European, I was also a fervent American. And any examination of this thing I loved called rock and roll made clear that both capitalism and America had played positive roles in its making. For me, that was the baseline. Capitalism and America did these things that were bad and these other things that were good, and rather than assuming that any residue of business practice or know-nothing chauvinism invalidated a cultural product by definition, you tried to knock down the bad and shore up the good. It was to annoy left-wing cheeseheads who felt otherwise that I entitled my signature venue the Consumer Guide.

Nevertheless, my political bent combined with my artistic opinions to draw me into a lifelong relationship with the grand-daddy of the alternative weeklies, which I'd started reading in 1957 as a fourteen-year-old Flushing High School "nonconformist." In an old avant-garde tradition, the *Voice* had augmented its elitist bohemianism with the pop consciousness of Gilbert Seldes and

Andrew Sarris well before the rock press sprang up alongside it. But culturally and economically, the paper lived off bohemian notions of consumption, which synthesized voluntary poverty with an aestheticized taste for the good life. Unlike the underground newspapers, the *Voice* was prehippie, deeply skeptical of pie-eyed sixties fantasy—its editorial bias has always been reform Democrat, and if anything it moved left after apolitical profiteer Clay Felker took it over from Ed Koch confidant Dan Wolf in 1974. It could hardly sidestep sixties ferment, however, and in 1966 published the first true rock critic, my longtime colleague Richard Goldstein. The likes of San Francisco's *Express-Times* and *The Boston Phoenix* emphasized music as a matter of course. And along with the early rock mags—especially Paul Williams's *Crawdaddy!* and Dave Marsh's *Creem,* but also *Rolling Stone,* whose review section was pretty far out under Greil Marcus's tutelage—the alternaweeklies redefined writerly journalism.

Part of this redefinition took place in the slicks, where the aforementioned Felker established the quasifictional immediacy of Tom Wolfe as a new industry standard. That the innovations of the rock and alternative press were so much looser was partly pie-eyed and partly bottom-line. Intensive Wolfe/Talese-style reporting requires rare talent and long labor, commodities that generally cost money, whereas confessional narrative, wild verbiage, polemical disputation, lofty thoughts, and the editorial "I" come cheap. Yet while the strictures against these journalistic no-no's are well-taken, not one is altogether barren as a literary method, and the sixties were ripe for all of them. Unable or unwilling to fairly reimburse their contributors, the alternaweeklies and rock mags gave them too much freedom instead, and in a precise analogy to the alternarock of the eighties, sometimes the indulgence paid off: writers (or bands) who had internalized a commercial form took risks with that form that few established publishers (or record bizzers) would have underwritten.

I returned to the *Voice* in 1974 determined to exploit these developments. As editor and writer, my aim was reviewing more sharp-witted and intellectually unpredictable than the reverential auteurism-once-removed by then ensconced at *Stone,* preferably touched with the gonzoism of Lester Bangs's *Creem.* I also expected to test my reportorial powers with celebrity profiles that didn't preclude critical analysis—and to expand upon the kind of career analysis *Newsday* had let me try with the Chuck Berry opus only slightly revised here.

I've ended up doing three kinds of music writing at the *Voice*. The Consumer Guide grades capsule album reviews that I later worked into alphabetized decade overviews. Theme pieces address genres, issues, scenes, trends, and the annual Pazz & Jop Critics' Poll. Most of my longer journalism, however, including everything I've collected for this book, is keyed to individual artists—almost always pegged, as newsies say, to an event, commonly an album release plus a show. In the seventies I would sometimes go on the road and report these—see my Clash and Lynyrd Skynyrd dispatches. But today I am known as one of the rare rock journalists who doesn't "do interviews." This isn't literally true—if I want facts only an artist can provide, I go for them. Yet although I have conversed with half the subjects here, I rarely quote them, and in only a dozen or so of the collected pieces does the contact play a role (providing data about Iris DeMent's religious history, say, or Sleater-Kinney's set lengths). Partly this is self-respect; people I do not regard as my superiors (which for me means almost everyone, as it should for you) have gotten very controlling indeed about "access," and as long I can do my job without begging, I will. But mostly I just prefer to keep my fannish distance. I know—real fans crave access. But they don't get it, and that leaves us equal. We all respond aesthetically to an information nexus comprising sound recordings, live performances, videos, printed mediations (reviews, press releases, interviews, features, sometimes entire books), and rumor.

Inevitably, sound recordings become the "oeuvre." But it's the nexus I write about. Of course popular music is a collectively produced "cultural practice." Of course its aesthetic impact is inflected by producers and backup musicians, managers and record execs, programmers and disc jockeys, interviewers and reviewers—and fans, above all fans. Rock critics knew all this well before Jean Baudrillard, and knew it was epochal, too. But for excellent empirical reasons that dovetail with journalism's crass and often reactionary commitment to celebrity, the music continues to be heard as the manifestation of an individual or group. And most of the time I write about the human beings rock and roll creates for me.

Highbrow philistines will assume that the reason you won't

find much close reading in these pages is that rock is too under-developed—harmonically, structurally, and intellectually—to support it. But the main reason is that I'm more interested in the human beings it projects. "Persona" is an overused term, and there's now a wide gap between consciously pop pop stars who specialize in it, Madonna being the paradigm, and alternative musos who cultivate anonymity instead, like Pavement or DJ Shadow. But usually it's personas we remember and return to. They're the prism through which we perceive work that supports note-for-note concentration but is designed for the casual attention it enriches. In general, sounds matter more and the rest less as an artist's heyday recedes. But the likes of Bette Midler and Janet Jackson as well as Madonna and Elvis cry out for other kinds of scrutiny. And from Loudon Wainwright to KRS-One, there are always artists who make music a means to an end that wouldn't be nearly as meaningful without it.

The tone and form I arrived at wasn't exactly what I'd envisioned. Good gonzo requires a loose-lipped head few writers can manage even if they get so blotto they can't type, and although I've filled notebooks on location from Akron to Abidjan, I've avoided the profile for almost two decades. What's left is sharp-witted and intellectually unpredictable when I'm on my game, which I find is greatly improved by a newshound's hunger for facts and a gonzo-inflected willingness to go out of my way for a laugh. Like Kael and Wolfe and Liebling—and unlike such academic titans as Raymond Williams and Lionel Trilling, both heroes of mine—I believe that humor is a prime virtue: good prose should make the reader snort or chortle if not guffaw. Nevertheless, *Voice* music writing has a reputation within the music world for being impossibly (and inappropriately) intellectual, and by the standards of the music world it is—even though that world is nowhere near as unlettered or unintelligent as too many academics ignorantly assume.

By the standards of the university, on the other hand, these pieces may seem rather middlebrow. Just because rock critics were onto the postmodern perplex so early, they rarely kowtow to it, and there's clearly a sense in which some of my rhetorical assumptions are academically disreputable if not just retro. I do not keep up with theory and the jargon that goes with it. Blatantly antigenteel though it may be, my criticism was belletristic before the term became a cause célèbre, and I wouldn't want it any other way. I'm a humanist who believes artists create art. I am for interpretation even if I explicate personas as texts. I make value judgments as a matter of course. Mixing guesswork sociology with approximate aesthetics, imbued with the utopian suspicion that justice has something to do with fun, I'm driven by a continuing quest for music that will serve some function or other in my life and yours—inspire, amuse, enlighten, calm, excite; help a person do the dishes or stay awake on the interstate, get through a bad night or a good marriage, know beauty and feel truth.

More than any other high or low subgenre—the sole exception is performance art, traceable through happenings back to dada—rock is expected by its critics to be, if you'll pardon the cant, "transgressive," or at least "subversive." Whether one's foundation myth proceeds from Elvis or the Beatles or Iggy Rotten-Ramone or acid house or vaguely conceived white-kids-who-dig-black-music, the turning point is assumed to be not merely a contested adjustment to emerging social realities and formal alternatives, as with the novel or abstract expressionism, but a progressive if not revolutionary disruption in manners, mores, power itself. And signaling or reflecting such a disruption isn't enough; quite frequently, rock is judged by how credibly it can be said to play a role in making change happen.

Inflated though rock and roll's sense of mission may be, this habit of thought has the virtue of keeping the music on its toes; as an early rock critic, I did my bit to promulgate it. But even in the sixties I also did what I could to let out some of its hot air, and over the years I've been impressed by what a burden counterhegemonic expectations impose in a world where the most consciously and cannily political culture—be it Bertolt Brecht or Cindy Sherman, Linton Kwesi Johnson or Bruce Springsteen—remains tragically if not ridiculously superstructural. When these expectations are piled on the utopian association of rock and youth, you have the name of a bad if paradoxically (or not) long-lived band: Pop Will Eat Itself. And so I find myself stuck in the middle again. I thrive on the shock of the new and am hardly above the shock of the novel, a distinction rock and roll makes hash of. Yet I know that when Danny & the Juniors declared that rock and roll was here to stay back in 1958, they were setting all of us up to get what we wanted and lose what we had. So while my continued interest in race and class may seem hopelessly sixties to post-whatever young antiboomers (not to mention fiftysomethings who have abjured their idealistic ways), I've evolved into a lot of things I had no use for in the sixties: an aesthete who enjoys music for its own sake, a seeker after intelligent entertainment, a student of the canon and the career, a guy with a tape player in his car.

Go back to the fifties or even the sixties and the rock and roll thrill is fresh and elementary: untrained young voices yearning toward a self-realization they're confident will be easy and a beauty they'll never attain, driven by a beat of unexampled candor and colored by electric guitars that can signify the pastoral and the futuristic inside the same gimcrack sonority. Plainly it's all bound up in what is called the blues. But my guess is that rock and roll's blues share more with the broad, primeval, international, preeminently melodic Afro-Celtic-American fusion posited by Peter van der Merwe's *The Origins of the Popular Style* than with the raw African retentions traced by Robert Palmer's *Deep Blues*. Because what's less plain but almost as telling is rock's ties, as both musical and social construct, to the pop music it found wanting.

That's reason enough to start with Nat King Cole, who has nothing and everything to do with any of this. I still believe in what that piece refers to as the great schism—still believe pop music changed utterly around 1955. But while, as is usually said, this change clearly expressed and unleashed powerful new racial and sexual forces, the thrust and contour of those forces has become increasingly obscure. Instead what I've come to hear most sharply is something that can only be called youth music: young adults enacting and reenacting, discovering and rediscovering, what in their teenage intimations of immortality they thought they already knew—their exhilarating capacity for pleasure and power, eros and agape, compounded by the rage and misery that seize them every time they realize these capacities aren't infinite. Inflected across thousands of stylistic permutations and thematic particularities, from Chuck Berry's impudently transgenerational post-blues racelessness to Sleater-Kinney's matter-of-factly transgendered postpunk militance, this structure of feeling is at the heart of rock and roll's irresistible energy and mysteriously renewable spirit. And conjoined with the stuff of rock and roll music—blues modality gunning for the hit parade, an unslakable appetite for rhythm, voices that prize verisimilitude—it has produced art richer and more durable than anyone except Danny & the Juniors fans expected.

In the beginning, the special magic of rock and roll is its countless freeze-frames of eternal youth and the promise of social regeneration that ought to be youth's reward, all expressed with apparent naturalness and spontaneity—an unimpeded, unratiocinated link to the wellsprings of creativity. But unself-consciousness is always a chimera, and in an information-laden culture like our own it soon proves a tough trick for ten-year-olds, never mind young adults or the old adults they fast become. So we end up valuing not just rock's purchase on youth, spontaneity, and renewal, all of which continue to pop up in the oddest places, but also the way it reconstitutes those staples in the presence of their opposites. Unexpectedly, rock and roll turns out to have a lot to say about aging as well—not about pretending to be something you're not, although plenty of fools try, but about retaining and refining flexibility and responsiveness as your emotions are weathered by loss and your physical plant decays. You learn that it's OK to become sophisticated as long as you don't lose your simplicity. Grooving or messing with rock's musical materials, seasoned troupers and overeducated young students of history conceive or reclaim or luck into admixtures, rediscoveries, and interactions that somehow don't crimp their access to direct emotion—even when they're painfully aware that direct emotion is the main thing they live for. Struggling for strains of humanistic corn accounted passé or oppressive by their betters, inspired amateurs make them live again. And every time these miracles come to pass, one's hopes for democracy are fortified against all the instances in which they've been smashed or distorted or cynically manipulated or just plain faked, often enough by rock and roll itself.

The nuevo-Athenian demos and the Frankfurtian "mass" are both hard to get hold of these days. Like every popular form since Greek tragedy, rock and roll has eaten itself over and over, accruing an ever-expanding body of historical reference and formal microdistinction, and like every modern commodity, it's been boutiqued from here till Fat Tuesday and megamarketed halfway to kingdom come. The sixties truism that located half the world's best music in the top forty has broken down as singles have evolved into video-driven promotional devices that invariably decline the utopian project of uniting a pop audience vaster than the sixties ever imagined, and that are generally anonymous dance fluff or sodden international ballads when they go all the way. As political meanings turn into superstructures built upon super-structures, social context counts for less. And while all too many sink sludgily into nostalgia, those who best love the music's usages and traditions are forced into the corner of aesthetics for its own sake. The realm Iggy Pop and the Flying Burrito Brothers long ago moved me to dub semipopular music, which loves pop materials to death without ever occasioning the materialization of a decent-sized populace, is visited these days by most serious fans and even the most anti-intellectual rock critics.

So forty years on, rock culture is more sub than mass. It is often argued—usually by small-is-beautiful folkies manqué, but with some truth anyway—that one secret of fifties rock and roll was local radio, which was motivated to seek out recondite local records and nurture vital local styles. Today local scenes are the special province of alternarock, hip hop, and dance music, three of the many niche styles now feeding a rock and roll mainstream with as many cross-currents as a bird's-foot delta. All have their deluded loyalists and scornful detractors, and all—like country and jazz, like Balkan and Zairean, like, I don't know, polka and Christian—are capable of producing records that will reach well beyond their own supposed boundaries into the heart of the rock and roll mystery itself. So where does that leave my theory of pop? In the dustbin of history, probably, although you never know and Janet Jackson has a good new album out. Where does it leave rock and roll? Somewhere between better than ever and doing as well as can be expected. Grown up all wrong yet alive and kicking, and for just that reason still offending straitlaced compromisers of every aesthetic and generational orientation.

These essays obviously don't circumscribe a canon—Louis Jordan, the Coasters, Thelonious Monk, Bob Dylan, Steely Dan, the Ramones, and Luamba Franco are all in mine. But I wouldn't want to narrow the field in any case, because that would obscure one of rock's prime strengths as an overproduced commodity—its cor-nucopia of minor artists (Loudon Wainwright III, Richard Hell), subjective faves (L7, Andy Fairweather Low), and unproven hope-fuls (Iris DeMent, DJ Shadow). The main reason I value quantity isn't that I find it so damn epistemic to immerse in the pomo media bath—just that there's good music all over the place. In some primordial part of me, with the sincerest respect for all principles of multivalence and different-strokes-for-different-folks, I suspect that bad music is bad for you—it's a kind of sin, a sin critics were put on earth to bear. Over and above living with aging, certain themes are endemic: race from the git, the sexual relationships embedded in courtship tropes, and especially all the ways vision and invention strive to make themselves legible—the means whereby homely genre exercises and bizarre personal experiments still do become "popular," as well as the travails that ensue when material rewards don't. But basically, my mission is to encourage readers to find good stuff and lay out a way to hear it. So these are all appreciations. I'm often sharp with artists I admire, but you'll find no debunks here no matter what Richard Thompson's publicist thinks.

Journalists who collect their writing often hold that it shouldn't be amended—not because they regard it as undying art (journalists are the most modest of mortals), or because they're lazy (of course not), but because its tie to the moment will be destroyed by too much fiddling. More often than not this is nonsense. I have enough faith in the moment to be certain that its aura isn't that fragile, and though all writing dates, I refuse to undermine the pleasure and credibility of this collection with moments whose occasion already obtrudes. Just as journalism strives to fabricate an illusion of immediacy, books demand a show of timelessness. And so I have revised as needed—changing language, inserting insights, weaving together different pieces on the same topic. This doesn't mean I've tried to sweep mistakes under the rug—I'm no longer as dismissive of glitter rock as I was in 1978 nor of movie stars as I was in 1991. But I have clarified clumsily expressed ideas, and as the compulsive editor I am, I've tightened, pruned, trimmed, and tightened again—most of these pieces are shorter than when they were published, by fifty words or fifteen hundred, which not only makes them more accessible but frees up space for a few more.

Organization is broadly chronological, with individual essays run together within ten thematic/chronological sections that I mean to flow, if not like the mighty Hudson, at least like the traffic on Second Avenue. Instead of finishing with the New York Dolls, still my favorite band, or Nirvana, who never could bear up under such strain, or Sleater-Kinney, who have only started growing up in public, I've returned to three artists I named the decade's greatest back in 1979—an unconventional call that's held up better than I could have hoped. Are Al Green, George Clinton, and Neil Young the greatest of all time? Of course not, and who cares anyway? They're just three very gifted human beings who were better heroes and better egalitarians than the competition. They've rocked their entire lives. And not one of them wasted more time than it seemed might be fun at the moment. Neither have I.

1

Where "Rock and Roll" Began

Across the Great Divide: Nat King Cole

Postpunk rock and rollers see musical history as a pomo junk pile—sounds, beats, attitudes, and images of varying status and pedigree, every one ripe for bricolage. Late hippies and early punks assume a permanent cultural battle between the authentic and the commercial. And those of us old enough to have undergone a conversion experience circa 1955 cherish the paradigm of the great schism. In the beginning, we believe, there was pop: leftover big-band singers crooning moon-June-spoon 'neath a cloud of violins. And then Elvis—or Chuck Berry, or Bill Haley, or if you want to get fancy something like Jackie Brenston's "Rocket 88"—moved upon the face of the waters, and all was changed in what was suddenly an us-versus-them world. In some vague way, which is all the concept deserved, we craved authenticity. But we didn't think authentic excluded commercial. Quite the contrary—it was rock and rollers against grownups for control of the hit parade.

Only nothing is ever that simple. The war was hard-fought, and for years, rock and roll coexisted with older pop. Many of us had show albums around the house, and we didn't control even "our" radio stations. The way *Billboard* figured it, Perry Como scored more top-forty records between 1955 and 1958 than any rock and roller this side of Elvis (and Pat Boone, who straddled the battle line with what must now be judged finesse). Then came Fats Domino and Ricky Nelson, but after them the biggest hitmakers were Frank Sinatra and Patti Page and the Four Lads and young

Johnny Mathis, who made the top forty eleven times between May 1957 and October 1958. Although most self-respecting Chuck Berry fans hated Debbie Reynolds's "Tammy" and Dean Martin's "Memories Are Made of This" and Morris Stoloff's "Moonglow and Theme From 'Picnic,' " fewer resisted pop flukes on the order of Gogi Grant's "The Wayward Wind" or Domenico Modugno's "Volare" or Perez Prado's "Cherry Pink and Apple Blossom White," which ranks second behind "Heartbreak Hotel"/"Don't Be Cruel" in *Billboard*'s fifties countdown. We were committed to rock and roll, but that didn't mean we tuned out the opposition—what makes a hit a hit is that it penetrates your defenses. Nor did our pop tastes boil down to simple like and don't-like. We responded to pop artists individually—for how they sounded, or who they seemed to be. At the time, I preferred the Four Lads (and Pat Boone, Lord forgive me) to Frank Sinatra, whose hit-parade stuff was often crap and who would have been over my head in any case. Patti Page meant nothing to me, Perry Como had his moments, Johnny Mathis I dug. And then there was Nat King Cole.

You'd never know it with Natalie's *Unforgettable* sweeping the Grammys and Nat's nipped-in-the-bud variety show trotted out by PBS like some high-middlebrow *I Love Lucy,* but Cole wasn't exactly a totem in the fifties. He was a very big singing star—his nineteen hits between 1955 and 1958 put him one below Como, who (unlike Sinatra and Crosby) outmatched him slightly over the entire decade. But he was also an anomaly. For eight years, Como was on TV every week, a grind Crosby and Sinatra were too big for. But Cole's show lasted approximately one season, a victim not of quality or ratings (which while unspectacular were above average) but of the unwillingness of national sponsors to back a black artist. And of course it was his race above all that made him an anomaly. Cole wasn't the first crossover artist. Louis Armstrong and Duke Ellington and Fats Waller and Louis Jordan had substantial (albeit inadequate) success with white consumers, and from Ethel Waters to Billy Eckstine, other black singers worked the pop vein. But Cole was much popper than any of them even though he began his professional life as the pianist in his own jazz trio, a trade some jazz fans never forgave him for abandoning.

In general, rock and rollers were more tolerant. If we'd known his piano playing, we probably would have blamed him for cocktail jazz, and like Sinatra, he put too much crap on the market. But he was a respected vocal presence. In this I'm pretty sure his blackness helped. With *Brown* v. *Board of Education* on America's mind, Cole obviously functioned as a reassuring token for the adult audience: "I loved him," recalls my mom, a Frankie fan who enjoyed Fats Waller. "He was so . . . self-effacing." And since rock and rollers were pro-integration in theory—at least up north, where the backlash was well down the road—Cole no doubt got points for skin color that Como didn't. But for all of us it began with his voice, which (like Sinatra's and unlike Como's, with the tremendously influential Crosby in between) remains one of pop's most remarkable. In his essential account of prerock vocalizing, *The Great American Popular Singers,* Henry Pleasants says he "cannot evoke the memory of his voice without the words to go with it." But for someone like me, who didn't tune in WMGM for "Ballerina" or "To the Ends of the Earth," it was different—I ignored the songs but absorbed their aural signature.

The attraction was in part physical, but on an unusually complex level—somehow what Pleasants aptly labels his "light bass-baritone" was simultaneously cool and rich, emery board and velvet. In his putative review of a new Cole bio, Leslie Gourse's cunningly entitled *Unforgettable, The New Yorker*'s Adam Gopnik observes that Cole's early records managed to combine the "two opposites of American pop culture as it developed over the next fifteen or so years—hipness and warmth," and he never lost the secret. His timbre and phrasing radiated an inimitable calm—kind, sly, intimate, classy, unassuming, utterly confident, and, most miraculous of all, not boring—that seemed inextricable in a way I couldn't articulate from what I would not then have called his blackness. Today I'd identify its racial component as an inspired personal amalgam of church-bred respectability and jazz-scene hip, but as a singer I'd call him the culmination not so much of Bing Crosby as of the crooning tradition Crosby established, which combined canny mike technique with the conversational rhythms of early jazz. To my fifties-trained ears, Cole remains the greatest of the crooners, and also, basically, the last—if he had an inheritor who meant a damn thing, it wasn't Natalie Cole but Johnny Mathis, "The King of Necking Music" and the most raceless star in the history of American pop.

With Natalie's "tribute" making 1992 the most reactionary Grammy year since Christopher Cross, generational and cultural warriors are slightly pissed at the man who sang "Mr. Cole Won't Rock and Roll." But forget it, Jake—it's the National Academy of Recording Arts and Sciences. Sure *Unforgettable* is terrible. Even shrewd antirockist Gopnik, who claims it's "not a bad record, either," immediately criticizes Natalie's "need to ornament her dad's records with a lot of overt 'emotion,' when the whole point of his style was that you got true emotion by seeming to suppress it." I'd amend that to argue that no matter how many stupid songs he recorded, Cole was too intelligent, and too tolerant, to set down rules about how one achieves "true emotion"—all he knew was how *he* managed to convey it. Natalie, on the other hand, is an ideologue of convenience and *Unforgettable* pure cultural politicking—with Nat, even such irritations as "Ramblin' Rose" and "Those Lazy-Hazy-Crazy Days of Summer" were at least of the era when nostalgia was every pop singer's stock-in-trade rather than the gauntlet it's become for his daughter and her admirers. Natalie's oversinging derives less from the soul ethos Gopnik chides than from the brassy, big-voiced showbiz swing Sinatra owned—which Nat essayed as he got older only because it was what pop icons did, and because he was always an agreeable man. I find the style dated myself, which isn't to belittle Sinatra, a greater singer than Cole or just about anybody else. But Pleasants is a fan of the stuff, and he believes that the bigger Cole's voice got, the less distinctively he deployed it.

Listening to Cole now is kind of like listening to classic countrypolitan. He doesn't drown in orchestral drama as regularly as Patsy Cline, say, but he transcends his arrangements less often than the insinuatingly Cole-like Willie Nelson, or than George Jones, who matches Sinatra's ability to sing through anything on a good take. If you can't bear schmaltz and schlock, Stash has compiled pleasant trio sets like *The Complete Early Transcriptions,* more affordable at four CDs than Mosaic's giant trio box. But most rock and rollers will forgo gems like "Gone With the Draft" and limit their "Cole-ectibles" to Rhino's *Jumpin' at Capitol,* which honors his forties style at a higher level of specificity. From jumps like "Route 66" to quiet nonsense like "The Frim Fram Sauce" to sweet, thoughtful chestnuts like "Embraceable You" and "When I Take My Sugar to Tea," it swings less politely and more intricately than the well-turned background music one might expect. And in 1956 Cole cut a trio album that Capitol has reissued with bonus tracks as *The Complete After Midnight Sessions,* which despite some dubious digitalization and a virtual absence of hipster jive is the peak his jazz-based fans say it is, mostly because the soloists who augment the trio—Sweets Edison, Willie Smith, Stuff Smith, and Juan Tizol—definitely aren't background guys.

What *After Midnight* lacks, though those who weren't there may dismiss it as my own nostalgia, is cultural resonance. I'm talking about the schlock and schmaltz. As much as any noncollector needs (and God knows there's lots more out there: he put twenty-seven albums on the *Billboard* charts) can be found on two competing Capitol compilations, *The Capitol Collector's Series,* a single CD, and *The Nat King Cole Story,* a double. Although fifteen of the twenty songs on the single are also on the double, the versions aren't identical—*The Nat King Cole Story* was a 1961 remake designed to take advantage of improved recording technology by approximating the arrangements of his early hits. You don't have to be an audiophile to appreciate the creamier sound, and that's not all, because as Cole matured his pipes did get stronger. This "Route 66" is as cushiony as the back seat of a Cadillac, its zoot-suit cool a fond memory. But I must confess I find the grain of his voice more seductive in its hi-fi edition. Cole was about comfort, among many other things.

Unlike Chuck Berry and the Stones, both of whom covered his "Route 66," I count as my favorite Cole song the one I've heard most over the years, though I didn't notice when it first hit in 1946: "The Christmas Song." Like my other favorites—by which I mean "Too Young" and "Walkin' My Baby Back Home" and "Stardust" and even "Unforgettable," not crap like "Ballerina" and "All Over the World" and "Non Dimenticar"—it shares with so much great pop, especially great black pop, the grace of making the bourgeois life seem kind. Which at certain times from certain angles it can be, you know.

1992

Let's Call the Whole Thing Pop:
George Gershwin

Since there's such a thing as being too open-minded, I'd better confess before I lie down and my brains fall out: I've been listening to show music. Please, not *new* show music. Nor do I own many vintage original-cast albums. But nobody who loves the pop tradition can avoid musicals altogether. The facts of production in the so-called classic era were straightforward: all the pantheon composers—Kern, Berlin, the Gershwins, Porter, Rodgers & Whoever—wrote primarily for Broadway and Hollywood. Check out Rhino's compilations on Gershwin, Rodgers & Hart, even Berlin (who actually published more "pop" than "theater" titles) and you'll hear almost nothing but songs introduced on stage or screen. The same goes for MCA's theatrical *George & Ira Gershwin: A Musical Celebration* and Mercury's rockish *The Glory of Gershwin,* not to mention the four painstakingly reconstructed unoriginal-cast recordings Elektra Nonesuch has devoted to Gershwin's theatrical oeuvre or the Broadway Angel souvenir designed for the million or two bon vivants who've caught *Crazy for You* at the Shubert and elsewhere since 1992.

Where the intractably populist Berlin and the supernally acerbic Porter are pretty much what they seem, Gershwin's august stature has always been more suspect—the concert-hall credentials that inflate his reputation among middlebrows ought to make rock and rollers wonder. Right—and Peter Townshend didn't really think *Tommy* was an opera, he was just having his little joke. Rock artistes like Sting, Peter Gabriel, and Kate Bush, to name only the most patently pretentious contributors to *The Glory of Gershwin,* aspire to any kind of stature you got, most certainly including Gershwin's, summed up neatly by the project's sideman-as-centerpiece, harmonica virtuoso Larry Adler: Gershwin made "the transition from pop to the concert halls. He could write popular songs, orchestral pieces and even, in *Porgy and Bess,* great opera." The problem with this theory is that no matter how often they're philharmonicized as sops to the national pride and the tune-mad rabble, *Rhapsody in Blue* and its arty successors have never entered the canon. Declares *The New Grove*'s Charles Schwartz: "His serious works are structurally defective. The orchestral and piano pieces are filled with repetitive rather than developed melodies, motifs, sequences, and ostinatos, and often sections are separated by abrupt pauses."

Ah yes, "repetitive rather than developed"—anathema for the classical gang, yet music to the tune-mad rabble's ears. So maybe we should cut Gershwin some slack. It's a good sign too that Alec Wilder, whose knowledge of sheet music is regularly mistaken for critical acumen by the classic-pop gang, carps without surcease about Gershwin's penchant for the repeated note—the "aggressive," "insistently cheery" " 'hard sell' " of songs all too well-served by "the advent of radio." After all, the much better critic Gerald Mast notes that for Gershwin, "the piano was a percussion instrument before it was a keyboard instrument," and in his uncommonly useful notes to the Rhino disc, Will Friedwald points out that where Richard Rodgers fashioned flowing melodies from discrete three- or four-note motifs, Gershwin motorvated his material by separating similar phrases with rests (for a simple example, hum the "You say potato" refrain of "Let's Call the Whole Thing Off"). Gershwin's beat was rarely elemental, and his melodies were far more elaborate than the folkish tunes of early rock and roll. But for sure he was hipper rhythmically than his fellow pantheon dwellers. And of course, I've been acting as if there were only one Gershwin. In fact, almost all of George's best work featured lyrics by a genius named Ira, the wise-guy foil to his brother's romantic seeker. I'll say potayto, thank you.

This isn't just a substantial body of work, but a substantial body of work you can have fun with, and it's shooting yourself in the foot to omit, oh, "Someone To Watch Over Me" or "How Long

Has This Been Going On?" or "They All Laughed" or "It Ain't Necessarily So" or "Bidin' My Time" or "I Got Rhythm" (or lots of others) from your bricolage. Old enough to have spun my parents' *South Pacific* seventy-eights for pleasure and groaned at the Tin Pan Alley filler on Milton Berle's show, I'm also young enough to have rejected everything I thought such music stood for. In 1994, however, that battle is over, because my side won. Classic pop was hardier than we knew, but its hegemony has been shattered; it's now a heritage, a resource, a gold mine. Rock and roll heroes unable to play it should know enough to play with it instead, and that goes double for mere consumers—including those young enough to think parent music is *Highway 61 Revisited* or *Never Mind the Bollocks.* The question is, in what form?

In a world glutted with rock songbooks whose offenses don't end with inconsistency and the blahs, two of the most enduring albums of the past decade rework major pop catalogues: 1985's *Lost in the Stars: The Music of Kurt Weill,* produced by Hal Willner before he got all insular and coy, and 1990's *Red Hot + Blue,* where postpunk took on AIDS and Cole Porter. The earlier record is avant by necessity, with Sting the bait for Dagmar Krause, Carla Bley, Van Dyke Parks, a then obscure John Zorn; five years later, sucked in by charity and postmodern panache, U2, Annie Lennox, Sinéad O'Connor, David Byrne, and the Fine Young Cannibals were all lending sales punch to an aptly nonhet and international lineup. But four years after that, *The Glory of Gershwin* looks like pure mutual congratulation society. For art it's very proud to add O'Connor and Elvis Costello to the above-named pretenders, leaving loads of shopworn commodities—Robert Palmer and Cher and Carly Simon, none of whom need worry about spreading themselves too thin, and Oleta Adams and Jon Bon Jovi and the long-lost Chris De Burgh, all of whom need wonder where their next promo budget is coming from—plus, for genuine chart muscle, Elton John and (urrp) Meat Loaf. And speaking of middlebrow pretensions, George Martin is charged with holding it all together. Rest assured that Adler's evocative, omnipresent mouth organ does not transform the Sid Bernstein of Abbey Road into Nelson Riddle.

None of this is as dreadful as one might fear. Martin is tasteful, give him that, and the material has long since proven its ability to withstand pop ego, which despite their aura of cautious respect few of these renditions do without. In fact, pop ego very nearly renders the collection listenable. In his superb survey of the musical, *Can't Help Singin'*, Gerald Mast adduces a schema that makes sense. Musicals began as revues, song-and-star showcases with little pretense to theme and none to plot. Inevitably, however, they evolved, with Kern's 1928 *Show Boat* pioneering the use of songs to advance story and character and Rodgers & Hammerstein's 1943 *Oklahoma!* the turning point—after that, songs and stars were expected not merely to advance the drama but to serve it. The result, Mast says, was both the flowering of a uniquely American art form and its decline. Although the art form rhetoric has always been a little overblown, let it go—the forties and fifties certainly produced a load of memorable shows. What interests me is the decline. Mast is suggesting that once tunesmiths began conceiving themselves as dramaturges and belters learned that their mission in life was conveying character, Broadway was no longer much of a spawning ground for songwriters and the singing stars they needed. This obviously wasn't the only reason for the power shift that ensued. But it does go a long way toward explaining why probably you and definitely I have never heard of and will soon forget the skilled nonentities whose Gershwin turns are currently competing with those on Larry Adler's genteel schlockfest.

The two Nonesuch recreations I've heard—the renowned *Girl Crazy* and the silly *Pardon My English*—lack any imaginable interest for nonobsessives. They're pleasant, amusing, and unbelievably mild. I wish I could say as much for the horrendous two-CD AIDS benefit, *A Musical Celebration,* which despite comic relief that veers between burlesque and backpat comes into focus when Mary Gordon Murray (is she famous? for what?) tears into the sensuous, questioning "Somebody Loves Me" like it was "Climb Every Mountain." Although the pastiched-together *Crazy for You* is justly chastised for reducing whole songs to two-chorus fragments, at least it favors razzle-dazzle it can handle over deep meaning it can't. Leading lady Jodi Benson has a sense of humor and sex appeal, a truncated "The Real American Folk Song (Is a Rag)" is better than none at all, and "What Causes That?" exits the cold cold ground a winner. But good, bad, or indifferent, all three projects seem strangely lifeless compared to *The Glory of Gershwin,* which exudes a personality they either lack or abuse. The rock bozos' command of pitch may be shaky, but they remain nonchalant about it, so that even the has-beens swagger like they have showbiz by the short hairs. A more daring conceptmaster could organize a more revealing collection. Yet something about their collective chutzpah suits the spirit of the brilliantly ambitious Eastern European Jews they've hitched their stars to.

Granted that Rhino's *Great American Songwriters, Vol. 1: George & Ira Gershwin,* featuring Chris Connor, Lee Wiley, Johnny Hartman, Dick Haymes, and other old-timers who wear their class with style, is far superior even though it's also far choppier (pity Johnny Mathis, who could have been a legend if only he'd replaced the Big Bopper on that Midwestern tour). Granted too that the very best place to get to know this stuff is on the kind of record that hooked me, where great songs go to the caliber of star and artist they were designed for—Ella Fitzgerald and Louis Armstrong's glorious, budget-priced *Compact Jazz* (twelve tracks, five Gershwins, Verve), or Fred Astaire's uncannily precise *Top Hat: Hits From Hollywood* (sixteen Gershwin/Berlin/Kern tracks, Columbia/Legacy). Nevertheless, it's a lot easier to survive in an archive than to thrive there. The Gershwins' pantheon was located smack dab in the middle of the agora, and it's nostalgic snobbery to believe the contemporary marketplace an uglier or more dangerous place. It pains me to admit it, but, well, Sting's "Nice Work if You Can Get It" is kind of droll. Dumbass ukulele and all.

1994

The Complete Work of B. B. King

King of the Blues got my attention by passing the boxed set test, a critical procedure not recommended to consumers because it requires prior possession of the commodity in question. The trick is simple: play the last disc first. Where *Queen of Soul* and *Clash on Broadway,* both by artists who've meant more to me and perhaps the world than B. B. King, start off promising the gift of eternal life and end up flailing for air, *King of the Blues* starts with its feet on the ground and its ass in gear and ends up—forty-two years later, mind you—with its butt still high. I was so impressed I checked King out live for the first time since the early seventies—introducing him at the Apollo to my editor, who was born the year King cut *Live at the Regal,* and to my wife and daughter two days later at a Westbury Music Fair matinee. The idea was to find out how he'd play two dissimilar audiences, only the turnouts weren't all that different: both were dominated by respectable-looking black folks getting on in years. There were more whites at Westbury, and, because David Dinkins was hosting a convention, more mayors at the Apollo. But age rather than race was decisive: even at Westbury, African-Americans were a clear majority, and even at the Apollo European-Americans outnumbered under-thirty-fives. The Apollo show was stronger mostly because it took place at night on a stage that didn't double as a merry-go-round. B. B. King knocked out all three generations I was talking to and everyone else within earshot. I swear he's barely lost a step.

At sixty-eight, King is an icon, and God knows he gets respect. He symbolizes The Blues for everybody from U2 to the State Department to *Sesame Street* to the Take It Back Foundation, which produced an all-star recycling video keynoted by his guitar. He can play big houses almost anywhere in the world. He has honorary degrees and accolades in the *Congressional Record;* he's the centerpiece of Charles Keil's pioneering 1966 *Urban Blues,* still one of the hippest academic popular-music studies, and the beneficiary of Charles Sawyer's fascinating 1980 *The Arrival of B. B. King,* as searching an authorized biography as any icon is likely to countenance. Although one never knows, you get the feeling Sawyer was given his head because the king of the blues had nothing to hide: all his faults are close to the surface.

Raised by a very extended family under typical Delta duress, King learned to sing in a sanctified church, but it was in a one-room schoolhouse that he took to heart the idea that remains his obsession—his obligation to make something of himself. He picked cotton and sharecropped and drove a tractor and jockeyed trucks before launching his career from Memphis, first as a local entertainer with a fifteen-minute radio spot, then as a full-fledged DJ who climaxed every show with his own music, and soon enough as the ultimate touring bluesman. You could say his marriages, both of which lasted eight years, succumbed to the usual stresses of the road, only it's the rare road musician who can claim three hundred forty-two one-nighters in three hundred sixty-six days, as King did in 1956. Granted, he was single at the time, but his schedule has remained almost as hectic to this day. Clocking over three hundred gigs a year, B. B. King isn't just a road musician—he's a textbook workaholic. He makes his home, such as it is, in Las Vegas, where for a long time his arcane taste in keno cards meant he always had to go out and earn more bread, and although both his marriages were childless, a problem attributed by one fertility specialist to a low sperm count, he took financial responsibility for eight illegitimate kids. This lifetime self-improvement addict doesn't really work for money—money is just an excuse. He works to prove his worth.

Unfortunately, one place King's hard-earned respect doesn't translate into cachet is the world of rock and roll. White acolytes from Paul Butterfield to Eric Clapton sang his praises back when he was unknown outside the natural confines of the blues, and soon he was wowing young longhairs at various Fillmores and college auditoriums. But as an honorable careerist, he was proud to play his blues to anyone, so at the same time he happily invaded Vegas and Europe and scored increasingly popwise minor hits. Gradually, his newfound visibility combined with his ingratiating polish to subsume all traces of chitlin-circuit myth, and after punk turned rock taste back toward the neoprimitive, a rock godfather lost much of his aura. His stylistic synthesis is at once so classic and so catholic that no one who gives it a fair hearing can deny its quality, but excitement is a more subjective matter—the first adjective in the disgracefully brief B. B. section of Robert Palmer's *Deep Blues* is "ambitious." This kind of faint praise helps skew King's generational demographic. But it hasn't cost him as much as it has rock and rollers who think all true bluesmen are starcrossed geniuses or good-timing rogues.

King didn't make a pact with the devil—he made a pact with an accountant, Sidney Seidenberg, who took over his management in 1968. Entertainment is his lifework, and for years his show has kicked off in high with Louis Jordan's "Let the Good Times Roll," which features portly trumpeter Jim Bolton shaking his booty and his Afro, pushing the crowd over the top before they know what hit them. But he has no apparent interest in the rock-friendly macho flash of the somewhat younger Buddy Guy. And unlike his somewhat older and much deader compatriot Elmore James, now revived on a strident, brilliant, Palmer-selected Rhino compilation called *The Sky Is Crying,* he's never tried to pickle his pericardium or play louder than God. For him blues seems less a matter of spiritual compulsion than of personal destiny—his musical heritage. He's just deeply proud of who he happens to be—a very diligent, very secular country boy.

To ideologues and ignoramuses, B. B. King's blues seem too suave, his lessons from cousin Bukka White buried in the past. And indeed, listen to *King of the Blues* and you'll hear sweet vocals, pop songforms, fancy horn sections, extraneous string sections, and the unfailing geniality of a Southern gentleman once removed. An incorrigible record collector and home taper, King puts a DJ's broad tastes into action, counting among his influences harmonic explorer T-Bone Walker and ear-busting riffer Elmore James, black jazzman Charlie Christian and European jazzman Django Reinhardt; it's typical that the violin-backed "The Thrill Is Gone," which sets off hypersensitive pop detectors, was originally a 1951 r&b hit for one Roy Hawkins, making B. B.'s biggest single a DJ's coup. But unlike most DJs (and artists), King's not shy about his dislikes. Here he is answering a Keil query about Lou Rawls, in 1966 considered the epitome of blues sophistication: "I guess I'm just a little critical about everybody, myself too; lots of records I hear today, mine too, don't move me much. I haven't heard him yet, really, but the sides I have heard gave me the same feeling as when I hear *Stardust* sung much too fast—do you know that feeling? He jives things a little too much for me." Almost three decades later, that judgment's drive to excellence and formal coherence are vintage B. B. Suave has nothing to do with it.

King's voice has deepened with age, but unlike his great rival Bobby Bland, who opened both shows, he hasn't lost his physical edge. Like Bland, though never to such extremes, he can be gritty and raw as well as smooth and contained; a favorite strategy is to start off with the pain in check—amused, thoughtful, at worst plaintive—and build to a shout of anger or a howl of realization. And though he no longer writes much, he has a songbook behind him—as both singer and showman, a knack for words is part of his tool kit. If he didn't invent the perfect "Nobody loves me but my mother/And she could be jivin' too," he had the presence of mind to copyright it, and from "Five Long Years" to "Paying the Cost To Be the Boss," he's bonded with the formerly minor blues theme of the provider who won't take no mess—or who'll make damn sure you know about it when he does.

But what marks every track blue is his guitar, known as Lucille, who for all her bell-like articulation and harmonic smarts hones his music to a minimum no matter what its excesses elsewhere. His time—I don't want to call it phrasing because that emphasizes off-rhythms, and King has a sneaky way of slamming the beat home—is an inexhaustible source of satisfaction. He adores the melody like another of his musical role models, Lester Young. And though his smallish, less than fleet-fingered hands may have determined his deliberate, uncannily speechlike style (which Sawyer likens to someone trying to overcome a stammer, as King did when he was a child), his brain and soul put it together. If he isn't Thelonious Monk, he has the same general idea, only within his own musical heritage: "You know, if I could sing pop tunes like Frank Sinatra or Sammy Davis Jr., I don't think I still could do it, 'cause Lucille don't wanna play nothin' but the blues." His playing alone won't suffice—as you soon figure out from *Spotlight on Lucille,* a circa-1961 instrumental showcase on Flair/Virgin, the gal needs to talk back. King the nonwriter hasn't sold his material down the river; from Leon Russell's icky "Hummingbird" to the Ira Newborn movie theme that's the only total failure in the box, pop forays are greatly outnumbered by DJ classics and made-to-order simulations of his style. But no matter what he's singing, she has the last word.

As someone who'd noted the remarkable consistency of King's mature albums, I should have figured he'd pass the boxed set test. If anything, the first disc, which includes only seven cuts from the Bihari-owned labels where he recorded for thirteen years, is the problem (Flair/Virgin's *Best of B. B. King* is a nice way to compensate). But there are plenty of bluesmen whose records provide a youthful rush, and from Muddy to Wolf, from John Hurt to John Lee Hooker, even those who maintained into their sixties were rarely so undiminished. In biographical context, the rich, solid, professional durability of King's craft takes on a poetry of its own. Blues is usually conceived as a means of transcending the rigors of the nine-to-five, and B. B. knows it's his job to let the good times roll. But it's just as apt to hear his music as an escape into work. No other rock godfather can make that claim.

1993

The Blank Slate: George Jones

George Jones is a singer before he is anything else—before he is a country artist, before he is a Southerner, before he is a legend, before he is a totem, before he is Dr. Jekyll, before he is Mr. Hyde, before he is the Possum, before he is No-Show Jones, before he is an alcoholic, before he is a man. He's the greatest of all country singers and one of the dozen or so greatest in any pop idiom these American ears can make sense of. Other vocalists of lesser endowment have been smarter and more satisfying—Billie Holiday and Louis Armstrong certainly. So perhaps have (the supernally endowed) Al Green or (the carelessly underrated) John Lennon, maybe even the young Mick Jagger or Bob Dylan (neither of whose IQ's proved of any use whatsoever in the little matter of avoiding self-parody). But although George Jones never got out of seventh grade, the formal and technical wisdom, cunning, and intuition of his best recordings is jaw-dropping. Since the advent of high fidelity, only two colleagues have yoked comparable musical intelligence to an instrument of such emotional complexity and physical range: Frank Sinatra and Aretha Franklin.

Please please please, no Mahalia or Elvis or Sarah Vaughan or, I don't know, Ethel Merman letters. I admit I'm being subjective, especially since I'm far from what opera people call a canary fancier. From Mariah Carey to Nelson Eddy & Jeanette MacDonald, the cult of the voice has been responsible for more bad pop than payola and John David Kalodner combined. But there are some voices that demand immersion, and if you have any feeling for country at all, this is one of them.

As Bob Allen recounts in the tough-minded 1984 biography updated last year as *George Jones: The Life and Times of a Honky Tonk Legend,* Jones came from a singing family—literally dozens of his aunts, uncles, and cousins would regularly raise the roof of the Baptist chapel his maternal grandfather built in the Big Thicket region of East Texas. His very first cries were said to have startled his mother with their clarity and resonance, and before he was ten, it was the special pleasure of his alcoholic father to come home drunk, roust his youngest son out of bed, and whup him with a belt until he sang Roy Acuff and Bill Monroe. A scamp who was spoiled by five older sisters, he showed no interest in honest toil, but there wasn't a musical challenge he wouldn't take on. He was singing for change on the streets of Beaumont by 1943, when he was twelve. He was in bars and on the radio by sixteen.

George Jones would appear to have no other gift but song. Until he was sobered up in the mid-eighties by eight hospitalizations and his fourth wife, his life was a horrendous mess. An affable fellow capable of Elvislike flashes of wild generosity, he was also known to flush money down the toilet, literally on several occasions and figuratively without surcease, and although he wasn't too badly used by producers Pappy Daily and Billy Sherrill, he never found a career advisor he could trust until the wife who saved him started managing him. His sole recorded political act is a George Wallace benefit with a previous wife named Tammy. And when he drank he was capable of damn near anything. He rarely got into one of his endless supply of getaway cars without a bottle, there were several near-misses featuring a .38, and I defy anyone who reads Allen's book to keep track of how many women get hit—after a while the brutality has a numbing effect. Robert Plant is Alan Alda by comparison. Frank Sinatra is Elie Wiesel.

I recount all this not to remind the ignorant that miscreant rockers and rappers have company in conservative Nashville, but to begin to wonder about the emotional resources of Jones's music. For if anyone epitomizes what country adepts like to call "white soul," it's George Jones, who unlike formal innovators Jimmie Rodgers and Hank Williams had no contact with black musicians coming up. In his voice admirers rightly hear the suffering, deprivation, heartache, and endurance of the white Southern underclass, all filtered through endlessly reworked tropes of good times gone bad and marital travail. But to leave it at that is to sentimentalize what Jones does and doesn't bring to a song. Listen close—as close as you can get without prolonged proximity to the Southern underclass, anyway—and ask yourself whether you have any sense of the man behind those close-set eyes.

Jones radiates none of the natural comfort of his honky-tonk antecedent Lefty Frizzell. Every song, every sentiment, feels like a *performance* that's longer on intensity than on comprehension—conceivably the performance of somebody who's afraid of getting whupped if he stops. Under the heat there's a coldness, and even the coldness can't be pinned down—you couldn't call Jones mean, like fellow sufferer Jerry Lee Lewis, or willful, like honor student Elvis Costello. His fleeting pleasures and undeniable pain aren't so much depthless as unfathomable, beyond measurement—maybe subcutaneous, maybe coded messages from the other side of the earth. Some great vocalists seem to sing from the head, some from the heart, some from the gut. George Jones seems to sing from the throat. As Nick Tosches put it in a superb profile, he has the aura of "a man whose unequivocal soulfulness abide[s] beneath an inert mind."

Far from diminishing his art, this vacancy is close to the essence of its genius. Its blank slate is his version of the limited means that render so many feats of popular culture heroic, his lucky or instinctive adjustment for an instrument that might otherwise seem too large to convey country's homely truths—a voice that even now tends to dwarf the deprivations it describes, making them seem simultaneously less immediate and more universal, a shared heritage. Yet he's never tried to exploit that voice for purposes of cultural upward mobility; it seems incapable of gentility or idealized beauty, and all of the uses to which Jones has put it have honored the only world he's ever wanted to inhabit. His respect for his wife Nancy and his sainted mother is inestimable, but hard country music alone has inspired his unfaltering fealty. Steeped in holiness hymns, in Acuff and Monroe, in Hank and Lefty, in every shade of musical emotion he'd grown up with, he was such an adept imitator that it took him over a decade to arrive at his own style. And nobody has yet surpassed that style—not its mournful off-melodies, not its effortless sweep of the octaves, not the thrilling shtick of its deep swoops, not its utterly idiosyncratic, utterly idiomatic phrasing and pronunciation, not its whiskey warmth and rough, sour-mash finish, not its rich palette that reduces to the colors of dirt except on the velvety maroon of the big ballads.

Jones is now so celebrated that outsiders no longer resist him the way I did when he paid a rote and probably scared-shitless 1973 visit to Lincoln Center with wife number three, and two recent two-CD sets go a fair distance toward rationalizing a catalogue of legendary inconsistency. Granted, Epic's forty-four-cut *The Essential George Jones: The Spirit of Country* does pass over eight tracks on the formerly definitive twenty-two-cut late-period *Anniversary—Ten Years of Hits* while duplicating seven tracks from Mercury's fifty-one-cut *Cup of Loneliness: The Classic Mercury Years* as well as eleven on Rhino's formerly useful *The Best of George Jones (1955–1967)* (most of them on the Mercury as well). What can I say? This sort of thing is part of the poetry of being a George Jones fan, every one of whom treasures some obscurity on an album purchased for eighty-eight cents at the Paducah Rexall's while waiting for a new alternator. (Mine include the late "Don't Leave Without Taking Your Silver" and the early "Eskimo Pie.") Honky tonk diehards will opt for the Mercury, which is certainly ace, not least because it kicks off with the insane, unjustly belittled (even by George) 1955 debut "No Money in This Deal." But honky tonk diehards aren't good enough for George Jones, who like Holiday and Armstrong and Sinatra (perhaps not Franklin) just kept growing as a singer. Having started out as a kickass Hank-and-Lefty acolyte with his own distinctive punch (summed up on Liberty's masterful *My Favorites of Hank Williams,* in print), he still has a penchant for tomfoolery—check out the Epic box's jocose Ray Charles duet "We Didn't See a Thing," or the Elvis Presley-Fred Flintstone tribute "Ya Ba Da Ba Do (So Are You)." Early on, however, his balladry contained the seeds of morose melodramas like "He Stopped Loving Her Today" and "Still Doin' Time," both extracted during his paranoid-schizophrenic coke-and-booze years by the single-minded Sherrill. Most singers' voices get lower as they age. Not many make the new depths seem like divine destiny.

Although I'd rather not say anything nice about his coke-and-booze years, I'd adjudge those two melodramas his very peak. Even during his early sobriety, which was undermined musically by Sherrill's decline as a producer, there were many great moments and one good album (1989's *One Woman Man,* in print). And since signing to MCA in 1991 he's settled into a studio groove whose chief negative is the predictability of MCA honcho Tony Brown's quality controls—1994's lovingly hyped *The Bradley Barn Sessions,* well-plotted duets with America's greatest living singer, is less interesting than 1979's taped-on-the-run *My Very Special Guests.* But he's making better records than Sinatra did in his sixties, and his second MCA album, 1992's *Walls Can Fall,* is his best since 1980's *I Am What I Am* (also in print, unlike *My Very Special Guests* and 1976's *Alone Again*). He's on the road with his manager a hundred and twenty nights a year at fees ranging from twenty to fifty thousand dollars, and although Tosches reports credibly that these days he "is far more enamored with his cows than with his career," his stop at Tramps in 1993 was everything a fan could hope except long.

At its most unfathomable, Jones's music is scary. His famous clenched throat is the sound of repression feeling—the sound of an individual and by extension a whole people determined not to understand the sources of his and/or its suffering, yet proclaiming the primacy of that suffering anyway. It's class pride transcending class antagonism and deflecting class solidarity, especially cross-racial class solidarity; it's a sinner's church-rooted pop segregated from African sources that are far more abstract than Afrocentrists will ever understand and no less real for that. White soul indeed. But I'll never forget a Jones show I caught in a Suffolk County roadhouse in 1982, on what the souvenir T-shirt called the Still Doin' Time Tour. It was pretty pro forma—just weeks hence, Jones would wreck one of his cars so it looked like everything else in his field of vision—but before he could escape he was obliged to do the title number, and he'd forgotten the words. After each line he'd lean across to a guitar-bearing flunky, who'd whisper the next line, which he'd then deliver. And each line sounded like his life— true, implacable, a force we all had to reckon with.

All discographical information is accurate as of early 1995. Recent highlights of Jones's incomprehensible catalogue include the reissued New Favorites of George Jones *(Capitol), the two-CD* She Thinks I Still Care: The George Jones Collection *(Razor & Tie), and the*

Melba Montgomery duet comp Vintage Collections *(Capitol). The first two include "Root Beer," the teetotaler's "White Lightnin'." The second two include "Let's Invite Them Over," a wife-swapping song that went top twenty country in 1963.*

1995

Black Face, Whose Voice? Emmett Miller

Lawrence Cohn's carefully remastered and annotated Emmett Miller compilation for Columbia/Legacy will certainly stand as the year's most audacious, educational, and just plain important reissue. Cohn's name comes first because *The Minstrel Man From Georgia* is his baby, an archivist's tribute to an entertainer who never translated subcultural renown into anything like fame, and who probably didn't glimpse his own historical significance even after Jimmie Rodgers, Bob Wills, and Hank Williams got rich exploiting his vocal innovations. Miller was a blackface performer who was still burning cork in 1949, pretty damn late in the history of a minstrelsy that went on too damn long. But I'm not convinced that, after surveying the current cultural climate, even the man they nicknamed "Nigger" would choose to represent his legacy with the racist repartee Cohn has stalwartly scattered over a twenty-track disc whose reason for being is musical. And although it's to Cohn's credit that he didn't try to conceal the insulting stereotypes, they don't make the music more fun.

Then again, fun is far from this record's only pleasure. What has fans shaking their heads is its eeriness, the otherworldly aura of a weird yet seminal voice from nowhere that comes as a total historical surprise. We accept that we'll never hear the huge cornet of Buddy Bolden or pin down the stylistic debts of Charley Patton's teacher Henry Sloan. But Miller's recordings are circa 1928, and 1928 is supposed to be codified—Armstrong and Ellington, Bessie Smith and Ma Rainey, Ralph Peer's Bristol sessions, Patton and Blind Lemon Jefferson, Jolson and Crosby and Ukulele Ike. So into this crowded and hotly contested canon strolls a twenty-five-year-old Southern carny-once-removed previously known from a rare bootleg album, the magnificent "Lovesick Blues" on 1982's *Okeh Western Swing,* the testimony of Wills and Williams, and a few pages of speculative mythopoeia in Nick Tosches's *Country,* where Miller is anointed "the greatest song stylist of his generation." Anyone who has first read *Unsung Heroes of Rock 'n' Roll* and then heard a few Treniers or Ella Mae Morse tracks recognizes that Tosches isn't the world's most reliable judge of talent. Yet now that Miller's music is suddenly more available than it ever was, what does the certifiably sane Francis Davis call him? "One of the most supple and rhythmically assured male jazz vocalists of the Twenties." He's no Armstrong; maybe even Tosches would go along with that. But he's well beyond Bing Crosby or Ukulele Ike, who ain't bad. It's unsettling, and exciting.

What's easiest to describe about Miller's singing is what's weirdest about it—his signature yodel, which can hardly be said to reduce readily to words, or even comparison. No Swiss or African model suggests its sound, and his imitators Rodgers and Williams don't come close to duplicating it. Of course, both titans deploy it selectively and decoratively, while Miller lives for its flights, breaking upward at will from a squeezed "normal" voice that sounds as if he compresses his larynx and then routes the vibrations up around through his nose—a voice something like that of his sincere flatterer Leon Redbone, but decisively higher. If Miller did indeed command the "warm, pliant tenor" annotator Charles Wolfe grants him, I don't hear it here, not even in the yodel-free rendition of the 1929 Ben Selvin–Ted Weems–Ruth Etting hit "You're the Cream in My Coffee" that the optimists at Okeh thought they might sell. Miller's own pop preference was for Jack Yellen and Milton Ager, authors of "Ain't She Sweet," "Alabama Jubilee," and "My Yiddishe Momme," who gave him "Big Bad Bill Is Sweet William Now." But he was plainly happier escaping into a realm of freedom that transcended his norm. And that wouldn't mean as much if on top of its strangeness the entire voice didn't also sound natural, at least to Emmett Miller—this wonderland is just my home, come on in and look around. Which in turn is a credit to the most indescribable feature of his style, that supple rhythmic assurance Davis finds so impressive—not provocative like Armstrong or any number of country bluesmen, just flowing the way speech would if speech swung, which sometimes it does.

And then there's a factor that has little to do with Miller per se: his backup band. All these sides were cut in New York, where Miller apparently made a living doing blackface at a time when minstrelsy had supposedly already gone south in more ways than one, and recorded with a bunch of jazz-age hepcats that included Eddie Lang and the Dorsey brothers. As far as Tosches could determine four decades later, these hard-working studio sophisticates barely noticed the rube who was turning them into "his Georgia Crackers" for the day, but the laid-back New Orleans derivative they fell into did them at least as proud as the work they put their names on. Wolfe notes that although the live Miller usually accompanied his songs on ukulele, there was nothing inappropriate about these arrangements—the Fitch troupe where he got his start was one of many to abandon minstrelsy's traditional string band for up-to-date horns. These settings almost certainly helped engender Western swing; since Bob Wills modeled his trademark interjections on bits of Miller's shtick and auditioned Tommy Duncan with Miller's "I Ain't Got Nobody," it's obtuse to assume the Texan simply snatched his country-jazz synthesis from the radio air. But there's a subtler consequence as well. By recording atop recognizable if simulated "black" backup, Miller augmented the impression established by his makeup—that his singing imitated a "black" style.

Anyone familiar with the great "Hound Dog" controversy is aware that even with plenty of evidence available, the racial identity of a song is an even more vexed question than the racial identity of a person. And with the music of minstrelsy, the evidence is almost entirely lost. The relative profusion of scripts for blackface skits is one reason the critical literature, which has piled up like hotcakes since Robert Toll's 1974 *Blacking Up*, concentrates on minstrel theater—which, as Miller's record suggests, was far more overtly racist than minstrel music. We do know that minstrelsy's pre–Civil War fiddle-banjo-tambourine-bones instrumentation was originally African-American, and assume that after the war, when actual black people got into the act, actual black music did too (although at the same time spectacle and the family audience were also cultivated). Some musicologists have found African-seeming syncopations in published minstrel songs; others have noted that even songs claimed by their authenticity-hawking originators to have been "copied" (stolen, ha ha ha) from blacks, such as Thomas Dartmouth "Daddy" Rice's genre-establishing "Jump Jim Crow," suspiciously resemble pop hackwork of the day. And with vocal production we're completely in the dark. Few white minstrels and almost no blacks were recorded, and the journalistic descriptions thus far unearthed are woefully unspecific.

So to assert, as several reviewers have, that Miller's singing style derives from Southern blacks (or even Southern minstrelsy) is pure speculation. Acquaintances report that Miller studied and emulated black speech, which he then demeaned—affectionately, thank you very much, but also with cruel, thorough parodistic condescension—in his comedy. But if his music is an imitation, how can it be that none of the many black bluesmen and songsters recorded in the twenties affects similar mannerisms? The closest I've found is Pine Top Smith's "Nobody Knows You When You're Down and Out" on Yazoo's new *Roots of Rap,* which not only isn't very close but is also entirely spoken. Fact is, the voice Miller's yodel most resembles is his own theatrical speaking voice—it recalls his character "Slam," the butt of countless jokes, rendered like many of minstrelsy's black dialect personas in an artificially high register probably meant to signify childishness. I'm speculating too, of course. But to me it sounds as if Slam embodied Miller's realm of freedom—that like millions of other white Americans, Miller projected onto blacks needs and possibilities he wasn't willing to take responsibility for. It sounds as if he needed that realm so much he felt compelled to make music of it. And as if out of that ignoble compulsion he created something new—maybe even something heroic.

1996

Brown Eyed Handsome Rock and Roller: Chuck Berry

The body of Chuck Berry's top-quality work isn't exactly vast, comprising three or four or perhaps five dozen songs that synthesize two related traditions: blues and country. Although in some respects Berry's rock and roll is simpler and more vulgar than its sources, its simplicity and vulgarity are defensible in the snootiest high-art terms—"instinctive minimalism" or "demotic voice." But the case for his artistic greatness doesn't rest on such defenses. It would be perverse to argue that his songs are in themselves as rich as, say, *Remembrance of Things Past.* As with Charlie Chaplin or Walt Kelly or the Beatles, their richness is a function of their active relationship with an audience—a complex relationship that shifts every time a song enters a new context, club or album or radio or mass singalong. Where Marcel Proust wrote about a dying subculture from a cork-lined room, Berry helped give life to a subculture, and both he and it change every time they confront each other. Even "My Ding-a-Ling," a fourth-grade wee-wee joke that used to mortify true believers at college concerts, permitted a lot of twelve-year-olds new insight into the moribund concept of "dirty" when it became his first certified million-seller in 1972, and the song changed again when an oldies crowd became as children to shout along with Uncle Chuck the night he received his gold record at Madison Square Garden. And what happened to "Brown Eyed Handsome Man," never a hit among whites, when Berry sang it at interracial rock and roll concerts in Northern cities in the fifties? How many black kids took "eyed" as code for "skinned"? How many whites? How did that make them feel about each other, and about the song? And did any of that change the song itself?

Berry's own intentions, of course, remain a mystery. Typically, this public artist is an obsessively private person who has been known to drive reporters from his own park, and accounts of his life overlap and contradict each other. The way I tell it, Berry was born into a lower-middle-class colored family in St. Louis in 1926. He was so quick and ambitious that he both served time for robbery in reform school and acquired a degree in hairdressing and cosmetology before taking a job on an auto assembly line to support a wife and kids. Yet his speed and ambition persisted. By 1953 he was working as a beautician and leading a three-piece blues group on a regular weekend gig. His gimmick was to cut the blues with country-influenced humorous narrative songs. These were rare in the black music of the time, although they had been common enough before phonograph records crystallized blues form, and although Louis Jordan, a hero of Berry's, had been selling something similar to both blacks and whites for years.

In 1955 Berry recorded two of his songs on a borrowed machine: "Wee Wee Hours," a blues that he and his pianist, Johnnie Johnson, hoped to sell, and an adapted country tune called "Ida Red." He traveled to Chicago and met Muddy Waters, the uncle of the blues, who sent him on to Leonard Chess of Chess Records. Chess liked "Wee Wee Hours" but flipped for "Ida Red," which was renamed "Maybellene," a hairdresser's dream, and forwarded to Alan Freed. Having mysteriously acquired a substantial portion of the writer's credit, Freed played "Maybellene" quite a lot, and it became one of the first nationwide rock and roll hits.

At the time, any fair-minded person would have judged this process exploitative. A blues musician comes to a blues label to promote a blues song—"It was 'Wee Wee Hours' we was proud of, that was our music," says Johnnie Johnson. The label owner decides he wants to push the novelty: "The big beat, cars, and young love. It was a trend and we jumped on it," Chess has said. The owner then trades away a third of the blues singer's creative sweat to the symbol of payola, who hypes the novelty song into commercial success and leaves the artist in a quandary. Does he stick with his art, thus forgoing the first real recognition he's ever had, or does he pander to popular taste?

The question is loaded, of course. "Ida Red" was Chuck Berry's music as much as "Wee Wee Hours," which in retrospect seems rather uninspired. In fact, maybe the integrity problem went the other way. Maybe Johnson was afraid that the innovations of "Ida Red"—the not-exactly-blues riffs way out front, with the ceaseless legato of his own piano adding rhythmic excitement to the steady backbeat—were too far out to sell. What happened instead was that Berry's limited but brilliant vocabulary of guitar riffs quickly came to epitomize rock and roll. Ultimately, every great white guitar group of the early sixties imitated Berry, and Johnson's piano technique was almost as influential. In other words, it turned out that Berry and Johnson weren't basically bluesmen at all. Through some combination of inspiration and cultural destiny, they had hit upon something more contemporary than blues, and a young audience for whom the Depression was one more thing that bugged their parents understood this better than the musicians themselves. Leonard Chess simply functioned as a music businessman should, though only rarely does one combine the courage and insight (and opportunity) to pull it off, even once. Chess became a surrogate audience, picking up on new music and making sure that it received enough exposure for everyone else to pick up on it too.

Obviously, Chuck Berry wasn't racked with doubt about artistic compromise. A good blues single usually sold around ten thousand and a big rhythm and blues hit might go into the hundreds of thousands, but "Maybellene" probably moved a million, even if Chess never sponsored the audit to prove it. Berry had achieved a grip on the white audience and the solid future it could promise, and, remarkably, he had in no way diluted his genius to do so. On the contrary, that was his genius. He would never have fulfilled himself if he hadn't explored his relationship to the white world—a relationship that was much different for him, an urban black man who was attracted to mechanization and modernization and had never known brutal poverty, than it was for, say, Muddy Waters.

Close relatives of some Berry riffs had surfaced on sides by T-Bone Walker, Gatemouth Brown, and others—especially, if Berry rather than the dim recorded evidence is to be believed, Louis Jordan sideman Carl Hogan. His tone and approach can be discerned in such Western swing touchstones as Bob Wills's (and

Leon McAuliffe's) "Steel Guitar Rag." But it was Berry who had the imagination to develop these stray note clusters into the basis of a music, uniting Ike Turner-style guitar-based r&b and neater country-style picking into a new electric sound whose sense of balance changed the world's ears. Alternating guitar chords augmented the beat while Berry sang in an insouciant tenor that, while recognizably African-American in accent, stayed clear of the melisma and blurred overtones of blues singing, both of which enter only at carefully premeditated moments. His few detractors still complain about the repetitiveness of his style, but they miss the point. Repetition without tedium is the backbone of rock and roll, and the components of Berry's music proved so durable that they still provoked instant excitement decades later. And in any case, the instrumental repetition was counterbalanced by unprecedented and virtually unduplicated verbal variety.

Chuck Berry is the greatest rock lyricist this side of Bob Dylan, and sometimes I prefer him to Dylan. Both communicate an abundance of the childlike delight in linguistic discovery that page poets are supposed to convey and too often don't, but Berry's most ambitious lyrics, unlike Dylan's, never seem pretentious or forced. True, his language is ersatz and barbaric, full of mispronounced foreignisms and advertising coinages, but then, so was Whitman's. Like Whitman, Berry is excessive because he is totally immersed in America—the America of Melville and the Edsel, burlesque and installment-plan funerals, pemmican and pomade. Unlike Whitman, though, he doesn't quite permit you to take him seriously—he can't really think it's pronounced "a la carty," can he? He is a little surreal. How else could a black man as sensitive as Chuck Berry respond to the affluence of white America—an affluence suddenly his for the taking?

Chuck Berry is not only a little surreal but also a little schizy; even after he committed himself to rock and roll story songs, relegating the bluesman in him to B sides and album filler, he found his persona split in two. In three of the four singles that followed "Maybellene," he amplified the black half of his artistic personality, the brown eyed handsome man who always came up short in his quest for the smalltime hedonism America promises everyone. By implication, Brown Eyes's sharp sense of life's nettlesome and even oppressive details provided a kind of salvation by humor, especially in "Too Much Monkey Business," a catalog of hassles that included work, school, and the army. But the white teenagers who were the only audience with the cultural experience to respond to Berry's art weren't buying this kind of salvation, not en masse. They wanted something more optimistic and more specific to themselves: of the four singles that followed "Maybellene," only "Roll Over Beethoven," which introduced Berry's other half, the rock and roller, achieved any real success. Chuck got the message. His next release, "School Day," was another complaint song, but this time the complaints were explicitly adolescent and were relieved by the direct action of the rock and roller. In fact, the song has been construed as a prophecy of the Free Speech Movement: "Close your books, get out of your seat/Down the halls and into the street."

It has become a cliche to attribute the rise of rock and roll to a new parallelism between white teenagers and black Americans; a common "alienation" and even "suffering" are often cited. As with most cliches, this one has its basis in fact—teenagers in the fifties certainly showed an unprecedented consciousness of themselves as a circumscribed group, although how much that had to do with marketing refinements and how much with the bomb remains unresolved. In any case, Chuck Berry's history points up the limits of this notion. For Berry was closer to white teenagers both economically (that reform school stint suggests a JD exploit combined with a racist judicial system) and in spirit (he shares his penchant for youthfulness with Satchel Paige but not Henry Aaron, with Leslie Fiedler but not Norman Podhoretz) than the average black man. And even at that, he had to make a conscious (not to say calculated) leap of the imagination to reach them, and sometimes fell short. Although he scored lots of minor hits, Chuck Berry made only three additional *Billboard* top ten singles in the fifties—"Rock and Roll Music," "Sweet Little Sixteen," and "Johnny B. Goode"—and every one of them ignored Brown Eyes for the assertive, optimistic, and somewhat simpleminded rock and roller. In a pattern common among popular artists, his truest and most personal work didn't flop, but it wasn't overwhelmingly successful either.

For such artists, the audience can be like a drug. A little of it is so good for them that they assume a lot of it would be even better, but instead the big dose saps their autonomy, often so subtly that they don't notice it. For Chuck Berry, the craving for overwhelming popularity proved slightly dangerous. At the same time that he was enlivening his best songs with faintly Latin rhythms, which he was convinced were the coming thing, he was also writing silly exercises with titles like "Hey Pedro." Nevertheless, his pursuit of the market also worked a communion with his audience, with whom he continued to have an instinctive rapport remarkable in a thirty-year-old black man. For there is also a sense in which the popular artist is a drug for the audience, and a doctor, too—he has to know how much of his vital essence he can administer at one time, and in what compound.

The reason Berry's rock and roller was capable of such insightful excursions into the teen psyche—"Sweet Little Sixteen," a celebration of everything lovely about fanhood, or "Almost Grown," a basically unalienated first-person expression of teen rebellion that sixties youthcult pundits should have taken seriously—was that he shared a crucial American value with the humorous Brown Eyes. That value was fun. Even among rock critics, who ought to know better, fun doesn't have much of a rep, so that they commiserate with someone like LaVern Baker, a second-rate blues and gospel singer who felt she was selling her soul every time she launched into a first-rate whoop of nonsense like "Jim Dandy" or "Bumble Bee." But fun was what rock and roll's adolescent revolt had to be about—inebriated affluence versus the hangover of the work ethic. It was the only practicable value in the Peter Pan utopia of the American dream. Because black music had always thrived on exuberance—not just the otherworldly transport of gospel, but the candidly physical good times of great pop blues singers like Washboard Sam, who is most often dismissed as a lightweight by heavy blues critics—it turned into the perfect vehicle for generational convulsion. Black musicians, however, had rarely achieved an optimism that was cultural as well as personal—those few who did, like Louis Armstrong, left themselves open to charges of tomming. Chuck Berry never tommed. The trouble he'd seen just made his sly, bad-boy voice and the splits and waddles of his stage show that much more credible.

Then, late in 1959, fun turned into trouble. Berry had imported a Spanish-speaking Apache prostitute he'd picked up in El Paso to check hats in his St. Louis nightclub, then fired her. She went to the police, and Berry was indicted under the Mann Act. After two trials, the first so blatantly racist it was disallowed, he went to prison for two years. When he got out, in 1964, he and his wife had separated, apparently a major tragedy for him. The Beatles and the Rolling Stones had paid him such explicit and appropriate tribute that his career was probably in better shape after his jail term than before, but he couldn't capitalize. He had a few hits that many (including John Lennon) believed he'd written before he went in, but the well was dry. Between 1965 and 1970 he didn't release one even passable new song, and he died as a recording artist.

In late 1966 Berry left Chess for a big advance from Mercury Records. The legends of his money woes at Chess are numerous, but apparently the Chess brothers knew how to record him; the stuff he produced himself for Mercury was terrible. Working alone with pickup bands, he still performed a great deal, mostly to make money for Berry Park, a recreation haven thirty miles from St. Louis. And as he toured, he found that something had happened to his old audience—it was getting older, with troubles of its own, and it dug blues. At auditoriums like the Fillmore, where he did a disappointing live LP with the Steve Miller Blues Band, Chuck Berry was more than willing to stretch out on a blues. One of his favorites was from Elmore James: "When things go wrong, wrong with you, it hurts me too."

By 1970 he was back home at Chess, and suddenly his new audience called forth a miracle. Berry was a natural head—no drugs, no alcohol—and most of his attempts to cash in on hippie talk had been embarrassments. But "Tulane," one of his greatest story songs, was the perfect fantasy. It was about two dope dealers: "Tulane and Johnny opened a novelty shop/Back under the counter was the cream of the crop." Johnny is nabbed by narcs, but his girlfriend Tulane escapes, and Johnny confidently predicts that she will buy off the judge. Apparently she does, for there is a sequel, a blues. In "Have Mercy Judge," Johnny has been caught again, and this time he expects to be sent to "some stony mansion." Berry devotes the last stanza to Tulane, who is "too alive to live alone." The last lines make me wonder just how he felt about his own wife when he went to prison: "Just tell her to live, and I'll forgive her/And even love her more when I come back home."

Taken together, the two songs are Berry's peak, although Leonard Chess would no doubt have vetoed the double-tracked vocal on "Tulane," which blurs its impact a bit. Remarkably, "Have Mercy Judge" is the first important blues Berry ever wrote, and like all his best work it isn't quite traditional, utilizing an *aabb* line structure instead of the usual *aab*. Where did it come from? Is it unreasonable to suspect that part of Berry really was a bluesman all along, and that this time, instead of him going to his audience, his audience came to him and provided the juice for one last masterpiece?

Although 1979's *Rockit* was Berry's best album in fifteen years, it was groove rather than songs that made it go. When he was sentenced to a second jail term plus an incredible thousand hours of benefits for tax evasion, the shock wasn't that a black artist was being robbed of his spirit, but that a black man was being deprived of his livelihood—the object of a persecution recapitulated in his legal battles of 1990, when local cops arrested him on "pornography" charges that were later dropped. A charter member of the Rock and Roll Hall of Fame who won belated Grammy recognition when he received a NARAS Lifetime Achievement Award in 1984, he was plainly a rock and roll monument, a pleasing performer whose days of inspiration were over. Yet two 1987 events proved him muscle and bone. One was the long-promised *Chuck Berry: The Autobiography,* which he'd started writing as long ago as 1959 and begun anew while serving his prison sentence in 1979. Berry claims it's entirely unghosted and that's how it reads. His pleasure in language isn't quite as palpable when he's not singing, but it's just as untrammeled, and the dirty parts make you wonder what he saved for the sequel, slated to concentrate on his love life. The other was *Hail! Hail! Rock 'n' Roll,* keyed to an all-star sixtieth-birthday concert that Berry actually rehearsed for—with a band organized by Keith Richards and featuring the long-absent Johnnie Johnson. As a record it's only a document—Berry's half-cracked timbre signifies natural bluesman, not perpetual adolescent. But Taylor Hackford's film is a wickedly funny and moving rock-doc, exposing Berry the money-grubbing control freak without devaluing his genius in the process.

Eventually Chuck Berry will die, and while his songs have already stuck in the public memory a lot longer than Washboard Sam's, it's likely that most of them will fade away too. So is he, was he, will he be a great artist? It won't be us judging, but perhaps we can think of it this way. Maybe the true measure of his greatness was not whether his songs "lasted"—a term that as of now means persisted through centuries instead of decades—but that he was one of the ones to make us understand that the greatest thing about art is the way it happens among people. I treasure aesthetic artifacts, and I suspect that a few of Berry's songs, a few of his recordings, will live on in that way. I only hope that they prove too alive to live alone. If they do, and if by some mishap Berry's name itself is forgotten, that will nevertheless be an entirely apposite kind of triumph.

1972–1975–1991–1997

Elvis in Literature: Elvis Presley

Elvis Presley is so everywhere that he gets as much space in *Books in Print* as Dylan and the Beatles put together, a full page that lists a hundred or so apparent acts of prose plus fakebooks, photo collections, catalogues, and so forth. Inexorably, he has become a literary hero, his meaning defined at least as much by the texts he's inspired as by those he's created. I'd regale you with humorous examples (Maia C. Magii Shamayyim's *The Spiritual Drama and Mystical Heritage of Elvis Aaron Presley?*) if Gilbert Rodman's *Elvis After Elvis: The Posthumous Career of a Living Legend* didn't so astutely survey a literature that also includes news clips, tabloid revelations, magazine pieces, journal articles, song lyrics, and fictional references without number. And as Rodman makes clear, these are only the verbal Elvis sightings; there are also paintings, sculptures, collages, comic strips, ads, Web pages, videos, roadside shrines, what-all. Including, you bet, music per se. Musn't forget music per se.

In the Elvis metatext sweepstakes, Rodman's ambitious precis tops even Greil Marcus's *Dead Elvis,* essays that became a book only because Elvis demanded nothing less. "Metatext" is my term, not Rodman's, but for better or worse—on the merits, better, but life is unfair—this theory maven deserves it. He can't cut the cultural studies posse off at the pass—not with Elvis a signifier so all-embracing that Madonna seems as austere as Mallarmé by comparison. I mean, if life is unfair, cultural studies is a Ponzi scheme. But unless you believe that none of its insights or methods is of any value whatsoever, then *Elvis After Elvis* is what the cross-discipline is for. Absorbing a vast array of representations, Rodman parses not only their differing meanings but their vastness itself, then lays out his findings in an unusually colloquial academic prose that conveys everyday pleasure in, respect for, and love of his subject. He's so likable you figure he must know what he's doing when he comes down hard on the jargon concept "point of articulation." And he does.

Rodman's thesis is that Elvis articulated the moment when rock and roll, a preexisting musical genre that would have developed without him, precipitated what many now call "the sixties." This is not an original claim. That "we" are all children of Elvis is assumed by Marcus and the immense school of exegetes inspired by *Mystery Train*'s "Presliad." But Rodman's presentation is gratifyingly coherent. All the political issues/metaphors/ ideas Elvis is understood to bear—race integrated/appropriated/ miscegenated/assimilated, sex as pleasure and gender, unmentionable class and its respectable cousin the American dream— are tucked into a long expository chapter called "Elvis Myths." In "Elvis Space," the faithful who use these myths are situated first in the imaginary community of their media-mediated devotion and then at Graceland, a geographical locus no other branch of fandom enjoys. Finally, fans meet society in "Elvis Culture," where Rodman first relishes every feelthy detail of the uncensored June 5, 1956 *Milton Berle Show* "Hound Dog," which he declares the point of articulation for all of Elvis's subsequent impact, then undercuts himself with the admission that his students are utterly unimpressed by the same video clip that fills him with awe: "where there was once a message so shocking that it seemed that Western civilization could not possibly survive its utterance, there is now no message at all." But rather than disavowing his own response, Rodman concludes that this incomprehension only proves how utterly Elvis changed the world: Elvis has normalized his own Elvisness.

Neat, eh? Yet nothing in this lucid schema is original enough to startle acolytes or overpowering enough to persuade snobs, and its very neatness insures the usual measure of benign distortion. Up against the fools, hacks, and academic con men who overrun *In Search of Elvis: Music, Race, Art, Religion,* in which Vernon

Chadwick collects presentations from the "six-day festival of learning" that was the University of Mississippi's 1995 International Conference on Elvis Presley, Rodman is a model of scholarly cool. But from his cultural studies hobbyhorse he's too ready to disregard Elvis's individual agency. It's fine to complain that Marcus habitually overstates Elvis's will and ability to produce unaided "a cultural formation," which is collective by definition. But Rodman risks losing sight of Elvis's incomprehensibly complex and protean persona.

Reading Karal Ann Marling's much slighter *Graceland: Going Home with Elvis,* for instance, you soon realize that Rodman's conception of Elvis's shrine, undeniable in outline, is a romanticized abstraction. The texture Marling's book has room for roughs up Rodman's idealization, and her expertise in the decorative arts (plus the phrase-making knack that complements it) makes Elvis's mansion on the hill seem a creation as well as a site. Graceland's "act of faith in serial novelty," she argues, synthesized the "intense concern for personal style" that made B. B. King notice a teenaged Elvis in a pawnshop years before he was famous and the fashion sense informing the "theme clothes" of the seventies—"carapace[s] of sheer, radiant glory." And she's franker than Rodman about the stereotypes that will surely rise again in reports of the twentieth-anniversary rites in Memphis this August. You can't miss them, she agrees: "the fat, the old, the unattractive, the hairsprayed, and the deeply crazy." But when Elvis was alive, she points out, he "remained in spirit a part of the have-not group on the other side of the wall." And now: "Jesus, or Elvis, speaks softly to all of them here in the garden of Graceland."

In a contradiction endemic to cultural studies, neither Rodman's left politics nor his wide-ranging references decrease his natural distance from the polyester regulars actually drawn to Elvis Space. Like most pomo types, he's drawn instead to the avant-garde, the abject, the radical, the intellectual, and the patently weird. Not that Rodman need pay any heed to the fans empowered by Vernon Chadwick's Southern-populist inclusivity— to the banalities of Elvis's cousin Gene Smith, "World's Greatest Elvis Fan" Paul MacLeod and his son Elvis, two different Danish archivists, or logorrheic Alvis artist Howard Finster (not to mention several professors of no other apparent distinction). *In Search of Elvis* strikes more telling blows for democracy when it steps back a little, as in John Shelton Reed's sociohistorical breakdown of the poor white South or Roger Manley's curatorial survey of the region's vernacular art.

Be thankful for Reed and Manley's garden-variety scholarship, which strides on undeterred by theory's disdain for history as a discipline—its doubts about the efficacy of facts themselves. Those doubts are why Rodman considers Elvis's political meanings myths. It doesn't really matter, he argues, whether Sam Phillips said "Negro" (as Jerry Hopkins originally reported) or "nigger" (Albert Goldman's calumny), or whether Elvis once opined that African-Americans were only good to buy his records and shine his shoes. All that matters is what people believe. The fallacy here is that what (seems to have) really happened affects what people believe. When Marcus launched his famous attack on Goldman's lie, he predicted that it would become official history, but instead, due largely to the fuss Marcus started and the research he followed through with, it is now widely discredited. So maybe, after yet more Elvis studies, black people will stop believing the apocryphal shine-my-shoes story—or maybe new evidence will prove them right. In the end, there's no denying the pomo view that each of us has his or her own Elvis, that Elvis as individually perceived is (like every other artist) a conflation of image, theory, personal bias, and oeuvre. But as we create our own Elvises, most of us are aided and comforted by the "real" one.

So for me, the oddest thing about Peter Guralnick's compelling and probably definitive biography *Last Train to Memphis: The Rise of Elvis Presley,* the richest spread of Elvis facts ever, is that in my own Elvis-making process it played no larger role than *Good Rockin' Tonight: Twenty Years on the Road and on the Town with Elvis,* a medium-cheesy tell-all as-told-to by Army buddy/factotum Joe Esposito and reggae woman/music scribe Elena Oumano. *Last Train to Memphis* is so masterful that, for all Guralnick's insistence on letting his research speak for itself, he inevitably portrays not the Real Elvis, but Guralnick's Elvis—or rather, since a second volume will complete a story that ends when Elvis ships out to Germany six weeks after burying the mother he adored, Guralnick's Young Elvis. Guralnick's Young Elvis is an irrepressibly energetic, heartbreakingly eager genius whose most secret dreams are thrust upon him. He's quick, impish, spiritual, serious, full of fun and full of music, with a gift for guilelessness that cannot possibly survive. He loves attention and he loves money; about sex, which he soon realizes is his meal ticket, he's more ambivalent. As the book ends, there's a sense not just of impending doom but of impending tragedy.

The main things missing from *Last Train to Memphis* are ideas and dirt. Both deficiencies reflect Guralnick's most irritating mannerism—his reluctance to make judgments, draw conclusions, generalize at all. In theory, this is formal rigor (report observations, not speculations); in practice, it's prim whitewash (if you can't say something nice about a person, don't say anything at all). It's why he'll never tell us in so many words whether Gladys Presley drank too much (as she seemed to toward her untimely end, which involved a mysterious liver ailment) or what the hell made her handsome husband tick (the two mentions of Vernon's chronic underemployment contradict each other). And since *Good Rockin' Tonight* asserts credibly that Elvis's mom "died of alcoholism" and glibly that Vernon "didn't treat her very well," I'd like to know, for no better reason than that I'm nosy. So I appreciate what Guralnick does reveal about Young Elvis's sexuality— enough to let the attentive reader imagine a guy who got laid a whole lot but was a little nervous about the act itself, so that he would lie around in bed for hours with his pick of the night's procurements, talking and making out (he was a "great kisser," girls report) before risking closure. The scene in which Elvis *doesn't* fuck a 1956 steady is breathtaking.

Even to get this far, however, I rely partly on *Good Rockin' Tonight,* which begins where Guralnick leaves off and depicts a much hornier guy. Esposito is mildly obsessed with Elvis's sex life because it messed up his own—as bad as an unlimited supply of disposable women was for his boss, it was terrible for the boss's cronies, who because they weren't famous might otherwise have developed real relationships. Asserting without prejudice that Elvis "was not the super-suave stud everyone thought he was," Esposito reports "voyeuristic tendencies," a "full-blown Madonna complex" (perhaps extending to Priscilla, who bore Lisa Marie exactly nine months after he married her), and drug-induced impotence in his decline. For a superstar, this is within normal range, reminiscent of both Frank Sinatra (probably more of a cocksman) and Chuck Berry (probably more of a perve). And to be blunt, that's a relief, because far more than the dreary details of his uppers and downers, Elvis's sexual history inflects the myth of a feral young Southerner whose twitching hips were the point of articulation for a seismic shift in American mores.

But having pursued Elvis's sexual history in the interest of substantiating Rodman's sexual myth, which codifies Elvis's first nationally televised opportunity "to dance, to twitch, to gyrate, to bump and grind, and to shake, rattle, and roll to his heart's content" as the moment when he and rock and roll (now joined at the hip) are "recognized as a threat to mainstream U.S. culture," I find myself unable to stop. Guralnick and especially Esposito provide raw material for a far more complex sexual persona. Super-suave or not, Elvis knew that with a few classy exceptions (Debra Paget, Hope Lange) he could score at will, but as a matter of form he put out a lot of sweet talk and boyish charm. A cut-up whose wit wasn't sharpened by the yes-men he joked around with, he was also a bullshit artist, because that was the way of courtship in his yes-man world. Maybe his love-making was feral (and maybe not), but his come-on wasn't. It was romantic, with dashes of levity. Isn't it striking that so much of the enormous store of Elvis music that *didn't* articulate a shift in American mores could be described the same way?

Since music is Guralnick's passion, it's no surprise that his descriptions of Elvis's painstaking fooling around in the studio flesh out Esposito and Oumano's welcome generalization that Elvis "may be the most underrated record producer in the history of rock 'n' roll." He was an artist who knew what he wanted and had a prescient notion of how to get it—by indirection, jamming until he hit upon the right feel and then nailing it, which is how rock and rollers have cultivated spontaneity ever since. This isn't an original claim either, and Rodman, who as an embattled postmodern academic has a stake in proving that Elvis doesn't get enough cultural respect, makes sure to pooh-pooh it: "If he was such a brilliant musician, then why did he make so much bad music?" Anyway, he didn't write his own material. But in his need to demonstrate that Elvis is no "*auteur*," Rodman falls into a trap that lurks for all who conceive him as the king of rock and roll.

In fact, Elvis's status as rock's only heroic *interpreter* (not counting, er, Jackie Wilson, the Shirelles, the Temptations, and Aretha Franklin, but bear with me) may just mean he isn't really the first and greatest of the rock and rollers after all. Maybe instead he's a missing link to the pop music he's also known to have loved (Dean Martin, Mario Lanza, the Ink Spots)—the very pop music he was supposed to have destroyed, so that whenever he tried it my generation saw a betrayal imposed by Hollywood, Colonel Parker, his evil twin, or his corrupt nature. As it is still unorthodox to mention, he shares more formally with Billie Holiday and Frank Sinatra than with Chuck Berry and Bruce Springsteen. And if Rodman doesn't think Holiday and Sinatra rank as auteurs, he doesn't know as much about popular music as a metatextualizer should.

This is not an argument for the primacy of music per se. One reason Elvis has become a literary hero is that as art recedes in time, it requires explanation, interpretation, contextualization, perceptual work—an aesthetic effort whose surprises are subtle and whose pleasures don't come naturally. With his Uncle Miltie epiphany forty years gone, Elvis is no more an exception than Norman Mailer or Jackson Pollock, neither of whom packs much shock value anymore either. Elvis caught more musical magic than philistines weaned on Holiday and Sinatra will ever comprehend, but much of it is almost as inaccessible to aesthetes weaned on Berry and Springsteen. And with all due awe for the yearning urgency of his rock and roll touchstones, it's willful to insist that on strictly musical grounds "That's Alright Mama" and "Hound Dog" and "All Shook Up" are epochal while "Great Balls of Fire" and "Be-Bop-a-Lula" and "Lonely Weekends" are not. It's what we know about them that makes the difference.

Elvis made a great many major recordings. And no matter what jaded undergraduates think, few rock and rollers of any era have moved with such salacious insouciance. But it's my best guess, based on raw aural information and patterns of pop history and everything I've read and observed and absorbed about artist and audience, that rocking or romantic, young or old, thin or fat, innocent or decadent, inspired or automatic, Elvis touches the millions he touches most deeply with that ineffable chestnut, the grain of his voice. From the pure possibility of both "Mystery Train" and "Love Me Tender" to the schlock passion of both "In the Ghetto" and "You Don't Have To Say You Love Me," no singer has ever duplicated his aura of unguarded self-acceptance. The very refusal of sophistication that renders him unlistenable to Sinatraphiles is what his faithful love most about him. Furthermore, listeners with looser standards in cultural articulation than those espoused by Rodman, Marcus, myself, or even Vernon Chadwick—listeners who think Elvis lit stops at supermarket gasps, yes-man as-told-tos, and maps of his mystical legacy—probably have a clearer pipeline to the meanings that voice might hold.

For finally, the decisive thing about Elvis Presley was that—to borrow a phrase so inevitable Esposito and Oumano can't have been the first to use it—he was an "extraordinary ordinary man." What's hardest for intellectual types to internalize about him isn't his momentousness. It's his accessibility. Eventually, common sense tells us, internalizing him will become harder for the faithful as well; already, common sense tells us, their experience of his accessibility reflects what they've been told about him, both orally and in texts of all kinds. But if Elvis is a literary hero, no one, patient reader, needs his literature more than you and me. He is a literary hero who confounds literacy itself.

1997

2

Where "Rock" Began

Spontaneity by the Seat of the Pants: Janis Joplin

Midway into the seventies, more than four years after the fact, I get the sense that many of those who survived her are just as happy Janis Joplin is dead. Not that they wished she would die, or felt any conscious relief when she did. The observers I have in mind stake too much on their own civility for that. But now that she is literally beyond the pale she is also out of the way. Formerly a nettlesome challenge to the numbing spiritual entropy in which so many chronic observers take comfort, she is now a neat, manageable metaphor for the failure of that challenge.

Midge Decter, reviewing Myra Friedman's biography of Janis in the *Times,* described that challenge like the lifelong entropy junkie she is: "the epidemic of antic despair that carried off our children in the late 1960's." Of course, as a cold war liberal who was present at the unveiling of the end-of-ideology ideology, she was a pusher as well as an addict. What about those without even an anti-ideology to support their habit? Those who were swept away by the utopian surge of the last decade only because they were unmoored by any conviction, and who now lie beached, more bruised than they care to admit but grateful just to be out of the water? Who take a snotty delight in reminding us that "the sixties are over"? In 1975, after all, this is a rather reactionary way of putting it. To me, it seems more pertinent that the eighties are coming.

But this is not a time when survivors willingly anticipate the future, and despite their current reputation as the years of gimme-now, the sixties were, at least for some of us. The single-minded voracity with which we partook of the present only reflected our complex notion of the future—we may have feared the worst, but not without hoping for the best, and life had prepared us to expect at least a happy medium. Does the belief that there is already a timewarped nostalgia for such a connection with the future inspire the marquee at Cinema 1, where *Janis,* a music documentary assembled by producer F. R. Crawley and editor-directors Howard Alk and Seaton Findlay, is playing to enthusiastic but less than sold-out houses? "The Soul of the '60s," it says.

It has become commonplace to downgrade Janis's mostly extraordinary albums because they do not live up to her myth. Whether we experienced it firsthand or aspire to comprehend it in retrospect, that myth matters more than the music. Hoping to grasp it, we resort to the biographies, but we find that Peggy Caserta's turgid porny and Deborah Landau's awe-stricken fan-book reiterate the myth instead of trying to recreate it, while David Dalton's purple haze falls so far short of its sincere ambition to transfix Janis's voodoo in language that it suggests that maybe the myth was garbled to begin with. And Friedman's supposedly sane and definitely respectable *Buried Alive* turns out to be a debunk, stuck in all the entropic platitudes about the danger and venality of the mythmaking process.

By its simple acquiescence to the powerful visual record, the film rights all that. Concentrating on performance without ignoring interview, the editors fiddle with chronology to make the conventional points about Janis's personal vulnerability, maturing musicianship, and liberating power. But these concepts structure the film—they don't rigidify it. Although I don't happen to agree with their implied analysis of Janis's musical "development," I was moved by how the argument respected the footage—no underhanded editing slanted its import.

More than records, more even than live performance, film was Janis's medium. The subject of as many interesting photographs as any celebrity of the sixties, Janis boasted one eloquent visual asset: her pug-nosed, acne-scarred, rubber-mouthed face. Her body was girlish, lovely, and the nudes she permitted when she felt secure about her weight prove it. But as with so many women who believe themselves fat, she probably could have proved it any time, and that we remember her as somewhat stubby reflects her own lack of confidence. She never managed to transform her body into a particularly graceful vehicle, for her sexuality or for anything else except frenzy; she looked OK doing kinesics around a mike stand or shaking a tambourine, but when she felt compelled to shimmy while the sidemen soloed, as she did more and more post–Big Brother, she risked blunting a message that had already become perilously broad. Far back in an arena, even from deep in the second balcony at the Fillmore East, her performance was reduced to raw emotion, beat, and energy— big voice, big backing, big body movements. It was only up close, or in camera perspective, that the sensibility that had won over her original fans came into focus on that helplessly articulate face. Janis could no more hide the intelligence there than she could suppress the play of moods that would sometimes overcome her. But intelligence wasn't what she or anyone around her was trying to put across, and very often it got lost.

Not that Janis was any sort of intellectual. She had a gift for the epigram and she liked to read a little, but her everyday pronouncements were updated beatnikisms. This distinction, which she insisted on herself, made her a child of the end of ideology. It meant that instead of utopian hippie politics, she knew none at all—beyond her fierce instinctual feminism. But not all intelligence is systematic or even verbal. Janis's was in her tone of voice and turn of phrase; she invariably invested the cliches she resuscitated with a paradoxically tender (even hopeful) skepticism that went otherwise unacknowledged.

This attitude carried over onto the stage. The first time I saw her perform, at Monterey Pop in 1967, I was not totally unprepared. I had run photos of her as a star of the "San Francisco underground" and marveled at her synthesis of blues and hillbilly inflections when "Down on Me" came on the AM radio out there. But I never figured on the banshee freak who stomped and moaned at me in the fourth row of the press section. She seemed an overwhelming natural force—a sort of contained disaster, like the floodwaters that irrigate the Nile valley. Yet this dionysian experience had its apollonian moments—I was delighted even as I was overwhelmed, and so was Janis. Midgrimace she would be taken by an almost humorous look, amazed at the flux around her.

Occasionally she chuckled. And as she walked off the stage she gave a happy little jump, like a nine-year-old who has just gotten a pony for her birthday. At one level, her entire ritual of spirit possession was obviously a conscious game.

Myra Friedman reports, rather pointedly, that Janis's famed spontaneity was largely posed: she preconceived almost every melisma and vocal aside and sharpened her off-the-cuff remarks until they crackled like folk aphorisms. Friedman acknowledges that this doesn't mean Janis never did anything spontaneous. But she doesn't trust spontaneity as a value, and obviously hopes to discredit it with her inside dope. My own skepticism is more tender. I distrust spontaneity, too, but regretfully, and I say that spontaneity was the subject of Janis's art. Again and again, she acted out what it might be like to experience a feeling as an impulse and move according to that impulse—and sometimes she actually did it.

Whether the acting out was neurotic self-concealment or high-minded mission—and chances are it was closer to the former—its limitations were always fairly clear. Janis's music never had the flow of a semispontaneous art like jazz. It was spontaneity as rebellion, tied to the will, the essence of the late sixties. Her most salient virtues were power, energy, strength. That's what it takes to grab an impulse by the seat of the pants. Perhaps her vulnerability was also so close to the surface because, once she'd grabbed on, the impulse just dragged her along. Her tragedy was that although her less salient virtues—intelligence, humor, compassion—affected the quality of whatever impulse she chose to tackle, she never found a context in which she could utilize and communicate this delicate causality.

At the onset of her fame, Janis's art was called "white blues." Its supposed subjects were the suffering and sexuality that blues, as the most basic Afro-American form, was thought to embody. It is only now that we can perceive these subjects as metaphors for a deeper and more general explosiveness, less tied to any specific black experience than we'd thought, and inquire why the white part of Janis's art, the country music she once sang for bar tabs in Texas, was ignored. Just as Janis's exaggerated cracker accent was essential to her white blues sound, so the stern morals and goofy, out-front drollery of country music were essential if submerged components of her white blues sensibility. Yet after Monterey she rarely got to sing anything that suggested déclassé country monotony.

Did you buy what is usually considered Janis's worst LP, the pre-Monterey compilation that she cut with Big Brother and the Holding Company for Mainstream? Put it on now—I bet it sounds stronger than you remember. The length of the tracks has obviously been curtailed, as has the band's tendency to carouse in feedback and other instrumental raunch, and the tinny audio is a disgrace: Janis was never recorded in a higher register, but she threatens to crack the cartridge whenever she gets up there. I suspect, though, that the sound that really bothered people was her own tinniness, which was deliberate. The heretically countryish detachment of some of Janis's vocals qualifies her passion; the songwriting undercuts intensity with humor. On *Cheap Thrills,* another foolishly disparaged LP, Big Brother drives Janis to a peak of energy; on the Mainstream album, the same band helps keep her sane and human by providing a musical outlet for her zaniness. This promising combination was never fully explored.

It's important to emphasize that going solo was not an artistic necessity for Janis. Big Brother continued to grow as a band into the seventies; *Be a Brother,* with Nick Gravenites, suggests the spunky, eccentric good nature of the Mainstream album in a more assured mood. It is my fantasy that a similar spirit would have made Janis's life and career a lot easier—by animating her humor, by nurturing the kind of spontaneity and compassion that grows up among friends, and above all by lightening the strain of stardom and professionalism on her voice and her ego.

This fantasy did not materialize for many reasons, more than a few of them connected to Janis's self-indulged personal insecurities. My own interest, however, centers around her advisors, from Albert Grossman on down, who I suspect of sidestepping the challenge of Big Brother because that challenge was aimed at the spirit of tasteful control that keeps advisors in business. The supposed self-expressiveness of the blues they could go along with—hone it, tailor it, art it up, and maybe its subversions will become so subtle that they cease to be an issue. But undercut blues with the repressed self-discipline and citybilly freakiness of displaced country music and power it with the rudest rock and roll in the Land of the Hippies, and suddenly three or four previously disparate underclasses are compounded. No liberal could deplore the idea of this conjuncture, but the reality obviously freaked the tastemongers right out, and they pressured their property to quit her band.

The film proves how much of a loss this was. Musically, Janis is at her most cohesive and her most torrential in the few Big Brother sequences. Not that she was ever "musical" in a way acceptable to Billie Holiday or Bessie Smith—or Myra Friedman, who makes sure we know she was almost a classical pianist. Her music depended on her voice box and her dramatic flair, an epochal combination that enabled her to uncover the violence of blues, but her phrasing was erratic and her melodic imagination all but indiscernible. Because her more musicianly backup units can't relate to this, Janis's best moments in the Kozmic Blues Band scenes can be credited to the audience, while what is riveting in the Full Tilt Boogie performances is the way she delivers monologues and asides.

As befits a world-class celebrity, however, Janis also expends creative juice outside of what would ordinarily be defined as her art. Some of the interviews in the film are as tired as her singing with Full Tilt Boogie, as Janis makes with the answers about "not just a veneer" and "if I keep singing maybe I'll get it." But once, with Dick Cavett, she exemplifies the interviewee's craft, putting across the kind of lines (about a groin injury) that Friedman makes clear were usually rehearsed, but also zipping in with a new-minted Janisism when she sees an opening. And her tenth high school reunion in Port Arthur is Janis at her most heartbreaking. There is beatnik-cum-hippie bullshit ("gettin' loose, gettin' together, gettin' down") and standard lie number four ("Everyone come to California and I'll buy you a drink"), but there is also Janis delighting in her celebrityhood with a gleeful "no comment" and rejecting a question of portly, Arthurian lameness only to muse some more and come up with a straight answer. "What do young people want today?" Long pause. "Sincerity and a good time."

In this sequence the line between the public and the private Janis is at its most tenuous. She is the conquering heroine, but by now her wallflower vulnerability is an established part of her persona. She knows she is being filmed, but her return to the settled-downs whose cruelty drove her to stardom constitutes a genuine personal crisis. At one point, a reporter asks, quite innocently, about her senior prom. Her voice, which has been unnaturally prim throughout, strains a little—"No, I wasn't . . . "—and then begins to break—"I don't think they wanted to take me." But because she is slightly out of control, she can recover by feigning (or is it pretending to feign?) total breakdown. "And I've been suffering ever since," she sobs. "It's enough to make you want to sing the blues."

To me, this performance is public art as rich as any of her music. It's unfortunate that it occurs in such a small arena, before an audience ill-equipped to comprehend it fully, but a lot of what Janis did was that way. That's what I mean by saying Janis never found a context, and it's one of several reasons her myth often seems out of reach today. The achievement of *Janis* is to remind us of the complexity of what Janis Joplin created. Her awareness of her contradictions coexisted with an art that tried to run them over—a subtlety often overlooked both by fans preoccupied with their own need to explode and outsiders who can't make sense of the music's power, much less its subtlety.

Include Friedman in the latter category. Solid enough in its own right, *Buried Alive* has been turned into the bible of a new rock and roll revisionism by commentators anxious to believe that the sixties were an aberration rather than an aborted spiritual necessity. This is appropriate, for just as Friedman the publicist disdained the star system she lived off of, so Friedman the rock and roll functionary was proud of her distance from rock and roll. Such dissatisfactions are common along art packagers, but few of them have been blessed with Friedman's unique literary opportunity. To be fair, few are blessed with Friedman's meticulousness or high IQ, either. But the inadequacies of the book lead to far worse distortions of Janis's work than Janis at her most self-destructive could accomplish.

In fact, the book's worst flaw is that it barely analyzes that work at all. Friedman's familiar middlebrow thesis is that a crucial cause of Janis's downfall was her inability to distinguish between herself, Janis, and her persona, the red hot mama she called Pearl. Thus the severe neuroses of the performer—which resembled those of a star as long-gone as Al Jolson, except that Janis had little aptitude for long-range calculation—become indistinguishable, for Friedman, from her performance. Friedman's account of these neuroses tends toward the priggish—a woman with easy access to pretty boys and a taste for other women probably had more fun in bed than Friedman wants to believe. But much worse is her insistence on identifying the personal excesses of "that child," as she once calls her heroine and client, with the risks of her work, rather than merely relating the two. No wonder the work is so badly understood.

Although it is manifest that Janis did not deliberately kill herself on October 4, 1970, she is commonly referred to as a suicide. "The word suicide must stand," declared Midge Decter, but no, it must be combated. For what it means is that anyone who takes major risks, in life and by extension in art, wants to die. That is the cold war liberal position—immerse yourself in contradiction, downplay the need to explode—and it simply will not do. These entropy junkies will tell us that it was the disorderly "children" of the sixties who were addicted to breakdown, but that's only because they refuse to imagine what kind of order might be fertile or even truly viable. A child of the fifties, Janis had a conditioned distrust of political programs, but she also knew the limits of the sincerity and good times she believed in instead—"the great Saturday night swindle," she called it. So she understood two crucial political truths: People are in drastic need of change, and they're going to make a hell of a lot of noise as a result. For very good reasons they're more cautious now, and I'm sure Janis would be too. But the chances are all too good that caution will get us nowhere fast.

The saddest thing is that it all ended when it had hardly begun. In the closing scene of the documentary, Janis is with Kozmic Blues in Germany, and there are lots of GIs in the audience. It is 1969. The GIs have short hair, but they signify their liberation with sideburns and beads. Janis implores them to get on stage. A few do, shaking ass a lot more awkwardly than Janis, each of them trying in his own silly rhythm to break out of whatever it is that binds him. As much as all the acid casualties and patricidal bullshit, this is what the sixties were about—not so much antic despair as desperate antics. It wasn't much, but it was good, and Janis helped it happen. She deserves to be eternally honored for that.

1975

Our First Bohemians: The Rolling Stones

Mick Jagger was never a rocker. He wasn't a mod, either. He was a bohemian, an antiutopian version of what Americans called a folkie, attracted to music of a certain innocence as only a fairly classy—and sophisticated—person can be. Unlike John Lennon and Paul McCartney (and Bob Dylan), his ambitions weren't kindled by Elvis Presley; his angry, low-rent mien was no more a reflection of his economic fate than his stardom was a means to escape it.

Something similar went for all the Rolling Stones. They opted out of the political movement that most young rebels found unavoidable in the late sixties: "What can a poor boy do/Except sing for a rock and roll band?" But not only weren't they poor boys then, they never had been—except voluntarily, which is different. Only two of them—bassist Bill Wyman, the son of a bricklayer, and drummer Charlie Watts, the son of a lorry driver—came from working-class backgrounds, and both were improving their day-job lots dramatically by the time they joined the Stones. The other three, the group's spiritual nucleus through the scuffling days, were in it strictly for the art. Lead guitarist Keith Richards, although he grew up fairly poor, revolted against his parents' genteel middle-class pretensions; rhythm guitarist and all-purpose eclectic Brian Jones came from a musical family headed by an aeronautical engineer and wandered the Continent after leaving a posh school; and Mick himself, the son of a medium-successful educator, did not quit the London School of Economics until after the band became a going proposition in 1963. So the Stones weren't rich kids; only Brian qualified as what Americans would call upper middle class. And never underestimate the dreariness of the London suburbs or the rigidity of the English class hierarchy. But due partly to their own posturing, the Stones are often perceived as working-class, and that is a major distortion.

Working-class is more like Elvis and the Beatles, who loved rock and roll at least partly because rock and roll was a way to make it. Their propulsive upward mobility thus became inextricably joined with the energy of the music they created; their will to be rich and famous was both heroic and naive, a key ingredient of the projected naturalness that was essential to Elvis and the projected innocence that was essential to the Beatles. For disapproving elders to dismiss this naturalness/innocence as mere vulgarity—without noting, as Dwight Macdonald did about Elvis, that genuine vulgarity has its advantages in earthiness—represented more than a "generation gap." It was open-and-shut snobbery, motivated like most snobbery by class fear.

With the Stones all of this was more complicated. Their devotion to music itself was purer, but insofar as they wanted to be rich-and-famous—and they did, especially Mick, who had always been into money, and Brian, a notoriety junkie—they were neither heroic nor naive, just ambitious. And insofar as they wanted to be earthy—which was a conscious ambition too, rather than something they came by naturally or (God knows) innocently—they risked a vulgarity that was mere indeed. Coached by Andrew Loog Oldham, the publicist-manager who undertook the creation of the Stones in their own image starting in the spring of 1963, they chose to be vulgar—aggressively, as a stance, to counteract the dreariness and rigidity of their middle-class suburban mess of pottage. Perhaps they aspired to the earthiness of the grandfather who passes wind because he doesn't fancy the bother of holding it in, but in the very aspiration they recalled the grandson who farts for the sheer joyous annoyance value of it—and then calls it youth culture.

It would be quicker, of course, to suggest that they sought only to live up to the earthiness of the rhythm and blues music they lived for. But although there's no doubt that Brian, Mick, and Keith were passionate about hard-to-find black records that were as crude and esoteric by the standards of English pop and beat fans as they were crude and commercial by the standards of old-bohemian English blues and jazz cultists, the Stones have never been very specific about what that passion meant emotionally. Only their affinities are clear. Elmore James was Brian's man, while Keith loved Chuck Berry, but they by no means defined the group's poles: One of the laborers in the rhythm section, Charlie, had jazzier tastes than Brian, while the other, Bill, was working in a straight rock and roll group when he joined the Stones in late 1962 or early 1963. Mick's preferences, predictably enough, were shiftier. As he once told Jonathan Cott: "We were blues purists who liked ever-so-commercial things but never did them onstage because we were so horrible and so aware of being blues purists, you know what I mean?"

What he means, one surmises, is that the Stones' artiness never deadened their taste for certain commercially fermented blues-based songs—not as long as the songs were pithy and hummable and would induce people to dance when played loud. But by mocking the blues purist in himself he elides purism's image potential. Symbols of the English r&b movement—thought in 1963 to be challenging beat (and hence the Beatles) among British teenagers—the Stones had it both ways. Their first big British hit, that winter, was Lennon-McCartney's "I Wanna Be Your Man." They scoffed virtuously at the notion of "a British-composed r&b number," but wrote their own tunes almost from the start, and ranged as far into pop as "Under the Boardwalk" and Buddy Holly in their early recordings.

It is sometimes argued that such modulations of sensibility belie the group's artistic integrity; in fact, however, the Stones' willingness to "compromise" their own proclivities meant only that they assumed a pop aesthetic. Most artists believe they ought to be rich-and-famous on their own very idiosyncratic terms; the Stones happened to be right. To sing about "half-assed games" on the AM radio (on Bobby Womack's "It's All Over Now") or glower hirsute and tieless from the Sunday entertainment pages was integrity aplenty in 1964.

Perhaps most important, the Stones cared about the quality of the music they played. If this music recalled any single antecedent it was Chuck Berry, but never with his total commitment to fun. It was fast and metallic, most bluesish in its strict understatement. Clean and sharp—especially in contrast to the gleeful modified chaos of the Beatles—this striking but never overbearing music was an ideal vocal setting, and if the guitars and percussion established the band's presence, the vocals, and the vocalist, defined it. Quite often Jagger chose a light, saucy pop timbre that also recalled Berry, but something in his voice left a ranker overall impression—something slippery yet unmistakable, as lubricious and as rubbery as his famous lips. (For a simple example, listen to his tone of voice on most of "I'm a King Bee"—and then to his half-playful, half-ominous pronunciation on the word "buzz" in "I can buzz better baby/When your man is gone.") Nor was this merely a matter of being sexy. Just as there was a pointed astringency to the band's music, caustic where Chuck Berry was consciously ebullient—the acerbic tinniness of Keith's lead lines, or Brian's droning rhythm parts, or the way the added percussion lags behind the beat—there was a hurtful tinge to Mick's singing, especially on the slow, murky originals ("Tell Me," "Heart of Stone," or "Time Is on My Side," composed by Jerry Ragovoy but defined by the Stones) that changed the group's pace the way ballads did the Beatles'.

Although the Stones' high-speed decibels were rock and roll, not rhythm and blues, they did appropriate many of the essential trappings of their music, like hooks and solos, from black sources. But despite his rhythmic canniness and cheerful willingness to ape a drawl, Jagger was no more a blues stylist or a blues thief than Bob Dylan or Paul McCartney. He simply customized certain details of blues phrasing and enunciation for a vocal style of protean originality. And while pinning down the voice of such a compulsive ironist is impossible by definition, his vocals are perhaps most notable for a youthful petulance that faded only gradually. His drawl recalls Christopher Robin as often as Howlin' Wolf; his mewling nasality might have been copped from a Cockney five-year-old. Jagger's petulance offends some people, who wonder how this whiner—a perpetual adolescent at best—can pretend to mean the adult words he sings. But that ignores the self-confidence that coexists with it—Jagger's very grown-up assurance not that he'll get what he wants, but that he has every reason to ask for it. Even worse, it ignores the fact that Meaning It is definitely not what the Stones are about. Jagger didn't so much sing Muddy Waters' "I Just Want to Make Love to You" as get it over with, and although he did really seem to wish us "Good Times," he made the prospect sound doubtful where Sam Cooke enjoyed the wish itself.

It seems unlikely that at this point the Stones were conscious about this. All of them, Jagger included, were attracted to the gruff, eloquent directness of so much black music; relatively speaking, they became natural, expressive, sexy, and so forth by playing it. What set them apart was Jagger's instinctive understanding that this achievement was relative—that there was a Heisenberg paradox built into his appreciation of this music—and his genius at expressing that as well. The aggressiveness and sexuality of the form were his, but the sincerity was beyond him—partly because he was white and English, and especially because he was Mick Jagger. He loved black music for its sincerity, yet he also resented that sincerity. He wanted what he couldn't have and felt detached from his own desire; he accepted his inability to sing from as deep in his heart as Sam Cooke, sometimes he reveled in it, but he wasn't sure he liked it, not deep in his heart. "An empty heart/Is like an empty life," he sang in an early lyric, adding nuance to qualification as always, so that even as it adhered to lost-love conventions, the song evoked the most basic condition of his existence.

Jagger is obsessed with distance. He forces the Stones' music to gaze across (and down) the generation gap and the money gap and the feeling gap and the meaning gap. But then, powered by the other Stones—all of them, like most of the Stones' fans, somewhat more simpleminded than Jagger—the music leaps, so that as a totality it challenges the frustrating, ubiquitous, perhaps metaphysical margin between reach and grasp that presents itself so sharply to human beings with the leisure to think about it. This dual commitment to irony and ecstasy makes the Stones exemplary modernists. Without a doubt, it has been their readiness to leap that has won the Stones their following. At least until the time of the punks, no one ever rocked on out with more ecstatic energy. But it is their realism, bordering at its most suspect on cynicism, that makes all that energy interesting and ensures that their following will never be as huge as that of the high-spirited Beatles (or of a techno-cosmic doomshow like Led Zeppelin, either). After all, not everyone wants to be reminded that it is salutary to think and have fun at the same time. But that is what it means to get up and boogie to "Street Fighting Man," or to party to a paean as bitter as "Brown Sugar."

Jagger's distance from the African part of his African-American musical heritage was especially liberating for white Americans. Whereas for Elvis and those natives who followed him the blues bore an inescapable load of racial envy and fear, Mick's involvement was primarily aesthetic. Since, as his English blues preceptor, Alexis Korner, once remarked, Jagger's chief worry was whether the music was "performed 'properly,' " he betrayed no embarrassment about being white. Not all Englishmen were so uninhibited: an obsessive like Eric Burdon emulated Southern intonations sedulously. But Jagger got off on being a white person singing black songs, and he put that across. His mocking, extravagant elocution, as wild as his hair and the way he pranced around the stage, was more than vaguely self-amused, achieving a power that compared to the power of its origins because it was true to itself.

For the English audience, however, the Stones' distance from the United States itself was edifying. Because English youth perceived American affluence and mass culture as sources of vitality rather than oppression, a natural perspective was built into all Beatle-era rock and roll, but whereas for the Beatles it manifested itself in fun, silliness, play, the Stones' version was more oddball and therefore more sophisticated. They wove a mythology of America around r&b novelties like "Route 66" and "Down Home Girl," then exaggerated every eccentricity with some vocal moue or instrumental underline. The image of the States that resulted was droll, surreal, maybe a little scary—enticing, but no hamburger cornucopia.

It was also a cleverly differentiated musical product that rose to number-two status in England upon the release of the first Stones album in mid-1964. Here, however, the Stones were number two only in publicity, well behind the Dave Clark Five and Herman's Hermits in sales and just slightly ahead of arty rivals like the Animals and the Kinks. Then came their seventh U.S. single, "Satisfaction." It was the perfect Stones paradox—the lyrics denied what the music delivered, with the vocal sitting on the fence—and it dominated the summer of 1965, securing a pop audience half of which was content to shout "I can't get no" while the other half decided that the third verse was about a girl who wouldn't put out during her period.

By then the Stones were Mick and Keith's band, although opening for Korner at London's Marquee Club in early 1963 they had been "Brian Jones and Mick Jagger and the Rollin' Stones." As vain and exhibitionistic onstage as Jagger, Jones later boasted of having been the group's undisputed "leader," a status he maintained, as Al Aronowitz observed, until it was "worthwhile for someone to dispute." Jones wanted to be a star so much he took it for granted; his relationship to the audience was self-indulgent and self-deceiving. But since outrage was essential to Jagger, Richards, and Oldham's product—aggro-sex image mongering, lyrics both indecipherable and censorable, and the longest hair known to civilization—and since Brian was the most genuinely outrageous (and crazy) (and generous) (and cruel) of the Stones, he remained essential over and above his musical input. He was the one people remembered after Mick—especially the teenybopper girls who were still the Stones' most visible contingent.

The Stones got the teenyboppers because Oldham was sharp enough to extend Little Richard's First Law of Youth Culture to his scruffy band—he attracted the kids by driving their parents up the wall. But although we can assume Oldham initiated his campaign of world conquest in a spirit of benign, profiteering manipulation, something more was in store: generational revolt on an unprecedented scale. In this the Stones were to play a crucial symbolic role. The key was a proliferating network of hip, collegiate Stones fans, heirs to the beatnik myth that had passed from media consciousness when San Francisco's bohemian community moved from North Beach to the Haight, but unaware for a few years of how many arty allies were thinking like thoughts nationwide. Call them predropouts, because dropping out then barely knew its name. And connect them to the bohemian revolutionary vanguard epitomized by the Diggers, who welcomed the Stones to San Francisco as brothers in struggle. Soon, many of these fans would consider the Diggers and do likewise, just as the Stones' teen hordes would consider them and do likewise later on. What it all portended was just what parents had always feared from rock and roll, especially this ugly group: youth apocalypse.

....

I remember the first time I ever saw the Stones perform, at the Forum in Montreal in October 1965. I purchased my tickets on the day of the show, and even from deep in the balcony got more from Mick's dancing and the droogy stance of the others than from the music, which was muffled by the hockey rink p.a. and rendered all but inaudible by the ululations of the teenage girls around me. It was only afterward, when I happened to walk past the bus terminal, that I glimpsed what had really just happened. There in the station were hundreds of youths, all speaking French, waiting to complete their pilgrimage by plunging back into the cold of northern Quebec. I had never seen so much long hair in one place in my life.

What was about to happen was an unprecedented contradiction in terms, mass bohemianism, and this is where the idea of "pop" became key. Pop is what the mod Oldham shared with the bohemian Stones, and what they in turn shared with the teenyboppers. Applied first to low-priced classical concerts and then to Tin Pan Alley product, the word was beginning to achieve more general cultural currency by the mid fifties, when London-based visual artists like Eduardo Paolozzi were proposing that a schlock form (e.g., science fiction pulp) might nurture "a higher order of imagination" than a nominally experimental one (e.g., little magazine). Youths like the Stones—who had never known a nonelectric culture, and who were no more wary of the modern media bath than of their own amps—automatically assumed what older artists formulated with such difficulty. Their pop sensibility led them to a decidedly nonslumming bohemianism, more unpretentious and déclassé than that of the twenties. This was the gift of mass culture, compulsory education (especially English art-school routing), and consumer capitalism to five young men who comprised a social sample that would have been most unlikely, statistically, to group around the arts forty years before. Not that the Stones were untainted by avant-garde snobbishness—in their project of rebellious self-definition, exclusivity was a given. They never figured they'd spearhead a mass movement that went anywhere but record stores. That mass potential, however, was built into their penchant for pop itself.

There were solid economic reasons for the rise of mass bohemianism. Juxtapose a twenty-year rise in real income to the contradiction in which the straight-and-narrow worker/producer is required to turn into a hedonistic consumer off-hours, and perhaps countless kids, rather than assuming their production function on schedule, will choose to "fulfill themselves" outside the job market. But traditionally, bohemian self-fulfillment has been achieved through, or at least in the presence of, art. Only popular culture could have rendered art accessible—in the excitement and inspiration (and self-congratulation) of its perception and the self-realization (or fantasy) of its creation—not just to well-raised well-offs but to the broad range of less statusy war babies who made the hippie movement the relatively cross-class phenomenon it was. And for all these kids, popular culture meant rock and roll, the art form created by and for their hedonistic consumption. In turn, rock and roll meant the Rolling Stones.

Of course, it also meant the Beatles and Bob Dylan and the Who and the Grateful Dead—and Grand Funk Railroad. But the Beatles' appeal was too broad—parents liked them. Dylan's was too narrow—as an American bohemian, he remained suspicious of mass culture and stayed virtually out of sight from mid 1966 until the hippie thing was done with. The Who and the Dead hit a little too late to qualify as myths, and proved too committed to the mass and the bohemianism, respectively, to challenge the Stones' breadth. And Grand Funk and so many others simply couldn't match the Stones' art.

From "Satisfaction" to the end of the decade, the Stones' aesthetic stature became more heroic. *Aftermath, Between the Buttons, Beggars Banquet,* and *Let It Bleed* are all among the greatest rock albums, and even the 3-D/psychedelic/year-in-the-making response to *Sgt. Pepper, Their Satanic Majesties Request,* remembered as a washout, is solid tunewise and legitimately tongue-in-cheek conceptwise—a first-rate oddity, its title the single greatest image manipulation in the Stones' whole history. After "Satisfaction" it was difficult to accuse the Stones of imitation; after *Aftermath,* their music came almost entirely out of their heads. Blues-based hard rock it remained, with an eventual return to one African-American classic per album, but its texture was permanently enriched. As Brian daubed on occult instrumental colors (dulcimer, sitar, marimbas, and bells on *Aftermath* alone) and Charlie molded jazz chops to rock forms and Bill's bass gathered wit and Keith rocked roughly on, the group as a whole learned to respect and exploit (never revere) studio nuance. In the fall of 1967 they split from Oldham, whose image-making services had become superfluous and whose record-producing skills they have since disparaged. They were making mature, resonant music by then—they permitted their pace changes some lyricism, they generated warmth as well as white heat, and Mick's voice deepened, shedding some of its impertinence.

By proclamation and by vocal method—he slurs as a matter of conviction, articulating only catch-phrases—Jagger belittles his own lyrics, an appropriate tack for a literate man who has bet his life on the inexplicitness of music. Nonetheless, Jagger's lyrics were much like the Stones' music: pungent and vernacular ("Who wants yesterday's papers"); achieving considerable specificity with familiar materials ("You got me running like a cat in a thunderstorm"); and challenging received wisdom more by their bite than by any notable eloquence or profundity ("They just get married 'cause there's nothing else to do"). But whereas the Stones' music extended rock and roll usages, Jagger's lyrics contravened them. He wrote more hate songs than love songs, and related tales of social and political breakdown with untoward glee. The hypocrisy and decay of the upper classes was a fave subject—many songs that seem basically antiwoman (although certainly not all of them) are actually more antirich. He was also capable of genuine gusto about sex (not as often as is thought, but consider the openhearted anticipation of "Goin' Home" or "Let's Spend the Night Together") and wrote the most accurate LSD song ever, "Something Happened to Me Yesterday."

But that was as far as it went. Traditionally, bohemian revolt has been aimed at nothing more fundamental than middle-class morality and genteel culture. That's the way it was with the hippies, certainly, and that's the way it was with the Stones. They did show a class animus even though it wasn't proletariat-versus-bourgeoisie ("Salt of the Earth" evokes that struggle no less sensitively than it evokes Jagger's distance from it), but rather the old enmity between freemen and peerage—and a penchant for generalized social criticism. They earned their "political" aura. But their most passionate commitments were to sex, dope, and lavish autonomy. Granted, this looked revolutionary enough to get them into plenty of trouble. The dope-bust harassment of individual Stones did keep the group from touring the States between 1966 and 1969. But their money and power prevailed; in the end, their absence and apparent martyrdom only augmented their myth and their careers.

Throughout this time the Stones were heroes of mass bohemianism. They lived the life of art, their art got better all the time, and as it got better, remarkably enough, it reached more people. But although their art survives, its heroic quality does not; the Stones betray all the flaws of the counterculture they half-wittingly and -willingly symbolized. Their sex was too often sexist, their expanded consciousness too often a sordid escape; their rebellion was rooted in impulse to the exclusion of all habits of sacrifice, and their relationship to fame had little to do with the responsibilities of leadership, or of allegiance. Not that leadership was Mick's—or any ironist's—kind of thing. All he wanted was to have his ego massaged by his public or bathed in luxurious privacy as his own whim dictated. This he got, but it wasn't all roses; it was also dead flowers. Early on, in "Play With Fire" or "Back Street Girl," say, he had attacked decadence with a sneer—it was something that happened to others, especially the idle rich. By "Live With Me," or "Dancing With Mr. D.," pop-star luxury had turned Mick into a decadent himself.

But because Mick was also a professional, his project of radical self-definition flourished where so many others failed. Most bohemians can find ways to waste themselves—it's often fun for a while, and it's certainly easy. But the bohemian art hero has a polar option: to persist and make a career out of it, becoming more exemplary as his or her success becomes more unduplicable. Jagger's talent, resilience, and sure pop instincts, combined with a boom market in creativity, made for a singular preeminence. Among the many who couldn't match up was Brian Jones. Despite what those who consider Mick a prick suspect, it is rather unlikely that Brian was forced out of the group because his attraction to the bizarre endangered Mick's self-aggrandizing aesthetic calculations. Quite simply, he seems to have fucked and doped himself past all usefulness. Brian was one of the damned by choice of personality. He drowned in his own swimming pool on July 3, 1969.

Two days later the Stones introduced previously hired ex-John Mayall guitarist Mick Taylor at a free concert in Hyde Park that served as Brian's wake, and that November they commenced history's first mythic rock and roll tour. They hadn't swept the United States—or anywhere—in three years; the world had changed, or so it seemed; Woodstock hung in the air like a rainbow. It seemed only fitting to climax all that long-haired pomp and circumstance with yet another celebration of communal freeness. The result was Altamont—one murdered; total dead, four; three hundred thousand bummed out. It seems more a chilling metaphor than a literal disaster in retrospect, as much the Grateful Dead's fault as the Stones'. But the Stones are stuck with it—if it is typical of their genius that their responsibility is difficult to pinpoint, it is typical of their burden that everyone who's into blame blames them anyway.

In the end, though, that's typical of their genius too. Whatever the specifics, the Stones acknowledge their complicity in a world where evil exists. Above all, they are anything but utopians. They never made very convincing hippies because hippie just wasn't their thing. Jagger's taste for ecstatic community was tempered by the awareness of limits that always assured the Stones their formal acuteness. A successful artist may epitomize his or her audience, but that is a process of rarefaction; it doesn't mean conforming to the great mean, even of the time's bohemianism. So while it is true that the Stones' flaws and the counterculture's show a certain congruence, ultimately Mick is congruent to nothing—he always leaves himself an out. He doesn't condone the Midnight Rambler or Mister Jimmy, he just lays them bare. His gift is to make clear that even if the truth doesn't make you free, it needn't sap your will or your energy either. As with most bohemian rebels, his politics are indirect. He provides the information. The audience must then decide what to do with it.

And yet that is perhaps too kind. Somewhere inside, the Stones knew that any undertaking as utopian as Altamont was doomed by definition. If their audience didn't understand it that way, it was because the Stones themselves, in all their multileveled contradiction, were unwilling to come out and tell them. They would suggest it, yes, embody it, but they wouldn't make it plain, because the nature of the truth is that it isn't plain. If a male fan wants to take Mick's struggle with male persona as an invitation to midnight rambling, well, that's the nature of the game.

After Altamont the Stones played with a vengeance. *Sticky Fingers* appeared in 1971 to trifle with decadence just when some retribution seemed called for, and on its two greatest tracks, it definitely did. "Moonlight Mile" re-created all the paradoxical distances inherent in erotic love with a power worthy of Yeats, yet could also be interpreted as a cocaine song; "Brown Sugar," in which (if you listen with care to a rocker so compelling that it discourages exegesis) Jagger links his own music to the slave trade, exploits the racial and sexual contradictions of his stance even as it explores them. *Exile on Main Street,* released in conjunction with the 1972 American tour, was decadent in a more realized way. Weary and complicated, barely afloat in its own drudgery, with Mick's voice submerged under layers of studio murk, it piled all the old themes—sex as power, sex as love, sex as pleasure, distance, craziness, release—on top of an obsession with time appropriate in men pushing thirty who were still committed to what was once considered youth music. Reviewed with some confusion when it came out, it was a certified classic within a year and is now remembered as their peak, the most consistently dense and various music of their career.

But as tuckered out as *Exile* initially seemed, it marked a peak only of the Stones' *recording* career—the one-decade marker in a showbiz saga destined to stretch on for several more. Like their partners in Altamont, the Grateful Dead, these quintessential rock and roll bohemians evolved into quintessential rock and roll professionals. *Sticky Fingers* and *Exile on Main Street* both featured Taylor, a young veteran of the rock-concert boogie jam, and session horn men Bobby Keys and Jim Price; in a way they are both triumphs of musicianly craft over the kind of pop hero-mongering that can produce an Altamont. But if that's so, then *Goats Head Soup* and *It's Only Rock 'n Roll* are musicianly craft at its unheroic norm, terrific by the standards of Foghat or the Doobie Brothers. Even the peaks—"Star Star" and "If You Can't Rock Me," respectively—had deja entendu musical and lyrical themes, and it's hard to imagine the Stones putting their names on tunes as tritely portentous as "Dancing With Mr. D." or "Time Waits for No One" in their prepro days. Only rock and roll indeed.

A similar distinction can be drawn between the 1972 and 1975 tours. In 1972, the mood was friendly. "Sympathy for the Devil" was not performed, the gentle Taylor wafted through the proceedings, and Mick undercut his fabled demonism by playing the clown, the village idiot, the marionette. Very professional, yet their most rocking show ever. In 1975, with ex-Face Ron Wood aboard in place of Taylor, they worked even harder, but rather than celebrating professionalism they succumbed to it. Jagger's hyperactive stamina was an athletic marvel, but his moves often looked forced, and although Wood and Richards combined for a certain bumptious dirtiness, the musical energy seemed forced as well. Yet the 1976 album, *Black and Blue,* was rock and roll that didn't deserve an "only," and the 1978 tour was an improvement, especially when Mick stopped prancing long enough to pick up a guitar and get fresh with *Some Girls.* Almost certainly the best album of their second and third decades, *Some Girls* was at once a punk-inspired return to the casual spontaneity of their early records and a disco-inspired demonstration of their pop facility. "Miss You," promoted in dance clubs with a remixed twelve-inch, proved one of their biggest singles. Never again would anyone assume they were has-beens. Here was professionalism at its best—creative ups and downs that engross an attentive audience as they divert a casual one. Not what we want, maybe, but what we can use.

As his teeth got longer, Jagger liked to argue that music wasn't the exclusive province of the young by pointing to long-lived Chicago bluesmen like his supposed inspiration Muddy Waters. But he never demonstrated a willingness to settle for Muddy's market share. His theme song became the wicked "Start Me Up," which keynoted both 1981's cannily crafted *Tattoo You* and 1991's powerful live *Flashpoint:* "Once you start me up I'll never stop." By the time of 1989's *Steel Wheels* extravaganza, hooked to that mechanically crafted album and by some accounts the most lucrative rock tour in history, Jagger covered center field at Shea Stadium more enthusiastically than baseball players twenty years his junior. But his star receded as his heresy was institutionalized. After the group jumped to Virgin for advances that gave accountants ulcers, Jagger surrounded 1986's offhand but winningly basic *Dirty Work* with ambitious pop solo LPs that disappointed musically and commercially. Meanwhile, the estranged Richards validated his withdrawal from a notoriously unforgiving heroin habit by cutting the 1988 Virgin album *Talk Is Cheap,* which outsold Jagger's 1987 *Primitive Cool.* And in the course of the decade, longtime fans gradually concluded that if Jagger was the Stones' brain and Richards was the Stones' soul, the group's self was its rhythm section, especially the incomparably terse and acute Charlie Watts, now widely considered the greatest rock drummer ever.

Only rock and roll? The Stones are the proof of the form. When the guitars and the drums and the voice come together in those elementary patterns that no one else has ever quite simulated, the most undeniable excitement is a virtually automatic result. To insist that this excitement doesn't move you is not to articulate an aesthetic judgment but to assert a rather uninteresting crotchet of taste. It is to boast that you don't like rock and roll itself.

1975–1992

God Grows Up: Eric Clapton

As Eric Clapton advanced through his Nothing but the Blues set at Madison Square Garden October 10, the paradox of the man was manifest to anyone with the wit to see—which didn't mean many of the sixteen thousand souls who'd paid up to sixty-five bucks to attend the last of three notably tough-ticket shows. Its median age over thirty, with more Asians than blacks and damn few of either, this crowd was clearly there to pay tribute, hailing a full-grown hero who'd outlasted his unfair share of hardship and now proposed to honor his debt to America's great music of suffering and survival. The aura of service was palpable. Gotten up in austere white cotton and work boots, barely speaking except for composer IDs, the forty-nine-year-old rock legend subsumed himself in the form he's always gone home to—through an eclectic tour of the genre that ranged from the acoustic obscurity "Motherless Child" to the Stax-Volt showboat "Born Under a Bad Sign," not a solo exceeded two choruses. Undeniably, Clapton has seen more trouble than any perquisite of privilege can wipe away, and long before his young son crashed fifty-three stories to a Manhattan sidewalk—hard on the death of his friend and rival Stevie Ray Vaughan in a helicopter accident that also killed three members of his own entourage—he'd proved that he loved, needed, and understood the blues. But that didn't mean this tour wasn't also a study in star power. Who but a Grammy-winning superceleb could so thoroughly indulge his taste for a historic genre he's never claimed he had the pipes for, increasing his untold wealth all the while? The minstrel photo that opened the auxiliary slide presentation underscored as much as it undercut. Was The Artist Formerly Known as God a humble votary? Or was he an arrogant fuck?

Like his chart-topping all-blues *From the Cradle,* the show was a mixed success. As you might expect, Clapton's problem is still vocal. Often taken to task for J. J. Cale and Don Williams imitations, all he's doing is leading from strength—the reserve he's at such pains to project is perfectly suited to a voice that's most masterful when it's murmuring. At its best, his singing has always suggested the kindness that can follow both sex and suffering. But trying as honestly as he can, he still doesn't have the lungs or larynx to sustain anything loud and raunchy, and that goes double on songs owned by somebody who does. So when he follows "Hoochie Coochie Man" with "It Hurts Me Too," all an admirer of Muddy Waters and Elmore James can do is follow "The hell you say" with "Oh it does not." The night I went, the low point was Howlin' Wolf's ".44 Blues"—taking on the genre's most seismic vocalist was arrogant fuckery to begin with, and to compound the offense the sideman with the bass drum failed to alert the band to the whereabouts of the groove.

Ultimately, however, the show shared with the album not so much a surfeit of gaffes as a paucity of gems. On record, a few collector-type discoveries augment the terse, incisive playing, especially Eddie Boyd and Willie Dixon's "Third Degree" and the copyright-control "Motherless Child." In concert, the thrills were in Clapton's always trenchant leads, the warm, clear, rapid runs of notes and slurs that he was wise and immodest enough to open wide as the show deepened—on Otis Rush's "Groaning the Blues," just before the close, his *two* two-chorus solos drenched the song in the kind of noise that only became permissible in blues when Jimi Hendrix and Clapton himself exploded the music's sonic parameters in the sixties. Live or digital, however, the pattern is identical: a passable singer honoring blues as song with more than passable renditions of material that should never be less than great.

To call blues historic is by no means to declare it dead. It continues to be the making of twentieth-century popular music, and as a distinct genre it lives on as a beneficiary of the boutique-style narrowcasting that now pervades pop marketing. Scores of blues albums on a dozen or so specialty labels are released annually, almost all by folks who manage to make a living off a hirsute clientele considerably less collegiate than its folkie counterpart of three decades ago. Although this world is home to myriad latter-day boogie bands, the majority of the artists are black, and the two most prominent—Buddy Guy and Otis Rush, Clapton precursors at fifty-eight and sixty—currently have major-label deals. Because the style is seminal and meaningful, much of this output is of discernible quality. But almost none of it answers the question of why anyone should go to the trouble of doing the discerning. It's as inaccessible outside its subset as polka, hardcore, or techno, at least in part because modernity's most durable musical materials no longer generate many topflight songs. Once in a while a journeyperson will vary one of the great old tune families with an irresistible groove or arresting lyric, but the only consistent working blues writer is Robert Cray, often disparaged by hairier-than-thous as too clean, too famous, or both.

In this context, Clapton's exercise of privilege accomplishes something for blues—less because he's a genius than because he's a rock star. As a star he can stick to covers and call it concept. Although I do wish he'd abjured chestnuts he's unequal to, there were so many great blues songs composed between 1915 and 1965 that *From the Cradle* stands as a treasury that will enlighten almost anyone and positively blow the minds of *MTV Unplugged* tykes who are lucky to have heard of Elmore James's kid brother Rick. As a rocker, meanwhile, he's free to roam the genre at will, translating far-flung finds into his own language—a language more catholic than the ones worked by even Guy or Rush, who by now have learned as much from his innovations as he did from theirs. So while it can't compete with good Cray, or with the newly compiled vault tapes of Skip James or Howlin' Wolf, the flawed *From the Cradle* is nevertheless one of the finest blues albums of the past decade. Except maybe for the live 1980 *Just One Night,* it's also Clapton's best album since 1974's quiet, supple, slightly homely *461 Ocean Boulevard* if not 1970's madly layered *Layla.* Well-behaved CD that it is, it splits the difference in monumentality, rendering sixteen songs in sixty minutes where *Layla* stretches fourteen over seventy-seven and *461 Ocean Boulevard* stops at eleven in forty-three. And musically it shares more with *Layla* than one might expect.

A promiscuous sideman whose monklike aura has never diminished his extravagant appetites, Clapton likes to get paid, and he's amassed a discography that's remarkably undistinguished for an artist of his caliber. In his self-protective self-deprecation he often attributes this to his own laziness or his need for a catalyst, but it's also guitar hero's disease: like many other guys whose hand-ear coordination is off the curve, he's a casual tunesmith and a corny lyricist, and his band concepts are chronically hit-or-miss. Indeed, *Layla* was created in just two weeks of debauched rich-hippie jamming with musicians Clapton stole from Delaney & Bonnie—augmented, of course, by drop-in Duane Allman, who joined the party two songs in and was told what to do with a will that struck the Georgia virtuoso as almost tyrannical. Anyone who suspects it's lost its luster by now, however, is advised to invest in the future with Ultradisc II's audiophile version, guaranteed to provide many happy hours in your golden retirement years.

Layla is a quintessential meeting of the guitars, a locked-in fusion of laid-back attitude and rock and roll energy. But it's also an anguished cry of unrequited love, and it's full of pop blues: Bessie Smith's near-standard "Nobody Knows You When You're Down and Out," Bill Broonzy's signature "Key to the Highway," Chuck Willis's pre–rock and roll "It's Too Late," and "Have You Ever Loved a Woman," written by the same minor New York pro who gave "Tonight Tonight" to the white doowop group the Mello-Kings. Listening back to these tracks, three of them very loosely conceived, what's striking about the singing is how unschooled and unself-conscious it sounds. Clapton was a blues adept who had already outgrown four famous bands, as sly about his image as any other ex-mod. But he was only twenty-five and as he suffered lavishly through his rejection by the wife of one of his best friends, he found himself in an environment so commodious that for once he could let it all hang out. The only way to classify the singing on *Layla* is "rock"; whatever adjustments he makes from song to song, Clapton always aims for one of those over-the-top displays of feeling that so many immature musicians identify with soul. This is a dumb idea, but when the spirit is there it can be profoundly compelling anyway, and it occasions Clapton's most significant and effective vocal performance. Cut before he'd perfected his intimate murmur, much less the earthy shout he summons on *From the Cradle*'s loud ones, *Layla* is why young hippies thought they had the right to sing the bell bottom blues. It leaves such categories as humble votary and arrogant fuck stuck on the ground.

    Layla was a moment of provisional truth, a promise Clapton couldn't keep in a life that by all reports has been full of them. He ended up marrying its inspiration, but that didn't stop him from sending her home from his no-gurls-allowed tour the next day—or, need I add, from breaking up with her several detoxes and uncounted infidelities later. If you think this hurt him too, figure it probably hurt her more. After all, it turns out he is rather the hoochie coochie man, with more notches on his dick than Muddy and Muddy's persona put together—he just doesn't sound like one, having always gotten more ass than a toilet seat as a shy, sotto voce genius instead. Whether this lifestyle continues I have no idea, but "Hoochie Coochie Man" or no "Hoochie Coochie Man," the mature artist he's trying to become has aspired to something more solid in both of the hats he's worn so far—namely, made-for-TV quietude and deep-rooted fortitude. Plainly, *MTV Unplugged* is why maturity has a bad name in rock and roll—it's complacent, sentimental, boring. Just as plainly, *From the Cradle* is why only young farts count an old man out—it's forceful, percipient, occasionally even surprising. And plainest of all, Clapton had more to tell us when he was a young fool in the throes of drug-addled romantic delusion than he'll ever get four fingers on again. His greatest truth was a lie—art is like that sometimes. And he saw deeper when he knew less than he does now—rock and roll is like that a lot.

1994

Genius Dumb: Led Zeppelin

Quiet as it's kept, critics didn't hate Led Zeppelin. That was just the old-hippie singer-songwriter stronghold *Rolling Stone,* where Jon Landau and John Mendelsohn convinced four preening assholes that the Establishment was against them. Most of us recognized what was obvious to Teen Planet—the irreducible whomp of "Whole Lotta Love" and "Immigrant Song" and *Led Zeppelin IV.* But we committed the pardonable error of not dreaming that the fools who created these sounds might comprise the greatest band in the known universe. Partly this was our heedless appetite for content—defined in part (oh, the shame of it!) as *verbal* content. Partly it was our occupational resistance to pomp. And partly it was the inconvenient paradox of good music happening to bad people. Moralizing by omission—it's a hazard of the trade.

I still don't know whether Led Zeppelin was the greatest band in the known universe, but I can certainly see that they might have been. They invented metal as surely as Hendrix invented electric guitar, yet like Hendrix they still tower over everything they influenced—often imitated, never duplicated, rarely if ever approached. And as with Hendrix, their triumph was preeminently sonic. Hendrix and Zeppelin are the great flowering of late psychedelic culture. Immersed in a grandiose mysticism that spurned the frontier folkieness, blues-boy grime, homespun doper wit, and Wild West local color of the original California strain, they bought the myth of the sixties as it is now misremembered, then sold it back with a coherence and vision that rolls right over such competing art-school wankers as Cream, King Crimson, and Pink Floyd. Led Zeppelin weren't just dumb, they were genius dumb. And so it is only appropriate that what made them classic was two of the three dumbest things about them. I still won't give it up to their Aryan, wild-man-of-the-north mythopoeia. But they sure could shriek. And hey, give the drummer some.

These days it is taken for granted that vocalists can function parallel to guitarists and drums can be mixed as lead instruments. And for better or worse, that knowledge begins with Robert Plant's vanity-of-vanity histrionics and John Bonham's sasquatchian tub-thumping. Was Plant soulful? Did Bonham swing? You might as well ask whether Aleister Crowley stuffed shark snouts up groupies' rectums. It wasn't about such corny values as soul and swing, which is one reason it was only marginally about the blues they raided so pitilessly. It was about their *own* corny values—their sense of scale, their addiction to power, their lust for a sound humongous enough to match their egos. Jimmy Page was the known virtuoso, John Paul Jones the stabilizer every movable madhouse needs. But Plant's inhuman vocalizations and Bonham's two-fisted clubfoot were the spirit and ground of their aural reality.

Maybe we were right to moralize. Maybe when we immerse in this reality we're reveling in romantic individualism at its most trivial and self-serving. On the other hand, maybe the pleasure we take in Led Zeppelin is just r&r—not rock and roll, dummy, rest and recuperation, a fantasyland grand enough to blot out a world that remains too big and uncontrollable no matter how much anyone moralizes about it. But either way it's amazing music. And either way it stands to remind us that one of the many differences between art and life is that in art, morality rarely means shit in the end.

1994

Jimi Plays History: Jimi Hendrix

Jimi Hendrix was a rock hero like no other, yet he symbolizes that radically individualistic breed if anyone does. A doomed avatar of sixties excess up there on Mount Rockmore with Janis and Jimbo and Brian Jones, all of whom he dwarfs in memory, he's the iconic guitar god whose vocabulary of postures, gestures, and facial expressions was transformed by style-setting photographers into an image bank for all axeslingers to draw on. Metal wouldn't be its grandiose self without him, he drove Miles Davis to fusion, and James Brown sires funk unaided only insofar as it doesn't turn funkadelic, at which point Jimi gets joint custody. If he has an heir, which he probably doesn't, it's Prince, the most protean and fecund pop star of the last quarter century.

But Hendrix bids for immortality on fundamentally musical grounds, and that is not the way of the rock hero. Influenced by Hendrix (who at least was funnier about it than Eddie Van Halen), we still envision the guitar god bent in expressionistic transport over his instrument. From Chuck Berry to Kurt Cobain, however, the real thing generally made history as a singer of songs; unless you want to stick Jimmy Page or Duane Allman in your pantheon, only master musician and reluctant vocalist Eric Clapton, a traditionalist where Hendrix was an iconoclast, resembles Hendrix formally. Due largely to his ingrained musicality, Hendrix was unknowable. It remains almost impossible to pin down this vague, gawky, and reticent genius, showman, and stud: his peace-and-love ideals, derived primarily from the freedom, beauty, and power he discovered in the electric guitar, mean too much and too little. And in the most obvious anomaly, he was African-American. There's no way to recount rock history intelligently without reference to Chuck Berry and James Brown and Prince. But the counterculture Hendrix represents so indelibly was white.

None of these generalizations would go undisputed by Hendrix's devoutly protective fans. Although the primacy of his guitar is undeniable, praise of his singing and songwriting is de rigueur. So I should emphasize that I'm not dismissing either, just pointing out that Hendrix didn't sing or write as compellingly as Berry, Cobain, or hundreds of others; if you don't believe me, compare Rod Stewart's version of "Angel," one of the few Hendrix compositions anyone's covered much—or try humming a few bars of "Love or Confusion" or "One Rainy Wish" or "Still Raining, Still Dreaming" if you even know what they are. And although only fools claim to comprehend the inner workings of this highway child who lost his adored party-girl mother at sixteen and didn't see his dad for the first five years of his professional life, few are willing to admit that even compared to Morrison and Joplin, who at least displayed a certain sardonic realism, he spouted a great deal of flapdoodle. As for race—well, as usual, that's when things really start getting complicated.

Chroniclers now express considerable embarrassment over how Hendrix's blackness was perceived in the sixties. There was the *East Village Other*'s generic praise for Hendrix's "beautiful Spade routine"; there was *Newsweek*'s "triptych of smirking, simian faces" working in, I swear, "the soul style of Ray Charles and Little Richard"; there was Albert Goldman's inevitable "great black snake"; there was even, yes, my own attempt to dub Hendrix at Monterey "a psychedelic Uncle Tom." (An index of the decade's high racial consciousness is that half the dis was censored by *Esquire*, which held that "psychedelic" was libelous.) Nevertheless, Hendrix's white associates insist not merely that he was beyond race, a multiculturalist ahead of his time, but that his late flirtations with the Panthers and such were the well-meaning gestures of a guy who could never say no, that his Gypsy Sun & Rainbows and Band of Gypsys bands were racially meaningless, musically misguided, or both. The problem even with the multiculturalism argument, borne out though it is by many published interviews as well as Hendrix's life, is that in part he was almost certainly jiving; a white person doesn't have to think he or she understands African-American reality to observe that blacks often soft-pedal their shifting racial animosities just so they can cope. Also, Hendrix's white admirers are disingenuous about their own needs. Is it odd that in a time that spawned both mass bohemia and black-power separatism, the symbol of that bohemia became its most prominent black proponent? Of course not. It reflects both liberal America's compulsion to convince itself that it has no race problem and the uneasy debt hip whites invariably feel they owe hipper blacks.

So instead of mystifying Jimi Hendrix as an emblem of tolerance, credit him with marshaling the intestinal fortitude and utopian smarts to decide that the strictures of racism were not for him. Feeling hemmed in by the r&b circuit where he'd honed his chops and shtick with the Isley Brothers, King Curtis, Little Richard, Ike & Tina Turner, Curtis Knight, Joey Dee & the Starliters, and an angelic host of semiapocryphal soul men, he was simultaneously attracted to nascent hippie notions of art and freedom. If Bob Dylan could sing for groovy white cats, why couldn't he? But the upstaging flamboyance Hendrix brought to tried-and-true stagecraft had already gotten him in trouble with his black taskmasters ("I'm the one who's going to look pretty," Little Richard famously said), and when he revved his moves so white kids couldn't miss them and let his hair and duds grow like wildflowers, the black audience was lost to him—especially since his music was loud, weird, noisy, and you couldn't boogaloo to it. By then, however, ex-Animal bassist Chas Chandler and ex-Animal manager Michael Jeffery had made Hendrix's blackness pay in the U.K., where he was packaged with his own connivance as a pop exotic from darkest America/Africa/Borneo whose willingness to please was guaranteed by befrizzed redhead Noel Redding on bass and pallid Elvin Jones fan Mitch Mitchell on drums. Thus did the chitlin circuit engender the iconic guitar-god look now identified with white "rock." And despite the Yardbirds and Who feedback forays adduced by overzealous integrationists, the proximate influences on Hendrix's music were black as well.

Exactly what blues Hendrix heard when is hard to work out. Although he was intimate early on with Chicago modernists

Buddy Guy and Otis Rush as well as Muddy Waters and B. B. King and got hands-on instruction from Albert King, he may well have come to country blues later, perhaps even with help from a girl-friend of Keith Richards. Moreover, the hornlike legato he took from blues isn't half the style of a man who often played two lines at once. Equally important—as Charles Shaar Murray establishes in the most striking argument of his astute *Crosstown Traffic*—were the rhythmic, tersely lyrical comps worked out by such soul gui-tarists as Bobby Womack, Curtis Mayfield, and Steve Cropper, with whom Hendrix enjoyed a five-hour session in 1964.

But it's wrong to box up this syncretist in any racial tradition, even the multifaceted one he absorbed touring America. The big-gest thing he took from black pop was its professionalism, its immersion in technical skill and tradition of legible innovation, which together set him on his own path. Rock's greatest impro-viser and consummate live performer, he proved a pioneering adept of the studio, where he jammed endlessly, rerecorded obsessively, and spent hours realizing spectacular, spaced-out aural fancies with engineer Eddie Kramer. Even more decisive were fourteen-hour days whiled away with his guitar—in bed, at table, in hotel rooms whose lights he tinted with multicolored scarves. Struggling always to turn sounds in his head into sound-waves in the air, he applied his enormous hands, indomitable play-fulness, and unsatisfied mind to an unchartable panoply of finger-ings, slides, taps, bumps, electronics, tuning changes, and special effects, many of which died with him. And in the course of this personal struggle he transformed twentieth-century music for every one of us.

Between the formation of the Jimi Hendrix Experience in October, 1966 and his death in September, 1970, Hendrix recorded what would have been a lifetime's worth of music for almost anyone else: four studio albums including two doubles, the second unfin-ished; hundreds of hours of fragments, groove sessions, and noo-dles; a myriad of concerts that merit attention for the simple rea-son that Hendrix regularly invented music where his lessers showed off. Nothing about Hendrix is more contested than this artistic legacy, which not only sounds good but still moves 2 mil-lion pieces a year. After decades of legal ugliness—in addition to skimming 40 percent of his minion's gross, Michael Jeffery was fond of dummy corporations, and many other high rollers and hangers-on have paper on Hendrix as well—Jimi's father Al is finally the boss, which is just. Musical control, meanwhile, has passed from Alan Douglas to Eddie Kramer, a significant change that should inspire any sane observer to launder the white flag and avoid crossfire.

On historical grounds, Kramer deserves the gig—more than Chas Chandler or any sideman, he was Hendrix's closest collaborator. But although Douglas doesn't care enough about songs and sinned mightily during his two-decade watch (never worse than when he and Warners deleted the excellent Kramer-compiled *In the West* and *Rainbow Bridge* to gain cheap authenticity points for later redubs and redundancies), since 1986 he's put out four superb new CDs: blunt and ballsy *Live at Winterland* and mod *Radio One* for Rykodisc, wild and woolly *Woodstock* and primeval *Blues* for MCA. The protofusion jams he proffered so proudly on 1980's *Nine to the Universe* are way too slack. But it would be nice to have jazz guy Douglas, who was getting important records out of Eric Dolphy and John McLaughlin when he met Hendrix in 1969, as well as pop guy Kramer, whose other production coup is Kiss, sifting through a vault that is now longer on moments of invention than finished works. It would also be nice to save the ozone layer.

The Douglas camp fiercely denies Kramer's claim that the inaugural release of MCA's Experience Hendrix imprint—remasters of the revered *Are You Experienced?, Axis: Bold as Love,* and *Electric Ladyland* and a reasonable stab at the mythic *First Rays of the New Rising Sun*—is the first time Hendrix's sixties master tapes have actually reached CD. Even if Kramer got the facts wrong, however, he got the music right. When I compare the vinyl *Experienced?* (my second copy, still in decent shape) and the CD MCA released when it wrested the Hendrix catalogue from Warner in 1993, the CD is discernibly tinnier. With the remastered version, on the other hand, it's like Kramer kvelled to *Guitar World:* "a veil has been lifted." As usual, the redigitalizations have their oddities; they could be bassier, and in the standard pattern, previously backgrounded tricks and instruments—Mike Finnigan's organ on *Electric Ladyland*'s "Burning of the Midnight Lamp," say—assume untoward prominence. But when Kramer boasts, "This is how Jimi always wanted to hear his music," I believe him. Although Kramer's remasters don't redefine the canon, for which we should be grateful, they enrich it. Their size and presence, clarity and precision put the huge impact and fantastic detail of Hendrix's music out front for schlubs like you and me.

As can't be reiterated too often, Hendrix's art wasn't about lyrics or meaning, lightning-quick notes or brainy changes, so much as it was about sonics. No one has described this nonlinear, untutored, very sixties accomplishment more succinctly than art historian Pepe Karmel in a *New Yorker* piece collected for Chris Potash's valuable *Jimi Hendrix Companion:* "Hendrix's music is really a question of timbre: the howl of feedback, the roar of distortion—all those elements that a musician would call 'coloration.' He got rid of chordal complexity so he could concentrate on tonal complexity." For this reason, the digital age has been augmenting Hendrix's legacy since the first live two-track remixes, with this release the culmination so far.

No matter how vivid the audio gets, however, even those of us who were there have trouble comprehending how epochal these albums were. Hendrix is the greatest electric guitarist in any idiom ever, and because he was about sound more than speed or chords, no one can clone him. Despite many thousands of rock simulations—most shallow (Frank Marino), many steadfast (Robin Trower), one sainted (Stevie Ray Vaughan)—his most legitimate inheritors are black guitarists who think like him more than they sound like him, including such jazz-schooled originals as Sonny Sharrock, Blood Ulmer, and Vernon Reid as well as the funk clan headed by Michael Hampton. But because his innovations are now lingua franca, the clarion chords of "Purple Haze" can't possibly shock us into reliving the unmitigated weirdness of *Are You Experienced?* What's struck me as I've reentered the first two albums— separated by all of six months, with seventy-five minutes of *Electric Ladyland* only a year away—is how unabashedly *pop* they are. Except for the 6:44 statement of psychedelic policy "Third Stone From the Sun," which impressed many potheads but has never blown my mind, only one of the eleven original tracks and six bonus sides lasts even four minutes; "Purple Haze" and "Fire" are under three, as are half the songs on *Axis.*

Yet *Are You Experienced?* sounded like no pop record anyone had ever heard. The thick, unending turmoil of Hendrix's guitar was without precedent, in rock or blues; even the few brilliant exceptions—the Who's feedback-drenched 1965 "Anyway, Anyhow, Anywhere," "Sunshine of My Love" and other Cream sin-gles—were jangly by comparison. The only reason it didn't seem utterly mad to make this articulated yowl the melodic bed for airplay-ready three-minute ditties was that no other pop form had yet been conceived, and if you listen for the conjunction today, the sense of coexisting incommensurabilities is pretty bizarre. These ditties didn't bother with verses, much less bridges, but as good English pop they did have hooks—most often sinewy, rau-cous power chords whose contained cacophony was then topped by a solo or outro. Teenagers who had been waiting for this break-through unawares since the first time they cursed out their par-ents welcomed the tunes that delivered it, then glommed onto the noise itself. Those more set in their formal ways took longer to realize that the noise was both catchy and rocking.

Not that it rocked like the Beatles or the Stones—or the Isley Brothers. Mitchell was a musical drummer, but he didn't com-mand much of a beat, leaving Redding to maintain the pulse because somebody had to. This weakened *Axis,* Hendrix's most song-conscious and lightweight album—full of great riffs, but how strong can it be if Redding's "She's So Fine" fits right in? Soon enough, however, the expansive pop structure Hendrix's sound demanded was in place, as the untrammeled mind-body some-thing-or-other of white blues and the San Francisco ballrooms coa-lesced into what was designated acid rock. By the time of *Electric Ladyland,* Hendrix felt free to translate to vinyl not a simulation of the show the Experience evolved as Jeffery slogged them all over the map, but an idealization. Less precious than *Sgt. Pepper* and less offhand than *Blonde on Blonde,* sweatier and more masterful than, to choose a neglected minor classic with similar spiritual ambitions, the Grateful Dead's *Anthem of the Sun, Electric Ladyland* is undiminished by the years. Where *Are You Experienced?* sounds both stranger and more natural, *Electric Ladyland* retains its magic, except that we now realize how historically fragile that magic was, which intensifies it. The album doesn't prove the sixties worked—they didn't. But it does remind us of what people hoped to find in them, and why they thought they might succeed.

"A sprawling, mighty mess," Greil Marcus declared after he'd had ten years to think about it, and clearly that was the idea—clearly the rockers, pop songs, riffs, grooves, jive poetry, blues tropes, New Age sci-fi, guest musicians, sound excursions, and bombs bursting midair were supposed to *evoke* mess. But we know too much about Hendrix's capacity for premeditation—detailed master plans of arrangements have been discovered, written out in words because Hendrix couldn't notate—to doubt the way its ebb and flow cohere as we relisten and relisten again. No less than DJ Shadow, Hendrix conceived a sound collage that he labored to capture in his head all at once, from beginning to end. *Electric Ladyland* is an aural utopia that accommodates both ingrained conflict and sweet, vague spiritual yearnings, held together by a master musician (for the intrinsic interest of the parts) who'd apprenticed in both American r&b and English pop (for the movement and shape of the whole). It's the rock concert of your dreams. It's a triumph of mind-body something-or-other. It demonstrates that life can be beautiful even if you don't clean your room.

Anything would be anticlimactic after that, and although Hendrix projected a second concept double, Kramer admits that *First Rays of the New Rising Sun* simply collects the songs Hendrix came closest to completing for it in 1970, after a lost year during which Redding went bye-bye and Jeffery milked his cash cow. By then Hendrix often regretted that he'd ever shown his fans the moves they demanded night after night; like many others only with more justification, he wanted to be a musician, not a star, which doesn't mean not a hero. Army buddy Billy Cox's bass steadies these songs—all known from the posthumous seventies releases, most marked improvements on the *Axis* norm—and Buddy Miles, who'd joined Cox in the short-lived Band of Gypsys, powers two tracks. But Jeffery never cottoned to Miles, so back came Mitchell, who was lively as always but not as funky as Hendrix might have preferred. Then again, Cox and Miles weren't ideal either. Ready to explore contemporary soul—"Drifting" is straight (or bent) Curtis Mayfield—Hendrix wasn't yet confident enough to seek sidemen outside the worlds where he was accepted. Forget Miles Davis—it's just as frustrating that we'll never know how he would have meshed with Duck Dunn and Ziggy Modeliste. We'll also never know why Hendrix took nine sleeping pills one otherwise uneventful night. But this not-quite-finished music should convince anyone that his death was a stupid accident.

Because it befell an active genius with more to learn and say and give, that accident was the cruelest tragedy ever to strike rock music. Hendrix was a space case till the day he happened to die, but he was also an intense, intelligent, generous man. He would have done some foolish things as he negotiated his multicultural fantasies while history contracted all around him. But this was a musician who made anything seem possible, a musician who has only gained in aura and vital authority. If his early canon seems startlingly pop, *Electric Ladyland* and, in embryo, *First Rays of the New Rising Sun* now give off a sense of world-historical sweep that's almost nineteenth-century in its magnificence. That kind of beauty is treasured by metalheads, and while I'm not twit enough to deny its presence in Mahavishnu Orchestra, Pink Floyd, Pulnoc, or Nirvana, I insist that in good rock and roll it's rarely attempted and almost never done right—that it has zip to do with what's invaluable about the Beatles or Dylan or James Brown and is barely approached by Hendrix's army of pretentious epigones. Admiring the Beatles and Dylan and James Brown as I do, I'm not sure I miss it, either. But I can't think of anybody it suits better than the wild man of America/Africa/Borneo. And I wish we could know where he would have taken it.

1997

Out of This World: Aretha Franklin

Aretha Franklin's great gift is her voice, but her genius is her bad taste. Admirers who try to ignore how she affronts ordinary notions of vocal decorum only prove that love is deaf. Phyl Garland's encomiums to her "dramatic instinct" and "fine sense of musicianship" tell us less about Aretha than the superlatives of the uncomprehending Rex Reed, who hates her: "Her delivery overpowers all semblance of order and dignity. Her phrasing is sloppy. She is probably the worst ballad singer I've ever heard."

In 1972, Aretha followed three dubious hits that broke a top-ten drought of three years—pro forma humankindness ("Bridge Over Troubled Water"), pro forma black consciousness ("Spanish Harlem"), pro forma rock and roll ("Rock Steady")—with *Young, Gifted and Black,* a pop album whose disconcerting disregard for the funky niceties showed rare promise once it was heard for the departure it was. Then she vanished. She canceled a tour; she threatened to quit Atlantic; and when her next album arrived, sixteen months later, it was nearly a disaster. Produced by jazz arranger Quincy Jones, *Hey Now Hey (The Other Side of the Sky)* was a document of genius out of control. Aretha's tendency to soar, ordinarily her chief asset, proved a liability as she sailed into the other side of the sky. The songs were long, and instead of ending they disappeared, just as Aretha had.

Less than a year later, Aretha celebrated *Hey Now Hey*'s fine follow-up album with a royal visit to the Apollo Theatre. Her performance was triumphant even if it also suggested that she had admired Bette Midler at the Palace without getting the joke. Her way prepared by six young *danseuses* whose implausible getups were trumped by their incredible interpretive gestures, Aretha entered in a spangled bikini-and-top-hat ensemble, her slimmed-down midriff covered with diaphanous gauze. Her faithful loved it. They loved the awkward bumps and grandiose grinds and outrageous costume changes. They loved the airborne grace of her hands and voice. And when she rocked out on "Dr. Feelgood" and "Spirit in the Dark," they rocked out with her. Apollo crowds aren't easily taken in; *les danseuses* elicited more than one howl of derisive glee. But this audience recognized that Aretha's silliest pretensions come from someplace strong and free.

The exact location of that someplace, however, remains obscure—the private passions of this notoriously reluctant interviewee are for all practical purposes unknowable. As the daughter of the renowned Detroit preacher C. L. Franklin, whose sermons made him a national recording star, she never experienced the poverty so many black performers have known too well, but neither was she insulated from it, and emotionally her life seems to have been hard. Her widely publicized late-sixties marriage to manager Ted White, whose take-and-take I briefly and uncomfortably observed while pursuing an abortive *Saturday Evening Post* profile in 1968, was no doubt unusually painful, and at thirty-two she is the mother of four sons, two of them teenagers whose existence is barely mentioned and whose paternity is never adduced.

But whatever else went on in her adolescence, Aretha Franklin was a precocious pianist and prodigious singer. At age fourteen, she was a gospel artist with Chess, her father's label, and at eighteen the great Columbia talent scout John Hammond brought her to New York, where for six years she languished beneath the ton of feathers that passed for pop-jazz sophistication around Gotham's studios. She did score minor hits in the early sixties, more on the pop than r&b charts, but it was only in early 1967, after the equally great Atlantic talent scout Jerry Wexler introduced her to several deep-fried Southern rhythm sections, that she found her adoring audience—blacks first, young whites almost simultaneously, and soon enough just about everybody. Deep-pocket drums and up-front Fender bass having boosted her voice into the irresistible force we know it to be, she whomped into the gospel chords of her youth and cut four classic soul albums in a year and a half. Only Otis Redding and Al Green, who sometimes seem dwarfed by the sheer size of Aretha's talent, have amassed catalogues of such consistency in soul proper.

Then again, Aretha's relationship to soul isn't all that proper. Redding and Green have trafficked brilliantly in white rock ditties and white pop trifles, but nothing as crude as "96 Tears" and "Niki Hoeky" on the one hand or as upwardly genteel as "Border Song" and "Eleanor Rigby" on the other. Only the former Columbia chanteuse would have covered Frank Sinatra's "That's Life," or consented to the big-band *Soul '69*, Wexler's stillborn attempt to counteract commercial genius's tendency to formulaic inertia while showing John Hammond that overarranging with bottom is overarranging with panache. Only the black-showbiz parvenu could have aimed the inspirational middlebrow detail of *Young, Gifted and Black* so lovingly and knowingly at the emergent class she'd been part of all her life. And only the jazz-funk cocktail pianist could have keyed the lounge intimacy and juke-joint lowdown of the almost hornless *Spirit in the Dark* to her own affectionate "Try Matty's." That cunningly stitched 1970 release stands just below the spectacular Atlantic debut *I Never Loved a Man the Way I Love You*, most of which should be consigned to any greatest-hits collection worth its title, as her finest album-as-album, although *Lady Soul* and *Aretha Now* have their savvy proponents and the rockin' *Live at Fillmore West* and gospel *Amazing Grace* their sentimental ones.

Produced once again by Jerry Wexler, Tom Dowd, and Arif Mardin (plus, this time, Aretha herself), *Let Me in Your Life*, which Aretha just feted at the Apollo, exemplifies a formula that subsumes pop as well as soul, gaffe as well as coup. It revives Leon Russell's "A Song for You" with a fresh electric piano part and a good helping of the indiscreet interpretation Rex Reed so deplores. But there is a moment when Aretha sings "I was hiding" as "I was hi—" (or maybe, God help us, "I was high"), pausing before coming in with the full "hiding" from some hidden cuteness chamber, that is mannered and godawful. On "The Masquerade Is Over" she sings a laugh after "laughed like Pagliacci" and gets in the way of the line. But the line is lousy anyway, and the laugh is liquid magic. At the end of "Oh Baby" she just wails, which at first sounds like more Aretha unmoored. Eventually, however, the Middle Eastern intonations she finds in herself add otherworldly feeling to an ordinary song.

The easy way out is to theorize that Aretha's childhood as a preacher's daughter is the source of her free-flying genius. But that obviously won't do. Although soul music is often excessive, it is usually excessive within rigorous formal bounds. So maybe the closest parallels are Ray Charles and Stevie Wonder, neither of whom grew up very sanctified, but both of whom are otherworldly in a literal way, because they are blind. Say that for Aretha Franklin the equivalent of blindness is a natural reticence closely linked to a lifetime of psychological hardship. Her sense of self is unsure, battered, but, projected through that vocal equipment, it overcomes. Aretha isn't content to interpret a song. She has to possess it, swooping and dodging unpredictably around the melody, flattening or emphasizing an unlikely phrase. There is something desperate in her inspiration, as if she's so eager to get it all out that she doesn't have time for niceties. Although sometimes her voice seems to flow like water seeking its own level, Aretha has plenty of musical intellect. She brings her own arrangements to the studio and obviously has a deep feel for rhythm. But she loses it sometimes.

So here's what Rex Reed is astute enough to mention but not soulful enough to hear. Overpowered meaning and sloppy phrasing turn out to be stamps of the singer's creation of personality. She doesn't so much sing ballads, many of which aren't worth her respect anyway, as transform them into lyric fancies. Order is provided by the grounded rhythm track. As for that missing semblance of dignity, well, hatred is also deaf. Aretha gathers dignity all the time—on the new album, for instance, she slips into songs conceived for assertive male personas ("Eight Days on the Road," say) as easily as she plays the sweet supplicant. Only occasionally has she commanded a wholly coherent and confident image of herself. Usually there are signs of struggle, moments of gaucherie. But if we know what's good for us, we'll embrace them as eagerly as she does. For we can always find some equivalent in ourselves.

1972–1974–1997

Nothing to Say but Everything, or, As Far as He Could Go: John Lennon

John Lennon's greatest work—greater than his persona, his marriage, even his music—was the Beatles. Obviously, though, he didn't create the Beatles alone. It's arbitrary to separate John Lennon the artist—the singer, guitarist, lyricist, composer, tape tinkerer, bandleader, author, actor, cartoonist, filmmaker, politico, publicity hound, comedian, and sage—from the culture of the sixties. It's conjecture to separate his Beatle image from the efforts of Brian Epstein, Derek Taylor, Richard Lester, or the thousands of journalists who turned him into copy. But it's just about impossible to separate his Beatle music from that of Paul McCartney, George Harrison, Ringo Starr, or George Martin.

Yet it was John Lennon who created the Beatles if anyone did. John's skiffle band, the Quarrymen, absorbed first Paul, then George, and finally Ringo, changing name and style along the way. Brian Epstein fell for John and then taught the world that, as Greil Marcus put it, "you did not have to love them all to love the group, but you could not love one without loving the group." John was the Beatles' chief composer and singer, edging Paul out statistically (by about 15 percent) and thrashing him aesthetically. The most outspoken of the Quotable Quartet, he was perceived as the leader by everyone including his three mates until acid went to his head. Years later, John talked as if the Beatles had already sold (him?) out when they walked into EMI; certainly, Brian Epstein's insistence on ties and smiles and George Martin's preference for

Paul's tuneful tonsils went against John's primal urges. But John did Brian's bidding because he also had a primal urge for money—and when money talked, Martin released Paul and John's "Love Me Do" (respectable debut) and then topped it with John's "Please Please Me" (Beatlemania!). Anyway, this was a group, and to have a group was John's most primal urge of all. A loner he wasn't.

That the Beach Boys and the Beatles each evolved a format in which four or five coequals shared vocals and played their own instruments is proof enough that the rock group was inevitable. Teenage fans of such leaders with backup as Bill Haley & His Comets or Buddy Holly & the Crickets were sure to create their own guitar-playing equivalents of the Ink Spots and the Ames Brothers eventually. But as it was we have one band led by a borderline catatonic who turned "In My Room" into the story of his life and another by a jealous guy whose chronic acute separation anxiety began when his mother turned him over to his aunt at age three. Lots of ordinary boy geniuses are natural leaders, but you can see how having his own group might have been a special comfort to John Lennon.

Like most skifflers, the Quarrymen picked up on the fad because it was easy and there. As soon as they could afford amplifiers they graduated from ersatz acoustic jug blues to ersatz electric hillbilly blues—rock and roll. This too was John's need. Paul was even more intense about fancy pop chords and corny pop tunes than he was about Little Richard. George's look was all rockabilly flash, but his music began with skiffle king Lonnie Donegan and proved even vaguer than that of most lead guitarists when he got out from under John's thumb. And while Ringo wouldn't have traded his back seat on the magic bus for any better drummer's solo spotlight, he recorded albums of country tunes and sentimental standards as soon as he had the chance.

None of this is to imply that Paul, George, or Ringo was an opportunist. No one who played rock and roll professionally back then (back before the Beatles, that is) chose the music casually, and stardom was a fantasy of the crazed. But John didn't merely love rock and roll. For him it was a passion, a calling, a way of life. Yoko Ono, prophet of total communication and love of his life, was the only artist who ever challenged the preeminence of Chuck Berry, Jerry Lee Lewis, and idol and predecessor Elvis Presley in

John's pantheon. John's sole reservation about rock and roll was that it couldn't say everything. And that was just what attracted Paul, George, and Ringo to his leadership. Most of the time, John Lennon believed that rock and roll *could* say everything.

In retrospect, the upsurge of rock and roll seems like the most natural thing in the world. It was sexy, it was lively, it was popular, it was real—who wouldn't love it, especially in the Fatuous Fifties? The answer is lots of people, including a good many fond but finally uncommitted teenage fans. And even when a kid did fall in love with rock and roll, it would rarely be forever—as a means to romantic fantasy or peer-group macho, the music tended to vanish into a nostalgic limbo once the job of growing up was done. But that wasn't how it was for the Beatles. Sure, they became entertainers for the same general reasons that egomaniacs everywhere go into show business (and the arts) (and journalism, too). But they became rock and rollers so they wouldn't have to grow up. Like a lot of war babies, these lads wanted to be sexy and lively (and maybe even popular) until they died, and good for them.

In John, though, the love of rock and roll went even deeper, and so the question of why he put so much of himself into it must go deeper too. One answer—simple, impolite, and almost certainly true—is that he had more self to put: more energy, more conviction, more emotion, more humor, more ideas, more sheer talent. But there's no way to understand John Lennon without understanding how he felt about pain, and for John pain meant his mother, Julia, so here's the story. When he's an infant his ne'er-do-well father deserts Julia, who meets another man and farms the baby out to her sister Mimi; when he's five or so his father claims him for a few weeks, then accedes to Julia, who again passes him on to Mimi; seven years later Mimi's husband dies and then, five years after that, Julia, who has always visited Mimi's frequently and whose home is now a haven of flaky permissiveness in his teen psychodrama, is run down near Mimi's house by an off-duty cop. She had John, but he never had her.

On balance, this is far from a horror story. John always emphasized that he enjoyed his childhood. He was working-class but not poor, a healthy combination, with a surrogate father or two and two mothers most of the time. And if reliable Mimi was less fun than Julia, the sisters shared three virtues: affection, animation, and good sense. But all those separations were just the thing to give somebody who didn't repress the whole business an uncommon taste for realism. Dead certain by age five that life wasn't just a bowl of cherries, he threw up a barrier of precociously bitter wit, specializing in cripples almost as soon as he learned to draw cartoons. And he was just as quick to develop a healthy aversion to hypocrisy. So it's fair to say that if he was attracted to rock and roll because it was sexy (affection) and lively (animation) and popular (affection, animation, and good working-class sense), he loved it because it was real—because it had soul and grit, a common touch and a tough lip.

John was a natural musician, just as he was a natural artist and a natural writer, an original without half trying. This ease of self-expression made him impatient with technique and formal discipline. One reason John ended up in music was that while he might (and did) fail his exams in English composition and even art, there were no O levels in rock and roll, no adult authority figures dictating standards. Rock and roll transmutes less into more as only a mass-produced, internationally distributed, electrically amplified folk art can, which means it makes the most of limited means as "higher" art cannot. But John's rock and roll would never have said as much as it did if he hadn't been crazy to make it say everything.

John was the undisputed leader of the Quarrymen when he first met Paul McCartney, who intimidated the older boy with his technical accomplishments—this snot-nosed tyro knew lyrics, he knew chords, he could tune a guitar. In short, he was a threat to John's preeminence, and John wasn't sure he liked it. But a week later Paul was in the band, and for the next decade-plus his unreconstructed boyishness, snazzy melodic ideas, transcendent harmonies, and insufferable pop treacle would clutter and inestimably enrich John's passion, calling, and way of life. Though it's safe to rely on the old rule of thumb that John was chiefly responsible for the songs he sang lead on, the fecund if often theoretical Lennon-McCartney songwriting partnership makes it especially hard to sort John out from the band. That's why it's important to remember that John deliberately encouraged this alien alter ego to modify and distort his music.

And though John was definitely the leader, he would never have led as fast or as far afield without Paul pushing from behind.

By 1959, with George on second or third guitar and John's art school confrere Stu Sutcliffe on bass, the ever-hustling Paul was describing the band's wares to a journalist he'd met in a pub without resorting to the dread words "rock and roll" at all—"modern music," he called it. And in 1961, with Pete Best providing the heavy off-beat Liverpool's beat boom required, the now Beatles brought their hodgepodge to Hamburg and whipped it into modern music—the music John would later say they sold out to become the biggest act in show business. The only extant recordings are some backups for one Tony Sheridan (after McCartney replaced Sutcliffe on bass) and the ragged, listless, all but inaudible *Live! At the Star Club* tapes, cut during their sullen Christmas '62 farewell to the Reeperbahn, with "Love Me Do" on the charts and the moptops dreaming of world conquest. So we can't test John's contention that the Beatles in Hamburg were at once tighter and more anarchic than they'd ever be again. But it's clear that it was only by choosing diverse material from their stage repertoire—including Paul's sappy "Taste of Honey," John's mad "Twist and Shout," and originals that were by no means pure rock and roll songs in the three-chord fifties sense, though we now regard them as classic rock—that George Martin defined what the world perceived as the Beatles' "sound" on *Introducing the Beatles.*

The Beatles grew up on rock and roll in Anglo-Irish Liverpool, with no racial, regional, or cultural stake in the American rockabilly and r&b and girl group and show-tune records they recombined. Their music arose from the odd circumstance of Lennon and McCartney, pop composers by virtue of the advanced chords Paul taught John, leading their own guitar band—a band that made its living hurtling top-volume barrages at sailors, teenage rowdies, women of the night, and other port-town lumpenbohos. Thus they evolved their own completely synthetic, completely organic version of the music—wilder than Little Richard, more civilized than Pat Boone, more complex and spirited than the Beach Boys. Where Brian Wilson begins his song of solitude with a gently ascending "There's a world where I can go/And tell my secrets to," gathering strength to tumble back down to "In my room," Lennon is faster, more confident: "There, there's a place/ Where I can go." The melody begins high and stays there, then drops a step. But John has better places to go than his room, and better ways to get there than Brian Wilson. Instead of continuing his descent, he modulates, taking the melody with him to cloud nine: "And it's my mind/And there's no time/When I'm alone."

Or so he claims. In its avowal of self-sufficiency this early song typifies his urge to say a great deal, serving the ironic complexities of his own half-schooled modernism within the conventions of the rock and roll love song. He often dismissed his early lyrics as off-the-cuff made-to-order, and it would be silly to read too much into them, but it would also be silly to think that any pre-Beatle rocker would have written a line as metaphysical as "And there's no time," awkward and ambiguous though it may be. An artist obsessed with separation can do worse than write love songs, and as a young husband John was already exploring the nuances of the one-on-one.

Sure he has his euphoric-to-cutesy moments, usually in his collaborations with Paul, though "I Feel Fine" and "Do You Want To Know a Secret" (which he had George sing) are John's alone. But he never allowed himself a love-at-first-sight goody like "I Saw Her Standing There" or "I've Just Seen a Face," and even such blithe moments as "I'm Happy Just To Dance with You" and "Ask Me Why" are touched with fear. Relatively complex themes—homecoming ("A Hard Day's Night," "When I Get Home"), reconciliation and betrayal ("No Reply," "Not a Second Time"), pain concealed ("I Call Your Name," "You've Got to Hide Your Love Away")—are dealt with in relatively complex ways. Early on he's writing "If I Fell," which fuses the yearning for tenderness and the yearning for revenge, and "Please Please Me," an oral sex song that precedes "Chewy Chewy" by half a decade. And before Beatlemania has crossed the line into psychedelia he's come up with "Help!" an outcry of raw polysyllabic need, and "Ticket To Ride," a female autonomy song that precedes the Redstockings Manifesto by half a decade.

Musically, too, John is an ironic primitive. He's the Beatles' most committed rock and roller, but he never just lets go like Paul on "Long Tall Sally," because both his realism and his belief that rock and roll can say everything impel him to undercut and overreach himself—he can never settle for just one meaning. So what is basically a very foursquare time sense is tempered by his nervously aggressive rhythm guitar signatures, many of them variations on the slightly syncopated rest-one-two-and-rest figures of "I Saw Her Standing There." Sometimes he tampers with a song's thrust just for the hell of it—listen to the vaguely Latin swing of "Ask Me Why" and "No Reply" or the broken-up intro to the reverberating "I Want To Hold Your Hand." Elsewhere, as with the stop-and-start verse that sets up the straight-ahead acceleration of "All I've Got To Do," he'll play up a song's drive with tension-and-release. Similar contrasts mark his mixtures of blues and pop chords and the way his harmonies sour Paul's ebullience. And they're present as well in the wicked, joyful pop-art jokes that are this band's birthright: the "Little Darlin' " la-la-las he tacks onto "Misery," the bacchanalian fadeout of "Please Mr. Postman," or the "Mr. Moonlight" travesty, with Paul on lounge-lizard organ, George on African drum, and John ripping up the vocal like it's rock and roll.

Needless to say, John did a lot more with vocals than rip them up—it was as a lead singer that he made the most of his greatest musical gift, his voice. It would be a mistake to attribute to one man a collective spirit in which the three little words "yeah yeah yeah" became a truth known only to young gods and the biggest giggle in the world simultaneously. But John's voice could certainly have created a narrower version of this fecund antithesis all by itself. Physically, his instrument didn't approach Paul's; it was rather nasal, with average range, strong but rarely rich. Technically, he lacked the rhythmic finesse and timbral liquidity of Jagger, the innuendo of Dylan, the surging purity of the American rock and roll originators. And I hesitate to just say he had soul, because one of his charms was that he never tried to "sound black." Yet soul is something like it. Maybe sincerity would be closer, but that's a strange term to apply to the class clown. So call it substance. However difficult it was to distinguish him from his mates in the early days of image saturation, it was the conviction and playfulness of his singing—cutting a passionate, decent emotional solidity with an extrovert's array of pranks, tricks, moves, and nuances—that made us feel there were real human beings in the grooves rather than cuddly toys.

Lennon found more vocal inspiration in rockabilly—Buddy Holly, Jerry Lee Lewis, and (once he hooked up with Paul) the Everly Brothers—than in the black rock and rollers he loved, and he certainly sounded white, partly because he was unashamed of his Scouse accent (not that he didn't drawl more when he sang than when he spoke) and partly because of his natural rhythm.

But his attack has something of Kansas City and the territory bands in it; it's flatter and more classic than that of any of the singers he covered, black or white. Although he definitely isn't above novelty effects, he's a shouter rather than a screamer, sweaty rather than hysterical and forceful rather than piercing, especially on his own straightforward rockers. His robust, steady assurance simply doesn't have much to do with Little Richard or Rockin' Jerry Lee; during "Please Please Me" and "When I Get Home" you can hear him shiver the timbre and beat the beat at crucial moments, like Joe Williams adding a decisive touch of urgency to a phrase. But there's something combustible just beneath the surface, and other times he goes to a scream instead, especially on remakes—in contained yelps for Larry Williams, all over the place on Barrett Strong's "Money" or the Isley Brothers' "Twist and Shout." While most white people singing black music overdo it—whether as gauchely as Pat Boone or as passionately as Janis Joplin—the intensity of John's covers rarely seems forced. When the Beatles outrock their exemplars, John is usually why.

But from a shout to a scream isn't the only way to go, especially for magicians and extroverts, and John proves it every time he camps up (or feminizes) a backup with a coy, lemonsugary purse of the lips. Although he can barely approximate the breathy vulnerability of a Smokey Robinson or Shirley Alston, his delicacy at ballad tempos is irresistible whether the underlying mood is purely plaintive ("This Boy") or lull before the hullabaloo ("No Reply"). The hammered vowels on a simple word like I-I-I-I-I augment "All I've Got To Do's"'s aura of longing, a trademark device, as is the scratchy moan that points up the pain of "Eight Days a Week." Even the silly coda to the silly "Misery" turns heartsick groan into sublime falsetto into comic sendup. By absorbing such vocal contradictions and playing them off Paul's more one-dimensional rock and pop modes, John dramatized the confusions of adolescence in a singing style emulated by fans everywhere.

Of course, the fans didn't think John was singing about adolescence in any case. They thought he was singing about life. And for the next five or ten years it appeared that they were right.

It is coming on Christmas 1965. In England, the Beatles have been more popular than the Christ child since early 1963; in the United States, where the craze started later, the group has released at least seven legitimate LPs—plus a few odd singles, one redundant soundtrack, an interview album, and the Tony Sheridan tapes—within about a year and a half. They have also starred in two fast, heady Richard Lester comedies, *A Hard Day's Night* and *Help!,* the first of which established them as the new Marx Brothers with a postcollege audience that in 1963 had been too old for rock and roll. They've said a lot of cheeky things to the press. And John has published two funny, nasty little books of stories, drawings, and verse, *In His Own Write* and *A Spaniard in the Works,* both replete with cripples, fantasy mayhem, solecistic spellings, and imagery that reminds critics of Edward Lear and suggests untapped lyrical possibilities. Enter *Rubber Soul,* with Our Boys tieless in suede and fisheye on the cover, and suddenly—not that there've been no portents—the world is about to change again. *Rubber Soul* is the Beatles' most unqualified triumph, the record claimed by their *Sgt. Pepper* faction and their Hamburg faction both. It is also the beginning of the end, if only because it carries the seeds of such factionalism.

The young John Lennon really was singing about life, but he was also really singing about adolescence. That is, he was making like an artist, trying to universalize his unique experience into a coherent rakka-rakka-rakka. A war baby in his early twenties, class-conscious but not classbound, beset since age three by an identity crisis less who-am-I? than where-do-I-belong?, and determined by nature and nurture to come out a winner, he found his form in rock and roll. Because he knew the difference between alienation and growing pains, he could infuse his deeper hurt with the giddy poignancy of teen trauma and vice versa. Because he knew the difference between alienation and anomie, he didn't automatically assign social significance to his problems; that was often essential to what he did, but only when he got pretentious did it take over. What made him special—what made him a youth gadfly as well as a youth symbol, and what made him a precocious adult—was his confidence that he could smash alienation altogether.

This confidence—which was intermittent, of course—reflected John's rise from a secure but never comfortable economic base; when he yelled out "I want to be free!" at the end of "Money," he added another level of spiritual ambition to the original. Such upward mobility was common in the boom years of the early sixties, but less so in England than elsewhere in the industrialized world; a working-class Liverpudlian with a sharp aversion to hypocrisy was well-suited to put its exuberance across with a little bite. And by 1963, something even more confidence-inspiring had entered his life. Having projected his longings onto the early heroes of rock and roll, he was able to invent an emphatically unalienated identity for himself, as leader/member of the Beatles. And then, with Beatlemania rampant, he found that the protective circles had grown even wider—adored by an enormous audience, he was also at the heart of a nascent subculture, which in England was temporarily dubbed Swinging London.

Even if this whole configuration had been frozen in a time capsule at its peak of perfection, though, John's confidence would still have been intermittent. And peaks of perfection were all too rare. For starters, he still wanted rock and roll to say everything, and up till mid 1965 he'd pretty much limited himself to happy love songs, sad love songs, assertive love songs, hurt love songs, idyllic love songs, enraged love songs, married love songs, and away-from-home love songs. What's more, like Elvis (and Valentino) before him, he had made the alarming discovery that there's nothing more alienating than stardom. He had no human contact with his fans and not much reason to want it—by definition they were incapable of understanding his dilemma, which was them. John was beleaguered by well-wishers and mendicants, on the job whenever he walked out his front door. Forced into more intimacy with his fellow Fabs than he'd bargained for, he found that the creative tension essential to any fruitful collaboration could get pretty irritating. And Swinging London—the cronies, business associates, starfuckers, and fellow celebs who were one portent of the hippiedom just over the horizon—proved hectic and disorienting. Marijuana, some say, entered the life of this longtime pill taker via a 1964 house guest who got his dander up in lots of ways—Bob Dylan. LSD was slipped into his coffee at a posh dinner party in 1965.

Convinced by mind expansion, rival songpoets, and his own insatiable muse to stretch his songs, John (with equal input from Paul and some from George) set about expanding the Beatles' music as well. In 1965, they were no longer the great bar band of 1962, but their playing had never been more assured and, although studiocraft was encroaching on their spontaneity, their records retained a bar band's spark. On *Rubber Soul,* the bar was definitely tonier—some cross between a cocktail lounge and a folkie rathskeller, with the Byrds, Dionne Warwick, and Dobie Gray's "The 'In' Crowd" on the jukebox. There was plenty of folk-rockish guitar, quiet when not actually acoustic, with George's sitar a stab at exoticism and Paul's limp "Michelle" proof that he believed in "Yesterday." But at a mean length of two and a half minutes, every other one of the fourteen songs had some snap. And the lyrics did nothing less than consolidate the conventional expectations of the Beatles' audience with the ambitious tastes of the Beatles' subculture.

Only three of them tackled new subjects. The double-reversed rockstar fantasy, "Drive My Car," and John's first aural caricature, "Nowhere Man," were openly satiric. "The Word," which notes that the message of his first love sermon can be found in bad books as well as good, is subliminally satiric. But such grown-up romantic advisories as George's "Think for Yourself" and Paul's "I'm Looking Through You" augment three of the most mature songs John ever wrote. "Norwegian Wood" is a comedy of manners in which John doesn't get the girl, although he may end up torching her furniture next morning. "In My Life" pledges life-long loyalty and more with a simple, elegant melody that's built to last. And in "Girl," the poor boy's putdown (cf. "Like a Rolling Stone") is sweetened with a lovesick vocal—in the line "She's coo-ool oo-ool oo-oo oo-ooh girl" he sinks from censure to swoon in midword.

Rubber Soul smashed a lot of alienation. Without reneging on the group's masscult appeal, it reached into private lives and made hundreds of thousands of secretly lonely people feel as if someone out there shared their brightest insights and most depressing discoveries. These honest, sharp, and resonant songs helped older admirers—the ones who would soon comprise a counterculture—feel connected to the world, and encouraged teenyboppers to mistrust comforting love-dove-above propaganda. But to John they were still genre pieces—rock and roll could say more, as he set about to prove on the B side of Paul's Lennonesque "Paperback Writer." Transmuting fatalism into mysticism into idealism, or else confusing the three, "Rain" unveils the druggy, vinyl-tower, war-is-over-if-you-want-it tautology that would keep John's working-class materialism at bay for the rest of his life. He complements this circular thinking with a sinuous, whining, Byrds-derived guitar texture and tops it off by playing a snippet of the vocal track in reverse. Psychedelia starts here.

And then, nine months after *Rubber Soul,* came *Revolver,* and psychedelia was in power. Even in the United States, where its impact was dulled somewhat by the inclusion of three of John's *Revolver* songs on *The Beatles—"Yesterday" and Today* two months before, it seemed, well, revolutionary at the time. With its string octet and French-horn solo and soul brass, its electronics and tabla and sitar, its kiddie sound effects and savage guitar breaks, its backward tapes and backward rhythms, its air of untrammeled eclecticism, mystic wandering, and arty civility, this was where the Beatles stopped being a bar band. What's most remarkable about John's presence is his vocals, because he's just about stopped shouting—his campy, kissy-lipped backup harmonies have turned into the near-prissy lead of a yea- and nay-saying oracle, lyrical one moment and bummed out the next. On the nowhere man's victory cry "I'm Only Sleeping" he achieves this effect solely with mouth and larynx, but elsewhere he double-tracks. And on "She Said She Said" and "Tomorrow Never Knows," the climactic side-closers that are John's only showcases on the U.S. release, a filter makes him sound like God singing through a foghorn.

This is not the voice of a lover because John is leaving what few love songs the Beatles are singing to his mates. From a man who'd snuck the word "trivialities" into "When I Get Home" two years before, "She Said She Said" is even more basic English than "She Loves You," but with a big difference: This time the simple diction conveys impoverishment rather than outgoing charity, satirizing mind-damaged, bad-tripping pretension and positing a tranquil childhood certainty against it. And "Tomorrow Never Knows" dispenses with pop song altogether. Incorporating violin snatches, mock war whoops, barrelhouse piano, and lots of run-it-backward-George into a rhythmic layout rooted in Ringo's off-center pattering and a static bass-and-tamboura drone, the song ignores ordinary verse-chorus-break structure. There's only the continuous downstream unfolding of the same melody going nowhere, like time, or consciousness, until it circles around to a conclusion that is also a rebirth: "Or play the game existence to the end/Of the beginning/Of the beginning."

In early 1967, the broken epistemology and childhood memories of "She Said She Said" meet the hallucinogenic "Tomorrow Never Knows." "Strawberry Fields Forever" takes us down to the depths of John's psychedelic pessimism, where even the innocence of ignorance recalled offers no respite. In "Strawberry Fields," nothing (but nothing) seemed real. On the A side, "Penny Lane," Paul recalls similar dislocations in his own boyhood, but for him they're only "very strange," quaintly picturesque in the unthreatening rain, because for Paul, with his hustler's self-assurance, psychedelia was costume, spectacle, and art-deco nostalgia—vaudeville for the mind. For George it was liberating, its exotic dangers neutralized by mystic formulas. For Ringo it meant longer card games between drum tracks. But for John it was experimental, synesthetic, deconstructive, chaotic, and ultimately frightening, not least because his group shared almost none of these perceptions. At the heart of the new subculture, alienation was the craze, but John was the only Beatle who went with the flow down in the flood. Testing his ever more fragile ego boundaries, he had already begun to surrender musical control to random juxtaposition and collage. His primary instrument had become the studio, and in some essential sense the Beatles had ceased to be any kind of band at all. But you'd never have known it. *Sgt. Pepper's Lonely Hearts Club Band* was about to turn them into artists for the world.

Depending on who you ask, *Sgt. Pepper* is either the greatest album of all time or Paul McCartney's folly—cute, contrived, dinky except for "A Day in the Life." But Paul had been doing wonderful work—"For No One" is probably the Beatles' finest heartbreak song, and even if it's sacrilege to say so, "Penny Lane" holds up as well as "Strawberry Fields Forever." Though *Sgt. Pepper* is a little stiff for rock and roll, Paul's whimsy peaks on "Lovely Rita" and "When I'm Sixty-Four," and John's brief contributions to two of Paul's songs catapult them into a complexity of tone that neither Beatle ordinarily approached on his own. The "I used to be cruel to my woman" section of "Getting Better," like the "Life is very short" bridge John added to "We Can Work It Out," illuminate Paul's aphoristic moralism with a flash of brutality, and in "With a Little Help From My Friends" John sums up pop psychedelia's balmy, life-is-ours-for-the-digging equanimity with a surprisingly warm, characteristically witty couplet: "What do you see when you turn out the light/I can't tell you, but I know it's mine."

The mood John projects on *Sgt. Pepper* partakes of the same life-affirming passivity. Turning the bricolages of his recent music into an all encompassing lyrical embrace, he "finds" the content of his songs in a drawing by his son Julian, a circus poster, and the newspapers. The first two come out as McCartneyesque conceits, and while the hectic "Good Morning, Good Morning" begins with a death, it ends with one of John's gnostic truisms: "I've got nothing to say but it's okay." Only the five-minute minisymphony "A Day in the Life," with Paul's wakeup routine imparting tragicomic import to the disconnected leads of John's dream journalism, fully expresses his personal turmoil. By saying "holes" where he should say "people" in the final verse, John names the emptiness at his center. Yet it was the last line of this popular masterpiece that people quoted: "I'd love to turn you on."

This was nothing new. Since "Help!" and probably before, Beatle fans had been reluctant to take their heroes' dark side seriously. They didn't know, and they didn't want to know—if separating John's art from his group, his image, and the culture of the sixties is problematic now, it was out of the question then. When the biographical facts were available at all, they were obscured by an overarching presentation that was optimistic as a matter of policy, and this wasn't all Paul's (or Brian's) doing: John was happy to play the stand-up guru. The Beatles' image was so powerful that it subsumed not only their life stories but their art itself; their tragic/absurdist ("heavy") tendencies were rarely taken at face value, serving instead to make the group's positivism seem more substantial. Sure there were rumors of internal friction, but the Beatles were the Beatles, our great symbol of the communal, and even the simple notion that John and Paul wrote songs separately scarcely creased our consciousness. Sure a lot of us got off on John's irreligious skepticism and mordant quips, but for most of his fans the transition from irrepressible cutie-pie to owl-rimmed hippie was wrenching enough. Sure "All You Need Is Love" was another pop art joke, parodying its own simplistic message from the "La Marseillaise" intro to the laughing horn phrase that follows the hook down the three-blind-mice coda. But it was also what all those entranced by the Summer of Love wanted to believe—quite possibly including John Lennon himself.

Six months later came Paul's real folly—*Magical Mystery Tour,* saved from its own preciosity only by the singles that made it an album, especially "Hello Goodbye," Paul's delightfully simple-minded play on the "She Said She Said" idea, and John's psyche-delic nightmare, "I Am the Walrus." John begins in a state of ego-less universality—"I am he as you are he as you are me and we are all together." But by the end his heavily filtered voice has dis-appeared altogether. When he sings the words "I'm crying," ech-oed at one point by an anonymous crowd, there's no sadness, just the matter-of-fact expression of an ego coming apart. Love was what John needed after all, not egolessness, and, sixties cant to the contrary, the two were anything but identical. Enter Yoko Ono. Enter and exit the Maharishi Mahesh Yogi.

At the time, John's breakdown songs seemed to prove that he'd learned to sing about life rather than adolescence—they explored an existential dilemma, and what makes dilemmas existential is their general human relevance. But existentialism has always been popular with college students because its central insight is avail-able to anyone who knows what it's like to be dead (as they say). And breakdown was enjoying a major generational vogue. For rea-sons having more to do with patterns of leisure consumption than with justice or the bomb, a fairly large, mostly young audience began trying to smash alienation chemically—to achieve con-nectedness by dissolving the ego's petty subjective prison. You were supposed to find yourself (and your brothers and sisters) by losing yourself.

Although acid took courage for John, who'd spend years building up an identity that would fend off painful truths about isolation to which his psychohistory had sensitized him, his thou-sand trips were also a surrender to his desperate need to expand his self as far as it would go. In the end, the psychedelic life was nearly a disaster for him personally. Artistically, his ingrained craftsmanship put him off the pulsating formlessness of San Fran-cisco, so that the epochal "Tomorrow Never Knows" clocks in at three minutes. But like all rock and rollers, John was a lyric artist, better at evocation than analysis, and though his vivid depiction of ego breakdown is important work, so is "There's a Place."

Yet by putting him out on his own, ego breakdown drove John to surpass himself. By the time of the White Album, much of which was written on their all-together-now jaunt to the Maharishi's India, he had abdicated. The group had turned into a solo project of Paul's that the others personalized with friends, family, and sidemen. John's boldest negation was "Revolution #9," an anti-masterpiece that took "I Am the Walrus" 's collage chaos to unpopular extremes. There were no chords, no melody, no lyrics; there were no instruments, no vocals; in fact, for eight minutes of an album officially titled *The Beatles,* there were no Beatles. Elsewhere, with a few exceptions—notably the baton-passing "Glass Onion" ("The Walrus was Paul") and the pacifist pastiche "Happiness Is a Warm Gun"—John signals that he's rebuilding from the ground up with a formally self-conscious return to basics. The tenderness and sweet simplicity of "Dear Prudence" and "Julia" are all but unprecedented; the dreamsong as insomniac mumble "I'm So Tired" is pointedly unadorned; "Everybody's Got Something To Hide Except Me and My Monkey" says just that. But the watersheds are "Revolution," which isn't what it says it is, and "Yer Blues," which is and a half. In its very rejection of left-wing rhetoric, "Revolution" implies that for him public (or subcultural) prominence carries with it political responsibilities. And "Yer Blues" announces the third phase of John's struggle to make rock and roll say everything—first Paul's received pop wisdom, then psychedelia's technowizardry and avant-decoration, now Yoko's antiartifice. He reasserts his ego in a spectacular renunciation: "Feel so suicidal/Even hate my rock and roll."

This may have felt like a truth when he wrote it, contemplating Yoko (whose terse, provocatively simplistic art directives had been bugging him for over a year) and rock and roll (permanent obsession) in his ashram fastness, but all it proved was how much he cared. A year later Yoko and rock and roll were his life and his ego was doing as well as could be expected. After the White Album, the Beatles started dissolving in public, played by cartoons in their third film while the fourth stalled in production. Their 1969 release schedule was a mishmash. "The Ballad of John and Yoko"—a Beatle song most assuredly, featuring Paul on bass, piano, drums, and backup vocals—competed with "Get Back" in June; "Give Peace a Chance"—composition still credited Lennon-McCartney but artist listed as Plastic Ono Band, the first official acknowledgment of what was going on—came out six weeks after that. In September, John played Toronto with one Plastic Ono

Band, cut "Cold Turkey" with a slightly different one, and decided he wanted out for real, though Allen Klein persuaded him to keep it to himself until more m-o-n-e-y could be squeezed out of attendant corporations.

Throughout this rich if confusing period, which ended with the release of *McCartney* and *Let It Be* in April and May of 1970, John divided his major work between political statements like "Come Together," "Instant Karma!" and "Give Peace a Chance" (far more rousing on *Live Peace in Toronto* than in its original bed-in production) and personal outcries like "Don't Let Me Down," "The Ballad of John and Yoko," "Cold Turkey," and "I Want You (She's So Heavy)." Either way the music is the most direct he's recorded, based on blues structures of irreducible simplicity. Yet if anything its expressiveness has intensified, and not because he's jazzing up the lyrics. Even when he wants a satiric tone, as in the sexually political "Come Together" or the Lennon-McCartney swan song "I've Got a Feeling," the wordplay is play indeed, with no nightmare surrealism lurking down below. And in his outcries, John says what he means as baldly as he can manage: "Get me out of this hell," "Christ, you know it ain't easy," "She done me good," "She's so heavy."

Physically, in measurable aural reality, you could say that what put flesh on these bones was John's voice, which hadn't returned to basics. John was rediscovering the chord changes he'd lived and breathed as a teenager, but he was no longer a teenager and he wasn't ashamed of it—he held onto his vocal technique. So every nuance and timbre he's mastered over the years is still on call—every taste of honey and spit of sand, every rasp and scream and coo. He exploits the studio's instant virtuosity to underline and accent rather than obscure and/or show off; the harmony vocal on "Don't Let Me Down" is either Paul in a fit of genius mimicry or one of the most gorgeous, tormented double-tracks ever recorded, and there are even hints of the filtered oracle in "Come Together" and "Instant Karma!" What enabled John to produce these sounds wasn't merely physical—plenty of sleep and a crack voice coach, or lotsa dope and some shredded nodes. Given his hard-earned skills, his margin was spiritual and conceptual. He glimpsed into the abyss of no self and with his old confidence concluded that singing mattered—even an occasional piece like "The Ballad of John and Yoko" sounds as if his life depends on it. But he would never have achieved this conviction without Yoko Ono—not just to prop him up and ease his isolation but to provide artistic direction.

Since the time he was in art school, John had been acutely aware of what cultural arbiters defined as his left flank—in art and politics both, he felt the challenge of self-declared vanguardists. Were they heroes making way for deeper communication and fulfillment than he and his rock and roll could offer, as they claimed, or just pretentious twits? Yoko's theories were a way out of this quandary. Her minimalist psychodrama and just-do-it neoprimitivism offended the craftsman in John, the more accomplished artist of the two technically. But at the same time Yoko's work suggested how rock and roll might say more—say everything important there was to be said—and at the same time reassert his eroded identity. Yer blues my foot—*his* blues was what they were. Less was more.

Of course, almost as soon as he made his commitment to Yoko he started doing pretentious things himself. But no matter how fatuous his various bagisms got, only the love-is-all-you-need moralism of John, Wisest of the Hippies was actually twitty. The rest—some of it at least educational (the return of the M.B.E. more than the bed-ins) or groundbreaking (the guitar solos more than the tape trips), some of it great rock and roll—was part of a demystification program. Having rashly dismantled some of his own anti-alienation devices and then watched the rest of the structure fall apart, the man who had once hidden his love away did his best to take it all off—to divest his life of its crippling defenses/dependencies and his stardom of its aura. If at the same time he had the presumption to play the political leader, that was part of the process. Fans had to become ex-fans, or something more than fans. They had to understand that smashing alienation meant affirming one's own energy, conviction, emotion, humor, and ideas—and suffering, because coming to terms with suffering is the only sure way to be strong. And once they'd achieved this strength, then the project of liberation would naturally continue.

John released his solo debut just in time for Christmas 1970. From the funeral bell that kicked off "Mother" it was a shock—an austere, agonized catharsis. Yet it was also the culmination of two years of growth, and it was also rock and roll. Less was more. *Plastic Ono Band* is hardly his richest music—on "Mother," Hamburg buddy Klaus Voormann plays less than one note per beat while Ringo is reduced to a metronome, and it goes on from there. But it's certainly his most powerful. With their three- and four-piece accompaniment, these monodic, pentatonic, preharmonic blues melodies fit the fundamental human afflictions at the album's root not just adequately but with a poetic justice that more civilized music couldn't match. And the album's starkness isn't always what it seems—without transgressing against form, John exploits our reduced expectations to enormous dramatic effect. Alien rhythms (12/8 in "Mother," 3/8 and 5/8 in "I Found Out") make the pain more jarring, and John has never sung more virtuosically. At first his voice seems to veer between just-the-facts recitation and primal ululation with no stops in between, but in fact all that's missing from his performance is fun. "My Mummy's Dead" employs a familiar-sounding filter to decidedly antioracular effect, while on the two love songs, "Look at Me" and "Hold On John," Lennon duets with himself. And after beginning "God" with a round of grit, he climaxes in a transported dream-is-over croon that's the most exalted, plainly beautiful singing of his career.

Superficially, *Plastic Ono Band* seemed an ad for primalist Arthur Janov, something on the order of "Know your pain and conquer the world." But it doesn't make salvation sound so easy. John emphasizes that the awareness of loss is ongoing. Through-out the album he presents himself as both parent and child—lit-erally (between Julia and Julian) and figuratively (to an audience whose disloyalties hurt him). In "Working Class Hero" he's both messiah and victim. And in "Well Well Well" his love for Yoko turns mysteriously sour for an evening. This working-class hero identi-fied so tellingly with the fucked-up generation of fans that followed him through teen trauma to psychedelic heaven to comedown (even junkie) hell to married-adult-in-love-in-a-troubled-world pur-gatory that not all of them wanted to know the details.

Whether applying kitsch sophistication to a crude guitar band (with Paul) or exploring a trippy technology that enabled everyrocker to come on like a highbrow (with acid), John had made the aesthetic connections of a born artist with no patience for discipline. *Plastic Ono Band* was his pinnacle, the kind of prim-itivism that only a natural formalist (with avant-garde advice) could have gotten to. But like most minimalism, it left only one way out. John's next album, *Imagine,* was a pop move and a populist bid—an attempt to turn on a larger, Paul- and George-sized audience to his psychopolitical program. Artistically and commercially, it was a major success. Even stronger compositionally than *Plastic Ono Band,* exquisitely sung, with Phil Spector's naive grandeur constrained by Lennon's lingering reductionist tendencies, it went number one on the back of its title single. But as the satirical ricky-tick of "Crippled Inside" proved, this was the end of the bare-boned form-is-content purism announced by "Yer Blues."

Soon John's struggle for identity began to falter. By early 1971 his working-class and artistic identifications had drawn him into the radical movement he'd once dismissed so smugly. But he quickly wearied of its strategic and ideological failures, not the least of them his and Yoko's agitprop album, *Some Time in New York City.* Though John's name is permanently linked to hopes for peace, his confusion about political means was chronic. Between his upward mobility and his distrust of intellectualism, he would always have been susceptible to the fatalism voiced most poignantly by this lifelong count-me-in/out/in activist in "Across the Universe": "Nothing's gonna change my world/Nothing's gonna change my world."

Of course, stability was as elusive as ever—primal therapy had betrayed its limitations as well. You can only know your own pain for so long before familiarity begins to breed contempt; therapeutic insights may last, but the thrilling intensity of the breakthrough always fades. After all, John's belief in himself had a codicil, something about "Yoko and me." No victim of separation anxiety can ever just believe in himself and be done with it. When his marriage got into deep trouble, so did he. It was 1980 before he made another strong album, though it's not as if there were no good songs between *Imagine* and *Double Fantasy.* "Woman Is the Nigger of the World" actually gained acuity over the years, as did several Yoko remembrances, and the versions of "Be-Bop-A-Lula" and "Stand by Me" that open *Rock 'n' Roll* showed where he was coming from. But most of that album was busy and spiritless, and his big hit from the period, "Whatever Gets You Thru the Night," is almost as self-pitying as its title. When the marriage was finally patched up, Beatlemania hadn't subsided—Broadway packagers were proving that—but John said the hell with it. Leaving the money to Yoko, he cooked and played with his new son and watched TV, content to be part of a home he was sure of. Had he conquered alienation? It seems unlikely. But love was all he needed, or almost all.

Like *Plastic Ono Band, Double Fantasy* began with bells, only these were smaller, brighter, like dinner bells. On this defiantly civilized marriage album, John again recast a classic form—the studio rock he'd hacked his way through in 1973 and 1974—to new expressive needs. The sound was rich and precise, replete with readymades from New Orleans r&b to James Brown funk, from magical mystery dynamics to detonating synthesizers. After five years off his voice sounded better than ever—sweet, tough, pained, reflective, calm, and above all soulful. It's possible, of course, that *Double Fantasy* would have been John's hello good-bye—that he would simply have returned to silence. But it's also possible that he would have continued translating contentment into clear, deeply felt albums, and his guitar solo on Yoko's "Walking on Thin Ice" hints that more daring music might also have been in store. I'd like to think that for however long he might have lived John Lennon would have made rock and roll say everything—everything he had to say, and nothing more.

With John Piccarella
1981

Why the Beatles Broke Up

The Beatles broke up because they were idealistic enough to be convinced of their historical mission and realistic enough to know they were no longer capable of carrying it forward. The Beatles broke up because they didn't see or care that the corporate life of a rock group could endure long after its collective life was kaput. The Beatles broke up because the couple is a more stable structure than the four-way. The Beatles broke up because three of them believed they were geniuses and only one of them was. The Beatles broke up because they thought they were immortal. The Beatles broke up because they couldn't stand each other anymore.

1996

James Brown's Great Expectations

I'd spent the weekend trying to convince John Rockwell that James Brown was the greatest rock and roller of all time, and my wife was getting bored. This was reasonable—rankings are a boy's kind of thing, very box-score. Still, when I came back and asked her who was the greatest novelist of all time, she saw what I was driving at before she could say Charles Dickens. I wanted her to tell me what she thought a novel should be. Without his mammoth technique—description, character, narrative pull—Dickens wouldn't be in the running. But if that's all there is, one could just as well name Balzac, Austen, Joyce, Dostoyevsky, Faulkner, even Lessing. By choosing Dickens, my wife was pumping more debatable virtues—reach, scope, heart, vulgarity, intuitiveness, yucks. And also, I should add, output—unlike Joyce or Austen, Dickens wrote a lot of books.

With the possible exception of yucks, Dickens' virtues loom large in James Brown's story, too—output and reach most of all. Over the longest peak ever mounted by a rock and roller, from 1960 to 1974, Brown recorded an enormous body of major music, including forty-three singles that made *Billboard*'s top forty. Elvis's career total is over a hundred, but the Beatles and the Stones and Stevie Wonder are also in the forties—as are Michael Jackson if you count his Jackson 5 leads and Diana Ross if you count her Supremes leads (and also, I admit, Elton John, with Pat Boone, Neil Diamond, and the sainted Fats Domino in the high thirties).

That's *pop* recognition for an artist who was always better understood by the black audience (well over fifty records in the r&b top
ten), *singles* sales for an artist who in 1963 pioneered the LP format
in r&b (and the concert-album format in rock and roll) with *"Live"
at the Apollo,* an artist who exploded radio's time constrictions
like he had disco in mind and left uncharted patches of paradise
at thirty-three-and-a-third revolutions per minute. Brown
cofounded soul and invented funk, and he's powered more good
rap records than teen testosterone and Olde English Malt Liquor
put together. A singer of epochal grit and grandeur, he did his most
daring work as a bandleader whose voice was past its prime. His
stance and message were more complex than any rock critic knew,
but we who now regard him as the greatest rock and roller of all
time are pumping music over meaning—and, meaningfully
enough, asserting that in rock and roll the musical component that
matters is, you know, rhythm. The song remains the same my
goodfoot.

Having plied Rockwell with wild estimates of Brown's ever-
burgeoning rep, I felt obliged to poll a cross-section of my colleagues, and at first I was disappointed. Robert Hilburn named
Elvis, then John Lennon, then Bob Dylan, with Brown somewhere
between four and seven along with Chuck Berry and Jimi Hendrix.
Jon Pareles, whom I'd taken for a music man, declared the question unanswerable if not meaningless (as it is), but added that in
any case Brown "doesn't have the verbal content" for the top slot.
Ever the wag, Greil Marcus unanswered by nominating Jan Berry
of Jan & Dean, who he claims did more with less than anybody in
the music. But deposed *Boston Phoenix* savant Milo Miles had it
Hendrix-Beatles-JB—"definitely number one among living Ameri-
cans." Dave Marsh, who contributed an evangelistic afterword to
the new edition of Brown's 1986 autobiography, responded: "First
I'd say it's a mistake to single out just one. Then I'd say James
Brown." Nelson George, whose brief reminiscence graces the new
Star Time box on Polydor, uttered just two words: "James Brown."
And Robert Palmer, who mentioned Brown's Georgia mentor Little
Richard before demurring from all great-man theories of African-
based music, saw my point. Choosing Brown, he suggested, was
like choosing Duke Ellington in jazz—honoring a "fundamental
structural remaker" rather than an "individual transcendent
genius" such as Charlie Parker. "So if you wanted to call him the

greatest, I wouldn't argue with that. He pretty much comes closest."

I got my first dose of James Brown theory when Pablo Guzman prodded me into reexamining JB's Polydor output for my seventies book, and even on that mixed evidence—augmented by Cliff White's U.K.-only *Solid Gold* best-of—I was half-convinced. A few years later, Polydor's White-compiled reissues—together with Eric B. & Rakim and "It Takes Two"—completed the job. But for Marsh and George the clincher was the four-CD, five-hour *Star Time,* which inaugurates a new phase of Brownmania. Polydor president Davitt Sigerson, once a damn good critic himself, projects a series of reissues that will gradually redefine Brown's body of work. Both *"Live" at the Apollo*s will remain, as will the hit-seeking *Roots of a Revolution,* White's dazzling portrait of the young hard worker as r&b polymath, and the patchier *Messing With the Blues.* For chartbound dabblers, a twenty-song best-of is due. Other albums will resurface whole, but Sigerson wants compilations to dominate—some obvious, some obscure, none both at once. He envisions collections of ballads, break-beat rarities, instrumentals from the Pee Wee Ellis and Fred Wesley bands, period overviews that "wash over you like a great African record."

Assuming full corporate follow-through, this is going to be something. Many *Roots of a Revolution* obscurities groove harder than the lesser *"Live" at the Apollo* titles whose studio versions fill out disc one of *Star Time,* and disc four intimates mortality at least twice. But *Star Time* is not only as definitive as these big-bucks boxes are always claiming to be, it's easily the best of them—an astute and generous reinterpretation of an oeuvre that doesn't break down neatly into albums. Its previously unreleased extended takes, which are numerous, never obtrude. And it doesn't come close to exhausting the artist's book. Though a third of it was recorded for King Records between 1965 and 1970—when a black icon infiltrated and then vanished from a pop radio that found "Say It Loud" 's black-and-proud rhetoric easier to take than "Mother Popcorn" 's black-and-complex beats—there's a hell of a lot more where that came from. In 1969 alone, Brown put ten singles on the r&b chart. Seven of them made top ten. Five had the word "Popcorn" in their titles. Only three are on *Star Time.*

I didn't need *Star Time* to convert me. But since Brown's peak was originally over my head and his output beyond my reach, I want to testify that it repays obsessive relistening. Brown's rhythms are arrayed so profusely across the octaves that getting to the bottom of them is irrelevant, and though the pop complaint that his music all sounds the same retains an aura of common sense, it seems ridiculous once you immerse—a way for white people to wish he'd remained the godfather of soul, which they have a handle on, instead of turning his genius to dance music that passeth all understanding. For starters, there's a separate vein of great vocal music. Accurately enough, we think of his voice as a rough, untamable thing—even the pop breakthroughs "Out of Sight" and "I Feel Good" are aggressively staccato. But listen to "Prisoner of Love" and consider what wonders a ballad collection might perform. Cutting a raw power that could give Ray Charles hearing loss is an idiosyncratic yet almost mellow clarity—not the sharp falsetto of a Wilson Pickett, though this unearthly screamer had some of that in him, but a timbre whose expressive resonance verges on normality. The resulting alloy recalls Bobby Bland without sounding like him or anybody else, including funk-period James Brown, and after a dozen or so years of three-hundred-nights-a-year touring it had disappeared from the face of the earth, leaving JB to his true work.

In Cynthia Rose's ambitious book-length critique, *Living in America,* Pee Wee Ellis reports that musicians called "topsy-turvy" bass-and-snare the "New Orleans beat," and that Clyde Stubblefield, who preceded the better-known Jabo Starks into a band they co-chaired for years, "was just the epitome of this funky drumming." This dovetails with Robert Palmer's belief that rather than inventing funk, Brown "codified" the stuttering drums and syncopated bass he'd first encountered fronting Little Richard's New Orleans–bred Upsetters. But I'd put it this way: Brown was the first musician with the vision and guts to put rhythm up top in a pop mix. He did it before soul was a byword, and even in black music nobody took up the challenge seriously until 1969, when nonpareil funky drummer Ziggy Modeliste led the Meters out of the aforementioned New Orleans. You can hear the beginnings as early as "Out of Sight" in 1964, but it turns out that "Papa's Got a Brand New Bag" was a more literal title than the rhythmically deprived knew. It was also Brown's first top-ten hit, late in the summer of 1965, and nowhere is it described better than in his autobiography: "The song has gospel feel, but it's put together out of jazz licks. And it has a different sound—a snappy, fast-hitting thing from the bass and guitars. You can hear Jimmy Nolen, my guitar player at the time, starting to play scratch guitar, where you squeeze the strings tight and quick against the frets so the sound is hard and fast without any sustain . . . I had discovered that my strength was not in the horns, it was in the rhythm. I was hearing everything, even the guitars, like they were drums. I had found out how to make it happen."

In an evolution of the ear, Brown's new bag has become the fundament of today's pop—for a decade or more, radio has inundated us with what he put into motion. So the funk titles that fill the three other discs of *Star Time* no longer all sound the same. Just as the songs of the typical popsmith break down into tune families, Brown's break down into groove families, but within the families there's plenty of individual variation—each intro delights the listener with a jolt as hooky as Motown or the Beatles, only it isn't "tunes" that provide the thrill, but riffs. These riffs connect on rhythmic rather than melodic shape (the rock and roll "tune" itself always relied heavily on phrasing), shapes elaborated in patterns perceptible and pleasurable to the mind's ear. Sure they're body music, but you don't need ants in your pants to enjoy them. In fact, often the elaborations are more harmonic than rhythmic. The one slight contradiction in Brown's description of how funk began is that most of the time Brown's jazzy proclivities surface in the horns.

That matters because *Star Time* proves again and again that jazz licks are essential to the unstaunchable freshness of his music. Pee Wee Ellis and Maceo Parker and Dave Matthews are no avant-gardists, but unlike permanent funkateer Fred Wesley, they play jazz on their own, and though by all accounts even these most crucial JB's did exactly what Mr. Brown told them, it was them he told. Avoiding both the solid comfort of Memphis/Muscle Shoals voicings and the busy ornamentation of Brad Shapiro and Dave Crawford's Philly charts, their twisty little furbelows add an acridly urban and perhaps even cosmopolitan wit and bite and backspin to Brown's already intricate beats—check *Star Time*'s nine-minute 1967 "Get It Together," which I'd never heard before, if you think I'm jiving. Texan Cynthia Rose believes Georgian James Brown is a Southerner above all. But the South is a big place and New Orleans is a singular one, and I say that if he hadn't recorded in Cincinnati and lived in New York his Southernness and even his second-line variations would have come out a lot more earth-bound, gutbucket, predictable. Brown's soul and funk are deep. But there's also a lightness about him, a transcendent impulse that's built into his concept rather than achieved momentarily in gospelized transport. He's a realist like Dickens, and he's also a formalist like Joyce. Such contradictions always mark the great ones.

Although Rose makes a case for the spellbinding incantation, in-the-moment specificity, and "all-out Southern surrealism" of Brown's "wordplay," and although his mastery of the colloquial is more than sufficient to his needs, "verbal content" is beside the point. So are the political vagaries of a self-made man whose ties to both Hubert Humphrey and Richard Nixon did even more to alienate pop hippies than his black pride. As an African-American conservative prepares to gut the Constitution, there's no reason to take Brown's black self-help philosophy as revealed truth. But it would be blind to deny that it has more currency now than people who couldn't do the popcorn ever dreamed possible, and not just with those who believe in other people's bootstraps. Even as he tells Dave Marsh that his three-year imprisonment "doesn't have anything to *do* with racism," there's no questioning James Brown's fervid racial commitment, and little doubting that at some organic level that commitment constitutes a species of inaccessibility—an irreducible identity that refuses universalist blandishments and continues to cost him respect.

"I'm not a rock'n'roll singer," says the greatest rock and roller of all time. By this he means not that rock'n'roll has been appropriated by the other man—a phrase he put on record in "Say It Loud—I'm Black and I'm Proud," twenty years before the rappers—but that rock'n'roll is old and he isn't. Even if he was born in 1933 (the books used to say 1928), this is an exaggeration. While no oldies show, his work-release pay-TV special—which began with 1986's "Living in America" and riffed long and loose on an updated version of 1978's "Jam/1980's"—was too iconic by half. But he's made some terrific music since his peak—the last six cuts on *Star Time* represent no serious letdown, and on 1983's *Bring It On* the ballads even sounded good—and it isn't impossible to imagine him doing it again. Some kind of funk-pop cross between *Our Mutual Friend* and *Ulysses* would be nice.

1991

3

Snatched from the Maw of Commerce

Stevie Wonder Is All Things to All People

Take One: Stevie Wonder Is a Fool

Stevie Wonder is a fool. I state it that way—baldly, without qualification—because the qualifications are so obvious that they tempt us away from the truth. I'm not saying he's a complete fool; in fact, I'm not saying he isn't a genius. But if you were to turn on a talk station and hear an anonymous Stevie rapping about divine vibrations and universal brotherhood, especially with that inevitable dash of astrology, you would not be impressed by his intellectual discernment.

Those who find small stimulation in both Leon Lewis and the Rolling Stone Interview probably regard this as a false issue. But I insist that it isn't, if only because Stevie's blather has more dimensions—about six in all—than that of the average Leon Lewis fan or rock and roll pundit. Foolishness is an annoyance; cosmic foolishness is an offense. Elton John and John Denver may be no brighter than the guy who tried to sell you Earth Shoes last week, but like most salesmen they do maintain a certain feel for the concrete.

Needless to say, I do not cite the Johns at the behest of my Ouija board. Elton John and John Denver, together with Stevie Wonder, are the pop music heroes of 1974 and perhaps the decade, and all three are united by simple-mindedness of a sort that seemed to have disappeared from such heroes a decade ago. Elton's fervent pursuit of stardom is a kick because he revels in music as well as wealth and fame, but unlike his spiritual models, the Beatles, he does not set up the playful distance that made avowed materialism seem nothing more than a precondition of its own transcendence. Denver purveys privacy with a smooth confidence that reminds us that James Taylor really can sing the blues and often seems to dislike himself almost as much as we do. And if Stevie's precursors—blind genius Ray Charles, love-crowd soul fave Otis Redding, Grammy perennial Aretha Franklin—never indulged in the sort of wary self-knowledge that makes for contrasts as intense as Beatles/John or Taylor/Denver, figure that his callowness came naturally in a child prodigy and say his real forebear was Sly Stone, who like so many rock (not soul) stars resolved the paradox of his personal power by pretending to inscrutability. And then note that Sly's public pronouncements are incoherent to the point of put-on, which opens that incoherence to further analysis, while Stevie's nonsense is accentuated by the earnest context in which it occurs.

As might be expected, the split between Stevie's embrace of oneness and Sly's union of opposites extends to their audiences: Stevie's is genuinely integrated, while Sly's is simply biracial, divided between the white hitters who have danced to black music for two decades now and the superfly blacks for whom Sly is the greatest hustler of them all. And it was Stevie's peace corps that turned out at Madison Square Garden last Friday. His third arena gig in this area since March suggested Sly-caliber hubris in a down market, with the added twist that all profits were to go to charity. But virtue was rewarded. At his Garden appearance in June, Sly couldn't fill the seats for his own wedding, which may turn out to be his countercharge in divorce court—a wife who doesn't draw. Stevie's show of agape, on the other hand, sold out. Sometimes the man's success is enough to make you believe in faith. Which may be the point, as we shall see.

It was a fine show, too—more electric, I'm told, than his Nassau Coliseum visit in September. It wasn't as thrilling as his first Garden appearance in March, which doesn't even qualify as a disappointment—counting on a repeat of such an epiphany would be like expecting to fall in love twice in the same restaurant. Last March, the only act who could have topped Stevie was Jesus Christ. He had come close enough to dying in a car accident the previous summer to make a lot of us realize how much we hoped of him, and then proceeded to surge across the radio to his sweep of the Grammys, when the record business finally acknowledged a small part of its debt to black music. The Garden concert was his victory celebration, and its sweet spirit, in all its integrated optimism, was like a one-night Summer of Love. The next day, everything looked like 1974 again, but for a brief time we could feel our power to defeat our own death wish.

But even on that great night, Stevie was far from perfect, because fools like Stevie cannot muster the kind of formal discipline perfection requires—he began too slowly, fooling around. Last Friday was even laxer. Wonderlove's warmup numbers dragged, the new star of the female backup trio was a very bad Sarah Vaughan, and Stevie didn't so much improvise on his synthesizer as doodle. The trumpet player's travesty on a doowop recitative almost ruined an otherwise inspired oldies medley. Stevie's joke buildup to "Three Blind Mice" was even lamer than Ray Charles's joke buildup to "Pop Goes the Weasel." And so forth.

More foolish than any of this, however, was the man's teachifying and preachifying. A third of the way into the set he paused to introduce the band and specify his own good works. The crowd buzzed restlessly, and Stevie was quick to reprimand. "For those of you that are talking," he really said, twice, pregnant pause and all, "relax your lips." Eventually, he got silence in the cafeteria just so two disc jockeys could list every charity and type of aid the night's proceeds would support. And then Stevie began to preach: " . . . pure love between all people, a love that is willing to give honestly and sincerely regardless of the color of your skin . . . " There was applause, whereupon Stevie reminded the skeptical that he is not a complete fool: "I hear that so many of you may clap when I talk about what I'm talking about. But unfortunately the only place where I find this love that I talk about is in my dreams, in the songs that I write . . . " It was as boring as church nonetheless, and when a black colleague whispered to me that all this folderol was really downhome sanctified, touching if not moving, I assented only in theory. And soon thereafter, Stevie began to sing "Visions."

I've often wondered about the visual imagery running through the songs of our blind genius. Maybe the visual bias of our thought and language forced him to go lookin' for another pure love, but it seems fair to surmise that only his penchant for cliches—for metaphors so hackneyed they become abstract—turns that love into the apple of his eye. Even in "Visions," a title that refers explicitly to the phrase "vision in my mind," he goes on: "I know that leaves are green/They only turn to brown when autumn comes around." If he's blind, how does the fool know the leaves are green?

It must be, however, that I really had been touched, if not by the undeniable fact that this star was actually giving away his money, then perhaps by one of his enchanting melodies, so much more compelling under the (note visual metaphor) focus of a concert than on record. I found myself moved by the "vision in my mind" idea, for obviously the man could enjoy no other, and suddenly I understood how he knew the color of the leaves—he had been told that it was so, and he had no choice but to believe. That was the definitive condition of his life. Much more than you or me, he was in contact with the unconscious acts of faith that get every one of us through every day.

I began by calling Stevie Wonder a fool because that is the kind of judgment we shy away from—after all, the man is blind, he is black, and we love him. But if he is a fool he is a sainted fool. His simplicity will not save us—what will?—but it will do us more good than the simplicity of John Denver or Elton John. We may enjoy their simplicity, we may find it useful—Denver did write "Leavin'" and "Sunshine on My Shoulder"—but we do not need it. It just may be that we need Stevie Wonder.

The persistence of hope that we call faith has always energized black music, and in Stevie Wonder this energy is intensified—because of his blindness, and because of his fortune as a survivor. He may sometimes be sanctimonious as well as sanctified; his musical expansiveness may puff him up; his dream of brotherhood for our grandchildren may cloud over the ironies of our condition more than he can ever understand. But he creates an aural universe—or maybe I should call it an aural condition—so rich that it makes us believe. His multiplicity of voices, his heavenly tunes, his wild ear humor, and even his integration of the synthesizer all speak of a free future not dreamt of in our philosophy. And it is not foolish to believe that the transcendence of philosophy is one reason we want music in our lives.

Take Two: Stevie Wonder Is a Masterpiece

The first notes of *Songs in the Key of Life* waft up from a choir of humming colored folk who might be refugees from Vincente Minnelli's *Cabin in the Sky*. Their music is mellifluous, placid, and elevated; it seems to epitomize (as Donald Bogle wrote of *Cabin in the Sky*), "ersatz Negro folk culture . . . passed off as the real thing." The catch is that this ersatz culture may be the real thing. For the leader of the choir, distinctly audible in the foreground, doesn't sound so innocuous; the other voices are obviously there to round out a quavery tenor of subtly disquieting indecorum. What's more, his mild uncouthness extends to the lyric. Within two lines, nine words—"Good morn or evening friends/Here's your friendly announcer"—he has committed two minor literary gaffes: the skewed parallel of "morn or evening" and the apparently inadvertent echo of "friends" and "friendly."

Fallacious or not, questions of intention arise immediately, as they so often do in popular culture. In order to understand what is actually going on here we must try to determine what is supposed to be going on. So if we've forgotten for a moment who this artist is, with his "serious news for everybody," we are now obliged to remember. This is Stevie Wonder. He is black and considers that an advantage; he is blind and given to mystic visions. His music is both meticulous and wildly expressionistic; his words combine a preacher's eloquence with an autodidact's clumsiness. And a small detail: in one of his best and favorite jokes, he impersonates a disc jockey, everybody's friendly announcer.

Who can gauge what intentions these credentials imply? Perhaps Stevie Wonder hopes to reclaim an unfairly discredited manifestation of black culture—the genteel Hollywood gospel chorus—with his blessing. Or perhaps the chorus—which, as it turns out, consists entirely of taped overdubs of Stevie's own voice—merely reifies the man's idealist notion of black spirituality. Perhaps the musical ambiguity is deliberate, the stilted language a gentle gibe at the "announcer," at Stevie himself. Or perhaps it's all just sloppiness. Only two things are clear. First, this man is too secure in his own artistic power to concern himself with such quibbles; he doesn't worry whether we think he's wise or foolish, careless or precise. Second, this music is so audacious and so gorgeous that it's pointless for us to worry about it either.

That is to say, among other things, that this album has presence and that its presence counts for something. After playing it obsessively for a few days, I put on WNEW-FM for a taste of the real world. As if in a dream, there was my friendly announcer crooning the song I've just described, "Love's in Need of Love Today." Why had I bothered to tune in, I wondered, when this lovely stuff was waiting on my turntable? But I bristled nevertheless when the official announcer referred to the album as "Stevie Wonder's new masterpiece." Words like "masterpiece" get thrown around too glibly in the music biz, and when you talk about someone's "new" masterpiece, you're very nearly implying that the someone is a genius (now where have I heard that before?) who just churns one out every year or two. As the virtues of rock and roll are not those commonly associated with masterpieces—works which, as Bob Dylan observed, are supposed to make everything "smooth like a rhapsody"—this seems unlikely. Yet I found myself in sympathy as I bristled. The irresistible beauty of this record calls for inept superlatives. In fact, Stevie Wonder has had me thinking for the better part of a week about just what a rock and roll masterpiece might be.

My first conclusion is that presence counts for a lot. A rock and roll masterpiece must be a pop masterpiece. Not pop as distinguished from rock—*Exile on Main Street* and *Layla* are two of the worthiest pretenders to the category—but pop as distinguished from aesthetic. This is an old riff for me, and I feel a little fogeyish coming down on it after arguing the primacy of the aesthetic for several years. I really do believe that Eno's *Another Green World* is a greater rock record than, say, Lynyrd Skynyrd's admirable *One More from the Road,* without benefit of sales, airplay, or (for that matter) blues chords and backbeat, and that something similar goes for *Ramones,* in many musical ways its polar opposite. But those are tours de force; they're too rarefied. Even efforts like Randy Newman's *Good Old Boys* (with an audience that acts like a cult) or Steely Dan's *Pretzel Logic* (solid gold masquerading as polished dross) are borderline. Or so I feel right now. For Stevie Wonder has reminded me vividly of the reason I've always paid attention to rock and roll, rather than potential passions like jazz or the novel—which is that rock and roll not only says something about masses of people but also says something to them. For the first time in too many years, a heterogeneous mass of people has

communed around a musical package of consistent and considerable aesthetic interest, and they have lent it their collective
authority.

I mean, lots of people ask me about this record—not pros or
fans, just contemporaries, give or take five years on the up side
and fifteen on the down. To an extent, their curiosity reflects a
suspense hyped up by titanic money battles and Stevie's studio
perfectionitis and then relieved by the evidence on the radio that
at least their anticipation would not end in letdown. But it also
reflects something more substantial. People care about Stevie
Wonder. And while it is impossible to credit this audience with
critical reserve—the double-LP was an instant number one—it is
also impossible, at least for me, to fault its faith. I was expecting
a letdown. This is one of those instances when the audience knew
better. That's one of the rewards of being a rock critic sometimes.

But it doesn't mean I shouldn't go ahead and do my job. The
only people I know who don't like this album are those who have
no use for Stevie Wonder, but many others seem confused by it,
and that needn't be. Granted that studio double-LPs invariably
dish up too much new stuff to digest comfortably, and that Wonder's cannily self-indulgent decision to add a fifth side (in the form
of a seven-inch LP-that-looks-like-a-single) has added to the sense
of surfeit. And granted that Stevie Wonder resists analysis consciously and even aggressively—in the first stanza of "Joy Inside
My Tears" he apologizes for using the nasty word "but," the analytic weapon that begins this paragraph. It's still possible to figure
out what kind of masterpiece this might be.

The answer, as one might predict, is that it is a flawed one—
not in the manner of Dylan and the Stones, who cultivated a rough
tone that made flaws inevitable, even welcome (smooth like a
rhapsody wasn't their idea), but by identifiable mistakes. There
are errors of commission on Stevie Wonder's new masterpiece. A
lot of it (the final refrain of "Isn't She Lovely," for instance, or the
homiletic "Black Man") goes on too long; there are many awkward
phrases ("founder of blood plasma"), forced rhymes ("red, blue,
and white"), and uncolloquial constructions ("for Christmas what
would be my toy"); "Summer Soft" and "If It's Magic" are quite
forgettable, I hope. *Talking Book* is closer to perfect. But on *Talking
Book* Wonder was coming off the Rolling Stones tour and pursuing their audience and music. A more complex and satisfying

delight—a delight that combines freewheeling energy with soft accessibility—is provided by an artist with the ambition to ride his own considerable momentum.

My reasoning, if that's what it is, is just what the announcer ordered. To put it in the jargon of a time gone by, I've overcome my negative vibrations. And that is the key to Stevie Wonder's prescription for life, what he means literally to denote when he says "love's in need of love" or warns against living in a "pastime [that is, "past time"] paradise," or, God knows, opines that "God knew exactly where he wanted you to be placed." Sometimes he almost seems to mean that bad thoughts are the source of all evil, an idea that declines to propose a surefire method of eliminating the bad thoughts—as Wonder acknowledges in "Village Ghetto Land," which serves as an empiricist postscript to the idealist "Love's in Need of Love Today" and "Have a Talk With God" by pointedly implying that poverty and happiness are often mutually exclusive. The man is no giant ideologically, but he does have a reasonably accurate idea of what's going down.

Ideology can hardly be his specialty in any case, because the locus of ideology is written language, whereas for Stevie books must talk. What makes the contradictory platitudes of his lyrics worth following is the rhetorical impetus of his music. Even in the accompanying booklet the words aren't as stiff and preachy as his worst moments have made you fear; sung or declaimed over a music much less vague and ballady than his worst moments have made you fear, they take on a convincing vivacity. It is no accident that the rich, declamatory one-man music of "Love's in Need of Love Today" is counterposed against the more intimately devotional one-man music of "Have a Talk With God," or that when the theme turns sociopolitical in "Village Ghetto Land," Stevie's synthesizer turns from African sounds to an ironic (though elegant) string-quartet minuet—the calm detachment of which is rudely interrupted by a jazz-funk instrumental from Stevie's Wonderlove band, which then moves into the boogieing black-music tribute "Sir Duke."

In themselves, the words—especially as brought to life by Stevie's high-spirited multivoice—have it all over the musings of Maurice White, or Eddie Levert reciting the verse of Kenneth Gamble; they're funnier and trickier. But as validated by the wit, pace, variety, and dimension of this music, they come close to redeeming the whole genre. They make clear that no matter how annoying the sociospiritual bullshit of Earth, Wind & Fire or the O'Jays may get, it still surpasses the escapist mythopoeia and greeting-card sentimentality that passes for poetry among too many white song-poets these days. If Bob Dylan scores an artistic punch with the rough tone, then Stevie Wonder is familiar with the artistic benefits of the genteel tone. He wants something like that gospel chorus in the sky—a chorus that has echoed through much of the most ambitious black music—just because of what it can say to masses of people. Sometimes he takes his advantage in a straightforward and seemly way—with synthesized strings, for instance, or with the beauty of that chorus itself—but sometimes he makes it work ass-backwards. Blame his literary gaffes and ideological inadequacies on confused cultural aspirations only after you acknowledge that it may only be through such indiscretions that the earth-shattering (or -mending) presumption of his music can be conveyed. A blind man who can envision a time "when the rainbow burns the stars out of the sky" or write a song called "Ebony Eyes" is like a black man who can stick Glenn Miller in between Count Basie and Louis Armstrong in a litany of music heroes. He doesn't even acknowledge limitations that some would hope were beneath him. As in most rock and roll masterpieces, the flaws are a part of the challenge, and of the fun.

1974–1976

A Boogie Band that Loves the Governor (Boo Boo Boo): Lynyrd Skynyrd

Early in the spring of 1975, before eleven thousand fans in Tuscaloosa, the members of Lynyrd Skynyrd were declared honorary lieutenant colonels in the Alabama state militia by the governor of that state, George Wallace. Although many country singers have been so honored, these were the first such "hard rock" stars. They were singled out, according to a press aide in Montgomery, for their declared willingness to assist the governor should he ever require their assistance—to raise funds on college campuses, say. The aide was referring not to charity but to politics, another rock first: the public support of Ronnie Van Zant, the Jacksonville, Florida trucker's son who is Lynyrd Skynyrd's lead singer, for the governor's presidential candidacy.

Van Zant's politics were not the reason Mark Vaughan, a University of Alabama student from Buffalo, New York, conceived and promoted this chauvinistic shebang. Vaughan just wanted an Alabama-style party, and he thought Lynyrd Skynyrd deserved recognition for yet another rock first: "Sweet Home Alabama," a top-ten state song. Of course, in addition to celebrating the state's skies and shoals and parrying the insults of Neil Young, this anthem does include a troubling reference to the governor himself: "In Birmingham they love the Governor (Boo boo boo)/Well we all did what we could do/Well Watergate does not bother me/Does your conscience bother you?" But Mark Vaughan says he doesn't know what these lines mean, and I believe him, because neither do I. I'll bet the governor doesn't either. In fact, I'm not even sure Ronnie Van Zant knows. Since they're attached to the most likable music ever recorded by an immensely likable, very Southern band, the question remains a compelling one. But confusing.

Yes, the whole business is confusing. As a loyal New Yorker, I was distressed by those lines until I caught the "Boo boo boo" part, first in concert at the Academy of Music, accompanied by raised fists, and then on record, where somehow I'd never noticed it before. What a relief: they were *booing* him! How comforting to reconceive the whole stanza as an attack on liberal self-righteousness, maybe the self-righteousness of Neil Young himself. Just because we're from the South, I could imagine Van Zant saying, that doesn't make us all George Wallaces, and you, you SoCal asshole, did you do all *you* could do? There were some Southern Californians mixed up in Watergate, isn't that so? Right on, Ronnie. The New South. I felt indicted myself.

If you've been following me closely, however, you have noticed that this explanation leaves one contradiction hanging. Why did the governor's aide believe Lynyrd Skynyrd would do benefits for the governor? The answer, I must report, is that Van Zant said so, and he does not seem to have been fibbing. This doesn't mean any benefits will materialize—they often don't. But the gesture remains, and if it confuses you, imagine how it makes me feel. I love Lynyrd Skynyrd, a band that makes music so unpretentious it tempts me to give up subordinate clauses. But before I can get down to this music, I am compelled to construct four paragraphs of tortuous rationalization, and still it is not over. Are even Southern boogie bands less simple than they seem? For Lynyrd Skynyrd does look like the next great one, far ahead of the pack of rebel-rousers now vying for the domain of the twice-decimated Allman Brothers.

What makes all the rationalization worthwhile is not that Lynyrd Skynyrd is a great Southern band, but that it is a great band that happens to be Southern. Loyalty to a region or a genre is a waste these days; quality is where you find it. Nevertheless, once you do find it, the specifics of that quality are charged with meaning. I can't share regional pride with Charlie Daniels, who has just scored a band-naming hit called "The South's Gonna Do It." And I don't trust, yet alone identify with, the flannel-shirts who wave

Confederate flags at Lynyrd Skynyrd when they're in New York—the most joyously unreconstructed of all Southern bands, Lynyrd Skynyrd flies the stars-and-bars on stage in Dixie itself, but is mannerly enough to put away its colors when touring up North. Still, if I love Lynyrd Skynyrd I'm obliged to come to terms with its Southernness. Which is why I spent the weekend after Lynyrd Skynyrd joined the Alabama militia watching the band play to crowds of seven-thousand-plus in Johnson City, Tennessee, and Roanoke, Virginia.

What has happened here is that *Easy Rider* has ended up in the South in a way Dennis Hopper never imagined. The free-ranging pastoral individualism that was at the heart of the pop counterculture is an American ethos that has always flourished in the South, countercultural in the deep and even ominous sense that it rebels against values that are analytic, modern, Northern. In the case of the Allmans, who ranged as far as San Francisco before returning to the Georgia woods to bring their music together, fundamentalist rapture takes on a psychedelic aura. The spiritual flow underlying their virtuoso raveups, buoying not only their exhilarating highs but their tedious lows, is the kind of thing that can induce a Northern teenager to wave a Confederate flag. Lacking both hippie roots and virtuosos, however, post-Allman soundalikes such as Marshall Tucker and Grinderswitch become transcendently boring and nothing else.

Lynyrd Skynyrd avoids this treadmill by working for good songs. Lack of virtuosos is a virtue of this staunchly untranscendent band. Its music is condensed rather than stretched until it disappears. When it rocks, three guitarists and a keyboard player pile elementary riffs and feedback noises into dense combinations broken with abbreviated, preplanned solos; at quieter moments, the spare vocabulary of the oldest Southern folk music is evoked or replicated. The standard boogie-band beat, soulish but heavier and less propulsive, is slowed down so that the faster tempos become that much more cleansing and climactic. In other words, as Ronnie Van Zant explained to me amiably on the way to the limo: "We're more commercial than the Allmans."

At twenty-five, Van Zant has led this band since meeting guitarists Allen Collins and Gary Rossington ten years ago in high school. As with so many Southern rockers, his demeanor onstage and off is casual enough to resemble torpor. But it soon becomes clear that he is shrewd, confident, and gifted. Van Zant's specialty is the intelligent deployment of limited resources, beginning with his own husky baritone. Although it is not as flexible or powerful as, say, Gregg Allman's, it is more subtle and evocative simply because Van Zant permits it to be: where Allman is always straight, shuttling his voice between languor and high emotion, Van Zant feints and dodges, sly one moment and sleepy the next, becoming boastful or indignant or admonitory with the barest shifts in timbre, or slipping up to falsetto head voice for an extra accent. A similar selectivity is applied to the group's material. The melodies most often come from the guitarists, but it is Van Zant who shapes them into songs. On the recent *Nuthin' Fancy,* two or three cuts sound like heavy metal under funk. Van Zant pleads no intent, but the fusion is typical of his ambition, and his talent.

Van Zant is so eager to broaden his audience that he sometimes grouses about the band's Southern rep, but those colors still fly in Dixie. The huge crowds in Johnson City and Roanoke clearly identified with the band as rebel brothers. At once straighter and more hippie (as opposed to hip) than the Skynyrd crowds up here, they had a lot more in common with their band than most rock audiences in 1975, ranging from naively hedonistic (guitarists Collins and Rossington) through sincerely hip (guitarist Ed King, the band's only non-Southerner, and rookie drummer Artimus Pyle) to slightly wiggy (keyboard man Billy Powell and bassist Leon Wilkeson). But the focus at both concerts had to be Van Zant himself.

Van Zant's hair is as frizzy as old corn silk, no Allmanesque tresses, and he has worn the same washed-out black T-shirt three of the four times I've seen him. He is stocky, short, but instead of trying to look taller he performs barefoot (though you have to look to notice) and tends to tilt the mikestand in a way that accentuates his height. Until he went off hard liquor—he says he used to drink a fifth or two of J&B a day but stopped cold when convinced it would ruin his throat—he liked to share his bottle with ringsiders. Van Zant makes the good old boy played by all Southern rock stars feel like the real thing. Using his persona to extend the undefended commonness of his voice, he makes even his most assertively banal ramblin'-man lyric sound credible—like real, defensive boasting rather than showmanship.

Not that all Van Zant's lyrics are banal. Many of them establish a droll and/or baleful distance from the more witless truisms of the good old boy ethos, like the satiric "Mississippi Kid" or the self-critical "Poison Whiskey." My favorite is "Gimme Three Steps," which like Charlie Daniels's "Uneasy Rider" is the tale of a man trapped in a saloon with somebody feeling nasty. But whereas Daniels's longhair delights in one-upping the rednecks, Van Zant is just a guy who has to balance valor and discretion like a philosophy professor. When the jealous lover with the forty-four turns to bawl out his Linda Lu, Ronnie turns tail out of there, in perfect time to a very catchy hook.

But although all this low-key cleverness is there to be shared with the band's fans, Lynyrd Skynyrd does remain a simple Southern boogie band. And it has to do "Freebird." The same call goes up in the South, where the Allmans are boys next door and Skynyrd is accepted on its own terms, and in the North, where the Allmans are still agrarian exotics and Skynyrd still an Allmans surrogate: "FREEBIRD!" "Freebird" is Skynyrd's automatic encore, a tribute to the late Duane Allman and the late Berry Oakley. It combines an assertively banal ramblin'-man lyric with a nonvirtuoso raveup in which all three guitars soar in effortlessly kinetic interplay, a perfect example of technopastoral counterculture transcendence. Its central image: male freebirds, like Duane and Berry, flying off on their motorcycles.

But freebirds are where you find them. Behind the arena in Roanoke, for instance, there was a sparrow that couldn't fly, and Leon Wilkeson intervened. Wilkeson is a zany who likes to joke about oral sex and wears a Boer War helmet that he calls his Nazi hat. He grabbed the bird just before it could hop under some crating, then cradled it sweetly in his hands while I went off for peanuts. By the time I got back it was soundcheck time and Leon decided to free the bird—not on the asphalt parking area, where we'd found it, but on a patch of lawn. The bird hopped off, very fast, spurning our peanuts even when we tossed them in its projected path. Leon returned to the arena and I watched the bird, which ate an insect or two before hopping back onto the asphalt.

We are cynical about such stuff up North, but in the South they like to believe. The comfort and tradition of the place is enough to make a person expect that freedom is just around some corner of time. Every rock and roller knows that the fruits of such faith have invigorated us up here, yet we continue to ask our stupid questions. Van Zant, an opinionated type, has even written a song about it. "Don't Ask Me No Questions," it's called, but its ending is conciliatory: he'll gladly talk fishing.

It was to forestall stupid questions, I think, that Van Zant brushed off the Alabama militia business when I first met him. "We say 'Boo boo boo,' " he reminded me indignantly. Our conversations were stiff until I complained politely about a kink in the Johnson City show that had also bothered him. He seemed to like that. In Roanoke the kink was gone, and the energy level of the concert palpably higher. Afterwards Van Zant and I were talking in his room and I asked him how the Wallace benefit rumor had started. Van Zant told me the rumor was true: he was sure three or four band members would be happy to help the Wallace campaign if it got off the ground.

This confounded me mightily; my query had been nothing more than a reporter's double-check. I asked lamely about the boos, and his explanation, which seemed to imply that the jeers were intended in some abstrusely satirical way, made no sense to me. I didn't have the heart to pursue it.

"Of course I don't agree with everything the man says. I don't like what he says about colored people." I believe that: Van Zant's "Things Goin' On" is a ghetto protest all the more powerful for its lack of specificity. "Chances are he won't even want us, he doesn't have much use for longhairs, y'know." I said nothing. "Course the real reason I'm doin' it is my daddy would whup me if I didn't." I began to talk about Wallace lies and a roadie interjected a few arguments. "Aw shit, I don't know anything about politics anyway," Van Zant said, and the discussion closed.

That may be close to the truth. In the cool, questioning light of reason I half believe that stuff about his daddy, too. But more important is a fact half-remembered from 1968—that most Wallace voters listed RFK as their second choice. Van Zant is opinionated: I like that. Better he should name his man than slither off into some apolitical void. His working-class impulses extend from his music itself, so much less mystical than the run of Southern boogie, to a gesture the band made in Detroit, where tickets were distributed free to the unemployed. I wish he would discover Fred Harris, but I can't blame him for liking George Wallace's populist image. And I don't really expect him to peer beneath it like some damn Yankee.

1975

Turn On, Drop In, Find Out:
The Grateful Dead

I tried to roll a joint before walking over to the Palladium to see the Grateful Dead for the first time in four years last Friday, but ended up asking my wife to do it. I'd never mastered the knack when I was in practice, and this would be the third or fourth time I'd smoked my own grass in—hmm—about four years.

I am, or have been, a certified Grateful Dead freak; I don't know how many concerts I've attended, but it has to be more than twenty-five, which for this record addict is a record. What's more, I never made a conscious decision to lag off. In fact, the last time I'd seen them, at Nassau Coliseum shortly after Pigpen's death in March 1973, I couldn't tear myself away from "Sugar Magnolia" and go write my review, though at Roosevelt Stadium in July 1972, I had left with some relief (and no deadline) during the same song. Yet somehow I never got back. I continued to admire Jerry Garcia's staunch countercultural communalism, but the band's spaced-out myopia became harder and harder to take as history got harsher and harsher. A parallel spaceyness was increasingly apparent in records I struggled—and eventually failed—to find praiseworthy. With Pigpen's r&b pulled out by the roots, the Dead's music was defined by Bob Weir's strained rockabilly when it touched earth at all—a sixties nostalgia trip in the attenuated country-rock mode of the middle seventies. So what if they ran their own indie label? I was better off savoring my memories.

It was basically to check out these memories that I went to

the Palladium. Antipsychedelic propaganda notwithstanding, Deadheads tend to be quite bright. But it should go without saying that the group inspires (and attracts) enlightened hipness rather than analytic acumen or musical savvy, which means that most of my acquaintances remain decidedly unconverted. When the Dead applied for State Department assistance on an Asian tour last fall, I found it impossible to locate cuts on either of two relatively strong albums that would convince a panel of open-minded jazz and folk professionals. In this skeptical context, Jon Landau's old charges about "absence of a lead singer with a competent voice" and "no drive" became quite vivid. I went home and put on *Live / Dead,* once one of my favorite records. It sounded aimless. Even *Workingman's Dead* lacked punch. I began to wonder whether my fanaticism had been based on anything more substantial than good dope and misconstrued vibes.

When we arrived at the Palladium at eight thirty, punctual by Dead standards, the music had already begun, and the vibes were unmistakable—hair was shorter, but the eyes had that old glow. The music sounded good, too; even skeptics find something nice to say about Garcia's guitar, and he was ringing through the smoke as we took our seats. The tune—from *Blues for Allah,* their worst, most recent, and biggest-selling studio LP—was predictably desultory. But when a Dead jam climaxes properly, Garcia's keen lines transfigure the surrounding babble into a strain of polyrhythmic rhapsody not ordinarily encountered at the Palladium or anywhere else. I was aware, as this climax recurred three times in the course of the song, that I was being subjected to the Dead's basic tension-and-release trick, but that didn't make me enjoy it less. Unfortunately, nothing nearly so exhilarating occurred during "New, New Minglewood Blues" or the always long-winded "Tennessee Jed." In fact, I was bored, and not in the spirit of friendly rumination I used to love them for eliciting—I was worrying how long they'd play. Not until Garcia's opening solo on a Donna Godchaux feature did anything catch my ear. I decided to toke up immediately. And immediately the concert got better.

But I swear that it really did get better. In any case, cheers and whistles from the audience increased in loudness and number, and mine were among them even though the effect of the dope was not to bring me into the music but to put me more attentively outside it. I noticed with some disapproval, for instance, that the ripple effect I'd always admired in Garcia's playing was achieved, at least this time, by an improvisationally elementary device. He was running triplets up and down the scale, four at a time, so that when he merely held a single note for two beats the contrast was arresting almost by definition. Soon I also noticed, however, that into all this repetition he was sneaking a few very attractive melodies. Then, for the final raveup, he suddenly attacked the guitar with a bluesish (almost Jamesian) slash that made all that rippling melody seem a diversion in subliminal retrospect. We'd been set up, and we loved it.

Joints were shared by strangers during the halftime intermission, a rite now rare enough to be newsworthy. But although the dope continued for the rest of the show, it was the two numbers that opened the second set—Gary Davis's "Samson and Delilah" and a long, slow "Sugaree"—that were the high point. Only the new "California" and Garcia's transmutation into Chuck Berry on the otherwise flaccid "Around and Around" finale turned me on. But when the cheering stopped it was twelve forty-five. My wife and I would have sworn it was an hour earlier.

In other words, although this was not (for me) a great Dead concert—great Dead concerts finish in total abandon—it kept me occupied the way nobody's concerts do anymore, not for two hours, much less four. Appropriately, my number one occupation was figuring out just what the Dead are and have been. Clearly, not your textbook Great Rock and Roll Band. They do lack drive; even at the climaxes they roll rather than rock. Their good drummer, Mickey Hart, is into jazz rhythms, and their ordinary drummer, Bill Kreutzmann, has never had the chops to push the band, although since Phil Lesh plays bass strictly for lyrical input and harmonic guidance, pushing the band would be uphill work for Steve Gadd or Keith Moon.

More complex is the issue of vocal competence. By their own standards, the Dead learned to sing—to project their voices— around 1969. Their physical equipment has never been overwhelming; even Weir, the loudest, has always wavered slightly. But insofar as they are incompetent, it is not as singers but as lead singers—they project voice but not character. They do add the appropriate emotional color to the words and notes, of course— weary plaintiveness, happy energy, whatever—but the color is there for musical rather than dramatic reasons; even when Weir shouts out "One More Saturday Night" there is something slightly detached about his ebullience. This deadpan quality is much more apparent in a typical performance by Garcia or Donna Godchaux, who has moved from pianist's wife to backup chick to part-timer in good standing. By instinct or design the Dead refuse to provide the easy psychological referents we seek in vocal music. What's left is the music itself. Performing personas—Weir's callowness, which becomes ever harder to tolerate as he passes thirty, or Garcia's beneficence—are inescapable for musicians on view for dozens or hundreds of individual spectator-hours. But even these tend to merge into the Dead's version of the ultimate reality.

The source of this vocal antistance is clearly the affectless cool of bluegrass and string-band singing. But it makes for surprising alliances. Yes and Cleo Laine, for instance, use the voice for emotional rather than musical effect. The Dead distinguish themselves from such showoffs by their vaunted modesty. Garcia and Hart and Keith Godchaux aren't averse to letting us enjoy their technical virtuosity, but always in the service of the larger pattern; in their own way, the Dead are as antivirtuosic as the Ramones. Or compare Television, say—or Eno, who in his considerably more abstract way also exploits rock and roll usages to build patterns that move between the reflective and the ecstatic. To me, such connections add an enlightening dimension to the Dead's status as musty avatars of the sixties counterculture. Were all those déclassé longhairs actually as avant-garde as they thought they were? The thought of finding out is enough to make me take up smoking again.

1977

Music for Smart People: Randy Newman

I want to say that what distinguished Randy Newman from the more popular rock artistes of the sixties was that he was smart. But it's possible all I mean is that he was Jewish. You'd have to be pretty stupid to think Janis Joplin or Jerry Garcia or Sly Stone weren't smart. But for sure they weren't Jewish. There were Jews all over the music industry—and also all over the political wing of the counterculture, from the Red Diaper Brigade to the Abby & Jerry Show. But unless you want to honor Jefferson Airplane, which I don't advise, or count the Brill Building grads led by Paul Simon and Carole King, who we'll call modern pop, only three sixties rock heroes were nongoys: Bob Dylan, who played the American wanderer with such single-minded denial that he became a born-again Christian before finally giving it up to Yahweh; Lou Reed, who disavowed the sixties, especially in their psychedelic guise; and Newman, who was like Paul and Carole with a sharper wit and a California bloodline. Following in the footsteps of his three soundtrack-composing uncles, two of whom won Oscars, he was a traditional American popular songwriter with ties to that tradition's most Jewish period, the so-called "classic" era of the Broadway musical, which was also its most "classical."

So it makes sense that although Randy Newman also loved American myth and also didn't fit the sixties very well, he was more secular-humanist about it than Dylan or Reed. Surrounded by know-nothings and phony radicals, he played the disillusioned, even embittered, liberal. For political types with their heads on their shoulders, which wasn't where heads put in quality time back then, his unabashed cynicism was a relief from revolutionary bullshit. But Newman was no intellectual, self-conscious or organic—just a classically trained wise guy who presaged nothing of moment in either popular music or cultural evolution. This was a rock and roller so compulsively ironic he made Mick Jagger seem soulful, only his style of irony was fifties middlebrow-modernist—compare the apparent and/or real stoopidity of the far more unreadable Ramones, or the postmodernistically pastiched Pavement.

Yet out of this recidivism Newman produced great albums, first and still definitive 1970's *12 Songs,* a half-hour collection of American miniatures whose commitment to minimal means is equally reminiscent of Sherwood Anderson and Metric Music, where Newman was indentured as a teenager. Although the shock of these songs was the acerbic, understated intelligence of their subtly orchestrated music and drawled, unassumingly misanthropic lyrics, what was smartest about them was how they skewered the apocalyptic-hedonistic generational, sexual, and racial pretensions of what was already a fading era—and how seamlessly they yoked the rock (and roll) of Newman's youth to the (classic) pop he had grown up around. The killer is the parlay of the 1932 "darkie" hit "Underneath the Harlem Moon" and Newman's own "Yellow Man," a family-of-family-men fantasy perfect for crooning in California internment camps after dropping the big one on Japan.

At their best, the much grander *Sail Away* (1972) and *Good Old Boys* (1974) are also about race. In their lead tracks, Newman bent his creaky mush-mouth to the personas of a flim-flamming slave trader and a redneck whose passion is "keepin' the niggers down," neither of whom seemed any less dangerous after the controversy they kicked off died down. Yet especially on *Sail Away* there were sophomoric moments that proved an omen. Throughout the seventies, Newman's smart-ass style of smarts served to distinguish him from his chosen peers, the self-righteous young millionaires of El Lay rock. Yet gradually and inevitably, it became an annoyance—or maybe just took over. As his song output was swamped by soundtrack work, his artistic metabolism no longer seemed equal to his jaundiced worldview. The results were occasionally brilliant and never ruinous, because Newman is one of those dour perfectionists who don't know what else to do with their principles except put them into their work. But basically, his cynicism was out of control.

By 1988's *Land of Dreams,* however, history had caught up with Newman's limitations. Reagan had been such a consummate performer the opposition could tell itself he was an accident. But the newly elected Bush was the president of cynicism rampant— not just twenty-twenty ambition and two-income subsistence, every organization man for himself and dueling tongues up the boss's ass, but erstwhile idealists embracing capitulation and calling it wisdom. We needed a cynic who could rub America's face in the shit it lived on, and Newman was the man for the job. One New Orleans song forced Big Easy boosters to explain away the part where Randy's relatives pretend to be Gentiles. (Interviewer: "Jews seem pretty assimilated in New Orleans, don't you think?" Newman: "No, they're not assimilated in America—not really. It's not our country.") Another had the locals celebrating their defeat of the Yankees in World War II. The humor of "Four Eyes," a frightening overstatement of the travails of childhood and the machinations of parental love, was mean to the parents and mean to the kid—as extreme as any Newman since "Rednecks." And on the truly inspirational numbers, the putdowns, the march of history goaded Newman to strike out at profiteers, supply-side bigots, the singer's latest girlfriend, his abandoned son, and, ultimately, "all the people of the world."

Fusing Newman's El Lay and Tin Pan Alley sides, 1995's decade-in-the-making theoretical musical comedy *Randy Newman's Faust* sure wasn't Goethe's. It was too earthy for Sondheim, too smart-ass for Rodgers & Hammerstein—Arlen & Hart, if anything. For Newman, musical comedy was the ultimate challenge, a test of professional skill that might complete the family circle and round out a prestige so phenomenal that when he asked his El Lay buddies for help on a studio version, not one balked. Don Henley, Bonnie Raitt, James Taylor, and Linda Ronstadt all just said yes, and were all revitalized by drolly awful characters who generated more jam than their own personas, personalities, or inner selves ever had. It's impossible to imagine any bunch of singing thespians approaching what these nonactors added to the material.

"We're a figment of their imagination," croak-croons the Devil, who's talking religion and could mean stardom too. But though Satan gets funnier lines and a more credible take on the problem of evil, the part of the former Prince of Darkness was clearly designed for Newman, because this Devil is also a whiner, a loser, a middle-aged lech. In Newman's *Faust,* the Lord, who most authors find harder to work with, steals the show. Newman has always loved God, his one great Jewish character not counting himself, and here he stole a page from *Green Pastures* and conceived him as "master of bullshit"—part snake-oil salesman, part charismatic politician. Finally permitted to con the masses as arrogantly and ebulliently as he knows how, Taylor locked into the role with easeful power, tremendous good humor, and just the right undercurrent of offhand malice. And Henley played the boneheaded young title character with the impregnable narcissism and lifelike nonchalance of an eternal adolescent. Where Goethe's Faust seeks omniscience, this jerk is too anti-intellectual to read his own contract. Even his blank self-interest is brainless—mixed with idealistic banality in a hapless mishmash. The Devil never sympathizes with his confusion. The Lord may. Newman does.

Faust was Newman's best album in twenty years because cast, plot, and genre pushed him past the limits of his irony and the wry, weary faux-blues croak that has always gone with it—the audience-pleasing theatrical truisms Newman absorbed while workshopping the show combined with the attendant vocal personalities to broaden his emotional range. Taylor exulted with a faux-gospel joy the auteur couldn't get near, Henley's dumb menace was devoid of the sly side glances that inflect Newman-the-singer's every phrase, and Raitt's unaffected feminist raunch wreaked havoc on his smart-ass games—her love song, designed as a flat-out lie that hangs the Devil's dick out to dry, becomes the only declaration of erotic faith Newman has ever brought to fruition. Economics aside, however, Henley and Raitt and Ronstadt lacked not only the acting chops but the fresh-faced insipidity to recreate on stage roles designed and destined for showbiz kids deploying their voice lessons, and while Taylor and Newman could certainly pull in ticket-buyers, they were more likely to win the lottery than put economics aside. You remember where satire closes on Saturday night. And where Andrew Lloyd Webber is counted a rock innovator. Broadway was good for Newman's art.

But in the end, Broadway needed Randy Newman far more than Randy Newman needed Broadway.

And even if *Faust* turned into *Cats* or *Rent,* it wouldn't be Newman's apotheosis. His apotheosis is his only hit, a novelty song submerged on 1977's *Little Criminals.*

I'd been waiting for "Short People" since 1969, when I devised a group called Shorties Liberation just as my head-on-her-shoulders inamorata was conceiving a science fiction novel in which progressive dolphins and chimpanzees struggled on behalf of their dumb (that is, speechless) but sentient fellow creatures in the vegetable king-or-queen-dom. For some reason, none of our Movement friends found these fancies as funny as we did. In fact, they often missed the point, and nothing about "Short People," which established its enduring artistic value when it was deemed "crass" by an organization called the Little People of America, indicates that they ever figured it out.

So although it's hardly appropriate, I'll try to state the dilemma without irony. As a result of inherited somatic differences sometimes compounded by dietary injustice, short people—like black people, women, and carrots—really do suffer. They are subject to physical intimidation; they are disadvantaged in most sports and many occupations; they face cultural impediments in their search for a mate. Black people, women, and perhaps even carrots suffer more. But it really is crass to joke around at their expense.

Nevertheless, that was, among other things, what Newman was doing—just as I was when I conceived Shorties Liberation. Humor is, among other things, a socially acceptable way of unleashing aggression. And what arouses as much socially unacceptable aggression as the grim logic of oppression—the suspicion of each advantaged person that he or she may bear a responsibility for all the suffering occasioned by the disadvantages of others? At the dawn of women's liberation, the militant feminist I lived with was wondering if it wasn't destined to end not merely in vegetarianism but in some cockamamy code that would require all food to die a natural death before its conversion to soylent green. Yet she could only lash out ironically, so that friends often failed to understand her altogether, probably because the truth was too painful.

By 1978, long before the great PC scandals of the nineties, many putative libertarians—the vast majority of them white and male, for some reason—resented all claims of oppression without shame. Since I was no fan of swastikas, fag-baiting, or chic racism, the anti-"Short People" reaction seemed a just if impotent response to a song that had been transformed from a wicked joke into a self-fulfilling masterstroke by its popular appeal. Just why was it, do you think, that a station in Buffalo played the thing for an hour straight? Because Randy Newman fans so detested intolerance that they longed to hear it squelched twenty times in succession? Or because someone was finally voicing the hostility they felt—not just toward the short people who took the symbolic brunt, but toward every minority to demand gingerly treatment since first Hiroshima and then *Brown* v. *Board of Education* turned the tide? That "Short People" aimed to squelch intolerance was the line taken by Newman's advisors as well as most of the well-meaning people who got off on the song. Offered as proof was the break, sung by those three paragons of right thinking, Glenn Frey, J. D. Souther, and Tim Schmit: "Short people are just the same as you and I/All men are brothers until they die." Live, Newman sang the break even more perfunctorily than the Schmeagles in his rough, mumbled, immutably sarcastic pseudo-Southern singing accent. A dozen or so souls would applaud as the liberal shibboleths passed by. But the cheers for "You got to pick 'em up/Just to say hello" were a lot louder.

Although what I'm saying ought to be obvious by now, I will once again try to restate without irony. The shibboleths are a setup. The platitudes about brotherhood are there to be shot down by the rabidly endearing know-nothingism of the jerk who gets the verse and chorus. This guy is so dumb (which from here on will mean stupid again) he doesn't even know why short people are offensive—they don't drive "little cars" more than anybody else this side of the NBA. But he walks away with the song.

The well-meaning will wonder how, if "Short People" did indeed insult short people, rather than achieving some clever but clear-cut "satire," one could in good conscience approve. Especially one who has suggested that the objections of certain militant short people lack neither merit nor poetic justice. They don't understand that what made the song worthy of censorship was also what made it a masterstroke. The protests proved "Short

People" 's strength. They were essential to the song's truth, because they made it harder to duck. If you enjoyed the song, you had to do so in the certain knowledge that your pleasure was someone else's pain—no doubt a hypersensitive crank, and a pushy one at that, but since all men are brothers until the day they die, a fellow human nonetheless. Then again, some of your best friends were short, and they thought the song was pretty funny, right? As Newman told the Associated Press: "Of course, no joke is worth hurting people's feelings, and some people are pretty angry about it. But I think it's only a tiny minority."

In 1974, Ralph J. Gleason, a well-meaner if ever there was one, got all tangled up trying to figure out whether Randy thought the Lester Maddox of "Rednecks" was as worthy a human as you, me, the song's "smart-ass New York Jew," or Ralph J. himself. Newman is sufficiently misanthropic that I doubt he liked Maddox much. But as the Amerisymp outsider he is, he did believe that when the Georgia governor got put down for being a dumb redneck, so that his racism only proved how dumb he was, other racist Southerners had a beef. Similarly, "Short People" did function as an anti-bigotry song, because its protagonist was portrayed as dumb. Hence, bigotry itself was dumb. And hence, bigotry was bad. But only if the dumb weren't equal to you, me, Ralph J., and that Jew.

This has always been the chief weakness of middlebrow-modernist irony, which protects the privileged from hard inquiry the way moralistic rhetoric did their predecessors. My editor, a smart person, was skeptical when I suggested that her pleasure was someone else's pain. The irony, after all, was so clear. But the nature of irony is that not everyone understands it. Dumb people—or smart people with a little touch of dumbness where the issue of height arises—don't necessarily get the joke. With Randy Newman, they rarely do. That's one source of his appeal—an appeal he broadened with a novelty one-shot not everyone and maybe no one understood.

Long before the song hit, one reviewer suggested alternate adjectives: not just tall, but thin, fat, old, young, white, black, red, gray, gay, and straight. Yet somehow he left one out. Which reminded me that a few years before, a painter friend of mine had figured out a way to tell Polack jokes. He changed them into artist jokes. Q: How do you tell the bride at an artist's wedding? A: She's the one who's braided her armpit hair.

So here's an artist joke for all you Randy Newman fans. I'm sure Newman would agree that I shouldn't call it "Jewish People." After all, "Jewish People" doesn't scan.

Smart People

Smart People got no reason
Smart People got no reason
Smart People got no reason
To live

They got great big foreheads
And ugly old clothes
They use great big words
That nobody knows
They're plottin' and schemin'
All of the time
Invented contact lenses
So you can't tell they're blind.

Well, I don't want no Smart People
Don't want no Smart People
Don't want no Smart People
'Round here

Smart People are just the same
As you and me
(Ave Marie)
All folks are equal
Eternally
(A Change Is Gonna Come)

Smart People got nobody
Smart People got nobody
Smart People got nobody
To love

They got dry little pussies
And scrawny little dicks
They got kinky little sex lives
That are sick sick sick
They laugh at you
But not at theirself

'Cause they think they're better
Than everybody else
They got too much brain
And not enough soul
Someday we're gonna bury 'em
In a big stupid hole

Well, I don't want no Smart People
Don't want no Smart People
Don't want no Smart People
'Round here

1978–1989–1995–1996

Time Waits for No One: Richard Thompson

Give or take a few backup harmonies, there's only his guitar and songs at first—better singers carry the burden. When the voice does emerge, five tracks in, it proves rather less supple than you'd expect of a twenty-three-year-old folk-rocker testing his solo wings on a bit of self-penned nonsense. His stolid, almost stentorian delivery does add a droll undercurrent to "Nobody's Wedding," a music-hall song disguised as a folk song. But the delivery isn't fully stentorian because it's also kind of thin, and in truth the fellow doesn't sound too comfortable in front of the mike. If anything, he sounds pained, like somebody telling funny stories on his way to an appendectomy.

The voice gains needed confidence and unneeded depth over the next ten years. But the vocal star is his wife, and she's the ideal complement. Where the whisky-soaked sobriety of Fairport Convention's Sandy Denny engulfed the young Richard Thompson, the former Linda Peters suited him like the sidewoman-who-broke-up-the-band she was. When she finally recorded a solo album, as she did after she jumped or was pushed into divorce, she proved as characterless as Rita Coolidge or Caron Wheeler. But as Richard Thompson's lesser half she was a vehicle of genius—his instrument, his conduit to humanity and godhead, his black Vincent '52. Singing her husband's compositions, which adapted the modes and dance rhythms and eldritch sonics of Celtic tradition to the dynamics and electricity of rock and roll, her straightforward, lightly grained mezzo-soprano became a thing of drama and mystery. Sometimes she was just playful ("I'm the one he spends his money on / We spend it one, two, three") or wicked mean ("Everybody don't like something and we don't like you"), but especially on the slower numbers, she joined cool compassion, plaintive clarity, and womanly sweetness (somewhere in there) into syntheses that seemed to breathe timeless wisdom.

Between his prematurely mature voice and his penchant for immemorial scales, this timeless business comes up a lot with Richard Thompson, smelling fishier and fishier as he puts his career on one year at a time. But with Richard and Linda—six LPs, four of them knockouts: the grimly jubilant *I Want To See the Bright Lights Tonight* (1974), the down and dirty *Hokey Pokey* (1974), the semimiraculous *Pour Down Like Silver* (1976), and *Shoot Out the Lights* (1982), which extinguished the debut's good times right down to its title—eternity remains the hyperbole of choice. Linda's solo album establishes that the secret wasn't her voice, and as far as I'm concerned, Richard's solo albums—six studio collections since the split, most recently Capitol's *Mirror Blue*—establish that it wasn't any intrinsic virtue of his songwriting either. So maybe it was the double-gendered songs he wrote with Linda in mind, or the songs he wrote when the Sufism they fell in love with before *Pour Down Like Silver* was the center of his life rather than the ingrained faith it became, or some synergistic combination of the two. Or maybe it was just that he didn't have to sing all the time. Doesn't matter, really. Because no matter how you slice it, something precious has been missing from his solo career, something bound up in the physical presence of a human being he shows no sign of remembering fondly. Richard Thompson remains an artist of admirable energy and undeniable substance, of deepening wit and virtuosity. He's a reliable, committed professional; he's even getting popular. And he's also very much a legend. But anybody who thinks he's timeless is living in the past.

Yet how else are we to understand the nonchronology of *Watching the Dark*, last year's lovingly compiled and annotated three-disc retrospective from Hannibal? The early-Thompson sequence I described above comes from the box, but it exists nowhere except my trusty CD changer. After leading with "A Man in Need" from *Shoot Out the Lights,* the set they're selling jumps to a ferocious live version of *Amnesia*'s "Can't Win," the first of five "1987–1988" selections; then it backtracks to three 1969–1970 songs, fast-forwards to five 1981–1982s, and so forth, forcing the clueless listener to contemplate the mystic unities of an artist who was never young and can never grow old. Producer Ed Haber, the most knowledgeable of the ever-expanding cult that's made Thompson its musical religion, contends credibly that a chronological sequence would have been forbidding in places, and complicated further by live versions and studio remakes. Yet I'm hardly alone in my frustration at the song order, which was determined by Hannibal owner and longtime Thompson producer Joe Boyd (who has faithfully, consumers please note, kept the catalogue in print). This is too bad; although the box is light on Linda, as Thompson no doubt wished, the previously unreleaseds shame the collector trivia that usually lards these things. Especially welcome are the searing goodtime guitarist of "Can't Win" and "Tear Stained Letter," rarely heard on record even though he's starred at Thompson's gigs for years; the genuinely ancient (or at least old) "Bogie's Bonnie Belle"; and a couple of new songs—the gentle, goodhearted "From Galway to Graceland," the cheap, satisfying "Crash the Party"—that would have toned up *Mirror Blue* considerably.

I'm far less convinced by the live 1983 "Calvary Cross," which first surfaced on Haber's *Gloom and Doom From the Tomb* fan-club cassette and anchors Greil Marcus's preface to Leslie Berman's historical essay. An opaque lament with coruscating guitar in all three versions I know, "Calvary Cross" is one of those songs that separates the believers from the admirers, particularly as regards Thompson's singing. The man is no Kris Kristofferson or Butch Hancock—leavened by Linda, his limitations were rarely even a distraction, and he's brought off solo albums from 1972's *Henry the Human Fly* to 1991's *Rumor and Sigh*. But not only does a little of his naturally somber, deeply inflexible baritone go a long way, it cuts into the credibility and simple interest of his more morose delvings for anyone who hasn't been touched by the spirit. So when Marcus asserts that lyrics weren't why the earlier versions of "Calvary Cross" "eluded" Thompson, most of us won't ever know what he means, because we can't truly hear Thompson singing those lyrics. For us, this renders moot at best Marcus's notion that "decades or centuries are brought to bear on the performance," that in this song "time stops," and calls into serious question his judgment that Thompson's songs show "little or no sense of development, maturity, refinement"—that his career can hardly be called such a thing.

Certainly that's not what Thompson thinks. Whether holding his nose at Haber's live prizes or telling *Rolling Stone* that a female partner is too constricting, he thinks he's better than ever, and the figures bear him out—*Rumor and Sigh* sold a hundred fifty thousand a lot faster than *Shoot Out the Lights.* Rakish in his boho beret, he's an unflappable fixture on the large-club-and-small-hall circuit, and replacing Linda as his musical confederate is L.A. folk-rock honcho Mitchell Froom, who's produced his last four albums. Like all keyb-rats, Froom has his schlocky tendencies, but the Thompson old-timers who think he's the devil incarnate are kidding themselves. I can't swear the written melodies are as modal as they used to be, but for all their aural gloss the Froom albums sound far less conventional than the compromised country-rock of Richard and Linda's 1978 *First Light,* the nearest thing to a bad record Thompson has ever made. The crucial difference—definitely a development, probably a refinement, not my idea of maturity—is the songwriting. For a decade now, close to half his output, he's made a specialty of crude men and brazen women.

Since Thompson has an eye, an imagination, a sense of irony, and a stable second marriage, there's no need to get biographical about this. More likely it's strictly formal, a fateful thematic confluence between the old ballads he loves and the classic rock and roll he grew up on. Like one of his dry-ice solos or a Briton stomp about an MG, it's a way he can go pop without perverting his vision or feeling like a jerk, and at his fastest he's damned good at it. So the problem with *Mirror Blue,* a lesser record than *Amnesia* or *Rumor and Sigh,* isn't that it's bedecked with no fewer than seven ah-sweet-perfidy-of-woman songs. It's that not one of them is as furious as "Tear Stained Letter" or as jocose as "Two Left Feet" or as exuberant and shameless as "I Feel So Good," which proceeds immediately to promise "I'm going to break somebody's heart tonight," slicing male piggishness open from the inside in what has become a typical narrative strategy; compare the cruising bruiser of *Amnesia*'s "Don't Tempt Me," or the sex-manual virgin of *Rumor and Sigh*'s tragic "Read About Love": "I do everything I'm supposed to do / If something's wrong, then it must be you."

Are these latter-day teds the real Richard? Let's say only in his dreams—and wonder when he'll get inside a female character, the way he did "The Little Beggar Girl" so many years ago. The closest he comes on *Mirror Blue* is a sentimental air called "Beeswing," honoring a flower child who didn't tie either of them down and now lives on the streets with a wolfhound and a bottle of White Horse, and the visionary Bonnie-and-Clyde burlesque "Shane and Dixie," in which Shane essays a murder-suicide to get their names in the papers and Dixie survives to marry the newshound who writes her up.

I'm sorry to say that neither surfaced at Thompson's Beacon show April 23, and that at least five other *Mirror Blue* cuts did, including "Slipstream," overwrought whether it's the diary of a stalker or a love song to God; "Can't Wake Up," the beloved as nightmare Medusa; and "The Way That It Shows," which sacrifices a rouge-painted conniver on the altar of eternal raveup. When he began his race for the finish line with "Feel So Good" and topped his encore with "Read About Love," I was reminded of Peter Gabriel storming MTV with "Steamroller"—when it comes to achieving climax, neither of these guys can resist waving his dick at you. I especially missed Linda on "Hokey Pokey," the greatest song ever written about cocksucking or ice cream—the male voice made the conflation seem less consensual. But none of this is to claim that I didn't have a good time as, backed by an un-Froomlike quartet featuring light-handed Fairport drummer Dave Mattacks and jazz-steeped Pentangle bassist Danny Thompson, Richard Thompson proceeded to reprise a lot of damn good material and prove himself the most dazzling rock guitarist this side of Robert Quine. Accomplishing fate and avenging Allah just aren't as high on his agenda as getting the respect he's earned and the cash that goes with it. So, fine—whatever its shortcomings, *Mirror Blue* deserves to sell its hundred fifty thousand.

Hell, it'll be perfectly OK with me if it sells *two* hundred fifty thousand.

1993

Father Alone Farther Along:
Loudon Wainwright III

Loudon Wainwright III is a minor artist by self-definition, as much a sport in the folkie world he calls his own as in rock's big tent, where he was anointed a New Dylan many years ago. What sets him apart is that "III." Even folkiedom has accommodated very few Northeastern Wasps, and from Pete Seeger on they've made it a point of honor to sublimate their patrician ties. Loudon Jr. was a *Life* essayist a tad or two tonier than Neil Young's sportswriter dad, and without benefit of audit I doubt the Wainwrights are as wealthy as, say, the Simons or the Taylors. But Carly's folks are Jewish even if assimilated German Jews, James's Southerners even if habitues of Martha's Vineyard. Loudon III, on the other hand, flaunts what will pass for ruling-class roots, playing up his Westchester country club for every laugh it'll get. By rights he should have been a novelist like Cheever or Updike, or, less grandly, one of those circumspect old–*New Yorker* short-story writers whose Anglo-Saxon names no lover of American vernacular can keep straight. Instead he learned to play an acoustic guitar just well enough to turn into one more singer-songwriter.

Luckily, he also learned to act before he dropped out of Carnegie-Mellon in 1967. Not only has this skill provided auxiliary income, it's the secret of his musical career. Although Wainwright's wild tongue-wags and screwed-up faces rightly irritate many, underlying them is the expert timing and presence of a pro who's been cracking clubs up for twenty-five years. He lives off his shtick, his patter, and his mother wit, and then there are his songs. More of these are funny than not, but most aren't solely funny and some aren't funny at all. A sixties grad who's hip enough to both enjoy and rue that pedigree, Wainwright is no Tom Lehrer or Noel Coward—he's not especially interested in (or good at) satire or nonsense. Instead he inflects his comedy with confessional singer-songwriter conventions. Hence his music. Sung with the thoughtful lyricism of which his throat and larynx are just barely capable, even melodies as functional as Wainwright's can evoke an emotion that puts the laugh lines in painful psychological context.

Nevertheless, another reason not to take him too seriously is that his is primarily an art of words and performance. Unlike competing New Dylan John Prine, or for that matter acoustic Bruce, he doesn't conceive his musical limitations as the voice of the common man. Plainly unsuited for the greeting-card factories of Nashville and El Lay as well, he instead reports on weird upper-middle class mores like Updike and Cheever before him—only without the trappings of literachoor. In other words, he's a minor artist with the self-knowledge to admit it—a specialist in the repressed yet materially and religiously unconstricted family life of an aberrant aristocracy.

Within this ambit he has evolved markedly. Despite his short hair and preppy clothes, he did exhibit an inevitable portion of twenty-three-year-old hippie sensibility on his 1970 debut. But on his third album—where he went top twenty with the misleading "Dead Skunk in the Middle of the Road," a fluke Clive Davis would pressure him to repeat at Columbia and Arista for the remainder of an increasingly frustrated decade—he balanced off his new beard with a familiar array of male foibles. Between major drinking, minor mayhem, rooting for the home team, and general romantic inadequacy, you can be sure Kate McGarrigle didn't just call him a fool for smashing his red guitar. The male fruit of their union would be celebrated on later albums with songs like "Dilated to Meet You" and the indelible "Rufus Is a Tit Man": "Put Rufus on the left, hon, and put me on the right/And like Romulus and Remus we'll suck all night/Come on, mama, come on and lactate a while/Look down on us mama and flash us a madonna smile."

Half of *Unrequited,* which includes that classic as well as several breakup songs, was recorded live, and it's no surprise that in 1975 he was already getting yucks with "On Park Avenue South/I punched my baby in the mouth." Given to mocking posthippies from their gurus to their bell-bottomed pants, Wainwright slipped easily into the role of the enlightened, or perhaps just ironic, male chauvinist, a.k.a. the crapulous, self-pitying, philandering prick. Not that he homed in on weak women—he's fathered two kids by the redoubtable McGarrigle and another by prima donna Suzzy Roche, whose finest albums with their respective sisters exceed his in both musicality and emotional substance. But as he passed thirty and then forty, his male-bonding proclivities made it harder to enjoy his tales of thwarted ambition, unrequitable love, civilized substance abuse, all-purpose cynicism, and, more and more notably, family life from every angle—husband, father, brother, son. Until a few weeks ago, I'd last sighted him in 1988 or so at the Bottom Line, where a claque of aging college boys howled uproariously in all the wrong places. One big hit was "April Fools Day Morn," in which Wainwright's mom cooks him breakfast after he spends a stinko night doing cruel and stupid things to everyone who crosses his path. It's one of those songs that invites you to admire an asshole for not merely knowing but *revealing* just how colossal his assholism is. Since the guys who buy this con are usually assholes themselves, I stay away from them as much as I can.

But as he passed forty-five, Wainwright kept evolving. The signal, cut in the wake of his dad's death, was 1992's *History,* but even though his fatherhood memory "Hitting You" could make anyone wince, in general its gentle tone surrenders too much of Wainwright's waggish iconoclasm. In 1993, however, the live and lengthy *Career Moves* concocted an adult version of Loud-O's bad self by cherry-picking his over-thirty output. And now *Grown Man* takes a wiser but uncontrite pushing-fifty into the studio for his best album of new material in twenty years. Irritated by the title song, which begins "You've got a grown man/For a boyfriend" and goes on to describe an evolved asshole, I resisted until the strongest stuff redefined it: a sarcastic meditation on aging recorded naked in the shower, a calm meditation on mortality's little ups and downs called "That Hospital," a vivid piece of self-loathing linking his dead dad's cheating ways to his own. In "A Year," he introduces a brand new, previously unannounced fourth child, a girl he elected—quite oddly, one has to point out—not to see for the first year of her life. And in "Father/Daughter Dialogue," he scripts a cutting plaint for his daughter Martha, whom he'd sent roses in "Five Years Old" (lousy present, Loud-O) and walloped in "Hitting You"—and who has just nearly been aborted in "That Hospital." Dad gets last licks—"The guy singing the songs ain't me," basically. But at twenty, Martha is already exulting in chops far lusher than either parent's. And she also gets the best lines: "You like to think that things are okay/By singing things that you should say," basically.

When I returned to the man's Bottom Line bailiwick January 20, those college boys had aged some more. Not counting a table I took for family, I doubt a tenth of the audience was under thirty, which given the material was understandable—I never expect people to put cash down on music that's over their heads. Most of the selections were of nineties provenance, and quiet stunners like "The Picture," to the sister I see is no longer managing him, and "A Year," about that fourth child, were intently received. The absence of "That Hospital" was perhaps a kindness to the backup chick who eventually materialized—Martha Wainwright, delivering her lines with passion even if she sometimes hid behind her hair. "Folk music Oprah Winfrey," the boss called it, and got his laugh. The way the tableau conflated Martha's autonomy and Loudon's paternalism seemed simultaneously deep and sick to me, until a while later Martha got a solo spot on "Question of Etiquette," the first song she'd ever written. Of all things, it was for her baby half-sister Lexie. Although Dad might split and Mom think the situation "bullshit," Lexie felt like family to Martha—and in a good way. If John Updike has anything deeper to say, he's being too coy about it. The same goes for kids like Pavement, or Oasis, or Raekwon, or Björk.

1996

Born to Be Mature: Bonnie Raitt

Maybe I should have stuck around Maine until Bonnie Raitt hit Portland, where the local rock critic adjudged *Luck of the Draw* "one of her strongest and most adult works to date," or driven down after vacation to catch her Atlantic City show. For a belated bigshot, after all, Las Vegas East and the boondocks are crucial arenas. Instead I met her halfway in Tanglewood, where compadres like Arlo Guthrie and Rip Torn and Meryl Streep cheered her on and forty-one-year-old Bonnie could have been kid sister to hundreds of the assembled appreciators. A special kind of kid sister, of course. Not wayward, exactly—just the interesting one, the self-starter who wouldn't play by the rules, ending up far hipper and more weathered than some lawyer or shrink or executive mom a few now-meaningless years her senior.

Bonnie Raitt isn't any more comfortable about aging than anybody else in this culture. "I guess I look older than I feel, and in a way it'll be a relief to reach an age where I can be all wrinkly because I'm *supposed* to be all wrinkly," she told Ken Tucker in *Entertainment Weekly*. More camera-shy than image-conscious, she almost ducked her *EW* cover shot: "You need young, *beautiful* girls to sell magazines!" But if the autumn of her years comes as a relief, it won't be for the reasons she thinks. In Tanglewood and Portland and New York and even Atlantic City, everywhere except her sweet home Hollywood, wrinkles are *supposed* to start around thirty-five, and like the exemplary Americans they are, most rock and rollers feel younger than they are till the day they die. What always made Raitt different wasn't that she looked her age and felt younger, but that she *seemed* older. Intensely interested in both sex and the lasting relationship, passionately political but skeptical about the usefulness of overtly political music, funny in a way some found adolescent and moralistic in a way some found dull, she took so long to go platinum not because of her famous scruples, but because she was selling something like wisdom long before most of her young contemporaries were ready to buy. She was born to be middle-aged. She's five or ten years on the good side of her prime.

Raitt's success is so just, so overdue, and so honestly trad that it'll make a lost generation of cynics hold their noses in perpetuity. She'll get her share of hit-seeking kids, and she'll hold on to their parents, including the youngish NARAS members whose votes gave *Nick of Time* its 1989 Grammys, the extreme flukiness of which is already shrouded in the mists of comeback myth. But between her blues loyalties and her ingrained professionalism, she was even more freaked by punk and disco than Linda Ronstadt, who at least has some bimbo in her, and throughout the eighties Raitt was half has-been and half never-was, permanently alienated from the aesthetic concerns of the smart coming-of-agers who'd formed her core demographic a decade earlier. Now sober and happily married in addition to engagé—the corporate sponsor of her tour program, JVC, has agreed to donate a portion of its proceeds to the local causes she's fund-raising for at twelve of her tour stops—she's got loads of brains and no sense of irony, just like always. Back when such smart-rock counterparts as Randy Newman and Steely Dan were embracing irony as forthrightly as its status as an ordinary mode of discourse dictated, she was refining and expanding the conventions of emotive, projective "sincerity" mined by pop stars from Al Jolson and Ethel Waters to Barry Manilow and Linda Ronstadt. Her thoughtful phrasing and gentle-to-gritty timbre, her understated dramatic presence, and the very songs she's chosen to sing have always made her "compassion" seem articulate and unsentimental without sacrificing cornball straightforwardness. And because she abjures that sacrifice, she's doomed to strike alternative tastemakers as too fucking wholesome no matter how much she wise-cracks and raunches it up. They'll forgive her wrinkles, but not her freckles.

That's one reason I wish Warners had programmed last year's *Bonnie Raitt Collection* with more guts. Country blues like Fred McDowell's "Write Me a Few of Your Lines" or Tommy Johnson's "Big Road," Sippie Wallace classics like "Mighty Tight Woman" or "You Got To Know How," protofeminist covers like Martha and the Vandellas' "You've Been in Love Too Long" or Calypso Rose's "Wah She Go Do," and beyond-folkpoetry strokes like Nan O'Byrne's "Sweet and Shiny Eyes" or John and Johanna Hall's "Good Enough" might have helped the benighted hear why people who laugh at Linda Ronstadt revere Bonnie Raitt. But they ought to be able to figure it out on the evidence. Although she's cut better albums in a month—*Give It Up,* recommended to anyone who fancies her bluesy phase, and *Home Plate,* for those with the heart to brave the El Lay wastes—this fifteen-year distillation makes its case.

My Linda Ronstadt digs haven't been entirely gratuitous, because Ronstadt (while a good friend, of course) has been Raitt's perpetual opposite number, setting a standard of vocal and sexual glamour that Raitt couldn't match even though she didn't much want to. The first side of the Warners compilation showcases the salt and subtlety she wouldn't give up, while the second points at a synthesis that was sitting there waiting for Don Was. As a past master of the punk-disco cusp, Was seemed like an off-the-wall choice to produce a Capitol debut nobody figured for more than a modest return, but like the postpunks who still love Kiss and early Genesis, this postfunk cynic had his seventies vices. Thus he could mastermind a blues-rooted pop whose intimate gloss owes more to cabaret—theater music like that of *Carousel* star John Raitt, only without the painful technical demands Dad's opera training was designed to meet—than to Ronstadt's punched-up studio-rock and overripe genre exploitations.

Raitt's vocal equipment is like her looks. She may not be *"beautiful,"* right, but she isn't a pretty woman just because she has a nice smile and makes the most of what the Lord gave her. And though you wouldn't call her textured contralto gorgeous or powerful, she certainly has a good voice. She can shout and croon, carry a tune and fill a room, with a timbre that still shows more curves then crevices; she's never reduced to talking her material like Lou Reed or snipping it together like Janet Jackson. The physical charms of her voice infuse the aura of care around her singing with a hint of sweet erotic possibility; she sounds like a loving woman who has the touch, soft and hard at the right times in the right places. And whether she's torching over layered keybs or locking a track in with her trademark slide (once a mark of feminist bravado, today it signifies devotion to tradition), her emotional detail has never been more precise. Raitt is not now and never will be one of the century's great singers. But the analogies are Frank Sinatra and Billie Holiday, or at least Tony Bennett and Dinah Washington, rather than anyone identified with rock or soul.

Though John Hiatt's "Thing Called Love" and Larry John McNally's "Nobody's Girl" have their striking moments, the sharpest lyrics on *Nick of Time* come from career interpreter and longtime writer's-block victim Raitt. The gender-bent cliches of "The Road's My Middle Name" are bent yet again by the artist's memories of the touring musical comedy star who's no longer married to her mom, and "Nick of Time" is as tender and terrific a song about pushing forty as anyone is likely to write you: "I see my folks are getting on/And I watch their bodies change/I know they see the same in me/And it makes us both feel strange" sums up the encroachments of mortality more succinctly than any kid could. For all its integrity, however, her comeback didn't win its Grammys challenging the industry standards typified by such wan El Lay homilies as "Cry on My Shoulder" and "Too Soon To Tell." It's honest, but safe. *Luck of the Draw* exacts more from the formula—it's not risky, but it's highly principled. Sooner or later, every song stands up and says its piece; the only reason Raitt's four contributions don't shine is that general standards are so high. If you count Rosanne Cash's *Interiors* as country, which you probably shouldn't, you'd have to go back to Donald Fagen's *The Nightfly* to find such deep and consistent session-pop.

There was ample opportunity to contemplate the new album at Tanglewood, where it furnished seven of the thirteen regular-set selections. You could say she's in a new phase: supposedly shy of breakup songs since tying the knot with actor Michael O'Keefe, she introduced *The Glow*'s "Your Good Thing (Is About To End)" as a reminder of the bad old days when "I was so pissed off I couldn't stand it," though "Sugar Mama" and "I Can't Make

You Love Me" weren't exactly lovey-dovey. But you could also say she was promoting her latest product, an instant chart-topper currently sharing the newly discovered old-boomer spotlight with Natalie Cole's rather more icky *Unforgettable*. What Raitt eventually joshed off as "the sensitive stuff"—the midset change-of-pace, four new ones plus "Nick of Time"—gained further dimension live, especially her own "All at Once," written in solidarity with a woman dragged down by a relationship. Unfortunately, the fast songs—even "Papa Come Quick," in which a teenaged girl runs off to East L.A. perdition from some godforsaken farm town—weren't quite as rousing as I'm sure Raitt hoped. This was a fine concert. I'm personally acquainted with individuals under ten and over fifty who enjoyed it far more than they'd expected. But it never took off.

Though Raitt still takes her songwriters personally, pumping Paul Brady as supportively as she once pumped poor Eric Justin Kaz, the level of craft in her material has both risen and diminished, and neither is a good thing. Good honest fun though it is, the insistent hookiness of former Bay Area new waver Bonnie Hayes, who has three songs on the two Capitol albums, doesn't come naturally to a mature cabaret-rock innovator, and though Raitt avoids the generalized banalities that the likes of Desmond Child feed to the likes of Michael Bolton, those banalities, flatter than Linda Ronstadt's ever were, drag her toward homily by association. Her second encore burnished two chestnuts of matchless literary quality: John Prine's "Angel From Montgomery," "All at Once" 's wise old big sister, and the gloriously episodic "Sweet and Shiny Eyes," a fondly remembered happy moment that can bring back your own altogether different epiphanies. Nostalgia-hater though I'll always be, they reminded me of what both Bonnie and I had lost.

I'm not talking about our youth, believe me, but maybe I should be. Uncompromised as her belated success may be, I know if she doesn't that you don't build rock and roll thrills on changing bodies or a good marriage. Her refinement of her formula is an admirable achievement in itself. But since she's still on the good side of her prime, I'd love to see her bring it up another notch or two—make it hipper and more weathered, so strong and adult it's disturbing. And if she doesn't, well, we'll both live. I hope.

1991

Two Rock and Rollers Who Won't Change the World: Pete Fowler/Andy Fairweather Low

Pete Fowler's mother is a schoolteacher's daughter, his father a retired railway worker who likes Enoch Powell. They sent all of their children to university, no easy thing in England; one of their sons is a nuclear physicist. Pete is a graduate of the London School of Economics and a Marxist. Now thirty-three, he makes his keep teaching high school in the mountains between Leeds and Manchester, and lives with two women and four children whose relationships to him I never got straight. He also writes a little rock criticism and has composed some forty songs. The first was called "The Miners' Strike." It was inspired by his grandfather, a miner who was still requesting up-to-the-minute reports on the coal strike of 1974 from his deathbed.

"The Miners' Strike" was released in England in 1975 as the B side of a single on Oval. The A side, "One Heart, One Song"—designed to be a hit, as A sides are—took six sessions to get right. "The Miners' Strike" was cut in an hour. The same renowned backup musicians—Gallagher & Lyle, Dave Mattacks, Pete Wingfield—worked on both sides, with production by Charlie Gillett, rock historian and co-owner of Oval. "One Heart, One Song" has a wonderful piano hook by Wingfield and a gentle, melancholy melody imbued with extra grace by Fowler, who sings like an over-thirty Buddy Holly, with all that intensity, ambition, and adenoidal quaver mellowed out; although it has the general feel of a love lyric, its real subject is the persistence of faith, its "baby" not some girlfriend but Fowler's own child. It wasn't a hit and I like it a lot—but not as much as "The Miners' Strike," as heartening and well-conceived a political song as I can recall.

"Have the miners won their fight? Are they marchin' through the streets?/Are the governments fallin' down/Terrified by the anarchy?" are the questions Fowler's grandfather asks, but the lyric doesn't record Fowler's answers. Instead, it follows him on a visit to his friend Billy's house and into bed with Billy's wife. A breach of solidarity to be sure, yet when Billy discovers it upon his return from the night shift, his first words are almost the same as the old man's—he wants to knows how the strike is going! "And though by rights I should explode/And kick you out into the road/ All I really want to know is/Are the boys in control?" Whenever Fowler asks a political question, his thoughtful singing style takes on a declamatory, inspirational edge. He fades out improvising phony slogans like "things are going our way" and "man the barricades" over the band's vamp. Wingfield provides another nice hook.

I think this is a virtually perfect cut; the words synthesize the undying hope and time-tested futility of the Marxian vision, while the music, deriving from the folk-tinged English country-rock originated by a more mortal Rod Stewart, locates the lyric in the bohemian political subculture it is a fable for. Admittedly, the subculture is a small one, especially in America, where the youth radicalism of the sixties rose and faded away without the beginnings of a class analysis. But the dreams of liberation it's about made their mark even among those who were chary of them, and I've never played Fowler's seven-inch for any contemporary who wasn't moved by it. It seems a shame, doesn't it, that almost no one has ever heard this record, and that Fowler may never make another?

Ah well, those who don't much care for coal miners may be thinking, who wants to know about protest songs anyway, and although Fowler's isn't exactly protesting I accept that. But let me tell you about another singer-songwriter, equally adult but much less "political," who works in the same rock and roll tradition: Andy Fairweather Low. In the sixties, Low (Fairweather is a traditional middle name in his family) led the Amen Corner, a British pop-soul group that was like America's Box Tops, only bigger— they've been classed with the Osmonds, an overstatement that gives the idea—and also not as good. While the gravelly power of the Box Tops' Alex Chilton merited comparison with young Stevie Winwood, Low's voice was reedy and adenoidal—sort of like the one Alex Chilton (and Steve Winwood) uses today, actually. But Low began to write good songs well before Chilton did. At first, these appeared as Amen Corner B sides. Then, in 1970, at the end of the teenybopper grind, the group reconstituted under the name Fairweather and scored a hit with Low's "Natural Sinner."

It was about then that Low became a refugee from the music business. Whilst topping charts and making girls scream, the Amen Corner somehow amassed fifteen thousand pounds in debt, even though its members only cleared expenses plus twenty to thirty-five pounds a week. RCA's Neon subsidiary gave the reformed Fairweather an advance that put them in the black, but the hits didn't keep on coming, and when Neon folded, Low declined to renegotiate with RCA, retreating instead to his native Wales, where he lived off savings and songwriting royalties. It was three years before he was heard from again, by way of a solo album called *Spider Jiving* on A&M. When asked why the delay, he told interviewers he'd been thinking very carefully about his next contract.

Low's three solo LPs are not what you'd call grabbers. The vocals crack and wobble, the beat is quiet, and the lyrics have a found, anonymous air. Perhaps boosted by Low's teen-idol history, they've done well enough in England, yielding both retail and turn-table hits as well as good reviews. But in the United States, *Spider Jiving, La Booga Rooga,* and *Be Bop 'n Holla* have disappeared with barely a trace. I warmly admired, mildly praised, and resolutely filed all three myself. And then my wife and I went on vacation, which for the past two summers has involved a cabin in a state park with a portable phonograph and some seventy-five "listening records" chosen in haphazard improvisation shortly before departure. Under these circumstances, with my normal store of thousands of albums cruelly reduced, I'm often driven to unexpected pleasures. In 1977, some semiconscious memory inspired me to take both *Spider Jiving* and *Be Bop 'n Holla,* and that was how Andy Fairweather Low entered my life.

Although time in the country tends to soften my tastes, it hardly attunes me to the high-gloss pastorale of city slickers like the Eagles and James Taylor or rusticated exurbanites like John

Denver and Dan Fogelberg. I mention this because some believe Low works roughly the same genre. *Spider Jiving* was produced by country-rock maven Elliot Mazer with a passel of Nashville stalwarts, and the next two LPs went to Glyn Johns, in the booth for the first Eagles album, and featured ex-Eagle Bernie Leadon and a host of sympathetic session men—for *La Booga Rooga,* almost the same crew as Pete Fowler's. But that's just one set of facts, damning only if you swallow the orthodoxy that countrified studio music can never be forceful or provocative. It's also a fact that Mazer's most prominent associate, Neil Young, is not a high-gloss type, and that Glyn Johns made his name engineering Stones records. Anyway, the English version of countrified studio music has never been as glossy as the American. If its practitioners can be heard on many records so desultory they make Poco seem endearingly pop, well, don't blame session musicians for the megrims of frontpeople. Because when the frontpeople have something unpredictable to say, the way rock and roll is so often made in England gives them room to say it.

Whether moved by the propinquity of their own folk tradition or by some general attraction to the eccentric, English rock musicians seem comfortable with a kind of rough-hewn spontaneity usually left to folkies here. They know that it's rarely enough to be "tight," an all but universal term of approbation among rock pros—you have to be loose, too. That's what pub rock was about, and the Kinks and the Faces and most British blues; it is the key to unknown weirdos like Kevin Coyne and wealthy crackpots like the solo Pete Townshend. And it is why Andy Fairweather Low can rock more convincingly than he did as an r&b teen throb and still create a laid-back impression. The groove may be more earthbound, the beat a little pokier, the vocal excitement toned down an octave, but there's a quirky punch to this music—especially in the grit and surprising turns of Low's singing, which has gained strength without getting pushy about it—that makes for great rock and roll. This is pub rock without golden oldies or genre experiments—without the explicit bows to history that were the signature and fatal flaw of a suicidally folky music. It's country-style music that's black as well as white. It's alive.

If you wanted to categorize you could call Low's records good-time, thus lumping him with Southside Johnny, Les McCann, Charlie Daniels, and for that matter Peter Frampton, once a rival teen throb with the Herd. But I counted it some kind of sign when my move toward Low last summer was accelerated by three separate over-thirtys—a fabric designer from south of Syracuse, a schoolteacher from the Michigan north woods, and a radical telephone worker from Manhattan—who interrupted conversation to ask who that was on the record player, an honor not accorded Television or Bonnie Raitt. "That's my kind of music," said the fabric designer, whose husband sang with Blondie when her hair was brown, and whose elder son is a drummer who admires Queen. "It's real rock and roll. You don't hear music like that any more."

I agree, I really do—although I also think I've never heard real rock and roll like it and I also think I've heard it all before, only not in rock and roll. That's because Low's version of good old eclecticism seems to weld (or maybe pin) together elements that originate for the most part in nonrock styles. So on "Spider Jiving," the cut that attracted my friend's attention, the guitar and bass that meet the Memphis Horns over an insistent but very unfunky four-four are both acoustic. On the next song, Charlie McCoy plays hornpipe harp over oompah drums. On another a pedal steel contributes a rock rhythm part and then echoes an r&b sax solo, all over a funk (not rock or r&b) beat. There's even a "Champagne Melody" that deserves the name. Of course it all sounds like rock and roll. What else could it be?

Whether it's good-time is another question. My idea of a good time these days is Elvin Bishop—Low is good-time plus, because he writes real lyrics even if they do sound found and anonymous. The secret is that they're supposed to; as with his music, their substance—their unassumingly obsessive speculation about man's fate—is bound up in their free use of verbatim borrowings from a shared language. Often, Low lights upon bon mots that have not quite turned into cliches—"dead to the bone," "ticket to ride," "too much of nothing." But in context even unmistakably hackneyed phrases like "no place to hide," "food for my head," "rhythm of life," "great pretender" have a way of regaining some of the acuteness they must have begun with to achieve cliche status. This effect is suggested by a play like "which way is down" or a line like "In God we trust but they make me sign my name." Low's inspired commonplaces are only heightened by their (deliberate?) lapses of syntax and falls from rhyme. He says he labors over them for months; his house in Cardiff is filled with little scraps of paper. "But mind you," he adds, anxious not to sound pretentious, "I write big."

Especially on the first two albums, the purport of Low's lyrics is as pessimistic as his music is cheerful. What depresses him often seems connected to the downs and ups of his decade in the music business, but because his metaphors are vernacular and his attack is allusive, his songs sound like the outcries of anyone who's ever felt outclassed, outcast, outranked, or outraged by the money boys. Low never whines or comes on as a misunderstood artist. His craft is so jaunty and his singing so heartfelt and humorous that even lines like "I don't need a reason not to rhyme" or "Insanity's keeping me company" are acts of affirmation. And then there's the music, which embodies the same strategy of victory through joy that blues singers have known for so long. One of his best songs provides an existential motto: "I can't stop dancing/ Dancing in the dark."

With some difficulty—he rarely answers the phone—I met Low for an unhurried Indian lunch in London last fall, and wasn't surprised to find him as likable as Pete Fowler the night before. The middle son of a dustman, Low left school under the influence of the Rolling Stones at sixteen. He'll be thirty in August, has been married for about five years, and would like to have children but doesn't as yet. Although in general he was as affable and spirited as his music, his bemused pessimism came out in a quizzical cock of the head that was almost a tic, especially when we talked about the biz. The failure of *Be Bop 'n Holla* to produce a hit had left him in commercial limbo, and even though he lived comfortably on publishing income and session money, this bothered him. He felt ready to make a more uptempo and hard-edged album—too many of his singles, he observed, "use the plaintive voice." And he didn't know when or how he was going to get the chance.

Artists in this situation usually grouse about their record companies; Low's criticisms were comparatively mild. But he felt in a bind. Plans to produce (and finance) an LP by a Welsh rock and roll pianist named Geraint Watkins on a rented eight-track had set him to thinking about doing his own, then hiring an independent promo man to push the single. A&M had nixed this because he owed them for past production costs and tour support; unless another label were to purchase his contract, thus starting the cycle of debt all over again, he'd just have to wait until A&M gave him the go-ahead or declined to put up its next scheduled advance. As it stood, Low didn't even think he'd care to take a flier on a U.S. tour—not that A&M was offering one. "I don't want to borrow any more money, not when it becomes such a liability, and it is at the moment. They say they give it to you, but . . . I mean, gifts are gifts."

I've devoted lots of space to two artists most of you have never heard of, and I hope a few more hear them as a result. But it would be missing the point to expect some undiscovered genius or superstar. One thing I love about both Low and Fowler is their aesthetic modesty; their music is crafted with ambitious commitment, yet isn't designed to take over the world. Both are rather adult rock musicians, and while the audience for good adult rock and roll, as opposed to rockish schlock, may not be terribly large, it's hard to believe that no one can devise a better delivery system than the one that has served these two so poorly. Of course, fiction fans have been saying something similar about the novel for years.

In the meantime, my friend the radical telephone worker, a haunter of record stores, reports that the only Andy Fairweather Low he's seen since last summer was in a Sears in Chicago. Fortunately, A&M (unlike CBS, Atlantic, Island) is cautious about deletions. So all three records are in catalogue, and if you know a nice retailer he or she might (a) order one for you without (b) charging you list when it arrives. *Spider Jiving* is the toughest, *Be Bop 'n Holla* the sexiest, *La Booga Rooga* the one I've played constantly while writing. As for Pete Fowler, my pet fantasy is for Arlo Guthrie to cover "The Miner's Strike." But last I heard, Arlo didn't want to make records anymore. It was costing him too much money.

1978

4

Smashing the State-of-the-Art

(If I'm Acting Like a King That's Because) I'm a Human Being: New York Dolls

There are people who love the Ramones or the Sex Pistols yet continue to find the New York Dolls deficient in melody or power or punch. "I guess you had to be there," they say, at once paying their respects to history and implying that those who were are no more fit to judge the resulting phonograph records than admirers of *Frampton Comes Alive!* It must be admitted, though, that seeing the Dolls on stage helped you understand their output, which comprises—not even crazies defend the live tapes and demo compilations—1973's *New York Dolls* and 1974's *In Too Much Too Soon*. They didn't play any better than on record, and—despite the theatrical reputation of "glitter rock," a reputation based on the attraction of photographers to unusual clothing and of David Bowie to mime—they didn't "put on a show" in the Alice Cooper or Bruce Springsteen sense. But they certainly tried to look like something special, and they succeeded.

Just as the impressionable listener was often deafened psychologically by the sheer rapid fire of the Dolls' music, so the impressionable onlooker was often blinded by the sexual ambiguity of their roles. It ought to be established, therefore, that the only time the Dolls ever affected vampy eyes, bowed red lips, and pancake makeup was on the cover of their first album. Ordinarily, their gender-fuck was a lot subtler. It did capitalize on a slight natural effeminacy in the speech patterns and body language of leader David Johansen and bassist Arthur Kane, but at its core was David's amazing flair for trashy clothes. The man was a thrift-shop genius. So Arthur, who was tall and ungainly even without his platform shoes, would squeeze his torso into a child's dress or put on a crotch-length hockey jersey over white tights; David would wear a shorty nightgown instead of a shirt, with fishnet stockings showing through the rips in his jeans; Syl would turn into Liza Minnelli doing a Charlie Chaplin impression.

Partly because it coincided with Bowie's publicly gay phase, this stuff seemed very significant at the time, and symbolically it was. But in retrospect it's clear that the rather sweet street-tough alienation projected by guitarists Johnny Thunders and Syl Sylvain and drummer Jerry Nolan was where the collective sexuality of the band was at. These were boys who liked girls; they shared the traditional rock and roll machismo, which is adolescent and vulnerable. What made them different was that their sweetness and toughness and alienation knew no inhibitions, so that where love was concerned they were ready for anything. By their camping they announced to the world that hippie mind-blowing was a lot more conventional than it pretended to be, that human possibility was infinite. Of course, between Arthur's instinctive awkwardness and Syl's clowning and David's pursuit of the funny move, they suggested in addition that human possibility was hilarious. And the band's overall air of droogy desperation implied that human possibility was doomed as well.

All this was conveyed from the stage without props or bits or any but the most elementary business—David and Johnny share mike, Arthur steps forward for falsetto phrase, like that. But in another way it was the real living theater. To be a Doll was to appear twenty-four hours a day in an improvised psychodrama, half showbiz and half acting out, that merely got wilder in front of the microphones. Arthur played the beloved weirdo and Syl the puckish jack-in-the-box; Jerry was the all-American dynamo who kept the machinery juiced. But the big parts went to David, whose mobile face and body accentuated the humor, smarts, and purpose not just of the lyrics but of everything the band was, and Johnny, who threatened constantly to detonate David's volatile handiwork. David was a benevolent ringleader; his exaggerated moues and gestures made fun of the whole crazy project even as they sharpened its meaning and established his authority. But Johnny was forever testing the flexibility of David's conception. He was a JD with a bomb sticking out of his pocket, careening from microphone to amplifier to beplatformed fellow Doll without ever (almost ever) knocking any of them down or ceasing to wrench noises from his guitar. He was Chaos personified, put on display virtually untamed for our pleasure and edification.

Of such stuff are legends made—and from such stuff does all this I-guess-you-had-to-be-there stuff proceed. The Dolls prove how easy it is to dismiss a legend as nothing more than that, especially when it's crude and raucous and flashy. That their music was consciously primitive was obvious; what wasn't so obvious was that it was also difficult. Even people who loved their records found those records hard to listen to—not because the concept (or legend) was greater than the music, but because the music wasn't merely fun. The Coasters and the Beach Boys and even the Rolling Stones were each in their own way avatars of fun-filled if alienated affluence. But the joy in the Dolls' rock and roll was literally painful; it had to be earned. The Dolls carried to its illogical conclusion the egalitarian communalism that was one logical response of fun-filled affluence to alienation. They refused to pay their dues, so we had to pay instead. These weren't Woodstock brethren—skilled, friendly musical specialists plying their craft in organic harmony, eager to help the energy go down. They were lonely planet everyboys, ambitious kids who'd drifted in from the outer boroughs of Communications Central and devised new ways to cope with information overload. Although they were addicted to the city, they knew damn well that "Somethin' musta happened/ Over Manhattan." And they wanted their music to sound like whatever it was.

Especially after a siege of pent-up urban frustration, I found no rock and roll anywhere that delivered comparable satisfaction. It articulated the noisy, brutal excitement the city offered its populace as nothing else ever had, and so offered a kind of control over it. The Dolls were at once lumpenkids overwhelmed by post-hippie New York and wise guys on top of it. They lived in the interstices of the Big Apple war zone on their wit and will, their music at once a survival tactic and a kind of victory. They never whined because it was fun making do, and they rarely complained about their powerlessness because they were too busy taking advantage of what ordinary power the city provided its citizen denizens—mobility and electricity especially. That's why it seems completely appropriate that their music evokes nothing so much as the screech of a subway train.

I'm not talking about lyrics—the lyrics were wonderful, and they do convey comparable messages, but not so unequivocally. It's the music that makes the Dolls hard to listen to, and the music that satisfies. Since neither album affords the kind of pristine sound quality that distinguishes cleanly between garage-band guitarists, it's impossible to be sure, but as I hear it Syl is the only Doll who doesn't add something unique to a sound that pits the competent-plus musicianship of David and Jerry against the rude thrashing of Johnny and Arthur. And it is the playing of Johnny and Arthur—one a primitive genius, the other a primitive klutz—that is the Dolls' contribution to musical history.

Johnny's offering was buzzsaw guitar charismatic enough to vie with heavy-metal fuzz in the hearts of rock and rollers everywhere. Ron Asheton of the Stooges and Wayne Kramer and Fred "Sonic" Smith of the MC-5 were the fathers of the style, going back to Pete Townshend's rhythm chords with the Who as opposed to Eric Clapton's lead licks with the Yardbirds, to the Link Wray of "Rumble" rather than the Duane Eddy of "Rebel Rouser," to create a drone-prone guitar countertradition that was not only loud but tumultuous. It was Johnny, however, who made buzzsaw definitively young, fast, and unscientific, undercutting the elephantine beat that had deadened hard rock since the early days of Led Zeppelin and the only days of Blue Cheer.

Despite heavy metal's ill-mannered pretensions, its glitter move was always (relatively) discreet because it was (relatively) discrete, often simply responding to the call of the vocal line with a neat, standardized electroshock phrase that incorporated both factory-approved sound effects and natural feedback. Not that there was no galvanic spillover—amplifiers were molested until they screamed in conspicuously unpredictable revolt. But for Asheton and Kramer and Smith spillover was the be-all and end-all. Exploiting their own continuous, imprecise finger action a lot more than the fuzzbox, they threw together an environment of electric noise with which everything else had to contend, replacing the deracinated call-and-response of heavy metal with music that was pure white riot. Without violating the primordial totality of this environment—if anything, the Dolls intensified buzzsaw's drone—

Johnny made it speak, gave it shape and idiosyncrasy and a sense of humor.

To be fair, Johnny couldn't possibly have made all that noise himself. Syl pitched in with a will and a wink, laying a bottom for Johnny's jerrybuilt ideas; you can hear his essential racket in its pristine state, a little bluesier than one might expect, on the guitar intro of "It's Too Late." But while a lot of guys could have done Syl's work for him, Johnny made up his own job, varying the tasks to suit his eternally teenaged sense of what was and wasn't boring. Often he created the impression of perpetual motion with intermittent music, as with the scalar figure that turns into a solo on "Jet Boy" or the fills of sheer sonic matter that surround Syl on "Looking for a Kiss" or the squawking licks that decorate his own "Chatterbox." The bursts of ersatz slide that he explodes at regular intervals through "Babylon" add up to a drone, while on "Subway Train" he breaks a whole drone into components, playing each half of a primal background riff for a full measure instead of alternating the two four times a measure as in workaday buzzsaw. And even when he provided a straight drone, he was too loose (or too sloppy) to leave it at that, and that was his gift. The crude variation on Bill Doggett's "Honky Tonk" that opens "Human Being" soon devolves into something more general, yet though it never quite regains its shape it never stops gathering force either; "Pills" thrusts forward on the almost tuneless phrase that Johnny repeats throughout the track. In both cases, the charge of the music is equivalent to the severely delimited (Johnny was obviously no technician and didn't improvise in the usual sense) expressiveness of his playing. Johnny was too restless (and too lazy) to master his lines absolutely. His mistakes are indistinguishable from his inspirations. Each of his solos and comments and background noises is a point in an infinite series of magically marginal differentiations.

If Johnny's contribution was the fruit of irrepressible individuality, Arthur's was the by-product of incompetent individuality. Johnny's untutored spirit found voice in technique, but Arthur (playing the instrument fellow bumpkin Ringo Starr declared "too hard") never got that far. You can hear how much bass he's learned between the two records, but it's not nearly enough to play around with. If he doesn't sink a blues line under Johnny's force field on (Bo Diddley's) "Pills" on the first album, it's only because he doesn't know one that fits; by the time of (Sonny Boy Williamson's) "Don't Start Me Talkin' " on the second he is double-timing an utterly conventional Willie Dixon part as Johnny sows discord all around him. In general, on the first LP he either echoes the rhythm guitar or just thumps along on a minimum of notes, sometimes difficult to distinguish from the bass drum. By *In Too Much Too Soon* his playing has definitely acquired a lilt, funky on "Bad Detective" and bluesy-tuneful on "Stranded in the Jungle," echoing the melody after a showpiece walk on "It's Too Late." But when he really wants to generate excitement, as on the climactic "Human Being," he resorts to the old thunderthud.

Arthur was the key to the Dolls' unyielding and all but un-danceable rhythms. Harmonically, he could have been a far more sophisticated technician without doing the band anything but good—tricky melodic hooks helped make their music lovable. But although the Dolls would have been tastelessly aggressive and urban even without Arthur, his inability to come up with a catchy counterrhythm, to supply the kind of syncopation that sets the body swaying, left them no room to be anything else. His style was anticipated to some extent by various protopunk pioneers, nota-bly John Cale, and he shared more than Johnny did with the pur-veyors of heavy metal. But Arthur Kane is the definitive punk bass-ist, the source not only of Dee Dee Ramone's wall of rhythm but of Paul Simonon's military intricacies. As for Sid Vicious, well, it sounds as if he studied with Arthur—Sid was the more confident player only because he didn't have to prove it could be done.

Admittedly, there's reason to wonder just how much Arthur was capable of proving: nobody else ever carried the Dolls' any-one-can-do-it gospel so far. Even among the English punks, only X-Ray Spex aimed for self-transcendence with such passionate inac-curacy. The responsibility of compensating fell to Syl. Syl's guitar was the band's fulcrum. By mediating between rhythm and mel-ody, a bass man's work, he picked up some of Arthur's slack. And if he had nothing unique to add to the Dolls' sound, he wasn't an ordinary circa-1971 hard rock guitarist either. Syl was a Doll because he was in love with speed, and he knew enough to coun-teract Arthur's inertia by keeping his touch unusually light. There's even a sense in which his ordinariness provided a modi-cum of conceptual stability, a common ground where the band's primitives could meet the musicians.

But Syl didn't have the drive to power the band himself, and if the forward motion had been left to Arthur, the Dolls might never have gotten anywhere at all. He just followed along, stating the beat in his own peculiar fashion, as Jerry Nolan provided the propulsion. Insofar as the Dolls believed in music cum music—in the power of rock and roll alone and unaided to provide salvation—Jerry embodied that belief. He was an ordinary rock and roll madman at heart—schooled in one-two-one-two, with the jumbo-size panoply of rolls, cymbal accents, and crossbeats at his disposal. He led the band in chops, but like so many punk drummers he never showed any conceptual commitment to the forced rhythms that are punk's mainspring. Not that this is surprising in a style whose innovators on the instrument—Maureen Tucker, who rejected the backbeat, and Tommy Ramone, so minimal he made Charlie Watts sound like Elvin Jones—had never struck a tom-tom in full earnest when they first tried out for their jobs. Ignorance can be the mother of invention too—it guarantees an uncluttered mind.

As it happens, though, drummers aren't required to use their minds much, not in rock and roll—they're just supposed to follow the right instincts (or orders) and play the right stuff. So however traditional Jerry's conceptual commitments, he played with obliging steadiness; although drawn to the backbeat, he submerged it, never funking around like, for instance, Frankie LaRocka of the David Johansen Band. This was essential discipline in what was supposed to be a definitively white style. The effects and rhythm changes were there when needed—Jerry provided more dramatic support for David than anyone else in the group—but for the most part held in check. There was no bombardiering or gratuitous noisemaking. In short, Jerry never showed off. As explosive as his sound seemed, it turned out to be surprisingly even in the moment-to-moment execution. His only self-indulgence was to play unceasingly, on every beat. The faster the tempo, the happier he was.

Jerry was not an original Doll—he succeeded Billy Murcia, a cofounder of the group with Johnny and Arthur who died of a drug overdose during the Dolls' first tour of England in 1972—and he always seemed a little simpler than the others. Syl, for instance, acted no less happy-go-lucky, yet at the same time projected a dirty old man's sagacity. But Jerry was street-smart without being street-cynical, so unfailingly eager that later, after he'd dyed his hair bright blond and helped compose a classic song about heroin for the Heartbreakers, he still seemed a naif clumsily astray in the rock and roll demimonde. He was the band's link to what people smugly consider normal emotions, and his musicianship did the same job—like any drummer who does his or her work well, he provided roots.

David Johansen was Jerry's obverse in all this, both as a public figure and as the band's other practical technician. The most worldly of the Dolls, the group's lyricist and conceptmaster, David took an undisguised pleasure in the ironic persona play that is the privilege and responsibility of rock's leading men. Although his style of humor was a lot more generous than Dylan's or Jagger's, he was as dedicated to the principle of fun as any great rocker since the Beatles themselves. But it seemed that this group might require more musicianly skills from its leader. With such a defiantly amateurish concept, wouldn't the conceptmaster have to do more than strike poses and think a lot if the music was to survive the force of its own forward rush? Without decoration and identifying detail, it might turn into instant blur.

A great vocalist like Little Richard could sing right over this endemic rock and roll problem, but more often it has been solved by means of hooks. These are usually tuneful little snatches of provisional significance that are composed into a song or added by some clever musician or producer, but in a pinch almost anything memorable will do. And because David's specialties were striking poses and thinking a lot, he was compelled to fashion more hooks out of less melody than a tone-deaf Eskimo. He did it, though—in constant consultation with his boys—and as a result the Dolls' music ranks not only with the hardest and fastest ever made, but also with the wittiest and most charming. A few touches on the Dolls' LPs must have been donated by producers Todd Rundgren (e.g., the two-tone double-track at the end of "Personality Crisis," not to mention the piano playing) and Shadow Morton (e.g., the soul girls on "Stranded in the Jungle"). But most of them were part of the Dolls' music long before it got inside a studio, offshoots of David's acting ability and of his encyclopedic fondness for rock and roll trivia. If Jerry's craftsmanship provided roots, David's bestowed spirit. He struck poses, he thought a lot, and he came up with what the group needed.

Even by modern standards, David was not a great vocalist. He was competent-plus in the post-Dylan manner—he had presence and rhythm and a teasing knack for enunciating just enough to whet your word hunger—but Little Richard he wasn't. His range was quite narrow and his timbre rather dry, and with the Dolls his singing was neither deeply expressive (that came later, when he went solo) nor acutely phrased. Yet his histrionic flair saved him, and not just live, where his rubber mug and felicitous gesticulations tended to overshadow his equally deft (and broad) vocal role-playing. His shifts of character and caricature on these records are an ongoing delight. "Personality Crisis," directed at a schizy imagemonger, pauses dramatically before David roars back with: "And you're a prima ballerina on a spring afternoon/ Changed on into the wolfman howling at the moon." Shape up, that's certainly his warning—but disapproval doesn't prevent him from whistling a birdie type tune (and doing a plié, although the rustle of tulle gets lost in the mix) after the first line, or awhooing joyously after the second. It is on the great novelty covers of *In Too Much Too Soon* that David really indulges his taste for this kind of impersonation—the high-stepper of "Showdown," "Bad Detective' "s all-too-scrutable Charlie Chan, and (most exorbitantly) the alternating Amos 'n' Andy reject and lover's-lane ass man of "Stranded in the Jungle." But on occasion he would momentarily change the gears of his basic vocal transmission, which filters a drawling pout through a tough, loud New York accent—as in the adolescent-reverting-to-childhood dudgeon of "you better tell me" on "Who Are the Mystery Girls?" or the maidenly "oh—all right" that closes "Private World." And every one of these personality crises helps decorate and identify the song.

But David's tricks didn't stop there. He stole mnemonic devices from everywhere and made up a few of his own; no wonder he wanted to work with Shadow Morton, rock and roll's greatest sound effects man. A cut might begin with a gong, a harmonica, sighs, some sloppy power chords, monkey chatter, handclaps, a whistle, a spoken intro, a shouted "One-two-three-four," a pouted "Oh . . . breakdown," or the greatest of all the Dolls' credos: "Aah-ooh, yeah yeah yeah/No no no no, no no no no." It might end with a gong, a harmonica, a sigh, a saxophone coda, a big fat kiss, a drum roll, a rifle shot, some climactic feedback, a shouted "Whatcha gonna do?," a pouted "oh—all right," or the greatest of all the Dolls' metaphysical questions: "Do you think that/You could make it/With Frankenstein?" The Dolls also loved to quote the classics—the Edsels' "Rama Lama Ding Dong," Del Shannon's "Runaway," the Shangri-Las' "Give Him a Great Big Kiss," Mickey & Sylvia's "Love Is Strange"—and would refer more allusively to anything from Jan & Dean to Chinese movie music to "I've Been Working on the Railroad." This kind of fooling around had a recontextualizing effect, of course—"Love Is Strange," for instance, pins down the meaning of "Trash"—but it also provided additional hooks, and time-proven ones at that. No wonder the group believed that if you were smart enough you didn't have to practice.

Since there are still people who label this kind of craft "gimmicky," as if that were a devastating insult, it ought to be emphasized that David's gifts as a practical technician went beyond what I've been describing. He knew how to use his voice (in the post-Dylan manner) and he knew how to put a song together (his compositions, which on the two albums comprise three written solo plus eight collaborations with Johnny, three with Syl, and one with Arthur, are moderately catchy in a generic way). As if to prove his competence-plus, he suddenly became a "better singer" who wrote "better melodies" when the more conventional concept of his solo career demanded it. Admittedly, I could have the order wrong—maybe increased competence is what David, whose father is an opera buff, would have preferred all along. But that wouldn't mean he was right. His melodies and his singing with the Dolls weren't merely adequate to the artistic venture—they were brilliantly appropriate to it.

Finally, David offered one additional accouterment—lyrics every bit as apposite as his music, lyrics that focused and aimed the band's thrust. His father may have been an opera buff, but his mother was a college librarian, and like the good rebel he was he betrayed and fulfilled his birthrights. Of course, in an era of pop surrealism, the bedlam of the Dolls' music had fewer precedents than the elusive logic of their words. But David's lyrics distinguished themselves from the post-Dylan norm by one simple expedient—they never sounded at all like poetry. It was to be expected that sometimes they wouldn't even sound like words—indecipherability was a rock and roll tradition David respected with a passion that passed all understanding. But the avoidance of imagery that declared itself to be imagery was a mark of sophistication that he shared with very few contemporaries, especially in America. Even a master of the colloquial like Robbie Robertson, that fervent opponent of "glitter rock," was capable of something as "poetically" obscure on the face of it as "The Weight."

The Dolls' obscurities were at once deeper and less considered. Often the inexactness of their words, like that of their music, seems unintentional, so that the opacities of "Subway Train," for instance, bespeak careless workmanship more than anything else. But David clearly regards ambiguity as a significant mode. How else to explain "Trash," in which "Please don't you ask me if I love you" is followed first by "If you don't know what I do," then by "'Cause I don't know why I do," then by "'Cause I don't know if I do," and the "life" in "Don't take my life away" changes at various times to "knife," "night," and "lights"? Yet so fetching was the hook—"Trash! Pick it up! Don't take my life (knife) (night) (lights) away!"—that you could hear the song dozens of times without ever puzzling over such quiddities. Especially as David performed them, all the lyrics offered some turn that earned a chortle of recognition, and the tendency was to leave it at that.

Since the phrases that stood out often signaled "decadence" and/or "camp," this tendency reinforced the impression that the Dolls were purely (and exploitatively) decadent and campy. Even when it was quite explicit, for instance, that David was looking for "a kiss not a fix," the song's shooting-gallery ambience (not to mention the way David used to tie off with the mike cord and jab himself in the bicep as he sang) wasn't calculated to imprint this on one's mind. And in "It's Too Late," which posits lessons from trivia history against the latest nostalgiac fads, the name of camp heroine Diana Dors has had more initial impact than the speed-kills putdown she's featured in. On the verbal surface, this is a band of kitsch-addicted, pill-popping teen Frankensteins on the subway train from Babylon to nowhere. Not only do they consort with bad girls, mystery girls, and other trash, they aren't even sure whether that jet boy up there wants to steal their baby or be their baby.

Like the Dolls' musical surface, this verbal surface offended many, but although the band certainly wasn't above sensationalism, their intent wasn't merely sensationalistic. Once again they were trying to create an environment that jibed with their experience. This was the modern world the Dolls sang about—one nuclear bomb could blow it all away. Pills and personality crises weren't evils—easy, necessary, or whatever. They were strategies and tropisms and positive pleasures, and David wasn't so sure that those who disapproved even deserved to be called human beings: "Well if you don't like it go ahead and/Find yourself a saint/ Find yourself a boy who's/Gonna be what I ain't/And what you need is/A plastic doll with a/Fresh coat of paint/Who's gonna sit through the madness/And always act so quaint/Baby yeah yeah yeah."

Well, nobody ever called him humble. But his arrogance is moral arrogance as opposed to the arrogance of power, and it's moral arrogance of the best sort, infused with comedy and a feeling for human limits. His basic theme is authenticity—sometimes as an explicit subject, as in "Personality Crisis" and "Puss in Boots," sometimes in tales of lost kidz like "Babylon" and "Subway Train"—in the midst of massage parlors, Vietnamese babies, and other seventies exposes, and his solution (counsel?) (message to the world?) is a little surprising only because it is so traditional. Johansen is a kind of cartoon prophet—a prophet posing as a bitchy scold. Don't you start him talking, he'll tell everything he knows. And what he knows is love l-u-v.

The only reason this denouement qualifies as any kind of big deal is the context, and David does go out of his way to avoid making a big deal of it himself. It's almost as if love enters his music by accident, because it happens to be the classic rock and roll subject. In "Bad Girl," when he tells the waitress who makes his heart hurt that he's "gotta get some lovin' 'fore the planet is gone," he reduces his worldview to a way to get laid; in "Trash," when he wonders whether his "lover's leap" will land him in "fairyland," he belittles his own proud (if ambiguous) pansexuality. But on the other hand, maybe the reason David is attracted to rock and roll is that it's always been a way to connect the cold cruel world with love l-u-v. Pills and personality crises may be OK up to a point, but they're obviously not going to get anyone past that point. In fact, the mood and message of these songs is not only expressly anti-phony (Dolls, not plastic dolls) but also expressly antidrug (just like Bo Diddley).

For the Dolls, the old answers can't be revived—the only conventional I-love-you songs here are Johnny's jokey, roughly affectionate "Chatterbox" and David's "Lonely Planet Boy." But the old answers can be adapted to the dangerous world where the Dolls' music finds its life, just as rock and roll itself can be reinterpreted to get rid of most of its sexy backbeat and twenty years of acquired polish. By the seventies, the love-suffering of "Lonely Planet Boy" was a hoary pop cliche and the love-nastiness of "It's Too Late" a virulent one. But the sardonically optimistic, quadruple-edged contingency evoked by songs like "Looking for a Kiss" and "Trash" and "Bad Girl"—so far from the self-serving transience of the rocky-road mythmongers and the fashionable equivocation of the sensitive singer-songwriters—was always unique to this band. In "Frankenstein" and "Vietnamese Baby" Johansen even moved from eros to agape, an agape that escaped the universalist mush of the music-as-brotherhood sermoneers because it was rooted in horror.

This was tough stuff in every way, and if the Dolls' record company couldn't put it to use, neither could the Dolls. The arrogance of power wasn't in their karma—they didn't lust after it enough to trouble themselves with the discipline it required. It took them much too long to learn that getting your name in the papers was not equivalent to world conquest, and in the end they didn't even win over the city that taught them everything they knew. After it became obvious that they weren't going to storm the charts, they did some touring and gigged sporadically for their sizable local cult, even hooking up briefly with Malcolm McLaren, who later devised the Sex Pistols in their honor. But their failure had put a damper on the New York rock scene, and before the punk audience had redefined itself at CBGB the Dolls were down to David and Syl.

As far as their legend goes, it's just as well that they were never forced to translate permanent insurrection into success. But the split meant the end of all their most invigorating tensions: between feeling and alienation, love and escape, craft and anarchy. Arthur, who'd fallen away early, surfaced looking very ravaged, first in a disturbingly Nazoid outfit called the Corpse Grinders and later behind Sid Vicious, of all people. David wrote deeply felt conventional I-love-you songs with an unconventional come-on-boys spirit and was joined by Syl in a band to match. And Johnny and Jerry became the soul of the Heartbreakers, who somehow managed to make junkiedom sound like laughs and fast times. It was on the Heartbreakers' *L. A. M. F.,* rather than *David Johansen,* that the old gestalt came through most emphatically. After all, what made the Dolls the Dolls was the way they energized negatives.

For me, the Dolls perfect—in a properly inexact way—a new aesthetic. Camp or no camp, theirs was not a case of "a seriousness that fails," of so-bad-it's-good. On the contrary, the Dolls were a miracle of pop, using their honest passion, sharp wits, and attention to form to transmute the ordinary into the extraordinary. Like the greatest folk artists, they plugged into an enormously expressive (and accessible) cultural given and then animated it with their own essence. But this was not a folk process—not orally transmitted, naive, somehow "natural." It was rooted in bookish ideas about art that were alive in the downtown boho air. Their music synthesizes folk art's communion and ingenuousness with the exploded forms, historical acuity, and obsessive self-consciousness of modernism. As culture, it is radically democratic and definitively urban; as art, it is crude and sophisticated at the same time. It epitomizes why rock and roll began and why it will last.

1978

Patti Smith Pisses in a Vanguard

Patti Smith is caught in a classic double bind—accused of selling out by her former allies and of not selling by her new ones. Maybe she's too famous for her own good. Habitues of the poetry vanguard, many of whom mistake her proud press and modest sales for stardom, are sometimes envious and often disdainful of her renown as a poet, since she is not devoted to the craft and they are. Music-biz pros, aware that *Radio Ethiopia* is already bulleting down the charts, remember that print exposure is the least reliable of promotional tools in an aural medium. Somewhere in between are the journalists and critics, who can now be heard making either charge, or both.

Cut to the artiste at her first Bottom Line gig in December, 1975, wearing a T-shirt that says CULT FIGURE. You can accuse Patti of taking herself too seriously, but you can't say she doesn't have a sense of humor about it. She knows that her audience—"my kids," she calls them, more maternal than you'd figure—has the earmarks of a cult. And she knows that she leads a critics' band. Patti herself has been a practitioner of rock criticism—"rock writin'," as she calls it, always having preferred celebration to analysis and analysis to censure—and lead mentor Lenny Kaye made his living that way until two years ago. She's always had critic fans, and these fans have spread the news, so that by now Patti has probably inspired more printed words per record sold than any charted artist in the history of the music—except maybe Dylan or the Stones.

Although Patti was personally acquainted with numerous critics, the nationwide journalistic excitement she aroused went far beyond cliquishness. Like Bruce Springsteen, she answered a felt need. The insistence of the record companies, booking agents, and concert promoters on professionalism had produced a subculture of would-be studio musicians who were willing to apprentice as touring pros just to establish themselves in a growing industry. Patti wasn't like that. She recalled a time when rock and roll was so conducive to mythic fantasies that pretensions were cutting into its artistic potential. Patti had her pretentious side, everybody knew that, but in her it seemed an endearing promise that she would actually attempt something new. Anyway, what other rock and roller had ever published even one book of poetry without benefit of best-selling LP? Nor was it only critics who felt this way. A rock audience that includes 6 million purchasers of *Frampton Comes Alive!* spins off dissidents by the hundreds of thousands, many of whom are known to read. People were turned on by Patti Smith before they'd seen or heard her. Even in New York, the faithful who had packed CBGB for her shows were only a small fraction of her would-be fans, and elsewhere she was the stuff of dreams.

The problem with this kind of support is that it is soft—a suspension of the disbelief with which any savvy fan must regard the unknown artist. Patti has always attracted a smattering of sensitive types who attend one show because they're intrigued by the word "poet" and leave wincing at the noise. But they don't count—it's the informed fence-sitters Patti could use. There's no way to know how many of the almost two hundred thousand adventurous fans who purchased *Horses* feel equivocal about it, but I can imagine half of them remaining unconvinced that the unusual lyrics, audacious segues, and effective vocals and melodies compensated for some very crude-sounding musicianship. These were people who wouldn't rule out the next LP—a genuine rock poet deserves patience, after all—but wouldn't rush out for it, either. For although Patti is a genuine rock poet, what she does—her art, let's call it—is not calculated to appeal to those attracted by such a notion.

Patti is far from the first published poet to have turned to popular music in the rock era. Recall with pleasure Leonard Cohen, who for almost a decade has been singing his verses in a tunelessly seductive monotone to pop-folk/European-cabaret backing, or Gil Scott-Heron, who declaims both poetry and songs over soul-jazz polyrhythms. Banish from your mind Rod Taylor a.k.a. Roderick Falconer, who in both his Sensitive and Fascist-cum-Futurist incarnations has attempted to sell his rhymes with the most competent rock musicians Los Angeles could afford. Or consider Rod McKuen and his numerous strings.

And then move on to three far more relevant poet-singers— David Meltzer, who is obscure, and Ed Sanders and Lou Reed, who are not. All are distinguished by a salient interest in those innovations of voice and prosody that occupy dedicated poets as opposed to versifiers good or bad. Meltzer, who recorded a mordant, playfully mystagogic LP out of flower-power San Francisco with the Serpent Power, can be found in Donald M. Allen's seminal Grove anthology, *The New American Poetry;* Sanders, the versatile avant-gardist who was the focus of the Fugs, was included in Ron Padgett and David Shapiro's *Anthology of New York Poets;* and Reed has been in Anne Waldman's *Another World* anthology. None of them is a major figure in these contexts, although Sanders comes close. But all of them craft poetry of a different order of sophistication from Leonard Cohen's melancholy anapests or Gil Scott-Heron's Afroprop.

And all have different ideas about music as well. Rather than committed professionalism for a preconceived audience, proper and predictable accompaniment for the verbal "message," the avant-gardists' music is strikingly amateurish, with all three bands using found drummers—poet Clark Coolidge in the Serpent Power, general-purpose bohemian Ken Weaver in the Fugs, and sibling-of-a-friend Maureen Tucker in the Velvets. Like the Fugs and the Serpent Power, the Velvets never hit very big, although like the Fugs they did sell a fair number of albums on sheer notoriety. Yet it now seems undeniable that they were one of the five great American rock groups of the sixties. Their music worked with Reed's words, not behind them; the two *united* were the group's "message." And eventually they inspired a whole style of minimal American rock, a style that rejects sentimentality for a rather thrilling visceral excitement. Patti Smith, who also appears in Anne Waldman's anthologies, consciously continues this tradition.

Because the minimal style is simple, its practitioners feel

hurt when it doesn't achieve instantaneous popularity. But it's hardly good old rock and roll. Unlike the heavy metal kids who are their closest relatives today, minimal groups have always eschewed self-pity and phony melodrama. They evoke factories, subways, perhaps warfare—all the essential brutalities of a mechanized existence—in a sharp rather than self-important way, providing none of the comfort of a staged confrontation in which a proxy teenager, arrayed in the garb and mien of a technocratic immortal, triumphs over his amplifiers. Minimal rock is too straitened to be comforting; it frightens people.

I obviously don't mean "minimal" the way an avant-garde composer like LaMonte Young or Philip Corner means it—more along the lines of "less is more." In this case, the maxim implies simplicity in an urban context and irony through understatement, all with populist overtones. Good old it's not. But though the melodies be spare, the rhythms metronomic, the chords repetitive, at its most severe this is still rock and roll, a popular form that is broadly accessible by the standards of a SoHo loft concert. Often the cerebral sting of the Velvets' ideas gets softened a little, especially with pop touches from the sixties—like the backup singing on "Redondo Beach" or the revelatory transition from Johnny's horses to "Land of a Thousand Dances." But the band's public pronouncements always suggested that something more was in store. Patti's fondness for both Smokey Robinson and Keith Richards is well documented; Lenny's production credits include Boston's poppish Sidewinders and the *Nuggets* compilation, which defines the original punk rock of a decade ago at its most anonymous and unabashed. But Lenny also christened heavy metal and has been known to say kind things about abstract shit all the way to the Art Ensemble of Chicago, while Patti's rock writin' included paeans to Edgar Winter as well as the Stones. Moreover, both have always been enamored of hippie-sounding notions about rock culture and the rock hero—Patti sometimes seems to prefer Jim Morrison to Bob Dylan. It is out of all these buts that the ponderous, postliterate, anarchically communal *Radio Ethiopia* was born.

Unlike almost all of my colleagues, whose reactions have ranged from liberated hostility to bitter dismay to affectionate tolerance, I am an active fan of Patti's second album. Too bad its one bad cut is its title cut and lasts eleven minutes, but I wouldn't be surprised if I reached a place where I even like that one. I've already gotten there with "Poppies" and "Pissing in a River," as I did long ago with the more pretentious stuff on *Horses*. If by bringing in producer Jack Douglas Patti intended to make an Aerosmith record, as some have suggested, then her intentions are irrelevant, as artists' intentions so often are. Personally, I believe she's smarter than that. She knows the Patti Smith Group isn't good enough to make an Aerosmith record, and she also knows it's capable of something better. It's priggish if not stupid to complain that *Radio Ethiopia*'s "four chords are not well played," as Ariel Swartley said in the *Boston Phoenix*. If they were executed with the precision of an Aerosmith, or a Black Sabbath, or a Chicago blues band, *then* they would not be well played.

For although there is no such thing as an unkempt heavy metal record—technocratic assurance, control over the amplifiers, is the soul of such music—unkempt rock and roll records have been helping people feel alive for twenty years. When it works, *Radio Ethiopia* delivers the charge of metal without the depressing predictability; its riff power has the human frailty of a band that is still learning to play. "Don't expect me to be perfect," Patti warned her full-house cult between skirmishes with the Palladium's sound system New Year's Eve. "You never know what our show's gonna be. But what it will be, even if it's fucked up"—and she fucked up herself momentarily, pausing vacantly as she tried to figure out just what to say next—"it'll be all we got."

At what turned out to be the concert of the year, Patti's "kids" looked to average out to college age—juniors and seniors rather than freshmen and sophomores. The crowd wasn't as loose as it might have been, but I liked its mix—a few arty types among the kind of intelligent rock and rollers who almost never come out in force anymore, a sprinkling of gay women among the hetero couples. When Patti came on, these sophisticates rushed the stage like Kiss fans, and eventually two women took off their tops and had to be physically dissuaded from dancing onstage. The climax was the true "My Generation," which began with Patti wrestling a guitar away from female roadie Andi Ostrowe and ended with Patti—joined, eventually, by Ivan Kral—performing the legendary guitar-smashing ritual that the Who gave up in the sixties. And that was only the ending. Because I'd never seen Patti's opening acts—Television (ex-lover) and John Cale (ex-producer)—out of a club setting, I assumed they'd have trouble projecting, but the Palladium theatricalized them. John Cale's obsessive riffs and yowls assumed dimensions unrealizable in a Bowery bar, and the transformation of Tom Verlaine into Tomi Hendrix is so near completion that the always indecipherable lyrics are now totally swallowed by the music of what was once an affectless song band of barely discernible instrumental attainment. That's what can happen to minimal rock—namely, increase.

When Patti first sought a label two years ago, her monetary ambitions were modest, but she demanded the absolute creative autonomy that new artists never even seem to care about anymore. This hippie quirk has meant, for instance, that Patti has run her own ad campaigns—she herself came up with the wonderful line, "3 chord rock merged with the power of the word." It has also meant that she exerts a producer's control over her records no matter who she calls in to advise her. The title cut on *Radio Ethiopia,* a white-noise extravaganza in which Patti yowls incomprehensibly and plays a guitar at Lenny Kaye, who yowls incomprehensibly on his guitar, really isn't Jack Douglas's kind of thing.

I'm a sucker for the idea I perceive in "Radio Ethiopia," a rock version of the communal amateur avant-gardism encouraged by the likes of jazzman Marion Brown. And it works acceptably on stage, where Lenny's delight in his own presence gets everybody through a lot of questionable music. But I've never found Marion Brown listenable, and I guess I'd rather see the "Radio Ethiopia" idea than play it on my stereo. The same does not go, however, for the other dubious artistic freedom on the LP, the swear words. In the wake of "My Generation" 's "We don't want this fucking shit" (on the B side of "Gloria"), Arista tried to convince the band to retitle *Radio Ethiopia*'s "Pissing in a River" and shuffle the words into something like (really) "sipping in a river," but Patti was adamant. It's almost as if her accommodations to radio, for that is how she understands the LP's heavy tendencies, had to be balanced by a blow for free speech, although I seem to recall her protesting about whether "the people" own the radio stations at her moderately disastrous Avery Fisher Hall gig last March. At the Palladium, we all received a flier offering Patti's side of the story: "We Want The Radio And We Want It Now." Perfect.

This crusade exemplifies the People's Park fallacy, in which one's allies, the members of one's cult, are confused with "the people." But the people are different from you and me—there's more of 'em. Broad-based rock-and roll alliances (Peter Frampton's, say) have rarely been of much use for anything as practical as a crusade, but I'm willing (even eager) to suspend my disbelief. The larger question is whether Patti can gather such an alliance. She appears to have the makings in New York, but not nationwide, primarily because her music is harder to digest than she is prepared to admit. Insofar as she can be said to be censored, it is because program directors now regard her as more trouble than she's worth and are faced with no public outcry to the contrary.

And yet wouldn't it be wonderful if she stuck at it and won? The swear-words-on-the-radio issue isn't as important as Patti thinks, but it isn't "boring" or "trivial" either. The airwaves really ought to belong to "the people," and the vast preponderance of those who listen to FM stations like WNEW or WBCN would welcome or at least tolerate a degree of linguistic freedom that the FCC, the owners, and the advertisers forbid. To pretend that this bucket in the ocean of our cultural impotence is boring or trivial is to construct one more defense against Patti's challenge. She dares us not to settle into our lives. She dares us to keep trying for what we want as well as what we need.

Patti Smith is a utopian romantic whose socioeconomic understanding is so simplistic that she can tell a Hungerthon that rock and roll power will feed Ethiopia; she is an autonomous woman who can cast herself cheerfully as a rapist in one poem and begin another: "female. feel male. Ever since I felt the need to/choose I'd choose male." Clearly, her line is not calculated to appeal to the politicos and radical feminists who actually live up to her challenge; it can also be counted on to turn off most intelligent, settled adults, by which I mean people pushing Patti's age—thirty. But Patti won't miss those uptights—she wants the kids. Her sense of humanity's potential is expressed most often in the dreamscape images of heavy rock: sex-and-violence, drugs, apocalypse, space travel. She theorizes that rock and roll is "the highest and most universal form of expression since the lost tongue (time: pre-Babel)." She believes that the "neo-artist" is "the nigger of the universe." In short, she would appear to be full of shit.

Well, so did Rimbaud, who, while no longer dominating Patti's cosmology, continues to exemplify her artist hero. I say artist hero, not artist, partly to avoid the absurdity of comparing poetry. But observers of the world of poetry inform me that some of the censure poets heap on her verse can be attributed to envy, and I suspect the same of the rock critics. As a reader who reveres Whitman, Yeats, and Williams and whose tastes in contemporary poetry—at those rare times when I have wanted to read it—have run to Creeley, Wieners, Padgett, Denby, I've found most of Patti's published work likable and some of it remarkable; *Seventh Heaven*'s "judith" strikes me as, well, a great poem, and one great poem is a lot. Still, I'll go along with the poet who told me he liked her wit and quickness but found her work unfinished. Patti reports that she works hard, tediously hard, on most of what she writes. But if it didn't seem unfinished at the end, like her rock and roll, then it wouldn't do what she clearly wants it to do.

In her search for a "universal form of expression," Patti rejects the whole idea of the avant-garde. Crowing about how Bobby Neuwirth and Eric Andersen encouraged her to write without ever mentioning Frank O'Hara, she obviously doesn't want to be associated with the avant-garde's limitations. But this in itself is a vanguard position that places her firmly where she belongs—in the camp of anarchists like Jarry or Tzara, as opposed to the unofficial academy of formalists like Gide or Mondrian. Avant-garde anarchists have always been fascinated by popular imagery and energy, which they have attempted to harness to both satirical and insurrectionary ends. The pop ambitions of this deliberately barbaric sometime poet and her glorified garage band are her version of the formal adventurousness that animates all artistic change.

One poet I spoke to posited rather icily that Patti reads Rimbaud in translation. This is more or less the case—and whether monists of the work of art like it or not, I bet it would be fine with Rimbaud. For although her verse may strive (with fair success) for a certain unrefined *alchimie du verbe,* it is Rimbaud the historical celebrity Patti Smith emulates—the hooligan *voyant,* the artist as troublemaker. Even the formal similarities—such as Patti's exploitation of the cruder usages of rock and roll, which disturb elitists much as Rimbaud's youthful vulgarisms did—are in this mold. If Patti isn't the artist Rimbaud was, she can compete with him as an art hero. Rimbaud, after all, would appear to have quit poetry not to make up for his season in hell but simply because he couldn't find an audience. That has not been Patti's problem.

One understands that even the most attractive art hero must actually produce some art, lest she be mistaken for Zsa Zsa Gabor, and that it is appropriate to scrutinize this art critically. Well, here is one critic who values it highly. Settled, analytic adult that I am, I don't have much use for its ideational "message," for the specific shamanisms it espouses—astral projection, Rastafarianism, whatever. But I'm not so settled that I altogether disbelieve in magic— the magic power of words or the mysterious authority of an assembly of theoretically unconnected human beings—and I find that at pivotal moments Patti quickens such magic for me.

The secret of her method is her unpredictability. To a degree this is assured by the overly ordinary technical accomplishments of her musicians, but even her intermittent reliance on shtick and irritating tendency to dip into onstage fallow periods help it along by rendering those moments of uncanny inspiration all the more vivid and unmistakable. Her comedic gift is so metaphysical, so protean, that sometimes her musings and one-liners, or even her physical attitudes as she sings, will end up meaning more than whatever big-beat epiphanies she achieves. But when she's at her best, the jokes become part of the mix, adding an essential note of real-world irony to the otherworldly possibility. "In addition to all the astral stuff," she boasts, "I'd do anything for a laugh." Thus she is forever set apart from the foolish run of rock shaman-politicians, especially Jim Morrison.

Forget Morrison, assign Jimi Hendrix's musical magic to another category, and declare Patti Smith the first credible rock shaman, the one intelligent holdout/throwback in a music whose mystics all pretend to have IQs of ninety. Because spontaneity is part of the way she conjures, she is essentially a live artist, but through the miracle of phonographic recording conveys a worthy facsimile of what she does in permanent, easy-to-distribute form. I don't equate these records with Rimbaud's poetry or Gide's fiction or Mondrian's paintings, although without benefit of historical perspective I certainly do value them at least as much as the works of Jarry or Tzara, both of whom survive more as outrageous artistic personages, historical celebrities. Since popular outreach is Patti's formal adventure, I might value what she does even more if I thought she could be more than a cult figure and remain her unpredictable, provocative self, an even tougher problem. But in a world where cult members can number half a million and mass audiences must be five or ten times that big, I don't. If you like, you can believe that her formal failure bespeaks her incompetence. I think it's a credit to her ambition, the hard-to-digest ugliness and self-contradiction of what she tries to do.

Now Patti must live with that shortfall, aim for her half million or three hundred fifty thousand as if they were worth all her will, and go on. Clearly she's determined to survive. She works hard; she's committed to touring although it wears her out; she tries to be punctual and cooperative. Bless Clive Davis's pretensions and hope that the two of them can play Patti's long tether out to the end and then cut it cleanly. Patti talks in terms of five years or maybe less. As a retired rock cult figure she'd make a great Zsa Zsa Gabor, only with real books. I can just hear the savants of 1982 dismissing her writing and undervaluing her shtick. But me and the rest of her cult, we'll just turn on the tube and get zapped.

1977

The Clash See America Second

N'I like to be in Africa
A beatin' on the final drum
N'I like to be in USSR
Making sure these things will come
N'I like to be in USA
Pretending that the wars are done
N'I like to be in Europa
Saying goodbye to everyone
                    —"Guns on the Roof"

'Course we got a manager
And though he ain't the Mafia
A contract is a contract
When they got 'em out on yer
                    —"All the Young Punks"

At five P.M. February 16, 1979, the first Chinese troops were advancing across the Vietnamese border, but in my ignorance all I was worried about was whether ice and snow would stay the Clash's equipment truck in the swift completion of its appointed round. From her command module at Cambridge's Howard Johnson Motor Lodge, manager Caroline Coon advised faith tempered by realism, so half an hour after the seven o'clock showtime I was inside the Harvard Square Theater, an eighteen-hundred seater that astonished promoter Don Law by selling out in an hour for an English band that was on only one commercial Boston radio station. I'm told every new wave band in the city was on hand, a hundred tickets right there, but even more numerous than punk types were short-haired, unstoned-looking (I said looking) versions of the kind of high-IQ fan Bonnie Raitt gets. This was a crowd that liked to read about music—I had my own moment of astonishment when someone asked for my autograph. But it was also a crowd that liked to listen—kids who hadn't been born when Bo Diddley first recorded recognized his beat as well as his name. In the row behind me sat Boston's pioneering new wave disc jockey, a mild young man with pink hair named Oedipus. A few hours before, he and several others had been fired from the only commercial Boston station—one of three major FM outlets in the USA—that was playing the Clash, but few in the audience knew it yet. There was that feeling in the air that we used to call good vibes, only the anticipation was sharper, the kilowatt potential more focused.

Sound check was just ending as I arrived. Recorded music, all titles announced, began with the Sex Pistols' "Anarchy in the U.K.," the Monkees' "Steppin' Stone," and reggae by Dillinger. At around eight the local opener, two girls and two boys called the Rentals, kicked off hard, dragged into some arty slow stuff, and revved back up to a climax entitled "Gertrude Stein": "Coca-Cola Coca-Cola/Pepsi-Cola Pepsi-Cola/Orange soda orange soda." Their set was not enhanced when eight Cambridge cops and a platoon of Don Law's beefy redshirts went after two punky nuisances who'd been hitting on people as if they'd read how in an old *NME,* ejecting them with the kind of enthusiasm we used to call brutality. After a literally brief intermission, Bo Diddley and an all-black trio surprised me pleasantly by rolling the audience down some funky grooves, easy blues lopes as well as variations on Bo's signature shuffle.

Less than thirty minutes later, the Coasters' "Riot in Cell Block Number Nine" blared out of the P.A. as the crew lowered a backdrop of stitched-together flags and the band advanced from the wings. Joe Strummer came on denimy, still bezippered and fatigued, but Paul Simonon's slash-necked red uniform was even more glamour-boy than the fishnet item I'd seen him wear in Leeds sixteen months before, while Mick Jones, his turquoise shirt unbuttoned most of the way down and turned up at the collar, seemed to have achieved most of the evolution from seventies to fifties punk—all of the Clash had slicked-back hair, but Mick's was almost d.a.-length, with sly teddy-boy overtones. Glaring riot lights searched out these details as the musicians paced the stage. Then Strummer and Jones sheared into the chords of "I'm So Bored With the U.S.A." and we were off.

No one has ever made rock and roll as intense as the Clash is right now—not Little Richard or Jerry Lee Lewis, not the early Beatles or the middle Stones or the inspired James Brown or the preoperatic Who, not Hendrix or Led Zep, not the MC-5 or the Stooges, not the Dolls or the Pistols or the Ramones. On a brute physical level, their combination of volume and tempo is unrivaled. Anybody with capital can turn up the amps, of course—the hard part, as an impressed Stanley Crouch theorized after the band's Palladium appearance, is for the musicians to turn themselves up even higher, something not even Robert Plant and Jimmy Page ever try for more than a minute or two. And fast heroes from Little Richard to the Dolls and beyond have known when to slow down, resorting to the change-of-pace much more readily than the Clash, whose dip into "Stay Free" and a speedy "Police and Thieves" induced no one downstairs at either concert I attended to sit, although by then fatigue had dropped a few. Even the Ramones do ballads and medium-tempo rockers, and the Ramones' formalist poses enable them to generate exhilarating music with almost no expenditure of interpretive emotion, while the Clash's dense and expansive song structures, freer stagecraft, and urgent verbal messages demand interpretation. For the Clash, every concert is an athletic challenge far out on the shoals of expressionism, whence few new wavers return without a mouthful of brine.

And as usual, Joe Strummer seemed to be spitting something out. But his muttered imprecations about orchestra pits and Harvard City Rockers were part of the fun, and if his largely incomprehensible intro to the obscure "Capital Radio"—only the first few words, "Complaint time, complaint time," emerged loud and clear from between his stumpy teeth—in fact referred to Oedipus, nobody (including Oedipus) let it get him or her down. Words, wonderful as they may have been, weren't the point. Clearly, these ticket-buyers were among the fifty-thousand-plus purchasers of the U.S. pressing of *Give 'Em Enough Rope,* on CBS's Epic label, and the almost fifty thousand who have made *The Clash,* on English CBS, the largest-selling import album ever in this country. Familiar with the five singles as well, they probably knew half the words by heart, which is all you can expect without crib sheets. But what gave the event its drama wasn't just the singalong cheers and outcries—"Guns guns shaking in terror/Guns guns killing in error"; "This is the city of the dead"; "Need a little jolt of electrical shocker"; "Clang clang go the jail guitar doors"—or the clamorous, life-giving onrush of the music. It was the natural theatrical force of Strummer himself, not so much exhorting the audience directly as alerting it to the symbolic world it shared with him. In his most characteristic move—which he can ease with a modified buck-and-wing or heighten by collapsing toward the floor—his shoulders hunch, his eyes narrow and peer upward, and his finger points as if bombs have just darkened the ceiling. His concentration is awesome. Even during instrumental breaks or the songs Jones sings, he is a fierce presence, scowling while he thrashes out his rhythm part or communing with drummer Topper Headon as if to get closer to the god of beats-per-minute.

On our side of the P.A., this was an ecstatic experience. But behind the fucked-up monitors, trying to make sense of the guitar Mick had borrowed after finally demolishing his decrepit '52 Les Paul, the band felt they were putting out a lousy show, and they brooded together as press and friends abided first in the auditorium and then backstage. Eventually Mick sauntered out and took me aside for a spliff. The last time we'd seen each other, in Max's last fall, we'd discussed fascism. This time Mick regaled me with a tale of love, hate, and Les Paul. "It was older than I am," he kept saying, and it had survived a broken neck at the hands of a stoned-hippie Dutch theater manager, but the night before, in Washington, after going out of tune throughout the tour—a friend who'd caught the band's U.S. debut in Berkeley complained about just that—it had started giving him shocks, one or two per song. So Mick, figuring one of them had to go, smashed the thing to bits; his first stop in Manhattan would be 48th Street. Telling me about it cheered him up. I asked after his mum, and learned she was flying in from Ironwood, Michigan, to see her boy play for the first time the next night. He'd be (1) breaking in a new guitar (2) at the Palladium (3) for his mother. Pressure drop.

There was a lull during which I wished Oedipus luck in what he regarded as a union-busting dispute. Then, suddenly, the whole Clash entourage was trooping off to the tour bus, so quickly that the seven minutes it took me to get my stuff from a nearby parking lot almost weren't enough. I was last aboard, with three of the Clash already behind closed doors in the bunk section. Only Topper Headon remained in the bow. I later learned that he'd suggested shoving off without me if I was going to be fucking late.

"Hello, I'm Bob Christgau," I said, sticking out my hand.

"Hello, I'm rude," said Topper Headon.

In England, the Clash are now much more than the great punk inheritors—they're a major pop group, complete with an album that entered the charts at number two and a bit of backlash in the only trade press anywhere that regularly accuses artists of undue commercialism. Not that that's the Clash's crime, exactly—it's more their failure to resolve contradictions that only they were brazen enough to confront forcefully in the first place. Like everyone else, they watched in frustration as punk disintegrated into faddish sectarianism. Despite their commitment to Rock Against Racism, their pilgrimage to Jamaica was summed up in a song about "a place where every white face/is an invitation to robbery." And worst, in a time of rampant nationalism in British music they softened on America. The producer of their second album ended up Sandy Pearlman, American ex-rock critic of Blue Oyster Cult fame (and Pavlov's Dog infamy), apparently nominated by Epic. While recording they split with manager Bernard Rhodes, a former used-car salesman whose hostile, obscurantist style—like that of his mentor, Malcolm McLaren—made it seem that he'd just as soon tour Patagonia as Pennsylvania. Then Jones and Strummer spent weeks mixing with Pearlman in San Francisco, and dallied in New York as well.

No one misses Rhodes, now etching himself on musical memory the way Mike Appel did with Bruce Springsteen—in court. New manager Caroline Coon has been close to the band personally as Paul Simonon's (somewhat) regular companion, but her credentials are far more substantial. She was both head of a hippie-era legal services program for drug arrestees and one of the first rock journalists to lay out the standard class analysis of punk. In short, her radicalism would seem to have deeper roots in a lived life than that of Rhodes, who has attacked the band's American overtures bitterly. Yet she clearly agrees with her group that American rock and roll is barely breathing and that no one is better qualified to resuscitate it than the best rock and roll band in the world. Not surprisingly, it was Coon the administrator, rather than Coon the ideologue, who was running what they called the Pearl Harbour Tour.

Sitting across from me in Waylon Jennings's plush outlaw bus, rented out of Nashville for the duration, Coon began to complain—for the first time in public, she insisted—about Epic. This was no shock. The parent company has always seemed quite unimpressed with English CBS's plum. After rejecting the band's magnificent debut album, first on the product-think grounds of sound quality and then because it had already sold so much as an import, Epic shilly-shallied for a long time with *Give 'Em Enough Rope*'s tour support. The corporate feeling is that the Clash will cost too much to break. The same money—between fifty and seventy grand for this abbreviated swing through presold locations (every venue was full), with thirty or so covering actual travel debits and the rest going into auxiliary promotion—could have been invested in a more established band, say a pretty good one like Cheap Trick, with a surer payback in additional units sold. Or it could be used to hype predictable new hard rock product like Trillion or the Fabulous Poodles.

Not that Coon was critiquing such bottom-line reductionism. Her beefs were more about day-to-day cash flow, and if she hasn't yet convinced Epic that these aren't musicians whose great dream in life is to puke on their grandmothers, she'd do well to take her wares elsewhere. Coast-to-coast by bus with one plane hop from Oklahoma City to Cleveland, eight appearances in seven cities in fifteen days, is a cruel grind. But the band stayed up, the crew works faster than any I've waited for in years, and even the snow-delayed Cambridge show went smoothly. I've heard a few reports of blown interviews, and the press doesn't seem to have made press conferences in California very interesting, but the group definitely made a sweeter impression than it used to when Rhodes was in there pitching. These were decent lads who knew what they were about. I've never encountered a more efficient tour.

I say this as someone who proceeded to spend over eleven hours en route to Manhattan. The first delay came when the driver spent an unaccountable stretch of time out of the bus. Eventually it developed that his bags had been stolen, a disclosure that stopped all conversation and so alarmed Headon, who'd suffered a similar loss on the fall tour, that he was soon whispering to Coon that maybe the few dollars he'd won playing cards could go to the driver. Still feeling Jones's spliff, I offered (over Coon's protestations) to put up ten bucks myself before discovering that I had only a five, four ones, and some twenties. Headon bid valiantly for twenty, got nine, and disappeared into the back, returning fifteen minutes later with a collection of about eighty dollars for somebody who probably cleared more in a week than any of them.

At around two, Jones and Strummer came forward for take-out food, and shortly after the fried egg and American cheese sandwiches, Headon set off a firecracker that scared the shit out of Jones. Both Headon and Strummer seemed genuinely concerned about this, and spent some time comforting their mate, patting his thigh and apologizing with surprising fervor. Then Jones and Strummer returned to the bunks and Headon, who'd been poking fun at my note-taking, told me how at fourteen he'd earned five pounds a night in trad bands around Dover, unable to leave the stage for a piss because he was underage. After years of tae kwan do his slight body was all sinew. His great dream in life was to break fifteen sticks, two skins, and a frame in one night without making a mistake. Only Billy Cobham, Headon told me, has ever broken a frame. Cobham, of course, is built like a fullback.

Soon the bus halted again, this time for real—the brake linings had frozen. A few of us sat around a restaurant until six, when I suggested to Strummer that he'd better get some sleep. There was room in back for me—Bo Diddley finds bunks confining and spent the night in a big corner seat—and I sacked out till eleven. When I got up, I found the following additions to the cursory jottings in my notebook:

Skiddley Daddeley
Hamster Fur
Webbed Feet
473 miles—Texas
Long Hair—Beards
Sid Vicious over . . .
Manhattan skyline.

It was not until four o'clock, back in my apartment, that I learned—from a friend, by telephone—that China had invaded Vietnam. As it happened, my wife and I had just been getting ready to make love; instead, we tuned to WINS and sat on the bed, holding hands and talking about the end of the world. Apocalyptic melodrama, I know—the world is never going to end. Of course not. But that was how it struck us at the time. And as the radio wound around to local news I was possessed by the need to get up and put on *Give 'Em Enough Rope,* the side that begins with "Guns on the Roof." I put it on loud. It made me feel better.

Like almost all Clash fans, I was a little disappointed in the follow-up to *The Clash,* which (tinny sound be damned) may well be the greatest rock and roll album ever recorded. I mean, ordinarily I seek verbal wisdom in books—what rock "poetry" really involves is slogans and images and epigrams, or else settings that transfigure ideas and emotions sorely in need of some transfiguration. But on *The Clash,* the words did more than specify the tremendous force (and subtler cleverness and difficulty) of compelling music. They made you think all by themselves. "The truth is only known by gutter snipes," Joe Strummer asserted in "Garageland," and although the street roots of this rebellious diplomat's son turned out to be hippie-squatter rather than dole-queue, his gutter truths were convincing and gratifying. The working-class youths he and Jones imagined didn't let their grim analysis get them down. Simultaneously (even clashingly) truculent and cheerful, cynical and fraternal, they refused to become immobilized; their actions may have struck more experienced (and privileged) well-wishers as primitive—"If someone locks me out I kick my way back in"—but at least they were actions. Here at last was art with access to a contemporary, white, English-speaking proletarian culture. It posited kids whose very determination to survive took guts and whose unwillingness to give up the idea of victory was positively heroic.

On *Give 'Em Enough Rope* this generous vision was stymied by perplexities all too familiar to experienced well-wishers. This major (and privileged) pop group sounded as wearied by the failure of solidarity, the persistence of racial conflict, the facelessness of violence, and the ineluctability of capital as some bunch of tenured Marxists, and I wasn't ready to settle—they'd amazed me by coming up with a new beginning, and just like my English colleagues I wanted them to amaze me again by carrying it through. But the familiar contradictions followed upon the invigorating gutter truths for excellent reason—they were truths as well. And at a time when two supposedly communist nations were girding up to ravage each other (not to mention me), I found that the way *Give 'Em Enough Rope* transfigured its old ideas and emotions was useful in a way I hadn't felt much need of before. The music channeled my fear into anger and lent me the spirit to do what I had to do. Which was go to another Clash concert, and if you weren't there I'm sorry. As Alan Platt put it in *The SoHo Weekly News:* "It would be a pity if the impending nuclear holocaust prevented you from seeing this band."

I found the vibes at the Palladium inauspicious, not because of potential H-bomb but because the edge of anticipation was dulled by curiosity-seekers—bizzers, celebs, plain old rock and rollers. Opening were the Cramps, who are finally achieving the contemptuous rigidity they have sought so faithfully for so long; I'm glad the Clash tried to hire local bands with women in them, and would suggest the Erasers, Nervus Rex, or even DNA next time. Bo Diddley was backed by an intriguing combo—four black men and a white woman guitarist—but without help from the show-mes in the audience couldn't make it jell. Yet from the moment the Clash came on the crowd was on its feet, and that this was only to be expected says a lot in itself. Perhaps heightened expectations were why the seen-it-all audience was still holding back a little at the encore of a performance the musicians themselves thought the best of the tour. That was when Strummer announced (quite undefensively, I thought) that New York was as tough as London. Shortly thereafter the Clash broke into a brief raveup on "London's Burning" that scorched New York good. I've run across those who were basically unmoved. But I've heard stuff like "swept away," "almost transcendent," "left me slack-jawed" from dozens of others.

Those not too familiar with the band were transfixed by Strummer, but the more knowledgeable raved about Jones, who had a hell of a night. In Cambridge his spare leads had worked almost subliminally, skimming the edges, but at the Palladium he cut through the tumult, intensifying both the concentration and the canny disarray of the music with his clangorous counter-statements. He also sang as if his mother might be listening, getting through the tricky "Stay Free"—a greeting to a mate out of jail that translates the band's new political wariness into personal warmth—without a clinker. What impressed me about Strummer was how his strumming drove the band, freeing Simonon's bass for the military embellishments he favors and allowing Headon the occasional Jamaican accent. Not that there's too much of that yet. These boys force the rhythm for sure.

I'd hoped the Clash would commemorate the onset of World War III with a propagandistic flourish, but it could almost have been any rock gig that happened to feature lines about wealth distribution and letter bombs. When Mick came center stage to sing "Hate and War"—"An' if I close my eyes they will not go away/ You have to deal with it/It is the currency"—he mentioned that the song had special meaning on the day China invaded Vietnam. And that was how he dealt with it. But after the concert, in a dressing room crammed with paparazzi bait, he flourished a paraphrase of the old Tempts' song: "If it's war that you're running from," he sang without a clinker, "There's no hiding place." Then he cited Nostradamus, not my idea of a reliable source, and offered his own prediction: "I figure they'll pick off two or three cities by the end of the year. Or do you think I'm doomsayer-mongering? Am I some kind of *nihilist,* Christgau?"

Obviously, people who go out and do what they have to do with so much determination aren't nihilists. A harder-line politico than me might even suspect they're getting too goddamn constructive. Do they want to turn into the Who or something? Well, in 1979 terms, maybe they do. This band revives insurrectionary international consciousness as a rock dream. And puny as any rock dream may seem in the face of World War III, that one is a long way from where we are. Epic apologists talk about how the Clash start out from "below ground zero" after all the punk stuff, but in fact the band has a deeper hole to deal with—the one in which the music biz, records and radio both, hoped to bury the kind of rock and roll that is an abrasive and/or inspirational force in people's lives.

I'm a skeptic, but I find it hard to believe that a band this good isn't going to dig its way out. Maybe they can even get to the place Strummer described a few months ago in London's *Time Out:* "All we want to achieve is an atmosphere where things can happen. We want to keep the spirit of the free world. We want to keep out that safe, soapy slush that comes out of the radio . . . All we've got is a few guitars, amps, and drums. That's our weaponry."

What else can a poor boy do? Lots of things. But these particular poor boys have their work cut out for them.

1979

The Great Punk Dandy at the Peppermint Lounge: Richard Hell

It was the only area appearance of rock bohemia's legendary symbol, but on June 25 the spanking-new downtown Pep was crowded with refugees from 45th Street—rock and roll youth out to get laid, lighter on hitters than the Ritz, but nowhere near as effete as Danceteria or as schlumpy-collegiate as Irving Plaza or CBGB. The one familiar face I spotted was that of Terry Ork, Richard Hell's original impresario. At two Hell came on with his latest band, who aren't called the Voidoids even though they feature Ivan Julian and aren't called the Outsets even though that's their name, delivering a brief intro in his patented kindergartner-on-the-nod drawl: "Hello ladies and gents—we were children once." Then they launched into "Love Comes in Spurts," the song Hell chose to kick off his debut album almost five years ago. As the set rocked on I noticed a few ravaged old-timers observing from the sidelines. I also ran into Giorgio Gomelski, the Rolling Stones' original impresario, who dubbed Hell "a symbol of elegance," spraying me with saliva as he did so.

As we collegiate schlumps often forget, it's not impossible to symbolize bohemia and elegance simultaneously (cf. Walter Benjamin on the flaneur). But though Hell apparently values his red top, which he wears on the cover of his follow-up album, it proved less noteworthy than the black leather and ripped T-shirts out of which he constructed the avant-punk antidandy back when Malcolm McLaren was strictly a haberdasher. Hell put on a strong show, but he made no waves in a casually dressed-up audience to which he related only as the professional entertainer he's never much wanted to be. Once he defined, and I quote, a blank generation; now he disparages, and I quote again, the lowest common denominator. Over a five-year haul, symbolizing bohemia can get to be depressing work.

At the time of *Blank Generation,* Hell really was the quintessential avant-punk. With no more irony than was meet, he presented his nihilistic narcissism not as youthful hijinks but as a full-fledged philosophy/aesthetic, and though he never quite put his heart into proselytizing, he was perfectly willing to go along with impresarios who considered his stance commercial dynamite—and to con others when the money ran out. Nor was he merely purveying a stance. Though it was the musicianship of Bob Quine—a much denser, choppier, and more nerve-wracking player than his romantic rival, former Hell associate Tom Verlaine—that made the Voidoids the most original and accomplished band of the CBGB era, Quine was and is a sideman, worth hearing in any context but lacking the visionary oomph to create one. The band was Hell's, and that it embraced former Foundation Ivan Julian, whose slashing leads I've misidentified more than once as Quine in a warm mood, and future Ramone Marc Bell, a converted heavy metal kid of surpassingly simple needs, says a great deal for his ambition and his outreach. That it sold bubkes, of course, may say just as much for his laziness and his hubris. But the problem didn't begin, or end, with Hell. The impresarios were just plain wrong.

So *Blank Generation* stands off in its own corner of the boho cosmos as the ultimate CBGB cult record. It had no apparent antecedents, and until *Destiny Street* was finally released by Marty Thau, the New York Dolls' original impresario, its only descendant was Lester Bangs's *Jook Savages on the Brazos.* If the new album feels just a little tired despite its undeniable attractions, it's not because Hell's musical concepts have been lowest-common-denominatored. With Material's Fred Maher replacing Bell and postpunk engineer (Y Pants) and bandleader (China Shop) Naux on second guitar, it's fuller and jazzier than *Blank Generation* without any loss of concision or toon appeal. Although producer Alan Betrock is a notorious pop addict, it was Nick Lowe who added ooh-ooh backups and cleanly articulated thematic solos to "The

Kid With the Replaceable Head," back when Jake Riviera was doing time as Hell's impresario; the version Betrock oversaw is chock full and coming apart, a real New York rocker. What's changed is Hell's head. He's matured, as they say, and I'm not sure it suits him.

The problem begins with the two theme cuts—the title parable, a vamp-with-talkover in which nostalgia and ambition are rejected in favor of the good old here-and-now, and "Time," in which an inescapable medium-tempo melody is attached to lines like "Only time can write a song that's really really real." Both are grabbers, and both soon let go, as music and poetry respectively. Elsewhere, the bohemian symbol's destiny seems bitter indeed, as a glance back at *Blank Generation* makes clear. "Lowest Common Denominator" is the only all-out putdown, but where "Liars Beware" reviled power brokers, Hell is going after scenemakers this time, no doubt the hitters and collegiate schlumps who've ruined his favorite hangout and orgiast's dream. In "Down at the Rock and Roll Club," "sexy love" was communitarian "fun," but now he prefers to "get all decivilized" at a "dropout disco" that sounds more like some after-hours hideaway than the Peppermint Lounge. In fact, all the old escapes have lost their charm. "Ignore That Door," a throwaway raveup that's the most sheerly fun thing on the record, opposes scag as unambivalently (vaguely but unmistakably) as "New Pleasure" praises it, and twice Hell complains of feeling "alone." So where "The Plan" and "Betrayal Takes Two" equated private sex with Faustian sin, these days the poete maudit manqué is looking for love that doesn't come in spurts. "Staring in Her Eyes" explicitly surrenders his narcissistic nihilism (and his "looking around") to achieve the bliss described in the title, which sure as shooting he takes to an unhealthy extreme: "Stare like a corpse in each's eyes/Till you never want to come alive and rise."

Admittedly, the song is affecting even at that, its lyricism intensified, as so often with Hell, by the yearning inexactitude with which he pursues its melody. And I sympathize in principle with Hell's new head, as you probably do. I just don't feel he has his heart in it. "Betrayal Takes Two" is a genuinely evil song, a seducer's alibi worthy of Kierkegaard before Christ, while "Staring in Her Eyes" is sweetly creepy at best—a little easier to sell, perhaps, and a real truth for the chastened Hell, but with less to express and hence less to tell us. And no matter what Marty Thau thinks, it won't be all that easy to sell. Hell might conceivably follow in the footsteps of David Johansen, the New York Dolls original, who now makes a decent living as a legend, but there's a big difference between the two—Hell's aversion to the lowest common denominator. He's just not a professional entertainer, and though his regrets over the multiplication and fractionalization of rock bohemia may be justified, his potential audience is no blank generation. Yet it was with that anthem that Hell tried to climax his show. It went over all right, of course—it's a good song. But the audience remained rock and roll youth out to get laid, and the Pep didn't look any more like a dropout disco when he was through.

1982

Pere Ubu's Right to Choose

Long ago and far away, David Thomas dubbed himself Crocus Behemoth, which sums up the persona and conceit—half Biblical monster, half shy harbinger of spring—that looms over Pere Ubu. Their riffs and rhythms scornful of boogie slack, Ubu was the flagship band of Ohio avant-punk, which soon funneled Devo, Anton Fier, and many other "new wavers" into the rock machine. Harsh, weird, and serious by seventies standards, they were also palpably playful and humane—even on their two urban-wasteland classics, 1978's *The Modern Dance* and 1979's *Dub Housing,* which begins "I've got these arms and legs that flip flop flip" and concludes the same thought with a jolly "Boy that sounds swell." It is Thomas's amused head voice and imperiously friendly organizing intelligence that defines the four Ubu discs on *Terminal Drive,* Geffen's uncommonly essential if typically excessive 1975–1982 reissue. And it was Thomas who conceived the jumble of Ubu-related arcana on the fifth.

Rather than the disinterested local best-of some civic-minded Clevelander should compile, the non-Ubu disc merely establishes that before 1975, the Ubu clan favor a raw rock and roll that has evolved decisively toward art-rock by 1980, when Thomas was masterminding the literary-cum-sonic fantasias *The Art of Walking* and *Song of the Bailing Man.* This less than foreordained development—his fellow seventies pioneers generally matured along rhythmic lines—made Ubu unique. Those who moan that the departure of mythic doomed songpoet Peter Laughner cost America its greatest punk band ignore both Laughner's commitment to Dylanism and his bandmates' commitment to musicianship, with synthmaster Allen Ravenstine and ubiquitous bassist Tony Maimone the conspicuous virtuosos in a highly proficient lineup. While "Final Solution" may be as convincing a punk anthem as "Blank Generation," its controlled tempos and complex dissonances set Ubu well apart from the scrawnier Voidoids, who were very much virtuosos by CBGB standards.

So what have we here? If "art-rock" seems insulting, you can say they're a striking "rock" band whose unminimalist forays into headlong desperation are one ploy among many. But I direct your attention to Thomas's penchant for wandering recitative, to the tedious instrumental atmospheres on the 1980–1982 disc, to the synthesizer itself. If Ravenstine's unprecedented animal and machinery impressions anticipate the sampler rather than emulating nineteenth-century warhorses a la ELP and Kansas, well, nobody ever said these guys were stupid. They're a *good* art-rock band, concrete and homely, as American as Captain Beefheart without the blues. The crucial difference is that Don Van Vliet grew up a desert rat where Thomas is a middle-class boy from the Rust Belt, eccentric but relatively urbane. A scold and a clown with a weakness for whimsy and the moral conviction of a Jehovah's Witness who never abandoned the faith of his father, Thomas no longer sounds angry, not even when he's shrieking or squealing the Laughner tirade "Life Stinks." In retrospect, he sounds as if he's playing at anger, trying it on with the bemused affability of a very bright guy casting about for a worldview nobody will say is stupid. True punks are possessed by existential rage. Even when he's flailing, the closest Thomas can come is existential indignation.

Still, the 1978 and 1981 concerts that compose disc four rock hard enough to leave the impression that Thomas's positive thinking doesn't emanate from the ether. Like Beefheart, he proved himself too willing to muck about in ecology ("Birdies"? "Petrified"?), but at least he likes his nature tame, and unlike Beefheart he's no misanthrope. If you decide that choosing life is the smartest worldview of all, as Thomas did by late 1979, a few touches of civilized wisdom help make the truism more interesting. But *Terminal Drive* proves once again that the positive thinker is never more interesting than when he's still figuring out where the life he's destined to choose will lead.

1996

Forever Rotten: The Sex Pistols

The deal was, if I would interview this band I like named Fluffy for *Spin,* their label would transport me to London, where Fluffy was opening for the Sex Pistols at a place called Finsbury Park. Now, as someone whose impulse was to skip the Pistols' revolting reunion even if John Lydon rang me up and begged, I shouldn't have been tempted by this offer. But I was—not because Iggy would be there too, not because after twenty-nine years as a rock critic it was about time I got to weekend in London, but because . . . well, because the perversity of the concept appealed to me. What better reason to catch the motherfuckers than that they were sharing a bill with Fluffy? So at the last minute I decided to take a flier.

Of the many things I didn't know about this gig going in, two loom large. No one could have comprehended that England would upset Spain in the European football championships the day before. But the other I should have had a bead on: Finsbury Park is where John Lydon grew up. In the standard texts—Fred and Judy Vermorel, Greil Marcus, even Jon Savage—little or nothing is made of this. The emphasis is on Lydon's rootlessness, a radical alienation that Marcus traces back to the dawn of the millennium. But Lydon's own *Rotten: The Autobiography,* which I wolfed down on the plane back, devotes almost seventy engaged, pungent pages to a childhood experienced mostly in that working-class North London neighborhood, where Irish battled English and, if they had any sense, befriended Jamaicans. Lydon is cynical about his working-class compatriots, who he considers "downtrodden" by their own passivity: "We're lazy, good-for-nothing bastards, absolute cop-outs." And he's never gushy about his strong, broad-minded, eccentric family—his mother beset by illness, introspective yet a rock, delighted by his Stooges and Hawkwind records, his father responsible, distant, his theory of nurturance limited to instilling his own toughness in his four sons. But The Man Who Can Be Rotten is proud of his roots nevertheless. He's been tight with his dad ever since his mother died in 1979. And as far as he's concerned, it was his Finsbury Park gang, including future teachers and craftsmen who are still his friends, who created the sensibility usually credited to Malcolm McLaren and the band he managed.

Lydon has despised McLaren forever, and although who invented punk is a stumper even disregarding their feud, it would be foolish to base any conclusions on his say-so. Nevertheless, I've long felt that of these two guys I wouldn't want my sister to marry, Lydon is the errant genius with his head up his ass, McLaren the wack poseur with hair on his palms. It's plain enough that the Sex Pistols—and the movement they inspired, which Lydon, typically, disowns for its conformism and pub-rock taint—needed both of them. But I go along with what the courts eventually decided: Lydon deserves the patent. When it's svengalis against performers, performers usually do, and without doubt Lydon gave shape to what was only McLaren's half-cocked fantasy. God knows what McLaren's Sex Pistols reunion would have been like—some fashion show in disguise, with faux-satirical attention to the genteel accoutrements Malc can't live with and can't live without. At least the comeback tour announced by Lydon, Steve Jones, Paul Cook, and Lydon's old antagonist Glen Matlock couldn't be any worse than Kiss or the Doobie Brothers.

Only of course it could. Kiss are crass by definition, the Doobies mushheads, and since nostalgia is crass and mushy, there's a fit there. Punk nostalgia, on the other hand, is a grotesque oxymoron. What can it mean to pine for a time when you were young and nihilistic? To look back twenty years to when you believed there was no future? The answers to these questions are not pretty: electric Luddism, "Live Music Is Better" bumper stickers, dress codes, chauvinism, disco sucks in a dozen guises, the censure of any pleasure not your miserable own. Add to these resentments the location of John Lydon's head as he heaped obloquy on his fans and denied that he had anything to do with rock and roll and you have a formula for the most tedious kind of ritual abuse. The only mystery was the exact form of the ensuing travesty. Would it be a rote replay of songs that had long since failed to dent the system they railed against? Or a wandering stop-and-go in which the musicians bollocksed their cues and cursed each other out as Lydon explained to the paying customers what suckers they'd been to show up?

Well, neither. What I forgot until I got to London was that in America the Pistols were subcultural exotics, while in Britain they were a native-grown mass phenomenon. To the amusement of the British press, which instantly declared the Pistols over because they were over, Finsbury Park wasn't just a concert—it was an all-Sunday festival that upped its draw by advertising nine bands old and new. And draw it did, albeit not like Kiss at the Garden—crowded for the Buzzcocks at four, it had spilled a near-capacity twenty-eight thousand twenty-two-and-a-half quid ticket-holders across the grass by the time Iggy appeared at seven twenty-five. Although the spike-headed thirtysomethings with baby buggies made for eye-catching photoplay, the age range of this very male (and very white) crowd was wide, say seventeen to forty-three, and amazingly, the generational spread was almost even, tilted only a tad toward the older end. But because 1977's art-punks and their techno heirs were too sophisticated to waste time on over-because-it's-over, it was uniform in another respect: class. These were the blokes who had stuck with punk long after Johnny Rotten threw in the towel, yelling along loudest when the P.A. blasted Sham 69's "Hersham Boys." The dominant style of the support bands wasn't Fluffy's minimalism of necessity but the expansive pop oi that linked veteran campaigners Stiff Little Fingers, still at it eighteen years after "Alternative Ulster" and "Suspect Device," to the hook-seeking 60ft Dolls and big-rock Wildhearts: guitars-bassanddrums, unison vocals and catchy terrace chants, fast martial rhythms shading or switching into thrash.

Dress was rough but sharp, with a tiny minority in costume and vintage T's scattered among the new souvenirs. There was some pogoing by old-timers contesting their mortality, spotty moshing, and no gobbing at all; especially given how much alcohol was around, the jovial concord with which stumblers were righted and shutterbugs mounted strangers' shoulders seemed utopian. And from what I could gather, the genial mood wasn't just I-have-survived. A vast majority of those present were into soccer, and England's victory on Saturday had put them in the full flush of the symbolic chauvinism only sports fans can wallow in. God fuck the queen and save Stuart Pearce, an old punk who'd won the day with a penalty kick against Spain after ignominiously blowing a World Cup match two years before.

Although all this is easy enough to figure out in retrospect, at Finsbury Park it snuck up on me. Jet lag, uneven music, yet somehow I was having a lovely time. The Buzzcocks got singalong like Pete Seeger, Skunk Anansie put me to sleep, the Wildhearts set off their smoke machine, and then I was holding my ground at my first Iggy show since the seventies. I've never bought James Osterberg's self-made legend, but at forty-nine he was every bit as pumped as I'd been hearing. Dry-fucking the amps, jacking a rocket-sized imaginary hard-on, parading his sinewy torso and shaking his skinny ass, body-surfing into the crowd to throw a punch or two, he wasted no ceremony getting to "Raw Power," "Search and Destroy," and "I Wanna Be Your Dog," and he never let up. "He's fucking fit, man," noted one student of the arts. "He's fucking fit," his mate responded. How did John propose to follow this?

Yet when the moment came it wasn't even an issue. After a decent forty-five-minute interval, guitaristbassistanddrummer took the stage and Rotten burst through a scrim of 1977 shock-horror headlines in a shiny laminated-linen suit, windowpane plaid with ridiculous shoulder pads. In an instant the crowd, which had only tightened seriously with Iggy, transformed itself into a roiling mass, an exuberantly physical yet far from hostile pogo pit. And suddenly it was clear that to the last Iggyite these people were there for one reason and one reason only: to see the greatest band in the history of the world.

The Pistols had changed the over-thirtys' lives with a few records and some phantom gigs; the kids had read about the same band in the first chapter of Genesis, shining light on the face of the deep. All of them had bought tickets, beaten Spain, and believed—so confidently and defiantly and intently and good-humoredly and unnihilistically that they could have transformed rote by force of collective will. But although there's not a single new song on the *Filthy Lucre Live* CD that preserves Finsbury Park for posterity, although tempos and arrangements are identical, rote has nothing to do with the music it revives. There are a few changes: Lydon cannily applies the deepened voice and declamatory techniques he developed with PiL to his Pistols book, and longtime professional musicians Cook and Jones get more sound out of their instruments than they once could. The general feel is bigger—longer on drama and shorter on passion. But beyond audience participation, what made this concert an unlikely triumph came down, as it so often does, to two commonplace mysteries: conviction and music.

Punk mythologists tell the world that Johnny Rotten was seer, jeremiah, and provocateur in his bones—that, as I wrote myself, "to call this band dangerous is more than a suave existentialist compliment. They mean no good." Lydon tells the world that Johnny Rotten was a role he created and played to the hilt. But of course, such interpretations are almost never mutually exclusive. If Lydon could only act and write the role because it was in him, no role is ever completely internalized, certainly not by a half-blind meningitis survivor alienated as much from himself as from everything else. At Finsbury Park, Lydon proved he could still pull this choice part out of his soul and gun its rants home like nobody else. His fury and wit strengthened by a new sense of entitlement, he reserved his contempt for the press, a predictable piece of business that served the crucial function of putting everyone (else) within earshot in the same boat. And as always, the timbres, cadences, and tone patterns of his unmistakable vocal sound marked and defined the noise beneath it.

What the noisemakers proved is that Lydon's (not to mention McLaren's) exultant contempt for their supposed incompetence— even in this era of good feeling, the story circulates that two decades worth of accrued skills compelled them to practice being "bad"—is mean, defensive bushwa. Lydon wasn't just politicking when he took to praising Jones in recent years. Few bands before or since have taken as much pleasure in or power from the pure and simple sound of rock guitar, unbedizened by the rootsy comforts of the pub strain Lydon despises. Cook's steady beats are his own, their deliberate speed pointing the way from Stones and Slade to the Ramones Memorial Expressway of the Clash and the Buzzcocks. And since before he was bounced for Rotten's chum

Sid, it was Matlock who provided much of the elementary humm-ability that sold the Pistols to the terrace-chant faction, his ability to actually play his instrument seems a major plus these days.

Never Mind the Bollocks will stand as a cultural landmark, epitomizing a moment of possibility that didn't pan out quite like we'd hoped. Beefed up and yanked out of history, *Filthy Lucre Live* reconstructs the landmark as mere music, in which form it could stand just as long. This music did dent the system after all, and I'm not just talking the obvious changes it wreaked on the music business. I mean the psychological space it provided blokes who had outgrown impotent posing and expectoration without gaining any future worth singing about—which didn't stop them from shouting every chorus as they jumped up and down. Although no subsequent reports suggest that the Pistols were putting out only to assure themselves of top-notch new product, New York isn't London and John is John. So I can't guarantee what will happen when this profit-taker hits Roseland. But as anybody who's even thinking about going already knows, guarantees mean shit in this world. Punk nostalgia sucks. The Pistols reunion is something else.

1996

5

Kings of Rhythm

Sylvester Is a Star

"You are a star/Everybody is one/You are a star/And you only happen once," Sylvester descanted over and over during one of the many high points of his Roseland visitation Memorial Day, and although this philosophy of showbiz derived from Sly Stone, it was tinged with Andy Warhol as well. Everybody is a star, all right, but sometimes only for fifteen minutes. I'm sure the songwriter, Sylvester's synth player Patrick Cowley, intended "you only happen once" as an affirmation of the irreducible uniqueness of all his "sisters and brothers," as he calls them. But coming from a performer who had finally achieved stardom in the most fickle genre this side of lions and gladiators, the ambiguity was inescapable.

I hadn't seen Sylvester since 1971 at the Anderson Theater, where he stole what show there was to steal from his fellow Cockettes, that ill-fated troupe of hippie drag queens about whom Gore Vidal devised the wicked line, "It's not enough just to be untalented." That wasn't quite fair to Sylvester, who let loose his rich falsetto in front of (black female) backup vocalists—he enlisted a retired Supreme and a retired Sweet Inspiration when his regulars cut out temporarily—and (white male) hard rock band. But even his admirers acknowledged that he failed to sustain a forty-five-minute set. Nor could his difficulties be blamed on image. As a black transvestite, he automatically gained the kind of instant recognition that is only a fantasy for most would-be artistes, and the

Cockettes' crowd no doubt found his persona a winning one. Uh-uh—the problem was music.

Admittedly, the getups Sylvester sported on his two 1973 albums—sequined pantsuit (b/w grass skirt) on *Sylvester and the Hot Band,* full-face drag with oversized jewelry on *Bazaar*—didn't help his music get across in the rapidly uptightening FM marketplace. Sylvester's funky internalizations of "Southern Man" and "My Country 'Tis of Thee" were pretty interesting debut stuff (although his Billie Holiday travesties put Diana Ross's innocent remakes in perspective), and the hard-rock showstopper that opened the follow-up was surefire boogie. But interesting wasn't where FM was at by then, and if Sylvester intended "I'm a Steam Roller" as a joke, the way James Taylor had, the result was much too funny. Sweet Baby Wanker moaning "churnin' urn of burnin' funk" was droll, but coming from a cartoon character who was one-fourth Sylvester and three-fourths Tweety Bird, the same words were completely ridiculous.

Physically, Sylvester was no match for the preeminent falsetto leads of the early seventies—Eddie Kendricks of the Temptations and Russell Thompkins, Jr. of the Stylistics—much less great predecessors like Claude Jeter, Clyde McPhatter, or the magnificent Smokey Robinson. But that doesn't mean much, because every good singer works with incomparable equipment. Thompkins could no more have duplicated Kendricks's sweet clarity than Kendricks could Thompkins's unearthly soft-edged fluidity. The main reason Sylvester sounded like Tweety Bird (even Flip Wilson's Geraldine once or twice) was that he was trying to convey a whole personality. He didn't conceive himself as a falsetto.

Women can sing falsetto, of course, but the soul falsetto tradition that traces back to Claude Jeter and the Swan Silvertones is definitively male. The typical falsetto "love man" sings in a woman's normal register but has no interest in her normal dramatic breadth—his highs come from one exalted part of his self, a place where both spiritual intensity and a transcendently tender sexuality reside. The overall effect is pure and miraculous, but narrow—that's how the purity is achieved. When a love man like Smokey Robinson does free a full range of emotion, he usually cheats by straying down into his natural tenor. In any case, Sylvester's aspirations were further out than Smokey's—he wanted to sing like a woman; he wanted access to the human gamut of a woman's feelings. And gradually he figured out that "soul" as opposed to "rock" was where to do this. *Bazaar* closed with Gram Parsons and Chris Ethridge's "She"—"She had the people all together/Singing praises of joy to the Lord above"—and by that album he was emulating the gospel ladies he idolized with fair success.

In a sense, Sylvester's failure to crack the rock audience in the early seventies paralleled that of Cissy Houston, Merry Clayton, and other church-trained hopefuls. He did suffer a few extra credibility problems, of course, but the fact that he was a man hurt his music even more than it did his credibility—because he sang one or two octaves above his speaking voice, he simply couldn't make all the rich womanly sounds his concept demanded. When he recorded again in 1977 under the soul-identified auspices of ex-Motown ex-Moonglow Harvey Fuqua, he was still plagued by this limitation. But on *Step II,* his 1978 album with Fuqua, he found the disco breakthrough he'd been seeking.

The B side of *Step II* is decent soulish stuff that progresses toward Sylvester's dream, although on its most effective cut he reverts to tenor. But the A side comes true. "You Make Me Feel (Mighty Real)" is a genuine classic, one of those surges of sustained, stylized energy that are disco's gift to pop music, and the singing puts it across. Sylvester still can't go three minutes with Lorraine Ellison, but he finds a public use for her brand of histrionic climax; he can't match pipes with Donna Summer or Gloria Gaynor, but he can make Madleen Kane and Grace Jones wish they'd stayed in pictures. In short, he shows primo disco potential, and on the follow-up *Stars* he exploits it unblinkingly, stretching his two incomparable tricks—for thrills, a supernal burst of sound too sweet for a shriek that he unlooses above his normal falsetto range; for romance, a transported croon—over a consistently satisfying four-cut dance album. The best track is "Stars," but the tour de force is a remake of Ben E. King's "I (Who Have Nothing)," the artificiality of which suits the schlocky lyric at least as well as King's much-admired virtuoso dramatics.

Sylvester and Fuqua have designed a music for live performance—their streamlined disco can be reproduced precisely by the singer and ten pieces, most definitely including his backup singers, Martha Wash and Izora Rhodes. At Roseland, Sylvester, a star at last—and performing for paying customers in this city for the first time since 1973 at Max's—did all the hits as if he could imagine no greater privilege. Simply made up, his hair hanging in scores of tight little braids, wearing a pastel-on-white tunic open past the collarbone, he personified what at first seemed like an odd choice for a Lennon-McCartney cover—a blackbird who'd been waiting for this moment to arrive.

An unassuming Latino who turned out to be WKTU's Paco introduced Sylvester with remarks equating disco and do-your-own-thing, and the crowd that had come out for the former hippie drag queen earned them—straight and gay, black and white and Latino and Asian, formal and sloppy and party and drag and costume, singles and (often demonstrative) couples. This crowd was bigger and broader than a cult, and obviously included casual ticket-buyers who had paid their fifteen bucks mostly to dance and hear songs they liked—"I (Who Have Nothing)" may have stiffed nationally, but in this disco town Sylvester is big-time. "Are you a girl?" one naif yelled out, to which Sylvester—whose demeanor was androgyne rather than femme—replied, "Honey, tonight I'll be anything you want me to be."

Sylvester does his own thing if anyone does, but like most great performers he seems to do it more out of love for his audience than for himself. I still found the material from the B side of *Step II* decent and no more; when Sylvester ventured beyond his bursts and croons into songs that required more detailed emoting, his voice still lacked luster. But the amazing thing was that Sylvester implicitly conceded this—that's why Martha Wash and Izora Rhodes were there. If he couldn't give the audience he loved the sounds he loved, then never mind ego, he'd give the glory to someone else. At the close of a rather colorless version of "A Song for You," he stopped and announced, "This is the part I like." After a brief pause, Wash and Rhodes went into a celestial harmony. Everyone else liked that part too.

Sylvester's first encore was the Gloria Gaynor arrangement of "Never Can Say Goodbye"—"the first disco song," he reminded us—but the second encore was the topper. After telling us we were in for "something very special," Sylvester led Rhodes, Wash, and pianist Eric Robinson in an otherwise unaccompanied hymn—"just simple, to let you hear our song." Before it began, he offered another reminder: "If it wasn't for this kind of music, all the fabulous background singers you hear in disco would not have happened." Roseland was quiet; people who had listened to Sylvester's set by dancing to it, which was certainly appropriate, stood and paid attention. I didn't know the song, but one line struck me: "I'm just a stranger here . . . "

Clearly, this is an artist with a sense of history and of his place in the world. He's been ambiguous recently about his sexual identity—jacket art has been toned down, and he's said he's reluctant to be too outrageous in middle America—but his artistic ambition gets clearer all the time. This man wants to honor and revitalize a female tradition roughly parallel to the one Claude Jeter articulated for men. He tells interviewers that *Step II* and *Stars* are only stages—the album he really wants people to hear is a live double recorded at the San Francisco Opera House that will include songs associated with such contemporaries as Thelma Houston and the Pointer Sisters.

I don't know whether he can master such music even with Martha and Izora backing him. And the critic in me worries about that. But the human being the critic is part of hopes Sylvester will happen again and again. He deserves it, and so, I hope, do we.

1979

Triumph of the Trifle: Ray Parker Jr.

The artist in question is not the future of rock and roll. He is a cottage industry and a consummate pro, a big-time studio bassist who made his move in 1978 and has turned out an album a year for Arista ever since. As his billing evolved from Raydio, a group name suitable to the halcyon days of airplay, to the simple, telling eponym Ray Parker Jr., he took to playing almost all the parts on his records himself, but this was in no way a claim of self-sufficiency. Ray Parker Jr.'s only great theme is getting laid, and as he's sure to remind us eventually, that takes two. Anyway, his small type invariably includes one of those "Special Thanks to . . . " roll calls that are de rigueur in the belly of the back-slapping, back-stabbing biz. On each of the last four albums, the list has begun with God and Clive Davis.

Parker has been a steady-state seller—all of his albums gold, none platinum. But artistically he's moved in a reverse parabola. *Raydio* was a paradigmatic star debut, a vocal group/funk band synthesis ripe with a young lifetime of material—I enjoy "Me" and "Betcha Can't Love Me Just Once," jokey boasts that establish his basic come-on, even more than the three chart records it was good for. But the follow-up, the well-named *Rock On,* was less of the same, and in 1980 the even better-named *Two Places at the Same Time* seemed to indicate that the synthesis wasn't holding. Sometimes fawningly pop, at others hyperbolically party-hearty, it was the kind of hither-and-yon effort that often signals commercial alarm. On *A Woman Needs Love*, though, Parker settled on his cute-assman identity. With the gain in clarity his songwriting rebounded, and now, with *The Other Woman*, he's produced what may stand as the pop album of the year—smarmy, even a little sleazy, and utterly charming.

Like *Raydio*, which makes it on staying power, *The Other Woman* isn't initially prepossessing. Its eight tunes favor the medium-tempo hippety-bump with which vocalist Parker, bassist Parker, and drummer Parker straddle pop, funk, and rock, and its lyrics play the angles shamelessly. If you take the customary instrumental, here entitled "Just Havin' Fun," as the soundtrack to a deceptively casual dance-floor flirtation, every tune focuses on fucking. Sometimes Parker is merely raunchy—"The Other Woman" and "Streetlove" are male and female versions of sex-for-its-own-sweet-obsessive-sake, and in "Let's Get Off" they come together. But at other times Parker gets serious, which is to say raunchy and romantic, upping the sexual ante not only on the patient proposition ("anyplace you like" refers to bodies, not apartments) and the behind-closed-doors plea ("Girl you never would believe/The calls I receive/Soon as you're away from home") but also on the leave-him-for-me speech ("Who do you call when you want to get it on?") and even the proposal of marriage ("Your stuff's so good I want my name on it"). There must be more to love than this.

Parker isn't prepossessing on stage either. At his first area appearance since 1978, sandwiched between two of the hottest acts in black music at Nassau Coliseum, he and his temp tour band—white drummer, white guitarist, Amerasian keybwoman, black bassist-dancer—finessed both Rick James and Grandmaster Flash by hardly putting on a show at all. Not that they just stood there—Parker exerted his prowess on four and six strings as well as coming on to the ladies, the others got brief showcases, and there was some sweetly jivey he-man business with the petite Amerasian. But their fifty-minute, eight-song set relied almost entirely on *The Other Woman* and probably constituted 80 percent of what they'd rehearsed. Which it turned out was just fine.

Soon I'd figured out that I still remembered all this wonderful stuff from a record I'd filed as a pleasant trifle, and experienced an appropriately small-scale pop epiphany. When trifles turn out this pleasant, I start believing that fun may be the meaning of life after all. The artist in question is that ever rarer prize, an inspired journeyman, which is to say that he exemplifies biz ideology at its best. In a subgenre whose practitioners hone their sexual personas as sharp as Cole Porter rhyme schemes, Parker can't be said to have come up with something new—the secure, sincere superstud is a role Teddy Pendergrass, for one, has exploited for years. But boy, does he go at it with flair.

It's a subtle flair to be sure. Only rarely does Parker come up with a conceit like the cowboy stanza in "Let's Get Off," where, after swearing to keep giddy-upping no matter how rough she makes the riding, he shoots his gun and loads up for round two. More often his articulateness is quite prosy—"You're intelligent/ And you're also very cute," or even "Nine times out of ten she's correct if she assumes/That marriage is the last thing on a man's mind." His music is just as articulately unobtrusive. And while he doesn't talk his songs, he has no need for the vocal pyrotechnics he couldn't muster—his stylishly textured, conversational timbre, halfway between a murmur and purr when he's really turning it on, is a cunning interpretive tool. For Parker does know that there's more to love than raunch—even that paean to raunch "The Other Woman" is also a warning about its emotional perils, and in other songs he lays out romantic nuance as if awaiting a call from Willie Nelson. He needs all his craft to do this coolly, like the smoothy he is. Sexual detail plus romantic detail is a potent pop combination, and he wants to keep it that way.

It's no accident that the shittiest time for pop music and/or good ol' rock 'n' roll since the early fifties is also the most racially segregated—Donna Summer and the Pointer Sisters are the only black artists in *Billboard*'s current top twenty-five. It's a double tribute to Ray Parker Jr., therefore, that "The Other Woman" went to number four. So is it churlish of me to complain that it deserved higher, or to suggest that the less successful "Let Me Go" is a top-five ballad if ever I heard one, or to wonder how many of the soi-disant pop fans reading this are aware of either? Well then, I'm a churl. Parker's entertainment value and invitation to suspended disbelief are a measure of how much target marketing and the hip-capitalist racism of AOR programming have cost us. When he climaxed his show with "The Other Woman," the absence of horn parts emphasized that groove's unmistakable debt to the Rolling Stones—not Chuck Berry or Muddy Waters, the Rolling Stones.

This was another small pop epiphany—we white folks owe black music a few, and even without Charlie Watts the beat was a lot more rousing than half of what the Stones were putting out last time they hit the Garden. It could never be the future I dream for rock and roll. But I can think of lots of worse ones.

1982

Working the Crowd: Bruce Springsteen / Michael Jackson

If you'd told me five years ago that I'd willingly spend the first weekend of August 1984 watching rock and roll in sports arenas, I'd have prayed for the souls of Strummer and Jones and wondered whether Debbie Harry would ever learn to dance. Such miracles seemed unlikely, but pop moves in mysterious ways: maybe "new wave" would breach the beachheads after all. And of course it has: if I'd so chosen, I could have gone to see the Pretenders at the Garden the following Tuesday. But instead I spent Tuesday's music time with General Public at the Ritz. Sensitive young people may find it tawdry, but the Ritz still seems made to order for beachhead-breaching "new wavers." Arenas are for Michael Jackson and Bruce Springsteen.

Rock and roll fans enter arenas for the company. Not that performance quality doesn't sometimes enliven (or deaden) the experience all by itself, and not that the great audience doesn't sometimes assemble under more modest circumstances—the thirty or so crazies who outlasted Flipper at their first Danceteria gig certainly qualified. But arena acoustics and sightlines can't enhance music, while arena crowds can, as the abysmal *Elvis as Recorded at Madison Square Garden* inadvertently proved to all those fortunate enough to witness his 1972 New York concerts in person. And as I learned two years later in the same venue from the transcendently competent Grand Funk Railroad and twenty thousand other citizens whose names I didn't catch, you don't have to be a full-fledged fan yourself to benefit. If the audience feels good about the artist and itself, it can generate magic. Chrissie Hynde filled the Garden on a tour promoted by MTV, an institution she's claimed she despises, and while I know I might have been pleasantly surprised, that contradiction boded ill. Michael and Bruce, on the other hand, did it their ways—very differently, though sensitive young people may well disapprove of both their methods, which weren't designed to captivate sensitive young people. We're talking mainstream America, what's sometimes called mass culture, with Michael riding Berry Gordy's showboat over a rainbow the black capitalist never thought big enough to see while Bruce slogged his way up that well-worn rock and roll road to a destination many have imagined but he alone has reached.

Michael has been in the biz since he was five, which isn't radically unusual, and internationally famous since he was eleven, which among black people is just about unique. His déclassé, millenarian religion and strict, close-knit, unpretentious family certainly helped shape his relationship to fame's pressure and privilege, but not as much as his talent, which no matter how industriously he hones it seems fundamentally unworldly. A fascination with pop fantasy from Oz to Disneyland to *Star Wars* suits an androgynous manchild who dances like a moonwalker and sings like a fairy, and that fascination extends to the fantasy world of stardom itself, a world into which he was thrust suddenly and permanently by "I Want You Back." By the time he was old enough to conceive his audience he was already one of the rare individuals who had one. No matter how much he learned watching Jackie Wilson and James Brown, his role models were the Hollywood icons who flickered to life in the screening room: Chaplin ("I just love him to death"), Astaire (who should be choreographing routines for him), and Hepburn (who became his friend in the flesh). Diana Ross, Paul McCartney, Brooke Shields, Ronald Reagan, Mick Jagger: he can't resist his colleagues in fame. While it seems unlikely that he anticipated *Thriller*'s numbers, there's no doubt the across-the-board stardom the album won him was more or less what he had in mind. Yet somehow—I'd attribute it to religion, family, and unworldliness all at once—he does retain an unmistakable if rather spaced-out aura of humility, mission, service. All he wants is the chance to entertain every single human being in the entire world.

Bruce bought his first guitar at thirteen, joined his first band at sixteen, cut his first album at twenty-three, and suddenly got real famous around his twenty-sixth birthday. An apostate Catholic, he spent as much of his adolescence as possible away from his father, a bus driver etc. who as it turned out wished his son all the best in his struggle to get out of Freehold, and despite his big strong voice and prodigious fluency as a lyricist his talent has always seemed subsidiary to his stick-to-itiveness. He never had time for day jobs, but he worked to escape surrounded by hundreds of friends and acquaintances who didn't believe a future free of the grind was possible, and most of them were right. In other words, he conceived his audience right in the middle of it. His role models may have been Elvis and Dylan, Mitch Ryder and Gary U.S. Bonds, but he identified so strongly with the guys he grew up with that he swore he'd never forget them. Many rock and rollers have contracted amnesia behind such vows, but with encouragement from a rock and roller with not much else in common with Bruce and his buddies—onetime critic Jon Landau, who's now produced and managed him for almost a decade— Springsteen still hangs out on the Jersey shore, living a distinctly "normal" life for a star of his magnitude. All he wants is a chance to speak to and for every one of his own.

Michael built his audience in the modern showbiz manner. Sure he practiced, sure he collaborated, sure he reached inside himself—sure he's a wonderful musician. And for all that, he's been a creature of marketing and multimedia ever since the Jackson 5 cartoons he had nothing whatsoever to do with. The brothers may have fled Motown to attain the creative control that made 1978's *Destiny* and 1979's *Off the Wall* possible, but the move also provided the distribution clout *Thriller*'s paneverything spread required. And let us not forget video, which the movie-mad clan has exploited since the dark ages of 1978. Bruce, on the other hand, has chosen the path of the traditionalist craftsman-auteur. Jackson Associates are no slobs in the studio, but Springsteen and Landau are crazed perfectionists, shuffling songs and risking technohubris not in pursuit of the hook or the beat but of sound and vision, sound and vision that evolve so slowly they appear to progressives not to change at all. Through seven years of pop ferment Bruce has resisted or ignored every trend, although with *Born in the U.S.A.* he has acceded to an Arthur Baker remix that still sounds like Spector to me and an overstaged Brian De Palma performance video. For all his bullheaded integrity, however, he's hardly held himself above the corporate. The record company, Rosie, gave him a big advance, and from the covers of *Time* and *Newsweek* in 1975 to the *Thriller*-financed promo blitz of 1984 he's backed up his own honest toil with the bosses' masscult machinery.

Mass culture: snobbish though the term may be, at the level of *Time* and *Newsweek* and CBS there's nothing else to call it. It's huge, traversing boundaries of gender and generation and class and race, and in theory it's homogeneous, lopping off inconvenient edges and corners so that one size fits all. Yet what was most striking about the sample masses of twenty thousand assembled at Madison Square Garden August 4 and Byrne Arena August 5 was how different they were. These really were samples; Michael and his brothers played to almost one hundred fifty thousand lucky customers in four shows at Meadowlands and the Garden and might conceivably have attracted ten times that, while Bruce reached over two hundred thousand in an unprecedented and quickly sold out stand of ten concerts in two weeks. That is, in this metropolitan area both artists attract audiences larger by a factor of ten or twenty—or much more—than an arena can hold. Yet if mass culture is really about traversing boundaries of gender and generation and class and race, the only way an elitist concept has any meaning for this democrat, then it may be that Bruce's music isn't mass culture at all.

Don't take this surmise for a backhanded putdown of Michael—it's meant to imply no musical superiority, and if the size of Jackson's success defeats him, he's hardly alone among mass culture icons. In fact, although in some ways it's easier to do good work down on the rock and roll road, many of Bruce's predecessors have fucked up badly enough to make Michael look as together as Paul McCartney by comparison. That Bruce seems to create "rock and roll" rather than "mass culture," however, signals the uniqueness of his achievement. The reason he doesn't classify neatly as mass culture is that his audience seems so homogenous: young white working-class men. But in fact it isn't. Perhaps 40 percent of the Byrne crowd was female, which is high for rock, with lots of women-together couples, which is almost unheard of. The age spread of fifteen years or so was also abnormally high, and it's my suspicion that there were too many collegiates and professionals there for the crowd to be called working-class in even the broadest sense of that nebulous term. That there's an irresistible temptation to pigeonhole his audience is first of all a tribute to Bruce, who has constructed a myth around the fate of the guys he grew up with that hits lots of different people where they live. But it's also a tribute to the audience, whose assent endows the myth with collective power. This is not to traffic in left abstractions, though they apply, nor to jive about vibes, though it would be unrealistic to pretend that an enormous charge of subliminal emotion wasn't what animated Bruce for four hours that night. It's simply to describe, quite concretely, an aggregate of fans who sang not just refrains but whole verses back to the stage whenever their spokesman gave them an opening, which couldn't have happened if hundreds or even thousands weren't singing along at almost every moment.

Springsteen has always been an extraordinarily vivid figure live, and though in the late seventies he fell into shtick—which he must still be subject to sometimes when he's not making his first appearance in Jersey in three long years—he's clearly firmed up his faith. Because his music has actually evolved, the records that gained him national recognition now seem relatively murky and overblown even to those who didn't mind those flaws at the time. Formally, the condensed songcraft that dominates 1980's two-LP set *The River* was the breakthrough, but *The River* didn't solve the problem that had driven him into both shtick and 1978's very overblown *Darkness on the Edge of Town:* the dawning realization that the trap he'd escaped not only continued to grind down the guys he'd grown up with but led him into a bigger trap, symbolized by a byzantine lawsuit with his ex-manager. Not until he sank publicly into the pits of *Nebraska* could he find the joyous release and honest laughs the dark-tinged rockers of *The River* never quite provided. We shouldn't underestimate the role of studio perfectionism in the ringing live intensity of *Born in the U.S.A.*'s sound, but on songwriting and singing alone it's an amazing feat. Not since *London Calling* has any album brought rock and roll's traditional affirm-in-the-negative to such a pitch of consciousness, and Bruce's outreach exceeds the Clash's by a factor of ten. It seems a simple thing—articulating the contradictions of freedom and powerlessness in America for teenagers who still believe they're born to run and adults who know where they end up. But nobody else has ever succeeded before cynicism or foolishness struck. And without doubt it's Bruce's passion for maintaining contact with his fans, his people, that has made the difference, to him and to them.

Such contact would of course be unimaginable for Michael, first of all because he's never had a "normal" life to maintain, but also because icons literally can't hang out, except in private with cronies and other stars—whenever they're in public, they're on. There's not much point in criticizing him for this, though I suppose that in theory he might have set himself the goal of becoming "normal" rather than the goal of becoming the biggest star the world has ever known. And thus there's not much point in criticizing the direction of his art—given his situation and his talent, fantasy or entertainment or escape will always be its vital center. But it is legitimate to examine the content of the fantasies, which can vary considerably, and also to ask in just what way they're entertaining.

Much has been made of the personal turn in Michael's recent writing—of the alienated paranoia of his love songs, of his identification with cinematic unworldlies like Obi-Wan Kenobe, E.T., and Dracula. But because the terrors of fame now rank among pop's most bathetic cliches, I still regard the Chinese-box humor of John Landis's "Thriller" video as Michael's most effective anti-star move, and feel obliged to point out that his lyrics have less than nothing to say about the alienation and fear that victimize so many of his anonymous fans. With the single exception of the discreetly valorous "Beat It," what impresses me most about his music is its intense sexual-cum-spiritual pleasure quotient. Connected to freestyle exhortations like "Wanna Be Startin' Somethin' " and "Don't Stop 'Til You Get Enough," which are designed to instigate the dancing that's always been Michael's calling and cause but can just as well be transferred to activities like sex and revolution, the soulful esprit of his singing and the depthless nimble wit of his rhythms take on the kind of universal significance that he aspires to and anyone can put to use: acute, invigorating, fun.

But such meaning was scarce at the Garden, and not primarily because the night I caught was by all informed accounts mediocre. Victory Tour mediocre is engrossing in a mild way—my mind wandered no more than it usually does for Neil Young or P-Funk or the Ramones. But the spectacle is not designed for highs. Comparisons to vaudeville and Vegas miss its rhythmic commitment, soul-circuit roots, and generic arena-rock usages, but Greil Marcus was wrong to dismiss it as "a standard rock and roll show"—as Nelson George suggests, only Earth, Wind & Fire has ever staged and lit and designed and choreographed so elaborately. Marcus was right, however, to characterize the evening as "a church social," "a Fourth of July picnic." Predictably, I suppose, opening night in Manhattan was less kiddie-studded and more celebrity-pocked than I'd been led to hope, but this was mass culture for sure: casually affluent, at most 10 percent black, and split down the middle sexually, with a concentration of on-the-town late-twenties and a visible sprinkling of interracial couples its only demographic peculiarities. The mood was surprisingly unhysterical—proportionately, I heard more high-pitched shrieks for Michael Stipe of R.E.M. at the Beacon two weeks before. And of course such congenial curiosity is exactly what anybody who wants to entertain the whole world is asking for. Perhaps Michael finds his world less scary in such company.

Me, I prefer my entertainment more thrilling. Ideally, rock and roll enlightens as it excites, with the two halves of the pleasure radiating back and forth in a kiss-you-kill-you Apache dance. But in the absence of dialectical synthesis a good shot of adrenalin will suffice. I wonder whether this master of albums and video, home media both, has any idea anymore of what it's like to sit in an enormous room and watch somebody try to entertain you. Of course, few acts manipulate the arena even as effectively as the Jacksons, who do earn points for effort with their solid-hue lasers and mechanical space monsters, but the musical translation went nowhere. Bruce's stolid beat projects (these days even propels) through the vastness he must fill, but the play of plectra and percussion that makes the Jacksons' records so compelling on the dance floor was doomed to get lost. Most of the words faded away by mutual agreement. And except in brief snatches, notably a minute or so of heart-stopping solo razzle-dazzle during "Billie Jean," the dancing that convinced America Michael was a genius didn't compensate.

And if performance and audience were of a piece, it makes a certain sense to fault Michael for both. Like so many who devote themselves to biggest, he's put less than his all into best. For comparison's sake, reconsider Bruce's wonderful but of course imperfect crowd. Though Jon Landau will probably be chagrined to read it, these native Americans do recall one rock and roll precedent, the Deadheads of the early seventies—not just in the way their unity transcends their heterogeneity, which is the good part, but also in the way their intensity delimits their heterogeneity. Bruce can't continue to improve his outreach unless he somehow extends it beyond the faithful, the full-fledged fans. But in Jersey, at least, tickets fell too fast to leave room for, say, sensitive young new wavers, whose curiosity might benefit from a steadying jolt of mainstream after seven long years of pop ferment, or, crucially, for black people, who I'm sure are even more turned off by his resistance to trends—particularly rhythmic trends—than are new wavers. Despite Bruce's public passion for r&b, my naked eye discerned more Afro-Americans in his band than in his audience, which may be why I sometimes got the queasy feeling that the rich Huck-and-Jim routines he's worked out with Clarence Clemons were slipping ever so slightly over toward Jack-Benny-and-Rochester.

These are imperfections Michael's audience—which piles middle Americans on a black base, mixing passionate star worship with bemused interest—might conceivably make good on and doesn't. The Victory Tour's thirty-dollar prices aren't as out of line as they ought to be; Marvin Gaye charged twenty-five at Radio City, though Bruce's top is sixteen. But they do seem to keep black kids away, and black kids would have made good company at the Garden. After all, they're the ones who've cared about Michael longest and deepest, who feel his success as more than an exotic accident of statistics and modern communication—and they're also the unnamed potential perpetrators who inspired the tour's massive-to-paranoid security outlay. As delighted as I am to see white America recognize a black hero, I'm not going to think the affection in which he's held means much racially until it gets generalized a little. I'm sure it wouldn't have been easy to engineer, especially for the football promoter who ended up running the tour, but two or three thousand freebies or maybe twofers in black neighborhoods might have done wonders—shored up liberal abstractions, added a buzz of unpredictability to the vibe, and increased the concentration of high-pitched shrieks if not spontaneous singalongs. A risk-free move? Not entirely, I suppose. Thrillers aren't supposed to be risk-free.

If I complain too much, please pardon the critic who came along on my willing weekend in the arenas—he has a big mouth and bigger dreams. Rather than expecting or demanding more from Michael, just say I'd like to see him make his own dreams bigger still, so that his star fantasies and his aura of service can come together. I doubt that the possibility would even have occurred to me if Bruce hadn't worked farther up that rock and roll road than seemed possible—and if he didn't think it was too late to stop now.

1984

Give Him Liberty or Give Him Death: Prince

In the eternal rock-hero sweepstakes, Prince will surely rank alongside Bruce Springsteen as Big Cheese of 1984. The skewed, soulful, synbeat-hooked "When Doves Cry" has already sold a golden-age 3 million singles, and the *Purple Rain* soundtrack could end up the year's best-selling album and is certain to finish in the money critically as well. Its nine tracks—three overdubbed by Prince in his traditional studio solitude, three laid down with the band he's now christened the Revolution, and three recorded live at Minneapolis's 1st Avenue, a hometown cross between CBGB and the Ritz—parade by with a verve, focus, maturity, and unerring hookiness that his previous five albums presaged but rarely approached. Never before has there been so much howling invention in his guitar or so much movement and muscle in his beat, and never before has he cooed, implored, admonished, rabble-roused, and just plain screamed with such resonance and force. The live cuts sacrifice a little too much tonguework and filigree, but for the most part *Purple Rain* is pure pleasure, which with this rock and roller as with no other is apposite and a half. Yet still I long to know—what does it all mean?

Admittedly, the rock and roller hasn't been chintzy with the hints—at 7 million bucks, the *Purple Rain* sighttrack is the most expensive video ever made. But the record is suggestive enough, beginning with a brief spoken preamble that permits Prince to revive the theological "controversy" he instigated on the 1981 album of the same name. It's reasonable to suspect that at the time nobody but his local clergyperson actually cared whether the inventor of erotopop believed in "God" or "Me." By now, though, people do care, and what's more, the man finally seems ready to answer his own question. As you might expect, he'll take it both ways. Addressing the worshiping multitudes in confident preacherly cadences, he intimates theism by promising "never-ending happiness" in "the afterworld." But he closes with a down-to-earth caveat that amounts to a declaration of practical agnosticism: "In this life things are much harder than in the afterworld. In this life you're on your own." Whereupon he sets off a truly frenzied invitation to the orgy entitled "Let's Go Crazy."

There is meaning here, I swear it, but this sequence reminds us first of all how tall Prince stands in the great long line of rock heroes who are full of shit. The tradition is of course a rich one. Even such raving realists as Chuck Berry and Bruce Springsteen pay it their respects and almost all of the music's visionaries, from Elvis Presley to the Honourable J. Rotten-Lydon, have based their careers on it. If the shit they're full of ain't fertilizer, then at least it's a healthy by-product—none of them could have given us so much pleasure or shown us so much of themselves and the world if they'd worried unduly about looking stupid. The stylistic revelations of Pelvis, Genius, and Godfather welled up out of their lifelong infatuations with themselves, and since the sixties the upside of Dylanesque and Lennonist foolishness has often been a surprisingly specific kind of satisfaction, a wisdom that's expressed in and reducible to words. But while Prince is canny enough to flaunt outrageous subjects and pepper his lyrics with buzzwords, his confused hippie-manqué ideas swamp his flashes of wit and insight. "When You Were Mine," "Little Red Corvette," and now "When Doves Cry" are among the most totally accomplished songs of the era, but anyone who wants to make similar claims for solid anthems like "Dirty Mind," "1999," and "Purple Rain," as Prince evidently hopes to, is full of shit.

If I seem to be implying that as a rock hero Prince doesn't go all the way, that depends on how much you expect from your rock heroes. Without doubt, the guy has the lineaments of a Significant Star. But because very little in his writing conveys the depth or breadth or good yucks of a George Clinton or Patti Smith, I want to put some heat on the ready assumption that given the limitations of the pop context he's somehow profound—that as an explorer of "tragedies and injustices" (to cite Milo Miles's skeptical formulation) he's got the stuff to lead a generation into the light. Let's face it: the tragedies he adduces invariably involve his own dick, which is also the keystone of his politics. If you set aside for the moment the racial distinctions he can't dodge despite himself—and do yourself the favor of overlooking the muddled "Annie Christian," where he comes out against Abscam and assassination—his thinking about injustice begins and ends with nuclear holocaust, which he's also against, albeit in an ominously passive way.

Why then is Prince taken seriously not just by poor ignorant teenagers but by associate attorneys, shoe salesmen, rock critics, and other reputable adults, myself included? The answer is music and image, where rock heroes happen and where Prince stands out not for what he says but for what he is—or rather, what he looks like, a "black" man. This pigeonhole troubles Prince; unable to follow the logic that classifies somebody who's 25 percent African as "black," he's spent his career trashing it. After earning his first gold album in 1979 as a brashly lubricious and utterly uncrossed-over falsetto love man, he nurtured the vocals, transmuted the persona, and leaned down hard on a stiff, steady, hard-rock four to create 1980's *Dirty Mind.* Thus he became the first commercially viable artist in a decade to claim the visionary high ground of Lennon and Dylan and Hendrix and (Jim) Morrison, whose rebel turf had been ceded to such marginal heroes-by-fiat as Smith and Rotten-Lydon. Immediately he lost half his black audience—that is, half his commercial viability. But he didn't lose his black identification, which while it cost him on the radio helped him in print. Then, in 1981, he redeemed himself commercially with the half-funky rebel-rock of "Controversy," which broke as a black dance hit and prepared the way for "Little Red Corvette," the triple-platinum *1999,* and 1984, the year *Dirty Mind* went gold and *Purple Rain* became a top-grossing movie and LP simultaneously.

Nevertheless, beyond "I wish there was no black and white/ I wish there were no rules"—a fond notion which his musical mélange both embodies and calls into question, since without black and white its ingredients wouldn't exist—Prince doesn't have much to say about race. As with Morrison and Smith, his passion is sex, which he associates with the redolent rebel-rock catchword revolution (a.k.a. no rules). As someone who's over-rated sex as a matter of principle for thirty years, I appreciate the impulse. Prince's unprecedentedly pornographic music is almost the aural equivalent of Marco Vassi's and the Mitchell Brothers' descriptions and depictions of fucking, sucking, and all their honey-dripping kinfolk; for me, especially in "Do Me, Baby" he's been amazingly effective at generating a raw genital charge. But like all pornographers he's better at inciting energy than at sug-gesting what to do with it.

In both ear and eye versions, *Purple Rain* is about what to do with it. Maturity, you know—that's why his voice has deepened, why so much footage is devoted to the oedipalia he sums up in a few deft lines of "When Doves Cry." The God-or-Me dichotomy is kept in play with cryptic Christian allusions (and messianic pre-tensions) that dress up the time-honored rock and roll battle between sexual abandon and sexual expression; "it's time u learned love and lust/they both have four letters/but they are entirely different words," a "poor lonely computer" is informed by "The Righteous Ones" in a typically heavy passage. The frantic self-indulgence of "Let's Go Crazy" gives way to a bitter on-again-off-again affair that climaxes in the compassionate resignation of "Purple Rain." From in-this-life-you're-on-your-own to in-this-life-heaven-is-other-people (and-you're-still-on-your-own)—not mere-ly for documentary expediency does the album go out with a live band working a live audience. This worthy message gains real-life authority and aesthetic edge in the context Prince has spent his career devising. And for total professionalism the songs that carry it are sensationally consistent. He's mastered the kind of raceless sixties-rooted pop whose revival "Little Red Corvette" broadcast with such brass and wit. Moves like the demurely complaisant "Thank you" that answers his "You're sheer perfection" in "Take Me With You," the cocky high speed of the brazenly redundant "Baby I'm a Star"—these signal an artist in full formal flower. But insofar as his messages are the outrageous ones he's been pur-veying since *Dirty Mind* (and those have to be there or the worthy ones won't hit), they've lost steam: "1999" is a more rousing dance lesson for the edge of apocalypse than "Let's Go Crazy," and "Head" and "Jack U Off" are more salacious than the ground-out "Darling Nikki" or the F-word vehicle and non-LP B side

"Erotic City." Prince may have gained maturity, but like many grown-ups before him, he seems to get a little blocked making rebel-rock out of it.

Nor does this maturity make him an original, even among professional sex maniacs. He's hardly the first libertine to have a thing about fidelity and possession or find let's-pretend-we're-married a hot fantasy, hardly the first to prove a moralist upside-down. One reason pornographers make such lousy advice columnists is that often when they decide that maybe it wouldn't be such a great idea for you to fuck your sister they remember that the search for freedom through sex is ultimately spiritual, and before you know it they get religion, sometimes in an unnecessarily literal way. This hasn't quite happened to Prince, but you can bet your ass it will if he lives long enough, which I wish I thought he believed he was going to.

Because in case you haven't cross-referenced to the purple sky of "1999," you ought to understand that the purple rain Prince hopes 2 see his on-again-off-again bathing in falls at the dawning of Judgment Day. We're all gonna die, and in the meantime we should have fun, and I'll love u if u let me—as impulses, images, moods people get into sometimes, these familiar sentiments are valuable, even visionary. But as a philosophy of life they're kind of limited. I find it significant that the "you" Prince always spells with such willful postliteracy is more explicitly singular, more eros than agape, than it tends to be when a live audience is brought into the equation. Worthy message or no, Prince has little talent for escaping the individual ego, which is no doubt why the quest obsesses him, and why in the end he's so filled with guilt. For like all too many seekers after self-transcendence/self-obliteration (through sex, music, drugs, politics, whatever), he anticipates Judgment Day a little too matter-of-factly—or is it eagerly?—to suit me.

Prince is one rock and roller who would do this practical agnostic's heart good by playing a few MUSE benefits. I just want to get through this thing called life.

1984

Magnificent Seven: Grandmaster Flash & the Furious Five

Since rappers promote their tags as jealously as graffiti writers, I'm chagrined to admit that sometimes I still have trouble telling everybody in Grandmaster Flash & the Furious Five apart. Maybe if I came from the South Bronx it would be different, but then, I couldn't even connect the Beatles' names with their faces until *A Hard Day's Night*—they were just THE BEATLES to me, and that was plenty. I've always had a fix on Cowboy, who favors the appropriate hat and flaunts a big, oily, orotund delivery, and Kid Creole, who's light-skinned and sharp-voiced. And Flash has never been a problem—he's the unsmiling Stevie Wonder lookalike who hunches behind the turntables and rides the others' shoulders. But Melle Mel (serious), Raheem (romantic tenor), and Mr. Ness (?) were a blur before the group's Pep gig in September.

From the moment I laid eyes on them in March 1981, however, I've had no doubt at all about GRANDMASTER FLASH & THE FURIOUS FIVE. Stuck between the Funky Four Plus One, whose "That's the Joint" remains rap's greatest record, and the Sugarhill Gang, the supposed stars of the show, they'd run away with rap night at the Ritz before Flash's first quick-cut. Their matching red soul-act suits (with piping for contrast and green ribbons for unity) gave immediate notice that showbiz corn was their vocation, but it was obvious just as fast that these menchildren (a) believed in what they were doing and (b) had their own way of doing it. They told us that they were only half of the show and made the old give-yourself-a-hand routine come true, because it really is the audience's response that turns the rappers' call into the party music it was born to be. They got to a blat I'd always taken for synthesized pseudohorns and proved that mixing equals musicianship—it was a revelation to see Flash produce that sound by dragging a record backwards on the turntable in precisely timed scrapes. They orchestrated a minute of silence for the Atlanta slain with the same concentration that illumined their fast-talking jive. They came up with choreography that brought Tempts-style footwork out of mothballs. And they went off with a capper that was both a star gang's grand boast and a street group's democratic credo: "Remember—seven men, two machines."

Yet amazing as that night was, my next three sightings were more so. May 9 at the 369th Regiment Armory someone flashed a gun and set off a stampede for the exits that interrupted Sugarhill's 1st Annual Rappers Convention for over an hour before my wife and I gave up and escaped, but we'll never forget Melle Mel's (I think) angry announcement during a lull: "We're all going to forget we ever ran!" And that display of positivity had nothing on their second Clash show at Bond's in June. The first night they were reportedly flustered by the insults and beer cups with which they were barraged by the assembled music lovers, but Friday they came prepared, wearing street clothes instead of soul suits and making very clear that they'd been proving their manhood since they were nine. Only a minority of the crowd was against them, but there was still debris in the air every few seconds, and damned if they didn't work it into the act, dodging like it was a new dance and firing cups back on the one. Furious for real, doubly intent in defiance of the distraction, they were a hell of a magnificent seven, and once again Melle Mel (I think) had the last word: "Some of you—not all of you, but some of you—are stupid."

Right now the Five enjoy a more amicable relationship with l'homme moyenne nueuo wavo, having proven their Art with a protest single that vied with "Abracadabra" and "Eye of the Tiger" on the city's overheated airwaves while taking on A Flock of Seagulls in its air-conditioned dance clubs. So at the Pep their theme was "Unity," and after a year on the road they could make it stick. The costumes were more grandiose and eccentric—very leather, very showbiz, very street—and so was the show itself, a pulsating, snakelike thing that included several quick-mix features for Flash, a modicum of kidding around, every single they'd ever made, and no band. It was raucous, participatory, and breathtaking.

From "Super Rappin' No. 2," their second release with Enjoy in 1979, the Furious Five have located rap somewhere to the rhythmic left of the hardest hard funk tradition, James Brown circa "Sex Machine" and "Mother Popcorn." They rock the body by pushing the beat (like Trouble Funk and the Treacherous Three) rather than teasing it by teasing it (like Spoonie Gee or Soul Sonic Force). This almost athletic physical excitement, this willed and urgent hope, has been the core of their real message no matter what party slogan or all-night boast they've set to it, and though they can't claim the tonal variety of a Trouble Funk, they establish considerable vocal individuality without entering the cartoon territory that is funk's comic blessing and romantic / realistic curse. Extreme pulse plus normal timbre—combined, of course, with Flash's mastery of rhythmic shape and the nonpareil Sugarhill band—have made them the definitive rappers.

But rap's commercial appeal proved marginal, and the hits didn't keep on coming. "The Birthday Party" (everybody has a birthday) was a clever follow-up to "Freedom" (everybody has a name), but only their raunchy remake of "Genius of Love"—not the Sugarhill Gang collaboration, not Flash's beat-box track, not even the seminal "Wheels of Steel"—enjoyed major sales success thereafter. Even so, Sugarhill matriarch Sylvia Robinson had to talk them into cutting "The Message" ("Why bring your troubles to the discotheque?" they asked Richard Grabel in *NME*), most of which was written by Sugarhill percussionist (and Columbia grad) Duke Bootee, and anyone anticipating a synthesis of the Gap Band and the Last Poets will pooh-pooh their debut album, *The Message*. Forget Funkadelic, forget James Brown even—these guys love Rick James and Stevie Wonder. They want to cross over. They want cash mon-ee.

Only it's nowhere near that simple, because they really do believe in what they're doing and they really do have their own way of doing it. I was put off by the new album myself. Here they were diddling around with vocal synthesizers (on their latest single, "Scorpio") and even singing instead of reprising "Freedom" or "The Birthday Party"; not counting "The Message" and a truncated "It's Nasty (Genius of Love)," only "She's Fresh," a borrowed funk showpiece featuring calisthenic bassist Doug Wimbish, three-handed drummer Keith LeBlanc, and a new universal party slogan (everybody loves their mother), was an instant hit at my house. But I'd already noticed that on "Dreamin," a song Raheem wrote for and sings like Stevie Wonder, he did actually display some vocal deftness, thus distinguishing himself from Kurtis Blow, Joseph Bowie, and the entire population of the United Kingdom. And then I registered a bit of dialogue in the break that goes like this: "Hey Flash." "What's up, Ness?" "Do you think we ever meet Stevie?" "I hope so, man." "Don't worry fellas, man, sooner or later . . . sooner or later."

I confess I'm a sucker for such fannish moments, and if you're not, why don't you go read William Gass or something? Its calculated guilelessness—which as all rock and rollers know is hardly a contradiction in terms—opened me up. I began to find "Scorpio" cute, and to take notice when their impressionistic interpretation of the Spinners' "It's a Shame" posited that cash mon-ee is the root of all evil. I even got to where I kind of liked Raheem's Jesus song.

The Message tries to be commercial—to touch bases with a broad demographic—but it's anything but formulaic. On the contrary, it's experimental, like albums used to be, and in the end every experiment justifies itself. Grandmaster Flash & the Furious Five would never have gotten this far on grim observations of ghetto life. They believe in positivity, in a hope that is willed and urgent. They make you wonder how much talent roams the streets of the South Bronx. And they make you grateful that they've done so much with theirs.

1982

The Beastie Boys Go Too Far

On the rap report card Kool Moe Dee stuck into *How Ya Like Me Now* back in 1987, the old-schooler proved an easy marker—only two of twenty-five pupils fell below Public Enemy at 80 B. The token nonentity Boogie Boys got a 7 or 8 in teach's ten categories for a 77 C +, and way below that were the perpetrators of history's best-selling rap album, the Beastie Boys, with a 10 in sticking to themes, an 8 in records and stage presence, and a 6 or 7 in vocabulary, voice, versatility, articulation, creativity, originality, and innovating rhythms. Total: 70, barely a C.

You can laugh off these grades, but with Moe Dee's arch-rival L.L. Cool J tied for fifth at 90 A, they did represent his sincere attempt to formalize the values of his fading artistic generation—values upended by Public Enemy and the Beasties. A career non-dropout who earned a communications B.A. while leading the Treacherous Three, Moe Dee idealized upright manliness; having come up in a vital performance community, he didn't consider records important enough to mark for hooks, mixing, sampling, pacing, innovating textures, and what-have-you. Like most rock and roll pioneers, he couldn't comprehend the upheaval he'd helped instigate: a music composed in the studio by copycats so in love with rap that they thought nothing of stretching it, mocking it, wrecking it, exploiting it—going too far, taking it up and over and out and around, making it better.

If Public Enemy were a threat—collegians with a radical program, arrogantly burying their pleasures deep—the Beasties were an insult: they dissed everything Moe Dee stood for. Sons of the artistic upper-middle class (architect, art dealer, playwright), they laughed at the education Chuck D made something of and Moe Dee strove for (two years at Bard, term at Vassar, two hours at Manhattan Community). Like millions of bohos before them, they were anything but upright, boys not men for as long as they could get away with it. As born aesthetes, they grabbed onto rap's musical quality and potential; as reflexive rebels, they celebrated its unacceptability in the punk subculture and the world outside. And of course, they were white in a genre invented by and for black teenagers whose racial consciousness ran deep and would soon get large.

The way the Beasties tapped the hip hop audience says plenty for the open-minded intelligence of their black manager and the black kids he steered them toward, but also testifies to their own instinct and flair—those few white imitators who aren't merely horrendous don't come close to the Beasties' street credibility. We were probably right to credit Rick Rubin with all the what-have-you that briefly made *Licensed To Ill* history's greatest rap album, but in retrospect one recalls the once fashionable fallacy that George Martin was the fifth Beatle. Certainly the Beasties' unduplicable personas and perfect timing were what Rubin's expansive metal-rap was selling, and most likely a fair share of the music was their idea. We didn't think they could top themselves not because they were stupid or untalented—except for a few cretins in the Brit tabloids, nobody really believed that—but because their achievement was untoppable by definition. Outrage gets old fast, and rap eats its kings like no pop subgenre ever.

Soon lots of things changed. The Beasties' street cred dimmed as "Fight for Your Right" went pop and Public Enemy turned hip hop to black nationalism. Due partly to the Beasties and mostly to how good the shit was, *Yo! MTV Raps* brought black rap to the white audience. History's biggest-selling rap single (and first number-one black rap album) was recorded in L.A. by a former repo man. After feuding with his black partner, Rick Rubin transmuted into a metal producer, and after feuding with their black manager, the Beasties became Capitol's first East Coast rap signing since the Boogie Boys. Chuck D. and Hank Shocklee undertook to mix up a since-aborted album of the Beasties' Def Jam outtakes. And if the Beasties' *Paul's Boutique* doesn't top *Licensed To Ill,* though in some ways it does, it's up there with De La Soul in a year when Moe Dee is showing his age and L.L. Cool J is holding onto his crown for dear life.

Avant-garde as rap, *Licensed To Ill* was pop as metal, foregrounding riffs and attitude any hedonist could love while eliminating wack solos and dumbass posturing (just like Kool Moe Dee, metal fans think David Coverdale has more "voice" than Johnny Thunders). *Paul's Boutique* isn't as user-friendly—no rock anthem like "Fight for Your Right" here, or street beats like "Hold It, Now Hit It" 's either. But give it three plays and half a j's worth of concentration and its high-speed volubility and riffs from nowhere will amaze and delight you. It's a generous tour de force—an absolutely unpretentious and unsententious affirmation of cultural diversity, of where they came from and where they went from there.

For versatility, or at least variety, check the names they check: Cézanne, Houdini, Newton, Salinger, Ponce de Leon, Sadaharu Oh, Phil Rizzuto, Bob Dylan, Jelly Roll Morton, Jerry Lee Swaggart, Jerry Lee Falwell, Joe Blow. Or the samples they exploit less as hooks than as tags, referents: Funky Four Plus One (twice), Johnny Cash, Charlie Daniels, Public Enemy, Wailers, Eek-a-Mouse (I think), Jean Knight, Ricky Skaggs (I think), and many others. For innovating rhythms, there are countless funk and metal (and other) artists I can't ID even when I recognize them. For vocabulary, start with "I'm Adam and I'm adamant about living large," or maybe "Expressing my aggressions through my schizophrenic verse words" (rhymes with "cursewords"), then ponder these pairings: snifter-shoplifter, selfish-shellfish, homeless-phoneless, cellular–hell you were, fuck this–Butkus. Not what Moe Dee had in mind, of course. But definitely what all avatars of information overload have in mind, or some of it: "If I had a penny for my thoughts I'd be a millionaire."

These Beasties aren't as stoopid or stupid as the ones Rick Rubin gave the world (or as Rick Rubin). In fact, one of the most impressive things about *Paul's Boutique* is what can only be called its moral tone. The Beasties are still bad—they get laid, they do drugs, they break laws, they laze around. But this time they know the difference between bad and evil. Crack and cocaine and woman-beaters and stickup kids get theirs; one song goes out to a homeless rockabilly wino, another ends, "Racism is schism on the serious tip." For violence in the street we have the amazing "Egg Man," in which they pelt various straights, fall guys, and miscreants with "a symbol of life": "Not like the crack that you put in a pipe/But the crack on your forehead here's/A towel now wipe." Hostile? Why not? Destructive? Not if they can help it without trying too hard.

Just to dis Def Jam—check "Car Thief," which also takes on the presidency—the Beasties couldn't have picked more apposite collaborators than L.A.'s Dust Brothers, one of whom coproduced the aforementioned number-one rap album. But where Tone-Loc's *Loc-ed After Dark* is simplistic, its beats and hooks marched out one at a time, *Paul's Boutique* is jam-packed, frenetic, stark. It doesn't groove with the affirmative, danceable swagger of Kool Moe Dee or L.L. Cool J, and its catholicity is very much in-your-face—as is its unspoken avowal that the music of a nascent Afro-centrism can still be stretched (mocked? wrecked?) by sons of the white artistic upper-middle class. Having gotten rich off rap, the Beasties now presume to adapt it to *their* roots, to make *Paul's Boutique* a triumph of postmodern "art." Their sampling comes down on the side of dissociation, not synthesis—of a subculture happily at the end of its tether rather than nascent anything. It impolitely demonstrates that privileged wise guys can repossess the media options Moe Dee was battling for back when they were still punks in prep school. After all, this deliberately difficult piece of product will outsell Moe Dee's own *Knowledge Is King.* One can only hope he's race man enough to take satisfaction in its failure to overtake L.L.'s *Walking with a Panther,* or *Loc-ed After Dark.*

1989

Looking for the Perfect Public Enemy

Unchic, fresh-faced, impossible to read classwise beyond student/ boho/B-boy, the fans who greeted the nineties in the dank Avenue C grandeur of the World were as racially integrated as any rock audience I've ever seen—fifty-fifty black-white plus a few Latinos and more Asians, with interracial groups and couples common. The date-night crowd broke down fifty-fifty male-female too, and made just enough New Year's whoopee to generate an infectious bonhomie. Whenever an anonymous voice would interrupt the dance records nobody was dancing to to try and stoke the PE fever already in effect, there'd be mild cheers followed by more patient joshing around. As twelve-thirty inched toward one-thirty and then two, however, some traditional rock restiveness surfaced. "BULLSHIT, BULLSHIT," "SHUT THE FUCK UP," "WE WANT PUB-LIC N-M-E," a few (mostly white) fans chanted. But when Flavor Flav yelled "Happy motherfuckin' New Year," any lingering fears disappeared. Public Enemy lives. It's even possible, as they insisted more than once, that they are family.

Live rap often flirts with consumer fraud, but PE has some moves—check Chuck D.'s prophetic rage and Flav's perpetual motion on the imaginatively gimmicked *Fight the Power Live* video. And though they hadn't gigged since the summer, what kept them from tearing the roof off the World was speeches, twenty or twenty-five minutes worth in an eighty-minute set, plus maybe the late start—rock-star power-tripping for a crowd that wasn't buy-

ing any. The music per se was hype, def; it rocked. "Black Steel,"
"Baseheads," "Bring the Noise," and "Don't Believe the Hype"
were riveting aural overkill in hectic motion, with Chuck racing
cross-country with the beat like Jim Brown pursued by the Great
Satan, a pace that didn't daunt the (mostly black) fans who followed him word for word from the moment he lit up the just-
released "Welcome to the Terrordome." But "Terrordome" was
the only preview of *Fear of a Black Planet,* now promised for late
February and don't bet on it. So the sense of historical urgency
that must always underpin Public Enemy's musical urgency was
left to the oratory.

A keyword was "controversy," the band's (especially Flav's)
favored euphemism for the shitstorm they've inhabited since last
May, when Minister of Information Professor Griff spewed anti-
Semitic canards into the tape recorder of black *Washington Times*
reporter David Mills—not just anti-Zionism run amok but pure,
sick, hate-filled paranoia, with Henry Ford's *The International Jew*
a prime cited source and the style of thought as telling as the
substance ("faggot"-baiting, a single man "owning" an enormous
corporation). Well before the shitstorm, the jealousies and
thwarted egos that tear at all newly successful groups had been
complicated by U.K. interviews in which Griff calmly posited the
righteous slaughter of gays and Israelis, and for weeks Griff's
status and the group's very existence were day-to-day. New Year's
Eve, however, Griff—who, dressed with the rectitude of a Muslim
at the mosque, allowed as how he wasn't the "partyin' type"—
opened the festivities. He announced another album due in February, from the misogynist free-speech advocates at Miami's Luke
Skyywalker Records: *Pawns in the Game,* by Professor Griff and
the Last Asiatic Disciples. After warning that "the U.S. government
got some shit comin' for both black people and white people"—
an AIDS plot, apparently—and pointing a finger at "the superrich,"
he told the whites in the audience: "Griff is not your enemy." And
he responded to the angry scrutiny "Terrordome" has excited in
the New York press: "You weigh and judge it for yourself. Deal
with the lyrics yourself. You think for your goddamn self."

Media devil that I am, I will of course deal with the lyrics
myself. But first I'll sneak in something about the music, which
would have made "Terrordome" an item even if Chuck had had
the decency to cut it four lines. Not since Hank Shocklee and

friends redefined rap with the thick allusions and police-siren sonics of "Bring the Noise" has the group achieved anything so striking, and the biggest advance belongs to Chuck, whose agile phrasing—he shifts angles three times in the twelve words of "What I got better get some get on up/Hustler of culture"—tempers the PE hardbeats with almost jazzy fluidity. Where the sloganeering "Fight the Power" goes on for a mere three-and-a-half minutes before breaking into its James Brown coda, "Terrordome" lasts a dense, unrepetitive five-and-a-half, over a hundred lines of personal mythologizing. Chuck has claimed the Griff crisis energized him artistically. For once maybe he wasn't bullshitting.

True, "Terrordome" 's more obscure references smell of rock-star insularity, a cross between "Subterranean Homesick Blues" and "Almost Cut My Hair." Because it's clearer, you could even argue that "Don't Believe the Hype" is a more effective transformation of self-promotion into PE's black-youth-as-public-enemy metaphor—while no outsider would call their ideology coherent, gradually Public Enemy has earned the right to be seen as a progressive public entity. Though a lot of "Terrordome" 's verbiage connects—Chuck is at least as gifted a poet as, let us say, Clash-era Joe Strummer—too much of it is incomprehensible except to insiders, and the big man's most generous moments, which he needs for mental health, are his simplest: "My home is your home," "Move as a team, never move alone," or, most effective, "God bless your soul and keep livin'." He's right to believe the song is far more critical of blacks than of whites or Jews or even the hated media. But the first black criticized would appear to be David Mills, and to go from Mills's whistle-blowing to Malcolm X's assassination is self-pitying, self-aggrandizing bullshit. However mixed the reporter's motives, he caught Griff in slanders that were intolerable—slanders Chuck himself has labeled "offensive" and even "racist" (though never "anti-Semitic") in his more measured moments.

And now, however much the tortuous moralism of the "Terrordome" controversy overstates the case and exacerbates underlying problems, Chuck has been caught in a comparable if less grave offense. Not with "Told the rab get off the rag," not unless you're so up in arms you think "rab" is an ethnic slur—by locating the rabbi in question at the Simon Wiesenthal Center for Holocaust Studies, *Newsday*'s Wayne Robins inadvertently establishes that the line is *not* directed at a group. But "Crucifixion ain't no fiction/So-called chosen frozen/Apologies made to whoever pleases/Still they got me like Jesus" wins the prize—even if Chuck believes the media crucified him and thinks "chosen" disses the Nation of Islam too and knows the Romans killed Jesus, even if the ignorant mother is only dimly aware that for more than a millennium anti-Semites have whipped up fear and loathing by charging Jews with the death of Christ. The syntax leaves him some outs, but the brute juxtaposition does all the damage that's necessary, forever associating Jews with deicide in the mind of every fan who knows his lyrics by heart. And if, as I suspect, Chuck wrote the lines without much thought and stuck by them mainly because he'd been told he couldn't—as one associate observed, "Essentially it boils down to a macho thing with him"—that just makes the offense worse. When you set yourself up as a political icon, you assume responsibility for the consequences of your actions. If, as Chuck had the guts to say about Griff last June, "You can't talk about attacking racism and be racist," you obviously can't defame and endanger a whole class of people to prove you're a big man, either.

But the hard question isn't whether "Terrordome" is anti-Semitic—it's whether that's the end of the story. I know both blacks and Jews who pooh-pooh the controversy largely because they're afraid overt anti-Semitism in Public Enemy's art per se will prove the last straw for many of the group's erstwhile sympathizers, as it clearly has. So now, having alienated readers who believe (reasonably) that the attacks on the group are inspired more by fear of a radicalized black youth and planet than by any impartial commitment to justice or (much less reasonably) that anti-Semitism gets too much press, I will alienate those who believe (reasonably) that neither leftists nor blacks take anti-Semitism seriously enough or (much less reasonably) that leftists will let blacks get away with anything. First by emphasizing that Chuck's offense is indeed indirect, allusive—he may be spreading anti-Semitism, but he's not advocating it; "Terrordome" is nowhere near as virulent as Guns N' Roses' "One in a Million," which even now has attracted far less opprobrium. And second by stating the painfully obvious: for any American leftist—not least a white male goyische leftist with immense debts to both blacks and Jews (and that means every one of us)—there is no contradiction more frustrating and tragic than black anti-Semitism. Of course, the only reason Jewish racism doesn't seem equally frustrating and tragic from a left perspective is that most Jewish racists have moved permanently outside any conceivable left consensus (though unlike the rest of white racism, Jewish racism at least counts as a contradiction—that's how much Jews mean to the American left). And even worse, one of the most frustrating and tragic aspects of black anti-Semitism is that it's understandable—not in any way justifiable, but understandable.

It feels shitty to moralize tortuously, exacerbating underlying problems, knowing no even-handed analysis is practicable. Not as shitty as living a life hemmed in by prejudice, I'm sure, but shitty enough. How can I expect to explain why I think black anti-Semitism is understandable (affluence, the myth of the media, landlords, Zionism and the Arabs, Israel and South Africa, competing holocausts, but every topic demands paragraphs, essays, books) in what's supposed to be a music piece? All I can do is throw up my hands against the inevitable crossfire and return to my review. Because if you'll remember there was a concert in progress. And though I had already reached my verdict on "Welcome to the Terrordome," I wanted to know what was going to happen next—not because I was on assignment but because Public Enemy still mattered to me. And why shouldn't they? Not only are they the most innovative popular musicians in America if not the world—harsh, turbulent, undercut by an irritating background buzz that proves an excitant once you adjust, turning urban stress into music, with relief of sorts provided by orotund preachifying and wild hilarity and a pulse that keeps your body so busy you forget to worry about breaking your neck. They're also the most politically ambitious. Not even in the heyday of the aforementioned Clash has any group come so close to the elusive and perhaps ridiculous sixties rock ideal of raising political consciousness with music. However mixed their motives, they have actually instigated a species of leftish Afrocentrism among second-generation B-boys—enough that they at least adorn themselves with leather Africa medallions instead of dookie gold.

And so I listened to Chuck's speeches—each preceded by the claim that he didn't want to give a lot of speeches—and was not surprised to find much of what he said simplistic and some of it a little scary. This was a man who thought it cool to try and be more unpopular than Jesus now. Of course he dissed the schools (what could we expect of institutions founded to help "WASP land-owners' sons" consolidate their power?) and journalism ("the media collectively is a devil") and Elvis (has Chuck ever revealed on what evidence beyond that of "redneck" origins he bases "Straight-out racist the sucker was simple and plain"?) and the American flag (as a white fan burned one, Flav drunkenly intoned, "I pledge allegiance to my dick, and to the pussy for which it stands"). The scary stuff was the talk about being "first-world" rather than "third-world," later fleshed out with the phony statis-tic that only 8 percent of the earth's population is white. Anybody who takes anti-Semitism seriously knows enough to fear majori-tarianism in any form.

Still, at a shitstorm press conference last June, Chuck had told us, "I don't even wanta get into the religion game, because I just think religion throughout the years has been a conspiracy by the world leaders to trick the people." "Right on," I muttered. He reminded me then of the smartest guy at a dorm-room bull ses-sion, and he still does. For sure it was reassuring to hear "capi-talism" used as a dirty word. And toward the end there was some-thing called the Jackass Theory—"Just Acting Caucasian Kills a Simple Solution"—that Peter Watrous got all the way wrong in his *Times* review. Chuck's pronunciamento wasn't about "blacks who 'act white' "—it was his promise that the day *whites* look at them-selves as human beings, rather than as whites, was "the day we'll let a little bit of our black nationalist pride slip." This I found unthreatening and well-put. Like Chuck, I believe that "white world cultural supremacy is not good." Guess I'll let blacks get away with anything.

Right—me and all those fresh-faced students/bohos who'd been chanting "BULLSHIT BULLSHIT" two hours before. Because somehow, there I was in the same old rock-dream time-warp, tak-ing in a talented egomaniac's radical rhetoric with an audience I liked more than I liked him. Rap shows at the World are notorious for drawing an element, to use a term making a fishy comeback. But though five different people of three different races were curi-ous as to why I was taking notes, the only hint of racial hostility I experienced, observed, or heard tell of was a baleful glance when I heckled Griff. Past disappointments teach us not to feel much confidence that what happened in the concert hall will have permanent ramifications in the real world, and Chuck is certainly more an icon than a politician—entertainment is what he was born for. But the Public Enemy controversy is obviously the Jesse Jackson controversy in symbolic miniature, reflecting all the anxiety that accrues when leadership in what miserable tatters remain of a viable American left passes out of the hands of well-meaning white people. I don't think "Hymietown" was a meaningless slip of the tongue any more than "so-called chosen frozen." Nor do I think Jackson has altogether transcended it. Does that mean his story ends there?

With a bare modicum of wisdom or consistency all you can expect of full-fledged politicians, it's a loser's game to put your world-historical hopes in entertainer-icons. All you can do is pray they offer some sustaining possibility or pleasure. Here is a political band riding the kind of groove only the greats ever get near. So to cop the title of Jack Thompson's *Swellsville* screed on Griff, Simon Frith, and the postpomo dilemma, don't go looking for the perfect Public Enemy. Although the sorry history of integration has once again convinced many of us that some sort of black-power program is essential to the most basic kind of black equality, the details of that program have escaped thinkers far more sapient than Chuck D. Yet "Terrordome"—and the audience gathered to greet it—convince me that he does more good than harm anyway. The best we can hope is that this latest setback will prove educational—the learn-from-our-mistakes/trials model. The worst we can fear is that it will serve to unloose the already overflowing backlog of desperation and paranoia on both sides of the color line. So as a well-meaning white person who can't (and wouldn't) be anything else, I continue to extend my vigilantly critical support. I don't like that phrase either—it's too stuffy, too tortuous. But in a world we never made, bullshit is something none of us can avoid.

1989–1990

An Autodidact's History of KRS-One

Having charged that the American educational system trained black kids to be white, KRS-One was doing his bit to counter the deprogramming. "Genesis Chapter 11 Verse 10/Explains the genealogy of Shem/Shem was a black man in Africa/If you repeat this fact they can't laugh at ya," began twenty-six attention-getting lines of "Why Is That?" the most controversial song on Boogie Down Productions' *Ghetto Music: The Blueprint of Hip Hop.* The exegesis concluded: "Moses had to be of the black race/Because he spent forty-eight years in Pharaoh's place/He passed as the Pharaoh's grandson/So he had to look just like him." In 1992, with Leonard Jeffries a liberal boogeyman and a black Cleopatra on the cover of *Newsweek,* the shock value has receded. But in 1989 it was sensational stuff, the tip of the Afrocentric iceberg, and because I cared about rap, Africa, America, political art, and the political artist in question, I felt moved to investigate.

I found nothing in Genesis 11 about Africa—the history it outlines starts in Mesopotamia, now Iraq, and proceeds to Canaan, now Palestine—or Shem's skin color. But Shem, Noah's firstborn son, is a crucial figure—the etymological if not biological forefather of the Semites, a linguistically defined grouping that according to my 1968 *Columbia Encyclopedia* encompasses the Arabs and many other peoples of southwestern Asia, among them the Hebrews, as well as "a considerable portion of the population of

Ethiopia." And soon—with the aid of a reading list distributed by his publicist, Leyla Turkkan, that included three titles she'd suggested herself—I started double-checking KRS-One's research. His citations were sometimes hard to trace. *The Pleasures of Philosophy* is one of Will Durant's more obscure titles, I've yet to find another reference to Kwame Nkrumah's *Hills of Africa,* and I learned from another bibliography that *The West and the Rest of Us* is by Chinweizu, not Chinua Achebe. But to my incalculable benefit—Walter Rodney's *How Europe Underdeveloped Africa* is as epochal as E. P. Thompson's *Making of the English Working Class*—I located and read five of his ten recommendations. And in the most peculiar of these—Rudolph R. Windsor's *From Babylon to Timbuktu,* published by a New York vanity house in 1969 and still in print—I reencountered Shem.

In effect, Windsor's "History of the Ancient Black Races Including the Black Hebrews" stakes a militantly African-American claim on the Judeo-Christian imagery that inspired the political generation of Martin Luther King, Jr., a quote from whom closes the book. His jerrybuilt exposition, sporadic sourcing, and chronic confusion between inference and proof are classic amateur scholarship. When he reads the Bible as history, or recounts an apparently nonbiblical tale about Moses and some flying snakes as flat fact, or leaps without warning from the Old Testament to 378 A.D. ("the Germanic tribes were on the move"), it doesn't do much for his tentatively proffered theory that the first whites were lepers (although note that he also suspects whites learned racism from the cruel "segregation" of lepers by Israelites and other black ancients). No way do Windsor's deficiencies make me suspect the Hebrews were white; they were certainly a lot darker than they used to appear on the flannelgraph in my Sunday school. But neither does he prove that the Hebrews—or the children of Shem, in the unlikely event that such existed—were black. And several of his key assumptions are challenged in a more authoritative book on KRS-One's list, Cheikh Anta Diop's *The African Origin of Civilization.* Where Windsor begins, "More than six thousand years ago in the land called Mesopotamia there developed the most remarkable civilization then known to mankind," the Senegalese scholar devotes a cogent chapter to demonstrating that Egyptian culture preceded Mesopotamian. As for the Hebrews, Diop regards them as a minor nomadic tribe who eventually carried the monotheism they learned from the Egyptians "to a rather remarkable degree of development."

"Why Is That?" wasn't based on Windsor, who only refers to Shem in passing. KRS-One told the Los Angeles *Times*'s Steve Hochman he'd been inspired to "personal research" by "Dr. Ben," as renegade Egyptologist Yoseph ben Jochannon is known. But when I interviewed the rapper after the March release of *Sex and Violence,* he couldn't recall Dr. Ben's name, referring me instead to Ella Stokely's *The Truth About the Hebrew Israelites. From Babylon to Timbuktu* he remembered, though, and when I pointed out how radically Windsor differed from Diop on the Mesopotamian question, his enthusiasm didn't diminish. "History is something that you should never base your argument on. Neither one of those guys was there. And neither was the reader. What would make me move would be what is right—what is right and what is wrong, who has gained and who has lessened, who has advanced and who has regressed and why. We should try to find the similarities in the argument rather than the differences in the argument."

This pragmatic view of scholarship may seem deplorable in someone who guarantees that no one will laugh at his "facts." It's the kind of thing that makes commentators as diverse as Playthell Benjamin and P.M. Dawn believe KRS-One has no right to appoint himself "The Teacher." But I can't say I share their indignation. Together with Chuck D., KRS-One created the ethos in which rap strives, as the cover sticker of *Ghetto Music* proclaimed, "to strengthen and uplift the mind." Much more than Chuck D., he's a voracious information gatherer, and as he understands the term, he qualifies as a teacher simply by provoking thought. But he's strictly self-taught, an autodidact actively hostile to academic standards, and he never forgets that he's an entertainer. He remains unique in rap not because he's so learned or positive or political, but because no other rapper has so straightforwardly exploited the didactic as a musical mode.

However much he hated school, KRS-One has the air of an inspired junior high school teacher—someone with a gift for putting across big ideas he doesn't altogether grasp himself. Even when he's boasting or telling tales, he cultivates the sound of a soapbox lecturer—an almost stentorian street voice instructing and declaiming over rhythms so controlled and utilitarian they never detract from the power and clarity of his words. There are a dozen varieties of indigestible experience contained in his blunt, hortatory, amused, slightly scornful New Yorkese. He's concocted some great yarns, and he's definitely a phrasemaker. But from "Listen to my nine-millimeter go bang" to "Disattach yourself from my penis," his lyrics show little of word-drunk delight that animates rappers as serious as X-Clan and Chuck D. He doesn't pun or invent argot, and his rhymes per se are often joyless afterthoughts—"grandson"/"like him" or "Africa"/"laugh at ya," which got its start in *By All Means Necessary*'s "Stop the Violence" and comes up again in *Edutainment*'s "Blackman in Effect." I wasn't surprised to learn that during his years as a Brooklyn Public Library-based runaway teen, he read no fiction—and though the first cut on his first album was called "Poetry," not much of that either. "Always true things—always reality."

No one in hip hop has nurtured a more thoughtful persona than KRS-One, whose proud black "humanism" long ago set him apart from positive rap's reflexive Afrocentricity. The image, and to an unusual extent the life behind it, has emphasized responsible activism. At the time of *Ghetto Music* and *Edutainment,* when he was the titular head of the Stop the Violence Movement, KRS-One's respectability had gone so far that he was widely perceived as Martin to Chuck D.'s Malcolm. He held forth on talk shows, published a *Times* op-ed piece; even today he lectures at colleges and juices H.E.A.L. (Human Education Against Lies), which put out the *Civilization Vs. Technology* album with his Elektra-backed Edutainer imprint last year. But KRS-One also invented gangsta if anyone did, and has worked to stay large in a hip hop community he defines as street and nonwhite. After 1987's tremendously influential *Criminal Minded,* on a label whose accounting practices discouraged RIAA scrutiny, three studio releases for RCA-distributed Jive went gold; *Live Hardcore Worldwide,* last year's *Criminal Minded* reprise, didn't. That makes *Sex and Violence* Boogie Down Productions' sixth album, an impressive total matched in rap only by hit has-beens the Fat Boys and Kurtis Blow, whose examples KRS-One has no intention of following. Humanist he may be; pop he ain't. Commercially, politically, *artistically,* he's true to his subculture, and like any cult artist he counts on a hard core of support: "You know it's funny everybody wants money/And material things from cars to chicken wings/When they sing they sing for the cash/They fail to realize respect will outlast cash."

Lyrically, where it counts, *Sex and Violence* is the strongest album of Kris Parker's sometimes frustrating career. Of course it's asinine to blame rape on see-through dresses, and of course the loose talk doesn't stop there. But it's pointless to expect MLK imitations from a guy who says "Ready for the revolution" when he answers the phone—who completes the catch-phrase "Stop the Violence" with the qualifier "in hip hop" (if not "and start the revolution") and believes "World Peace" must be "taken." Beneath the thoughtfulness lurks a rhetorical provocateur, never more in evidence than on a record that seems designed to piss everybody off at least once. Drug dealers fare better than "barbarian" schoolteachers, Clarence Thomas and Colin Powell are "the devil," and insults are leveled not just at fronting gangstas, wanton women, and sucker MCs but at Muslims of convenience spouting "original man" dogma ("The first man with the first tan on the first land with the first plan?/Who gives a damn?"). Sticklers for academic detail will be pleased to learn that he's cut down on the history lessons. But they won't like it when he calls English "the language of the devil." I sure don't. No wonder this Anglophone versifier takes so little pleasure in words per se.

Pleasure has been a problem for KRS-One since his partner and mentor DJ Scott LaRock was killed trying to break up a beef in 1987. He's too stingy with beats; sometimes I think he moans so much about pop rap and gangstas "only tryin' to rock the party" because he knows suckers are showing him up. But as the deep intricacy of such polar opposites as De La Soul and the Bomb Squad coalesces into yet another arcane pop dialect for yet another far-flung coterie of cognoscenti, Kris Parker's musical austerity—"I could rhyme to a snare and no bass or just a kick," he told me—is showing its strengths. The new album is catchier than the BDP norm without sacrificing trademark simplicity, and a clear, authoritative, charming, even sexy show at the Ritz was only set in relief by the labyrinthine wordplay and busy beats of the younger FU-Schnickens and UMC's—both fun, both overpowered by the old-school headliner. But because subcultures evolve—big more incomprehensibly than small, teen more inexorably than adult, none more rapidly than hip hop—it seems possible that BDP's street respect has peaked. *Sex and Violence* has stalled well short of gold, and it features enough original-is-still-the-greatest bluster to suggest that KRS-One worried about this in advance. Seizing the stage from his perceived pop-rap rivals P.M. Dawn was a bully-boy PR stunt aimed at the hardcore audience he believes in—which he then reprised by berating black teenzine journalists at a press conference called to announce a cease-fire with his perceived Afrocentric rivals X-Clan.

Not yet twenty-seven, KRS-One seems certain to remain a revered rap elder, like Kool Moe Dee with far more weight and charisma. It seems equally certain, however, that BDP will never command the juice of Public Enemy. And if on the one hand that's only fair—BDP flat-out ain't as good as PE—it's also a loss. Kris Parker isn't a more scintillating or satisfying artist than Chuck D. But he is more street and more bookish, more indigenous and more idiosyncratic, more suggestive. Having lived his adolescence first as an off-and-on runaway, then as a homeless frequenter of the parks, subways, and libraries, finally as a shelter resident pursuing educational opportunities for his bed and board, he's got stronger ties to the criminal-minded and the deep poor than Chuck, who no matter how much he hung out remained a middle-class kid with a business head and a college ID. But he doesn't fit the ghetto-bastard stereotype—the academic demands of his college-educated mom were one of the things he rebelled against. He thinks for himself. And like so many autodidacts, he has truths to tell whatever the quality of his facts.

In his music and his public pronouncements, KRS-One insists that like all "African-Americans" he's African, not American. "To call yourself a nationality that is killing you is self-destructive," he told me after acknowledging that he'd never been to Africa. "Why not call yourself the part of you that is alive? Why show respect to the side of you that shows you no respect, no honor, no morals? It's how I feel, my love for bass and heat." Nevertheless, the free hand with which he assembles his shifting patchwork of ideas and attitudes recalls the naive, rootless, arrogant appropriations of American culture—the kind he regularly brands "theft"—more than the syncretic adaptations of Africa, which has spent most of this millennium digesting the usages of Islamic traders and Christian conquerors. He's unimaginable anywhere else but here.

No way are the two equal in genius, but I'd even call him brother to one of the most American of all artists—there's something Whitmanesque about KRS-One. Alone among the rappers who say what's up to God, he seems motivated by a religious impulse, a syncretic pantheology drawn from many scriptures: "You gotta study the Koran, Torah, Bhagavad-Gita, the Bible, five baskets [?] of Buddha, Zen/And when you've read them shits, read them shits again." And though there's a vaguely Buddhist/Hindu idealism to his railing against "material things from cars to chicken wings"—in his greatest song, "Love's Gonna Getcha (Material Love)," even loved ones qualify as "things"—he's not the ascetic his sporadic distrust of sex might tempt you to suspect. His advice in re big butts and smiles bears the stamp of personal experience, he obviously eats more than his vegetarian share, and he's no teetotaler even if he rarely cracks a forty. His belief that God resides in "self" or "consciousness" (the first tenet of Harold Bloom's "American religion") reflects a general disdain for the church matched only by his disdain for the schools—a style of radical individualism with a long and honorable history in specifically American nonconformity. If you want to dismiss Mr. Stop the Violence as a hip hop hypocrite, if you think good mystics don't brandish Uzis or go around beating up other mystics, so be it. Does he contradict himself? Very well then, he contradicts himself. He is large—he contains multitudes.

The Teacher doesn't generate too many errors as egregious as the ones that pop up in the *Civilization Vs. Technology* book, a now-aborted H.E.A.L. project that says Andrew Jackson wrote the Declaration of Independence, or in the lecture he contributed to Joseph Eare and James Spady's *Nation Conscious Rap*, which quotes the Oxford dictionary's definition of *black* as follows: "reflecting no life; from lack of life; like coal or soot; completely dark; dark skinned black or Negro (not human); dark sea . . . " In fact, the first mistake apparently originated with his coauthor, California Afrocentrist Zizwe Mtafuta-Ukweli, while the second is a botched transcription that mishears KRS-One's spoken *light* for *life* and incorporates his sarcastic aside about Negroes being considered inhuman into the purported dictionary text. To his credit, KRS-One showed enough scholarly pride to seem embarrassed by both when I pointed them out. But "lyrical terrorism" remains his favorite flavor. He drops science and/or nonsense to demolish faith in authority, pumping pride by any means necessary.

So where "Why Is That?" cites Genesis, a year later "Black-man in Effect" scotches the myth of the (Mesopotamian) Garden of Eden with the now accepted (though long controversial) thesis that human life originated in East Africa—and then serves up a classic piece of strained inference by contending that the golden age of Greek philosophy is also a myth because Greece was at war then. Some of KRS-One's more outrageous tropes—like the idea that beef passes along the fear and stress steers die with—are familiar counterculture baloney; others—the various black Hebrews, notably Noah and Jesus, who march through his work, or the obloquy heaped on Aristotle for stealing his shit from Egypt—are Afrocentric commonplaces; still others—like his esti-mate that "80 percent of American business is created illegally," or his charge that Lincoln didn't free the slaves—he may have concocted himself. But none of them is prima facie wrong the way Jackson writing the Declaration of Independence is wrong—they may be crackpot, but they're not inarguable. And for KRS-One, arguability is all.

His Lincoln spiel, for instance, relies first on the incontesta-ble fact that Lincoln didn't fight the Confederacy to end slavery, and second on the plausible theory that the purpose of the Civil War was to make America safe for capitalism—for universal slav-ery. Invariably, however, it gets bogged down in semantic quibbles about whether people you define as slaves can ever be free, in narrow readings of the Emancipation Proclamation, in conflations of Lincoln and his allies or ancestors that slander the Illinois pol by suggesting he owned slaves himself. This is typical. As long as he's got a leg to stand on, KRS-One will go out on a limb—as his failure to read the printed texts of his lectures makes clear, he's above mere detail. His goal in this case is eradicating the image of a white Great Emancipator from brainwashed minds, especially black ones. And in the end, this doesn't seem at all deplorable to me. I prefer my own inexpert view of a flawed and undeveloped Lincoln impelled by circumstance into extraordinary spiritual growth, and I wish KRS-One would give this morally complex per-sonage as much slack as he gives crackmongers. But as an alter-native to Lincoln the pop-educational icon—to the compassionate saint many believe in—KRS-One's Lincoln-the-hype-job serves a corrective function, especially coming from an artist who's at pains to point out that "a large sum of white people died with blacks" fighting racism (even if he also believes the baloney that "the media" don't want anyone to know this).

Put it this way. Lincoln was an opponent of slavery who thought the abolitionists went too far. He temporized until he had no choice; in twentieth-century terminology, he acted like a liberal rather than a radical. KRS-One disses him because he wasn't an all-the-way antiracist, while I suspect it was a good thing Lincoln was who he was—the right man to accomplish a goal the abolitionists could only prepare the way for. I wish KRS-One could project himself, and his audience, inside a white nineteenth-century ideology that reduced all blacks to simpletons if not savages—a racial myth even more suffocating than today's. But that would be asking even more of him than he asks of Lincoln. KRS-One is also who he is. He's an anti-authoritarian autodidact whose most undeniable gift is musical. He's a bigtime reader who pulled the H.E.A.L. book because he decided his audience would want to own it but not read it. And he's committed to combating a Eurocentrism that won't go down without a fight. Sure Linton Kwesi Johnson and the Disposable Heroes have more perspective. Now all they need is some rapport with the hip hop community.

I prefer KRS-One's slackest science to the corrosive outpourings of an Ice Cube—the precept that rampant emotions are proper material for art and rampant ideas aren't is romantic ideology at its thickest. Nevertheless, he's most mind-boggling at his most criminal-minded. Whether transporting ordnance in "100 Guns" or losing a crack empire in "Love's Gonna Getcha" or escaping through the basement of an Afrocentric bookstore in "Bo! Bo! Bo!" or just blowing a few faces off in the infamous "9mm Goes Bang," his narrators never moralize. In the first two songs, the cops get their man; in the last two—both pre-*Edutainment,* both featuring a protagonist named KRS-One—the protagonists either get theirs or stay out of harm's way. Win, lose, or draw, KRS-One's cold eye is worthy of Burroughs or an African trickster tale—without succumbing to the callousness of the Geto Boys, say, he seems unfazed by illegality, violence, crime, evil itself. In addition to quashing sentimentality, his refusal to flinch enhances his subcultural credibility. Only liberals love a moralizer.

Not that KRS-One doesn't dis crack like every other rapper in the universe. But he's not exactly scandalized by it. "How many people here go out and work every day?" he asked the Ritz. Everyone cheered. "How many work legally?" he went on. Two-thirds of the house cheered. "And how many work *illegally?*" he concluded. The other third cheered just as hard. Presumably, not every illegal was dealing, much less dealing crack. But as *Sex and Violence's* "Drug Dealer" puts it: "I go on tour/Now who do you think picks up the bill?/A hard working fireman?/Chill." The same song calls on "drug dealer[s] black and Hispanic" to "stop killing one another" and put their earnings "back into black," investing in legitimate businesses the way their supposedly myriad white predecessors supposedly did, and ends by urging a roll call of posses to join the revolution. Sure he'll talk to college students (who turn out to be mostly white, he's said); it's a lucrative sideline, for one thing. But this is a man who expects the revolution to start with the homeless and who went on MTV to advise the L.A. rioters to organize. His intellectual and emotional ties to the street determine the message he presents. And the same connections exert a crucial and salutary influence on the tone and texture of his art.

Often I just don't care whether KRS-One's lyrics are right or wrong, beautiful or ugly, good or bad. I'm just amazed by the hyperactively heterodox sensibility underneath. On *Sex and Violence* the haywire social engineering—the shocking "Drug Dealer" ("Rise up") and the bizwise "How Not To Get Jerked" ("People like to buy your spirit") and the anticapitalist "Who Are the Pimps?" ("Pick up that money, hoe")—is only the beginning. There's also sociopathic antisucker mayhem from gangsta sidekick Freddie Foxxx and assorted threats of violence. And there's the mad, utterly tasteless "13 and Good." This tale of statutory rape—the thirteen-year-old is the daughter of a police chief who'll let KRS-One bang her as long as he can bang KRS-One—is a little too fantastic (and dumb) to match up against his great criminal-minded songs. But it ends with lines that speak for all of them and a dozen others: "The moral to the story/Is that there is no moral/You finish the story for me/When you're livin' your life every day in the hood/Wakin' up in the mornin' makes you feel [whereupon the track closes on the first word of Chic's "Good Times," sampled to humorous effect throughout]."

KRS-One's increasingly pragmatic view of history is likewise street-defined. He's decided that whether his fans are criminals, college students, or both, they aren't even going to read his illustrated *Civilization Vs. Technology,* much less Walter Rodney's *How Europe Underdeveloped Africa.* And while it's possible that he's merely destroying faith in teachers and clergy who might lead the benighted out of the darkness, I'd say that faith was long since destroyed by forces no rap star could counter. On the street no less than anywhere else, black Americans are damn well aware that Eurocentrism does them dirt. And no matter what continent your ancestors came from, perform this simple test before you swear you've outgrown the prejudice: ask yourself whether you still think of 500–1000 A.D. as "the Dark Ages." Do you really keep it in the forefront of your consciousness that the period was definitely darkest for nondark people—that at the same time urban civilizations most of us have barely heard of were in flower throughout the Islamic world and in the northern part of an as yet un-Islamicized sub-Saharan Africa (not to mention Central America and eastern Asia, areas where I remain even more ignorant)? I'd remember KRS-One's latest slogan before fully crediting white academic protestations that all such errors are behind us: "If you don't know the history of the author you don't know what you're reading."

In most things—especially a neglected subject like Africa—we are all autodidacts; broad expertise is a privilege of academics, most of whom are too dull to take advantage of it. So anybody who thinks at all relies a lot on guesswork, common sense, and trusted sources—authors whose history he or she knows. Based on my uncommonly extensive yet oh so limited reading, I'm not persuaded that Egypt was as Nubian or Greece (or Israel) as Egyptian as KRS-One and narrower Afrocentrists believe. But I'm also not persuaded that the similar hunches of such scholars as Cheikh Anta Diop and Martin Bernal are as wrongheaded as evenhanded-looking reviews in the *Times* and *The New Republic* have made them appear. Neither Diop nor Bernal trained as a historian or archaeologist, so racism aside, there's turf at stake—academics always dismiss extradisciplinary research until it becomes undeniable. It's my guess that the Nubian hypothesis—which holds that the wellspring of Egyptian civilization was in black Upper Egypt rather than the Nile delta—will eventually make inroads with the Eurocentric scholars whose immediate predecessors attributed everything admirable in ancient Egypt to a vague and at bottom absurd "race" of dark-skinned "Caucasians" from somewhere in olde Mesopotamia. Ah yes, the fabled Hamites. You've heard of Shem? Well, meet Noah's nextborn, Ham. As recently as 1950, men of learning all over academe were hyping his etymological progeny. And you can be sure they'll change their minds again.

Occasionally I run into interested parties who've been piqued by KRS-One's pronouncements and want to know what I've found out. When I detail this error or that distortion, they are usually more than piqued—they're offended. I'm not. The political generation of Martin Luther King is receding into the past. We will not see its like again. And though it was always silly to try and make Martin Luther King out of a talented rapper whose political mouth remains bigger than his political head, I'm happy he's working. Even if KRS-One is a confused philosopher, he's a complex artist. He speaks to a radically disillusioned generation that has seen its expectations raised higher and dashed lower than Dr. King dreamed. And compared with other political rappers who address this demographic—X-Clan or Movement Ex or Paris or Poor Righteous Teachers or Sister Souljah or even Public Enemy—he's hung onto an image of generous humanity that seems consistent and sincere without surrendering the racial consciousness essential to his spiritual survival.

So even if Bernal and Diop and Chancellor Williams recede into total obscurity—well, as any drug dealer black or Hispanic could tell you, racism is never far to the side in this society. If it makes KRS-One's fans feel better, why shouldn't they believe that Cleopatra was black? Is that gonna be what makes them beat down the wrong white guy because some jury they can't get their hands on has finally pushed them over the line? Until they can rely on the information fed them by KRS-One's cliched targets (schools, church, media, government, ho hum), we—which in this case means "responsible" intellectuals of every color—have very limited bitching rights.

Not long ago I told Nelson George that his new basketball book, *Elevating the Game,* left me with the same reservation as his music history, *The Death of Rhythm and Blues.* On the one hand, both celebrate the integration of black creators into American culture. On the other, both regret the passing of segregated institutions that produced specifically black ways of shaping the world. Somehow, I told him, he had to resolve that contradiction.

Without missing a beat, Nelson answered that the contradiction was permanent—that it would never be resolved in our lifetimes. The moment he said it, I knew he was right. I was chagrined that I'd never figured this obvious truth out myself. And I was glad there were still African-Americans who struggled to straddle both sides. KRS-One is one of these heroes. To hell with complexity—it's as simple as that.

1992

6

Between Punk and a
Pop Place

A Voyage to Liliput

Before I even laid hands on the thing, I was crowing that there was a Liliput compilation out, but more often than not I got the same response:

"Who's Liliput?"

Fortunately, there's a simple answer. Liliput was the best all-female rock and roll band that ever existed. And now, at long last, their entire studio output is there for the consuming. I do mean there, too—way over there. Two CDs worth of *LiLiPUT,* forty-six songs lasting some two hours and twenty minutes, can be obtained by U.S.-based music lovers in one way and one way only. You send a thirty-dollar check to Off Course Records, P.O. Box 241, 8025 Zurich, Switzerland, and Off Course sends you the record. Got that? So go do it. When you come back I'll tell you why.

First, though, I guess I'd better explain why you never heard of them. Granted, if you were around during those halcyon postpunk years, which makes you a registered grownup by now, there's a reasonable chance the name rings a bell. More likely, though, you remember Kleenex, which is what the group was called on the 1979 Rough Trade singles "Ain't You"/"Hedi's Head" and "You"/"Ü." In the small world of postpunk DOR, and specifically at Jim Fouratt's seminal club Hurrah, those were very big little records. Amid so much darkly asexual male posing, it was an up to hear a woman shouting "Ain't you wanna get it on?" and "Push it in and push it out"—even if Liliput's claim that they were talking on-off buttons is strongly supported by otherwise incomprehensible syllables that do indeed add up to "radio." Anyway, Kimberly-Clark has better lawyers than Jonathan Swift, so the less momentous if equally brilliant Rough Trade singles "Split"/"Die Matrosen" and "Eisiger Wind"/"When the Cat's Away" were by Liliput—or, as they preferred, LiLiPUT. The change didn't hurt the band's music, but it was murder on name recognition. So was their failure to release an album until 1982—by which moment in Britpop hypertime, says Rough Trade's Geoff Travis, they were good for maybe eight or nine hundred sales there and fewer here. And of course, their safe European home didn't enhance their legend or their word of mouth. A Swiss band who sang mostly in English, they played out plenty near home and got to England twice. Bassist-founder Klaudia Schiff has visited the United States as a painter, a pursuit that puts more bread on the table; guitarist-archivist Marlene Marder has never been to America at all.

Kleenex/Liliput might also have crossed your field of vision in two other ways. Greil Marcus wrote an *Interview* column about the compilation—the sum of its English-language coverage, Marder tells me. Marcus, a close friend whose musical judgments haven't coincided significantly with mine since Reagan ran amok, also has a piece on them in his bedside book *Ranters and Crowd Pleasers*. Occasionally, too, the band snags fanzine mention as riot-grrrl foremothers. But with their records rarer than the Raincoats' or the Slits', even the few under-thirtys who dimly recall the name—every one female in my informal survey—have no idea what the music sounds like.

That's partly because it sounds like nothing else. It's "punk," all right—fast guitar-bass-drums, minimal chords. But even pre-"Ain't You," it isn't *that* fast. One way or another, the self-taught female players (not singers) to emerge from the punk explosion all sought recourse from its high-testosterone momentum. Travis associates Kleenex drummer Lislot Ha's herky-jerk pulse—"that clattery, non-rock and roll quality, somewhere between free jazz and rock and roll"—with Palmolive, who drummed for both the Slits and the Raincoats, the latter while they headlined Kleenex's 1979 U.K. tour. Travis reckons that Ha was simpler; Raincoat Ana Da Silva recalls that Kleenex seemed "slightly more traditional in structure, in the rock and roll sense." I'd put it less negatively. I'd say that of the three all-female postpunk bands, Kleenex/Liliput accomplished the most because they were willing to integrate their boho artiness into a version of rock and roll form, and also because they could play what they heard in their heads.

It's a little startling, isn't it, to realize that there were only three such bands? Others that come to mind, Essential Logic and the Au Pairs and Delta 5, were more in the singer-plus-backup mold, while New York's Bush Tetras comprised a female guitarist, bassist, and singer and a male drummer. (By the time they recorded *Cut,* the Slits had arrived at the same gender distribution, and Liliput too ended up with a male drummer sitting in sometimes.) Equally noteworthy is that not one of the bands just named made it past 1984. Sexism must have had something to do with this, both as overt prejudice and as the life-pressures that come down harder on women than men. But most of the women in these bands were bohemian dabblers riding a cultural moment that lost appeal as it lost steam—artists as opposed to musicians. Punk's anyone-can-do-it ethos gave them room to work, and except for Greil's beloved Essential Logic, every band I've named created at least a few undeniable songs in the available space. Play the Slits today—or check the Raincoats catalogue on Geffen, where Kurt Cobain has proven an ace lobbyist—and you'll hear explorations that go somewhere; primitive though the playing is, it was arresting then and has gained resonance and meaning since. Play *Li-LiPUT,* however, and you'll hear a rather large body of enduring music.

An oeuvre wasn't what I expected. I expected the singles and a few finds and maybe more stuff as nice as the 1982 album (confusingly entitled *Liliput*). What I got instead was eight songs that, combined with the first three singles, would have constituted a debut LP approximately as consistent as, oh, *Ramones,* an album I sorely underrated at B+ in 1982, and a comparable follow-up (*Some Songs,* Switzerland only, 1983). Plus the sui generis "Eisiger Wind"/"When the Cat's Away." Plus, OK, some filler—material any contemporary singles-only band would dole out coyly for years. For indie DIYers so poorly remembered they've been dropped from *The Trouser Press Record Guide,* this is a whole lot of quality work. The retrospective divides it neatly between disc one, singles/outtakes 1978–1982, and disc two, albums 1982–1983, and aurally there's a split as well—things get dreamier and more experimental with vocalist Astrid Spirit, now a practitioner of some Asian massage therapy Marder doesn't understand. But despite the three lead singers—serious, deep-voiced Regula Sing fronted for the first ten sides, playful young Chrigle Freund for the next twelve—and the addition of various saxophones and Spirit's violin, it all sounds like Kleenex/Liliput. And it all sounds like nothing else.

The band's trademark is what we'll designate vocal arrangements—the greatest collection of nonsense sounds since doowop. And while I feel constrained to note that my two favorite bands also excelled at this trick, the Dolls and the Clash were pikers by comparison. Liliput utter oh-ohs and ee-ees and dtoeng-dtoengs and especially woo-woos, shrieks and whistles and grunts and groans and screams and yelps and kissy-sucks and animal cries. Sometimes they sound like soccer fans, sometimes like cheerleaders—oi boys, oi girls. Always their phonemes and prephonemes fit, as chorus or comment or response, and always they surprise. Taken together, these sounds constitute musical substance, not musical decoration—the inspiration for Marder's guitar rather than vice versa.

Marcus's claim that these are "noises males would have been ashamed to make then and would likely be ashamed to make now" seems a stretch in a world with room for Pere Ubu. Still, young male rock and rollers do worry about their "manhood." Like their vulnerability, rockboys' playfulness is usually achieved or constructed, so too often it comes out cute. This all-woman band is almost never cute—on "Hitch-hike," which explains "She had no money to pay the train" before switching off to "Don't touch me . . . Let me be," one hook is provided by a rape-alert whistle. But from that first "Ain't you wanna get it on?" they've projected the sense of spontaneously enjoying their difficult lives. A unique and perhaps uniquely female sense of fun defines their music, their message, their vision. Marder, who's now a promoter and indie retailer, was the musician in the group, the saxwoman who volunteered to take over at their inaugural gig after the guitarist with the penis bolted. At first, she says, the all-woman thing didn't seem important, but "everybody asked"; Dangermice, the band she formed after she and Klaudia and Astrid went their separate ways (and which finally broke up when she decided she'd rather read a good book than perform every weekend), was all-woman too. And why did Liliput disband? "We tried to research new things, but we didn't really know how to go on. We didn't know whether to have a career and go into the music business or just have our fun and go on at our own pace." I repeat: "have our fun."

It would be misleading to suggest that this music goes down easy enough for lazybones. Pop addicts may find it tuneless, beat addicts grooveless, and many of the album songs have an improvisatory aura—a sense of people picking their way through naively untoward musical ideas without expecting closure on the other side—that does recall *Cut* and *The Raincoats*. Liliput are always more imaginative and less halting, though. Anyone with the sense to object to arty impulses in practice rather than principle, to believe that the world would be a far more interesting place if they worked out as often as they're said to, should find this band's complete works an inspiration. And anyone who thinks the only path a riotous girl can tread is that of craft and common sense definitely has another think coming.

That address again: Off Course Records, P.O. Box 241, 8025 Zurich, Switzerland. Thirty bucks postpaid. Have fun.

1993

Simple Because He's Simple: Marshall Crenshaw

Never blessed with instant recall for Mann-Weil chord changes or guitar licks from old Hollies records, vague on details when people complain that this song is obviously Buddy Holly and that one obviously Lennon-McCartney (which ones? I don't remember), I miss Marshall Crenshaw's references, if he's making any. Charges of self-consciousness and calculation and retro slip right by. So when I first heard *Marshall Crenshaw*, I filed it mentally under power pop, in 1982 a dated but still useful catchall, and though I found it a little bland I tested it out the only way I knew how—I played it more. Soon it became clear that whether he'd made them up in his dreams or pilfered them from his vast record collection, Crenshaw had the tunes most power poppers only claim. I didn't just say hi to these tunes as they paraded across the room—I actively longed to hear them again. In my critical lexicon, tunes you want to hear again are called "good." The more you want to hear them, the "better" they are. And if they keep getting "better" when other people impose them on you—radio programmers, say, or your wife—they may conceivably be "great."

So if I call Crenshaw subtle, I don't mean, for instance, that rather than exploiting the music of his betters, his quotations and allusions (if he's making any) link disparate realms in recombinant blah-blah-blah, although they may. I'm trying to do justice to that first album, which seems simple because it is simple, yet continues to unfold long after you'd think its byways played out. Listening back, I realize that Crenshaw accomplishes this not with the snazzy bridges and key changes of the traditional pop arsenal, but by repeating lines at odd junctures or bringing in the chorus again when you're anticipating another verse. And what's just as important is that I've enjoyed these tricks dozens upon dozens of times without once wondering how they were done—without noticing that they were tricks at all.

Marshall Crenshaw was a surprisingly profitable debut, yielding a top forty single and selling some two hundred fifty thousand copies in the last and flattest of the biz's dinosaur years. *Field Day*, which didn't do half as well, was a misconceived sequel. With Steve Lillywhite doctoring Crenshaw's efficient trio (Marshall on guitar, brother Robert on drums, Chris Donato on bass) until it boomed and echoed like cannons in a cathedral, the production seemed designed to prove that Marshall wasn't retro; what it demonstrated instead was that however genuine your commitment to the present, you can look pretty foolish adjusting to its fashions. But eventually Crenshaw fans noticed that song for song *Field Day* was the equal of its predecessor. I prefer it, actually.

Put it this way. *Marshall Crenshaw* is something like a perfect album—a perfect summer album, easy and exuberant. As far as history is concerned, it's Beach Boys rather than Holly / Lennon. The songs are nearly all classics of sorts, and what they evoke is classic as well—endless, timeless, ageless, seamless teenage summer. And yet it's neither retro nor cutesy; its associations are elusive, achieved not through lyrics about Chevys or vocal cartoons, but indirectly, by way of slides, twangs, stray languid phrases that conjure without being explicit. The tone isn't sappy, either—on the contrary, it's sly and slightly snotty. "Cynical Girl" is one giveaway. He knows you may think she's simple, or maybe cinnamon until you read the title, but there's a deeper hook: he's deliberately using the word wrong, sort of. He's just looking for someone who won't settle for "The Usual Thing," another giveaway, even a credo. The way "Mary Anne" starts right on the crest of a climactic riff and stays there with a few asides throughout the whole song is a structural gimmick that is also a credo of sorts. The album as a whole is multiple-climaxed. Again and again the music takes off with a soaring sweep, leaving an erotic blast that seems to come from nowhere you could point to in this unraunchy, personaless person.

Field Day starts right off with its own all-climax song, the airplay hit "Whenever You're on My Mind," and suffers no shortage of exuberance, but the songs crest differently. Though individual melodies are as natural as ever and even more conversational, they move rectilinearly, and Lillywhite's hyped-up guitar and drum sound tends to crimp Crenshaw's voice. There's less soaring, and on "All I Know Right Now," placed in the homestretch with a melody that sounds like a summing up, the expected total breakout never comes. *Field Day* is autumnal, strewn with broken or reconsidered promises, crumbling cities, long relationships—new tastes of disaster, new feats, new excesses, new pleasures. "Why not try till we die?" goes the album's greatest refrain, and that's definitely the mood. Despite appearances, "Monday Morning Rock," another credo of sorts, isn't about what a relief it is to get back to work after a hard weekend in the clubs—it's an exhortation (to his girl, but also to the whole block) to lock the door and have sex first. And the rectilinear discipline has its advantages over the expansiveness of the debut. What gives you goose bumps isn't the swoops so much as the placement of a harmony or the dissonance of a guitar. The constrictions on Crenshaw's voice bring out its center—he's less croony, more personal, warmer.

But although close listeners eventually heard all this even if they didn't figure it out, album three was two years coming. The T-Bone Burnett-produced *Downtown* betrays telltale signs of commercial anxiety—studio hands replacing road band, one track given over to, uh-oh, Mitch Easter. Only I can't discern its commercial strategy, misconceived or otherwise. I suspect that's because Crenshaw said the hell with it and just tried to make the best record he could. An ex-critic at Warners remarks that it sounds played rather than produced, which is true despite the unfamiliar musicians (who remain pretty constant throughout), and the most passionate Crenshaw fan of my acquaintance is partial to its vocal highlighting. These effects are extensions of the naturalistic illusion that is Crenshaw's aim in life. This is a smart man bent on defying analysis.

Walking into Toad's Place in New Haven as Crenshaw's now five-piece band bopped through the syncopated chorus of their opening number, *Downtown*'s negligible "(We're Gonna) Shake Up Their Minds," I got my Marshall buzz. Whether airy and precise or heavy on the drums or jammed loose like this warmup, Crenshaw's gigs always brim with the same unassuming, putatively effortless vitality; they seem to grow out of the bandstand. That surge of grace is his trademark, maybe even his message. As far as I'm concerned, Crenshaw doesn't try to recreate anything; if he's sometimes too respectful of the past—introducing a slightly wimpy cover of Ferlin Husky's "Gone," he claimed fealty to the entire 1957 hit parade—he's in no sense stuck there. One reason his debunkers can't decide whether he's ripping off Buddy Holly (nice boy, wears glasses) or John Lennon (played him in *Beatlemania,* wears glasses) is that he loves the music of the fifties the way sixties rockers did before they fell victim to hippie condescension—not as living tradition but as living music.

With its played-not-produced intimation of process, music in the making rather then music as artifact, *Downtown* gets this unpretentious message across, but not without sacrifice, because it lacks pretensions to live up to. You pick your exception and I'll pick mine, but basically there are no weak lyrics on the first two albums—no banalities, no false moves, no duds. The debut brushes by the everyday phrases that are the stuff of songwriting to add a twist or make an oblique point, enabling Crenshaw to capture a magic ur-adolescent innocence without acting the simp. On *Field Day* he grows up with a bang, and Lillywhite's drum sound reinforces the record's depth, conveying both Crenshaw's sense of doom and his will to overcome it. Nothing so complicated happens on *Downtown.* Because he really wants this one simple, it's filled with the kind of songs those who consider Crenshaw one more retropopper always thought he wrote. They're well-crafted, fully imagined, and the commitment and understated sexual urgency of the singing makes them real—"Little Wild One (No. 5)" is no less compelling and more detailed than the Isleys' "That Lady" or Hot Chocolate's "You Sexy Thing," and "Yvonne," which he describes as "about sex," is a classic name song. But even the pointedly mature "The Distance Between" has a fairly arbitrary happy ending, which you'd figure from the way it stresses "When it gets right down to the bottom line." An earlier Crenshaw would have glanced right off that tired trope.

Maybe lyrics that say what they seem to say are a commercial strategy. But more likely they're there to reinforce the message. Which as I said is music. And which is always what you want from "pop" geniuses who never become all that popular.

With Carola Dibbell

1983–1985

Aching to Become: The Replacements

I mean, fuck art—you would have kicked Bob Stinson out of your band too. A reformed arsonist who shat in the ice bucket, wandered Minneapolis with his diaper dangling, and greeted strangers "I'm in the Replacements, got any coke?" he was and no doubt is an unsatisfied man. Existentially unsatisfied, and professionally unsatisfied, because before Paul Westerberg learned songwriting by doing, the Replacements belonged to Stinson by seniority and talent. But after six years of outvomiting three guys who still show no sign of equating marital bliss with the new sobriety, his substance abuse became too much for them. Westerberg told *Spin* that when they were cutting their 1986 Sire debut *Tim,* "He didn't know the key of A from his left foot, so I'd sorta show him where to put his hands. 'Just kinda start there, Bob.' "

Whereupon—and here's the thing—Stinson would detonate his crazed guitar, juicing the notes with a little something extra and probably wrong, defining a band whose idea of inspiration was crashing into a snowbank and coming out with a six-pack. Not so unavoidably, I admit, on the real good *Tim* as on the real great *Let It Be,* which made major labeldom possible. Who knows, maybe Westerberg was already filling in when Stinson was incapacitated, the way he did on *Pleased To Meet Me* after Stinson was cut loose. He's got his own artistic interests, and he probably doesn't miss Stinson any more than the programmers who've positioned "I'll Be You" not just twixt Lou and Elvis in *Billboard's* "modern rock" top five but at the top of the "album rock" heap—over 38 Special, Chris Rea, Julian Lennon! Nor has the demon airplay been appeased at the expense of guts ball. With new guy Slim Dunlap reaching bell-like through serious clamor, "I'll Be You" tastes like the 'Placemats of old, comparatively speaking—something those who accuse *Don't Tell a Soul* of sellout, an irrelevancy that's hard to prove in court, as well as of maturity, which nobody can deny, would have trouble explaining if they noticed it.

But that's not to claim "I'll Be You" is anywhere near as post-hardcore as, say, "We're Comin' Out." There, as on most of *Let It Be,* Stinson's guitar is a loud, unkempt match for Westerberg's vocal, only at the end it breaks into pure cacophonic outro—which after a trick pause gets a coda from Westerberg, plunked unsteadily on a pianner. The latest phase of a slow evolutionary process, *Don't Tell a Soul*'s basic guitar move is much classier: Dunlap plays hooks. On "Back to Back" Westerberg sings "Back to back" and Dunlap doubles a four-note cadence, on "Achin' to Be" Westerberg sings "She's achin' . . ." and Dunlap chimes in two-one two-three—like that. The hooks aren't always so simplistic, and they're usually catchier than what Twin Cities cult journey-man Curtiss A gave Dunlap to work with, but a decade-plus after the dawning of power pop the device reeks of the mechanical; except in country music, where formula is part of the charm, it's tough to bring off without sounding corny or manipulative. At its worst—I vote for "Achin' To Be," which starts off "She's kinda like an artist" and never once slaps itself upside the head—*Don't Tell a Soul* is both.

With his usual guts-ball flourish, Westerberg kicked off the first of two sold-out Beacon shows last Thursday with the early snot-rocker "Color Me Impressed" and followed with the rawest thing on *Pleased To Meet Me,* "I Don't Know," where Westerberg shouts "Should we give it up?/Or should we give it hell?/Are we making a fortune?" etc., and after every line the rest of the band duhs back "I dunno." That "I dunno" is like a signature for drummer Chris Mars and Bob's little bassist brother Tommy Stinson, proof enough that hooks don't have to be tuneful or cute, and for sure none of the twenty-six songs they roared through in their hundred minutes could be called well-tailored. The reconstituted Replacements fulfilled their chaos quota with relish. That they didn't forget the defensive sexist-classist "Waitress in the Sky" also indicated that they haven't succumbed to good taste quite yet. But in the kind of promotional effort Sire couldn't count on circa *Tim,* they did go heavy on recent originals, and *Don't Tell a Soul* did provide too many of the valleys that are part of the scenery at any concert-length thrash. Dunlap was happy to play noise, but his hooks were audibly in place, and on some of the older material—"Unsatisfied," for instance—the guitar parts were enunciated with a force and catchy clarity worthy of Squeeze or the dB's. And not counting a blues feature with opening act Johnny Thunders, the one cover I recognized was a typical fuck-you stroke from a band that used to delight in reviving AOR gold from Zep to BTO: the Only Ones' new wave classic "Another Girl, Another Planet." It sounded fabulous.

So if the evening's raucousness offered succor to the die-hards who insist that their Replacements have not matured no they haven't, it was also a step in the aforementioned evolutionary process. As well it should have been—would you want Bob Stinson in your life? It's just too bad that Westerberg isn't as good at maturity as he was at snowbanks. He's always had a genius for vague rallying cries—*Let It Be*'s keynote "I Will Dare," or "Bastards of Young," which brought the encore to a properly raucous climax. But he's always balanced them with gripes and putdowns whose shameless specificity is summed up by the immortal titles "Tommy Gets His Tonsils Out" and "Gary's Got a Boner." Not counting the Who homage "I Won't" ("I w-w-w-w-w-won't"), the closest he comes to an old-style speed-anthem on the new record is "Anywhere's Better Than Here," which leads off side two as a sop to the band's old fans and old selves—Westerberg says he only writes fast ones for Tommy now. Elsewhere the vagueness has gotten more thoughtful, and stupider. Hook lines like "We'll inherit the earth/But we don't want it" and "Telling me questions/And asking me lies" vent the know-nothingism of a Cadillac salesman's son who's been the consummate middle-class misfit since he didn't graduate from high school. And the most trenchant thing about the love songs "Back to Back," "Darlin' One," and "Achin' To Be" is that they take up time on the record. "Here's a sensitive, mature song from a sensitive, mature group," was how Westerberg defensively introduced the last. He's a defensive guy, right. But that doesn't mean no one's attacking him.

Forced to generalize, I'd call this your basic rock and roll dilemma—the music of youthful confusion/anger/exaltation comes by wisdom awkwardly and with difficulty. But since I'm old enough to be Westerberg's father, I can claim to appraise his gifts objectively. Lou Reed and Linda Womack and plenty of other rock and rollers have something to say about marriage and moderation and such; so far, Paul Westerberg has something to say about youthful confusion/anger/exaltation. Clearly, the subject doesn't engage him the way it used to—he associates it with suicidal excess, for one thing. But, so far, this sane decision is fucking up his art. And that's not quite all he wrote.

The opening act was an old hero of Westerberg's, the subject of one of his earliest songs. "Johnny's Gonna Die," it's called, and a real guts ballplayer would have included it Thursday: "Johnny always takes more than he needs/Johnny always needs more than he takes." I love Johnny Thunders myself, and when I last saw him four years ago I thought he'd never play an interesting set again. On Thursday, he played an interesting set—though much of it was about cleaning up, he seemed as crazed and sly and retarded as ever. His reemergence was the latest chapter in the lesson rock and roll has been teaching me all my life, which is that you never can tell about chaos. So you never can tell about the Replacements. Or about Bob Stinson either.

Bob Stinson died in 1995—four years after Johnny Thunders.

1989

Living Legends: The B-52's

My past three months have been saturated with B-52's, almost like I'm a fan or something. That's because my daughter Nina has been a fan if not an addict ever since the dreary Saturday when I jaw-boned her into watching the *B-52's 1979–1989* video compilation instead of *Mickey's Magical World.* The video overplays the band's double-platinum comeback *Cosmic Thing,* and doesn't entirely convince the critic in me—the visual tricks seem secondhand from such art-worlders. But I hereby attest that it holds up to repeated repeated repeated viewings: custom doesn't stale Fred Schneider's moues or timing, and his voice has been working out. Nina's personal audio compilation, slanted toward the debut album (represented on the video only by a live, early "Rock Lobster"), has proved equally eternal. They're pure pop after all. In heavy rotation, they keep on coming like "Billie Jean."

The B-52's were New York's last great club band partly because they were too all-embracing for its club scene. Not only did they flaunt Athens as regional epicenter, they precipitated the fun-versus-art rift that set dancers against coolies, folkies, and pig-fuckers throughout the eighties. But they weren't killers enough to cash in, and after 1980's *Wild Planet* their albums languished commercially and critically even though there were great songs on them—songs people danced to. And then, just after *Bouncing Off the Satellites* was finished in late 1985, Ricky Wilson died.

Schneider was the unflappable natural comedian; Cindy Wilson and Kate Pierson provided spirit, soul, and deep closet; Keith Strickland was the drum-beating dynamo straight out the kudzu. But in this ad hoc party band, Ricky Wilson was the amateur genius whose self-taught guitar tunings made the whole bassless meshugas hop, skip, and jump—the main reason Chris Spedding and Robert Quine swore by a tacky little dance band from Athens G-A in 1978, and the main reason the dance band was still recording great songs seven years later. Already shaky, the B-52's disintegrated when AIDS got him. You don't just go hire a new inspired autodidact.

Then, some two years later, a miracle occurred—Keith the drummer, who'd long doubled on bass and keybs, taught himself guitar, and slowly the band regrouped. But though Keith gets the interpersonal chemistry right, he's not Ricky, and *Cosmic Thing* proves it—for all Fred/Cindy/Kate's renewed belief in their concept, its only properly wacky triumph amid much honorable fun is the universalist-in-your-mind "Roam," written by band friend Robert Waldrop. Which must just prove that Ricky Wilson was too good for this world, because *Cosmic Thing* broke riding a Keith throwaway: "Love Shack," the party-hearty anthem they always claimed they wanted, not all that different in ethos from "Party Out of Bounds" or "Butterbean" except that it's utterly untwisted. Like Bonnie Raitt's "Runaway," to choose a comparable market ploy from the depths of rock history, it's not horrible. But put it in heavy rotation and you'll tune out pronto.

Still, my nuclear family wasn't about to miss Nina's heroes—Fred so funny! Cindy so female!—when they swept back through metro New York for the third time this year: Radio City before the album showed legs, then Earth Day, and then the Meadowlands preceded by our choice, the Jones Beach Theater, a space made for the greatest beach band of the era. Never having seen the beach band at a venue more all-embracing than CBGB, I had my doubts about the tailgaters downing brews in the parking lot, but though I'm sure my new date swayed my objectivity some, the show was pretty transcendent. Angularly minimalist no longer, this proudly cushy new wave seven-piece (long-lost ex-Waitress Tracy Wormworth on bass, ex-everything Pat Irwin on everything) entertained without shame or surcease. Fred led the ensemble through its paces with an aplomb rendered bittersweet by his age lines and the trouble he's seen.

Downplaying their platinum, the B-52's presented themselves as a band with a history—three from *The B-52's,* four from *Wild Planet,* "Mesopotamia," "Song for a Future Generation." And given how wildly the young audience greeted these blasts from the past, I got the idea that they've come back from the dead as living legends. This is some kind of spiritual triumph. The hippie references that always seemed risible riding beehives and beach buggies make sense now. Urging the tailgaters to get involved at the Greenpeace table, these campy postpunks are as deeply into health food and waste disposal as any sixties diehard in the biz. They're happy goofballs because they're *glad* they're not dead. And they damn well have a right to be.

1990

Sonic Youth Sell Out

Unlike so many "alternative" bands who lose in-crowd cachet as ordinary rock fans learn to love them, Sonic Youth have indeed sold out. Slowly, steadily, relentlessly, they've abandoned a bohemian aesthetic for a commercial one; although both tendencies are discernible throughout their work, the progression has been unmistakable. The band itself is divided on what this might mean—"I just don't think about progress," Kim Gordon claims, although as Thurston Moore points out, the bass melodies an earlier Kim couldn't have put her fingers on are emblems of "growth," no two ways about it. For someone like their former label exec Gerard Cosloy, who claims archly that they've sunk to "the mushiest, most feeble pop tunes imaginable," the progression is a regression. But for someone like me, who only believed the hype when 1986's *Starpower* EP edited the two catchiest tracks on *Evol* for pop-tune legibility and added a Kim Fowley cover for title and concept, DGC's new *Goo*—their first true major-label effort despite *Daydream Nation*'s thirty thousand dollar budget and unintentional Capitol distribution—is yet another giant step. It's as far from *Daydream Nation* as *Daydream Nation* was from *Sister* was from *Evol* was from *Bad Moon Rising*. And I say that as somebody who thought *Sister* was as far as they had to go.

Proudly recorded in a Times Square studio so classic or antiquated it uses only tube equipment, *Sister* is the album Sonic Youth's disillusioned old acolytes and runaway new bandwagoneers come together on. It's anarchic and murky, but the epiphanies it pulls out of the chaos aren't isolated moments of apparent clarity—rather than emerging from the mix-mess, they're embedded in the composition, however unpremeditated that composition may have been. Not one track is perversely uncatchy, not one runs over 5:04, and as an added sop to normality the death porn is kept under control. Yet *Sister*'s prevailing mood is still pretty demented, a consciously clumsy attempt to regain a semblance of balance on the other side of the edge: "I'll join you tonight in the bottom of the well/Feel around in the dark until you get the idea."

Also, *Sister* doesn't move too good—not only is it clumsy and murky, it's clunky. Steve Shelley—the hardcore tub banger who became their fourth and forever drummer in 1985, after Richard Edson (former Konk, future Jarmusch), Jim Sclavunos (former Jerk), and Bob Bert (future Pussy Galore) had ground to their respective halts—has never been as symbolic as his predecessors, whose musical contributions were limited to on-and-off timekeeping and properly rockish sonic input. He's always had a motor function, one that powered Sonic Youth's commercial turns as much as Kim's and Thurston's religious impulses. But even the songful *Sister* was relatively static, carried more on guitar riffs than on drumbeats. That was the big change on *Daydream Nation*, which though it stretched thirteen tracks over two vinyl discs felt far popper than *Sister* because it generated a groove. Finally the longest-running reinventors in avant-punk history were fucking not just with rock—with the kind of music you can put "art-" in front of—but with rock and roll.

To be fair, though, the thirty grand also helped, and I presume David Geffen's bottomless coffers helped some more this time. I haven't heard the band live since before *Bad Moon Rising*—early on I thought (correctly) that they sucked, after which they discouraged my attendance by calling for my assassination at gigs, and their recent forays into respectability haven't prevented them from thrashing and droning until long past my bedtime. So I can't judge the oft-restated caveat that no record can convey the way "the massed overtones produced by their altered tunings hover and dart above you, making you hear things that aren't there." All I know is that the CD version of *Goo* peals and clangs with the clearest recorded version to date of a guitar sound that has always been their reason for living and their excuse for telling the world about it. Though they share their rep as destroyer-saviors of rock and roll with many others, nobody else has stuck at it so faithfully, and their major-label bio makes the most of their steadfastness: "Actually we feel we're very traditional," sez Thurston. "We bolster and progress rock tradition. We respect it. But we don't go back to it." Unless you concoct your rock myth out of life on the edge, permanant rebirth, and related vanguardist cant, what this rep has always signified is a guitar band exploring and exploiting alternatives to the recombinant roots of smart-garage convention. This time I mean alternative, too—no quotation marks please. Later for Sonic Youth's philosophy of life. They're a great-sounding band.

You won't catch me equating amplified guitars with rock and roll at this late date—I still hear the future in beats, technology, history-hopping internationalist bricolage. But that doesn't mean amplified guitars aren't great-sounding. They've dominated the music sonically for thirty-five years, and with true believers adapting the scales of every musical culture in the world to their urban flash and grunge, they're going to be around. So what's worn out isn't a sound—it's the blues-based chords, changes, and structures associated with that sound. Enter Sonic Youth's famous tunings, which anyone can tell are produced by electric guitars and anyone can tell are weird. Early on this weirdness was subsumed in willfully simplistic or gratuitously shapeless songs, but as the band gave ordinary rock fans more to grab hold of, the scalar perversions went into relief. The chords sound even more recondite with their reassuringly elementary relationships out front, and more so yet when they underpin the rhyming four-line segments of putatively feeble pop tunes and ride a mix that for the first time makes rhythm players Shelley and Gordon sonically competitive with guitarists Moore and Lee Ranaldo.

Ranaldo, who still cultivates a warm spot in his hot heart for Glenn Branca, has been heard grousing about this latest concession to market forces, but he can save the self-expression for SST, sole distributor of his solo research, which like Kim's Harry Crews one-off and the collective's Ciccone Youth travesty remains readily available to the in crowd. For the nonce, the Sonic Youth trademark is reserved for commercial purposes. The most memorable songs of Thurston and Kim's anarchy period concerned mad sex and the Manson family. And though *Goo* does include a boring

four-minute coda for Ranaldo and a tone poem about go-cart racing and a UFO fantasy and a raveup from their anarchy period,
their most memorable Geffen-financed songs concern responsible
love. "Titanium Expose" even makes a stab at pinning down what's
nice about marriage (which Kim and Thurston seem to understand better than John and Exene ever did)—and, wouldn't you
know it, the star-fan nexus.

When bands start dwelling on that rock and roll road, it usually means they've run out of material. But Thurston's hard-riffing
"Dirty Boots," which depicts him "making out with a bitch in a
coffee truck" before singing the praises of that blues-based "jelly
roll," no more reflects his modestly profitable touring experience
than his Spahn Ranch ditties reflect his memories of Squeaky
Fromme's jelly roll. Its subject is one of the countless professional
bands (ZZ Top "in a van," he says in the press kit) whose realm
Sonic Youth has now entered. And of Kim's three rock-life songs,
only the title number is remotely predictable—for one thing, her
rock dreams are about women, women she identifies with. "Tunic
(Song for Karen)" is intoned in the voice of Karen Carpenter playing drums in heaven, finally free of her brother and her mother
and her treacherous flesh. And in "Kool Thing," a fan sings "about
and to her favorite rock star," played by none other than Chuck
D., who can never again be accused of lacking a sense of humor.
"What are you gonna do for me? I mean, are you gonna liberate
us girls from male white corporate oppression?" she asks, but all
Chuck can do is pronounce slogans in his oiliest voice: "Tell it like
it is," "Word up," "Fear . . . fear . . . black." The fan isn't disillusioned, exactly, just canny enough to keep her distance: "I don't
wanna/I don't think so," the refrain repeats, and then repeats
again.

Goo is another fan, someone who used to hang with the in
crowd. With her "real tattoo" and "green underwear," she's hipper
than the "Kool Thing" girl, though in another sense she's dumber
because she's so cool, so passive—"she can play the drums in
two," but "what she does best is stand and stare." Since Goo was
the name of a character in a Raymond Pettibon movie before getting her own 2:18 punk raver, you have to wonder whether in some
sense that's her on the cover, a black-and-white Pettibon cartoon
soon to greet curious teenagers from every mall Geffen can infil-
trate. Supercool behind shades, cig, and guy, a tough chick tells

her story: "I stole my sister's boyfriend. It was all whirlwind, heat, and flash. Within a week we killed my parents and hit the road."

A boho fantasy, of course—a boho fantasy about pop culture. Say Goo represents Sonic Youth's fans; they've decided the girls are more interesting and promising than the guys, and one way or another she's all of them, from the tattooed love dolls of the Anti-Club to the mall baby who's intrigued, to use the *People* term, by the tattooed love doll in home room, and also by the idea of killing your parents. Say the band has come to suspect that these two poles aren't all that far apart. Living on the edge because that's where you wound up is just life. *Goo*'s commercial aesthetic, strong-willed pop tunes yoked to a weird guitar sound designed to scare off cowards and the truly retro, won't fully satisfy the in crowd's need for epiphanies that emerge from chaos. Nor will it make the world safe for self-expression. But then, neither did their bohemian aesthetic. All we and they can be sure of is that it progresses rock tradition one more iota. And that it sounds great.

1990

Curse of the Mekons

Late in 1989, the Mekons released their first major-label effort since *The Quality of Mercy Is Not Strnen,* thrown against the post-punk wall by a bright-eyed U.K. Virgin in 1979. Funk-influenced intellectual leftists like their Leeds compadres the Gang of 4, the Mekons seemed worth a go back then. But that debut LP never even came out in America, and the ambiguously entitled follow-up was on the left-identified U.K. indie Red Rhino. Subsequent labels have included the Leeds indie CNT, their own Sin imprint, the U.S. indies Twin/Tone and ROIR, and Sonic Youth's temporary resting place, Blast First. Blast First is partners with the best-selling Anglodisco indie Mute, just now beginning U.S. distribution with Elektra, but the ambiguously entitled *Rock 'n' Roll,* a.k.a. *The Mekons Rock 'n' Roll,* was on A&M via the Twin/Tone deal engineered by a&r hotshot Steve Ralbovsky, formerly of EMI and CBS, now a senior VP at Elektra. The Mekons were one of the properties that attracted Ralbovsky to Twin/Tone, and though the eccentricity of the group's recording history only begins with their foot-loose corporate connections, *Rock 'n' Roll* crunched hard enough to pass as a major-label effort—hard enough to inspire fantasies of sales in the middle five figures.

But the project misfired even before release, which was held up while the A&M legal department fretted over the unauthorized Elvis pic cunningly concealed on the cover, and to the predictable dismay of both sides, U.S. consumption topped out at around twenty-three thousand. Talk to founding Mekons Tom Greenhalgh and Jon Langford and you'll hear the sad old stories of fans who just couldn't find the thing in the shops; Blast First president Paul Smith, who became the only manager the band's ever had shortly after the record came out, complains about paltry tour support, about nonexistent ads in *Forced Exposure* and *Your Flesh* and *Musician* and *Spin*. There are counterarguments, however. A&M couldn't stand Smith, whom nobody claims is easy to get on the phone, and promotionally, what touring the band did do was ill-designed—it allowed no time for advance work, and instead of first selling themselves to label honchos in L.A., the Mekons finished up there and immediately returned to Europe for more dates. By the time they came back that spring, *Rock 'n' Roll* was dead meat, and when they told Ralbovsky they wanted to cut another album right away, he suggested they have some fun with an EP instead. Honoring this request to the letter, they dubbed the fourth EP of their oddly configured career *F.U.N. '90:* buncha covers, ghost vocal from early fan Lester Bangs, Anglodisco-style pulse that came as a shock after *Rock 'n' Roll*'s Clashlike aggression. A&M was baffled, and pissed.

So were the Mekons. In fact, they felt on the verge of breakdown or breakup, and when they flew over to play Tramps last November, they asked out of their contract. I won't bore you with the crossfire except to note that A&M insists the Mekons demanded sales in the hundreds of thousands and the Mekons deny it, and that A&M refused to let them go. Abandoning the clever scheme of withholding *The Curse of the Mekons,* which they'd cut on advances from Twin/Tone and Blast First, the Mekons eventually sent master tapes to A&M only to have them rejected as "technically and commercially unsatisfactory"—commercially for the obvious reasons, technically because the tape arrived too late to release before alternative radio went home for vacation (not for sound quality, as the indignant Mekons believed). The album then reverted to the Amerindie limbo of Twin/Tone, which to no one's surprise failed to find another major-label distributor. If the group can get their catalogue back in return, *The Curse of the Mekons* may yet surface as their Twin/Tone swan song. Otherwise, their tenth album will only be "available" here as a Blast First import.

This is lamentable—even tragic. Since 1985's *Fear and Whis-*

key, the Mekons have put out as much good music as anybody in rock and roll. Informed opinion differs—Lester Bangs beams up *The Quality of Mercy,* Greil Marcus still pumps 1982's *Mekons Story* worktapes, and 1986's *The Edge of the World* is much loved—but for most of their cult (and also Langford, though not Greenhalgh) the peaks are *Fear and Whiskey* and *Rock 'n' Roll.* The former marks the moment when a commune that harbored upwards of sixty enemies of the state in the eight years following Johnny Rotten's con began to resemble a proper band, with former Rumour drummer Steve Goulding the linchpin, and also when their long since unfunkified anarchy turned hillbilly. Even *Rock 'n' Roll* is drenched in fiddle, and though Langford says that record was merely an attempt to reproduce their raucous live energy in the studio, it functions as an exuberantly embittered celebration/critique of rock 'n' roll as capitalism's big beat. Commercial oblivion spoils the aesthetic effect. And of course, that's not all it spoils. Oblivion is no f.u.n. for artists, especially artists working popular forms with putatively political intent, and it's hell on their protein intake. Materially, the Mekons have fuckall to show for their critically acclaimed studio output—Hüsker Dü made more money. At least people should be able to buy their records.

Far better realized than either of the Twin/Tone albums that got them to A&M, *The Curse of the Mekons* is more sour than bitter and worth the hunt nevertheless. "This is our truth that no man shall stop," Greenhalgh warns soddenly near the top, and both "Sorcerer," about brainwashing, and "Funeral," about the death of false socialism, have plenty of truth to them. But unstoppable they obviously aren't—the country stylings of Ms. Sally Timms, who delivers the drugs-in-history lecture "Brutal" and a painfully crystalline reading of John Anderson's "Wild and Blue," are more convincing in the end. Though the Mekons threaten "magic, fear and superstition," they never approach the goth-metal overdrive of their Leeds compadres the Sisters of Mercy. By the final cut, they're reduced to exhuming Jesus from Loch Ness to thank him for their beers, their careers, and the ditty at hand. Like all their records save *Rock 'n' Roll,* this one fleshes out their anarchist principles by abjuring power—it's messy, slightly inchoate, as unreconstructed and befuddled as their politics.

After all, how clear-eyed are they supposed to be in the year 12 A.T., having disseminated their message cheek-by-jowl with

Madame Medusa for over a decade? At some level they must suspect that reifying their incoherence into a proper career—making records that rock when they're supposed to rock and grin when they're supposed to grin, putting the same riffs and jokes across night after night—would be an obscenity. Who wants to make a living preaching to the converted when the converted are such a miserable minority? Who stands a chance in bloody hell of teaching disillusioned R.E.M. fans what real disillusionment is? Of the very few bands who've stuck it out longer than Johnny Rotten— longer than Hüsker Dü, even—these guys and gals are the most undefeated and the most lost.

Both Langford and Greenhalgh land the occasional cheapo production assignment, and Langford had enough capitalist in him to put down an advance from his 3 Johns side project on a house in Leeds, where one of his roomers likes to embarrass him by calling him "landlord" in front of his friends. Greenhalgh gets dole money and the occasional art or worker's education gig. Langford scripts installments of an anarcho-surrealist rock history cartoon. The computer-trained Timms holds down real jobs, currently "in an administrative capacity at a telephone dating service." And Goulding, the closest thing to a professional ever to put down roots in the band, scraped by on session work until he moved to Chicago to get married and, Timms reports, take up copywriting.

The vagueness of their take on the dilemma that is their material/professional/creative life is striking in such theoretical sophisticates, though not in such hard-drinking bohemians. Greenhalgh says he only wants "a little money to make things easier" and attributes the band's longevity to its propensity for "the short-term view." Bitterly, Langford imagines arts council funding in an England where Shakespeare is looking like a charity case. Timms, Langford's sometime companion and a definitive contributor on vocal chops alone by now, also mentions this utopian fix, but retains a grip on the everyday: "People want some sort of security. You get to about thirty-two or so and it's not the same sleeping on people's floors." Although they grant that they could make a living at it if they were willing to tour like troupers, they're not that masochistic. "We'd survive," says Langford, the only principal who still resides in Leeds, "but I don't know what we'd survive as." Even Greenhalgh, who warms most readily to such a prospect, would want to do it their way: not opening for the Pogues or whomever, but setting up a "Club Mekon" for more or less extended stays in more or less friendly locales.

Relieved of the psychic weight of A&M, which came down to vibes as much as biz, they're very together at the moment, touring Europe for a month with the Blue Aeroplanes' drummer and the peripatetic Tony Maimone. Timms ventures that even if she were to go so far as to have a baby the Mekons wouldn't really get in her way. But as far as she's concerned, "Jon and Tom are the Mekons," and Greenhalgh acknowledges that he's "been considering as carefully as possible whether to carry on doing it." Even Langford, who says he's positive they'll "just go on doing it," admits that he "can see a time when we might still pack it in." All naturally look to the hard-won numbers of the equally unconventional Sonic Youth as a way out. But Sonic Youth live on the road, and unlike the Mekons have a truly distinctive sound to sell. Greenhalgh likes *Curse* because it's "enigmatic, a bit more open and broader" and even Timms, who loves the Mekons' records—"They all bring in different strains, there's so much to get out of one album"—allows that they're "rough sounding," not something you put on just "to listen to." They're not obscure, but they raise the question of just how commodifiable attacks on commodity can be—even when they're acerbic, multileveled, tuneful, and you can clog to them.

So hope for the best. Hope that on prestige and roadwork and newfound luck the Mekons escape Amerindie limbo and reach the middle five figures—the sixty thousand U.S. sales Twin/Tone's Paul Stark says will keep a band going and A&M's Julie Panebianco reckons is a good start. Forget that the majors' habit of cherry-picking middle-level acts is what's pushed indie capitalism into limbo—let younger bohos suffer for a while. And though Panebianco says she's never met a band willing to stop at sixty thousand, or even "a really happy number" like a hundred thousand, pray that after fourteen years the Mekons could be the exception—and figure that given the miserable minority they're cursed with in the year 12 A.T., they'd better be.

Since 1991, the Mekons have put out several records, none as well-regarded as Curse of the Mekons, *which was never officially released Stateside. They've also recorded many side projects and collaborated dubiously with avant-garde hot shots Vito Acconci and*

Kathy Acker. Langford and Timms got married, not to each other, residing in Chicago and Brooklyn, respectively. Then Timms got unmarried. Greenhalgh is still in London. Their current labels are Quarterstick, an affiliate of the Chicago indie Touch and Go, and Chicago's anti-Nashville Bloodshot.

1991

7

They Are the World

West Africa Not Africa, Europe Not the World: Salif Keita / Youssou N'Dour

Since adulteration is the essence of pop, it should pain no one to admit that the great African pop styles aren't purely African—and that alien elements often determine their place in the sprawling transnational marketplace where they're compelled to compete. By re-recasting the relatively untouched and nonetheless bastardized ("Latinized") Afrobeats of Cuba, for instance, Zairean soukous became the big music of Africa itself. The longstanding attraction of South African blacks to American blacks—originally, of downpressed British colonials to idealized English-speaking freemen—was one reason mbaqanga ended up striking a chord with Paul Simon fans. Similarly, it computes that the most ambitious avatars of Afropop crossover should hail from West Africa—the Islamicized, Francophone region that stretches from Mali down through Senegambia and Guinea to the client state that's proud to call itself Côte d'Ivoire.

Inconveniently for you and me, the commercial conquest envisioned by Senegal's Youssou N'Dour and Mali's Salif Keita doesn't have much to do with airplay in Indianapolis. Europeans may dream of greenback dollars, but for French West Africans, Europe itself is the promised land. Sheer proximity assures a core audience of uprooted Africans there, as well as access to whites who rub shoulders daily with African culture while Afro-America remains a media myth, sexy but secondhand. Just as important, France's assimilationist colonialism has predisposed West African upwardly mobiles to all things Gallic—they identify progress with Paris, evolving naturally toward Europop ideas. Islamic and French individualism having brushed off on their griot traditions, the singers of the Sahel are prepared psychologically and technically for Western-style stardom; they're ready to go alone into the world and express themselves. Far-seeing syncretizer and local demigod Sunny Ade proved irreducibly Africa-specific up against a similar challenge—away from Lagos or Kinshasa, he turned into a little king, pining for the certainties of home. N'Dour and Keita are comfortable as citizens of the world. If Americans are to enjoy them, they'll have to be comfortable as citizens of the world too.

Leave your romance of the primitive where it came from— our pop visionaries may rebel against nondescript working- or middle-class backgrounds, but N'Dour and Keita were born to lead. His mother a griot who married up and/or out, N'Dour was a prodigal son, leaving home at sixteen to become a musician. Compromising, his father sent him to Dakar's École des Arts, where he lasted a year and a half. In 1977, he joined Senegal's top dance band; in 1979, at twenty, he started his own, and has been his nation's biggest star for a decade. He first recorded in Europe in 1984, tested the United States in 1986, and has toured for profit and the glory of Amnesty International with his well-known mentor Peter Gabriel.

Keita is an albino born to the Malian nobility—an extreme outsider and an extreme insider. Declining a teaching career, he defied the rules of his caste to set out for Bamako and become a singer. After picking up pointers in the state-supported Rail Band, he began in 1973 to adapt the modern, Congo-inflected dance music of a more frankly commercial musical group to traditional Malian forms and instruments. Soon the Ambassadeurs were a sensation—his sensation. They emigrated to Côte d'Ivoire in 1978 and recorded an obscure album in the United States in 1980. In 1984, disappointed by his progress, Keita moved to Paris and went solo.

N'Dour's and Keita's grand ambitions are powered above all by their grand voices—Keita's a sweet, rough rush, N'Dour's clearer and lither, both soaring on a soulful muezzin wail. But their very different biographies also recall countless self-made rebels of nineteenth-century Europe, back when the artistic calling was nurtured by inherited position just negligible enough to seem more duty than privilege, a constraint in a world of infinite challenge. In the Africans' case, however, the alienation from their ordained roles, the need to live in the whole world, doesn't preclude patriotism—in fact, it grows out of their patriotism, their longing to see their people enter the future.

Certainly they're entertainers—both got famous leading dance bands, and N'Dour especially seems ready to do whatever the international music business requests. But they're also intensely serious, not to say pretentious—men with a mission more severely defined than pop visionaries on the scale of Bowie or Prince could imagine. Soukous is a signifying good-time music of forward-looking vivacity and complexity, and Zairean echoes from seventies Bamako and Dakar can be heard in Keita's and N'Dour's most Euro-inflected music. Well before they left Africa, however, their focus was specifically, ideologically *West* African, and it still is. So say they're griots for a postsoukous era. It sounds like bull, I know, but they really are like preachers or storytellers even when their songs aren't narrative or hortatory (and most of the time they aren't). Sure they can meet the rhythmic requirements of contemporary pop. But groove doesn't matter as much to them as structure and message—drama.

American African music fans, for whom beat if not polybeat is what it all means, have more trouble with these priorities than the Europeans who took to Keita's 1987 *Soro*—though it should be noted that Keita's onetime Rail Band cohort Mory Kante soon had a much bigger hit with the discofied traditional "Yé Ké Yé Ké." Overseen by Afro-Parisian kingpin Ibrahim Sylla, *Soro* comes with an inner-sleeve trot that from a non-African viewpoint rarely justifies the meaning-heavy arrangements—mostly instructions to Keita's people, and especially his caste, on adjusting to a "topsy-turvy" world in which "lovers tear each other to bits" and "lords no longer enjoy the privilege of slaughter." And judging from the annotated press-only translations, the omission of a lyric sheet from his new *Ko-Yan* isn't exactly a blow to world peace. The lead cut on the A, keyed to a Bambara word that means "at one and the same time life, fortune, power, reputation and the devil," and the lead cut on the B, keyed to a Bambara word that "refers at one and the same time to the King, power, alcohol and drugs," are hard to render into English, not just linguistically but culturally. The celebration of Mali's riches, the praisesong, the metaphysical homily, the title tune that translates as "What's Going On"—every-thing except the bitterly cryptic black protest "Nou Pas Bouger" seems curious international fare. Even as an exiled enemy of his nation's caste system, Keita hasn't abandoned his royal respon-sibilities—he's singing to Malians, or maybe West Africans, and hoping others will listen.

Perhaps because he recognizes this paradox, though, *Ko-Yan* has the grace to correct *Soro*'s melodrama for groove. The music is still very much composed rather than spun out along a line to infinity, but the production goes lighter on the abrupt bright bursts of horn, the atmospheric kora colors, the synth-simulated whistles and pans and balafon. Keita's voice, often in tandem with a strong female chorus, rides the rhythm in a partial return to the dance music of the Ambassadeurs. This fusion could teach non-Malians more about the complexities of modernization than his lyrics ever could, and if that sounds like bull again, why kid around—it probably is. As well-suited for world fame as Keita may be in theory, he's too stern, too driven, too Malian, and just pos-sibly too old to have a serious shot at pulling off the transforma-tion—not in Europe, and definitely not in the United States.

About ten years younger than Keita, his personal struggle not so wrenching, N'Dour is less world-weary, more the expansive universalist. His 1987 *Nelson Mandela*—a textbook title, both radical-sounding and irreproachably conventional—was more danceable than *Soro*. But it also overreached like over-the-hill Wil-son Pickett, and *The Lion*—produced by Peter Gabriel henchman George Acogny, with input from Springsteen pianist turned new age fusioneer David Sancious—strives even more assiduously for effect. Reviewers may drool over its indigenous rhythms. But though old N'Dour hands play bass and drums, it's no more a rhythm album than whatever Peter Gabriel opus you care to recall. Since Gabriel does play "rock," that's not to say *The Lion* isn't a rhythm album at all. But there's no apter way to describe it than as a very good Peter Gabriel record. And if you can't get with that, go back to your hip-hop or soukous or acid house.

Granted, I wouldn't have developed a tolerance and then a taste for it myself if duty hadn't goaded me on, and I have no idea where it will find a market if Peter Gabriel fans are as limited as I suspect. But a market it most certainly deserves. Gabriel's m.o. is to pump up rock and third-world sonorities with grandiose settings and structures and put them across with a big beat, and N'Dour does it better. Forgiving the horn parts—just compare the Senegalese lines on 1984's *Immigrés*—his arrangements are on the whole less forced. His voice is more powerful and pleasing. His beat is indigenous enough. And his lyrics are better. In Wolof, French, and English, with French translations on one side of the inner sleeve and English on the other, they have something to say to everyone—where Keita writes to Africans, N'Dour writes for them.

There are the usual useless saws ("Truth will always win against deceit," "You should help those with less than you"), and the compassionate tale of lost virginity concealed is overwhelmed by its portentous synth-wash-and-percussion accompaniment. But there are also at least three cross-cultural advances. N'Dour, who is dismissed as a "ladies" ' singer by some Senegalese (men, presumably), advises his four-year-old daughter to follow her "destiny" rather than her "heart" (which suggests how he weighs vocation and self-expression in his own path to glory), and collaborates with Gabriel on a feminist anthem far more explicit than anything on Stella Chiweshe's *Ambuya?* or Miriam Makeba's *Sangoma.* It's a little simplistic, as anthems tend to be. But most African music is so deeply male chauvinist that to hear N'Dour sing "Changing your ways, changing those surrounding you/Changing your ways, more than any man can do" is to believe his mission is a humanitarian one—not many male singers in Europe or America have voiced a more convincing solidarity. Nor have many artists of any provenance written more complex songs about shaping history than N'Dour's "Old Tucson," an almost reverent description of three museums—a slavery museum in Africa, the NASA museum in Washington, and his favorite, "the museum town of Old Tucson."

"One of the most wonderful days of my life," N'Dour sings in impenetrably accented, arhythmically recitative English. "I found myself in the real world of the Westerns/I had seen in the cinema." And suddenly N'Dour's ambition—to grasp the past, change the future, and master the very media to which he's always been subject by accident of national origin—comes to seem heroic in its magnitude. Pray for him. And tip your hat to Peter Gabriel while you're at it.

1989

The Black Sea Giant and the Lion Queens: Mahlathini and the Mahotella Queens

> I hear that Gallo have just moved to some fancy new building. Do you know where Mahlathini lives? Do you know that he doesn't even have a bicycle? So much of the music around South Africa today is because of Mahlathini, and he walks to the bus stop, he walks to the train.
>
> —Hugh Masekela, in Muff Andersson, *Music in the Mix* (Johannesburg, 1981)

Things have gotten better for Simon Nkabinde—whose professional name is said to mean Jungle on His Head, after the witch-doctor dreads he no longer wears, which complemented the "groaning" "goat voice" that suddenly emanated from deep in his bowels at age twelve, or eight; early on he also performed as Boston Tar Baby, Black Sea Giant, Warrior with a Tomahawk. He hit a low point when disco invaded the townships. But by 1983, long before Paul Simon donned gumboots, West Nkosi had him back in the Gallo studios with the reconstituted Makgona Tsohle Band and the original Mahotella Queens, and many of those unforgettable tracks ended up on *The Indestructible Beat of Soweto*. Now Mahlathini enjoys a career as a cultural treasure among Azanian blacks, especially Zulus, whose pride of origin isn't discouraged by white fascists who believe their deathlock on urban South Africa is strengthened by anything that promotes tribal ways. He's also got a cult in France, England, and at long last North America, where he opened a month-long tour with Makgona Tsohle and the Queens June 21 at S.O.B.'s.

Of course, there's no way for an outsider to tell how materially rewarding his resurgence has been. Nkosi, a gifted saxophone/pennywhistle player who became the top Gallo a&r man on Mahlathini's shoulders, is the businessman. And Mahlathini looks like he's seen some serious shit. On his passport he's fifty-two, which with hits dating only to the early sixties is completely plausible, but some believe he's older. When he climbed on the S.O.B.'s stage at ten (three A.M. in London, where he'd woken up the previous day), he seemed bone tired, and without a hint of dissipation—just fifty-two years of hard time. Yet as soon as he reached the mike he was the image of virility—assuming Zulu postures I later realized I knew from Johnny Clegg, spreading his arms in benevolent grandeur, stabbing the air with fist or finger. His bass lead was broad and powerful, and my worries that its edge had gone the way of all flesh disappeared on his second number, when he brought out the groan—a deep, penetrating sung roar that seems to filter sound that begins in his diaphragm through a special resonator in his larynx. Amazing on record, this voice is unreal live. No wonder they thought he was a witch doctor.

Mbaqanga is at once more hectically urban-upbeat and more respectfully tribal-melodic than its jazzy and folky predecessors, marabi and kwela. It's also far more Azanian than competing pop styles. Nkosi is big on authenticity even though Makgona Tsohle is hardly innocent of Afro-American timbres and rhythms; Mahlathini makes much of his bush upbringing and experience leading a troupe of traditional wedding singers. Both emphasize mbaqanga's "message"—not "just 'love, love, love' and 'I love you,'" Nkosi boasts. What this means in practice, near as a non-Zulu speaker can determine, is that they berate Soweto's mean streets and extol the moral certainties of tribal life, sex roles prominent among them: from his lionlike voice to his sinewy gestures, Mahlathini is emphatically male. If that were the end of it this regression would be too bad but not fatal. Drawing on premodern cultural resources that are almost invariably male chauvinist, lots of rock and roll is reflexively sexist in much the same way, and that doesn't mean it can't also be liberating. When the dominant culture pillages your heritage, you have no choice but to try and recreate it from the ground up. How successful you are depends on who does what with it in which context. At S.O.B.'s, the doers were the Mahotella Queens.

Keyed to Marks Mankwane's guitar-riff fakebook, Makgona Tsohle are mbaqanga's greatest studio band, and something to look at—Joseph Makwela's unmatched argyles were almost as impressive as his unshakable bass. Mahlathini is a gift from God—just compare the wonderful and nonetheless dwarfed groaners on

Shanachie's *Izibani Zomgqashiyo,* recorded in 1977 by four competing Mahotella Queens. But these big-legged matriarchs—Hilda Tloubatla, Mildred Mangxola, and Nobesuthu Mbadu, all of whom returned to music in 1983 after long child-rearing layoffs—ruled the show. They warmed up the crowd with a close-harmony Mandela tribute, a piety that could get them in trouble in the wrong context, and then a band-backed dance number, taking over briefly again when Mahlathini rested after three songs. More often than not they sang the melodies, leaving the Lion of Soweto to knock the crowd back with his gruff interjections, irascible commentary, and climactic afterwords. And physically they were all over the place—leaping, shrugging, crouching, cavorting, redefining grace as effort, matching the leader move for muscular move. Granted, they have from five to eight years on him, but they also have more weight to throw around; playing their heft and their tough, knowledgeable faces for strength and vitality rather than resorting to comedy, they projected not femininity but self-sufficient femaleness. In a culture where middle-aged people aspire successfully to the slim carelessness of youth, they were a revelation—I can think of nothing in show business like them.

Not that the Queens, who began as dancers, would be as gripping without Mahlathini. They're fine singers, but their male counterpart is absolutely extraordinary—it's he who makes you gasp or pound the wall, who propels the show they carry over all linguistic and cultural barriers. And of course, the show changes when it crosses them. I can't be certain what it signifies for those immersed in Zulu culture—maybe every exchange is village shtick, or maybe the idea is that the traditional male gets the last word on three modern women. In America, though, I'm sure that this particular mbaqanga does more than internationalize and hence renew r&b usages—it's the image of custom in dynamic flux, almost the obverse of the secondhand traditionalism any musical tourist ought to be wary of. Mahlathini's *The Lion of Soweto,* on Earthworks, proves he didn't lose his potency during his '70s troubles; his later *Thokozile* exemplifies Nkosi's confident case for mbaqanga as invigorating alternative pop. But it's Celluloid's dramatically balanced, aurally resonant *Paris-Soweto* that best captures the gestalt I had to see to understand. Bring your daughters when this battle of the sexes passes through—I'm bringing mine.

1989

The Goat-God in History: The Master Musicians of Jajouka

On October 14, 1995, in a not quite sold out Town Hall, the Master Musicians of Jajouka commenced the first New York set of their centuries-old history with essentially the same music that had blown Brian Jones's mind back in 1968. Playing in unison or trading two simple melodies, six identical double-reed pipes/shawms/oboes—rhaitas, Stephen Davis calls them in his 1993 "novel" *Jajouka Rolling Stone;* other sources say ghaitas—gave forth a ferocious din that skirled phoenixlike over the wittingly imprecise patterns and sporadic licks of the six drummers. Soon I was caught up in a precious feeling—that never before had I encountered such a sound. Unfortified by kif, a preemptive glance at Davis's book, or a craving for a more vital life, my interest in the music's oft-told magical capacities was limited. But I sure did dig the noise.

Through the magic of technology and human commerce, I'd heard similar sounds/noises before. I wouldn't have been there if Point Music's rerelease of *Brian Jones Presents the Pipes of Pan at Jajouka* hadn't been good to my earhole in a way the vinyl version wasn't back in 1971, when I played it twice and filed its caterwaul away thinking sour thoughts about exoticism, necrophilia, and the satisfactions of the blues-based backbeat. I'd adored Ornette Coleman's 1977 *Dancing in Your Head* despite "Midnight Sunrise," where he wisely drowns out Robert Palmer's clarinet and Jajouka's unnamed and treated implements, and barely noticed the Rolling

Stones' 1989 "Continental Drift," where the Master Musicians' "Moroccan instruments" and Farafina's "African instruments" vie for special-effects time. And in 1992, when Bill Laswell emerged from the Atlas range with the Master Musicians' strongest recording, Axiom's *Apocalypse Across the Sky,* I filed *its* caterwaul away thinking sour thoughts about cultural imperialism, megalomania, and the sweet comforts of European tuning. That I could connect in 1995 says more about my increased familiarity with Middle Eastern modes than about Jones's record, which the doomed blond fool tweaked big-time in the studio, leaving it markedly inferior not only to the Laswell but to Joel Rubiner's 1972 *Master Musicians of Jajouka,* now available on Genes. But no record captures the loud power of the rhaitas live. And I swear this was a strictly acoustical phenomenon. Bou Jeloud had nothing to do with it.

As is known to those who have sampled the lore—which Davis lays out sapiently enough even if he does rename preservationist Rubiner "Joel Fischer," impresario Rikki Stein "Ricky Stone," and so forth—Bou Jeloud is the Jajoukans' goat god. Literally, he's a Berber youth in a smelly pelt, like the one whose wild saltarellos climaxed the Town Hall show. In myth, however, he guarantees fertility to those who have grown up in his neck of the mountains—and links those Jones branded the "psychic weaklings" of the alienated West to Hellenic wholeness, to Roman Lupercalia, to what the folks at Genes call "primal energy," to any golden-age metaphor that suits a seeker's fancy. In short, this tiny local style comes to the international marketplace burdened with more bullshit than any music can bear. From Bowles and Burroughs to Ornette and the Stones to scribes like Palmer and Davis, who made a bundle on a seminal Led Zeppelin biography long after he'd offered up his soul to these more obscure adepts of power, its support roster is monumental. And the claims surrounding it are grand enough to wreck it for ordinary secular humanists.

No one goes so far as to argue that Jajouka replicates the cultic strains of the storied past, but the talk does get heady. Jajouka's crucial propagandist was Brion Gysin, an intimate of Bowles and Burroughs whose life was changed around 1950, when he climbed up to the hidden hill town with a friend from Tangiers who was tied to the Attars, now the Master Musicians' ruling family. Davis, who talked at length with a one hundred fifteen-year-old still entranced by the peachlike asses of fondly remembered goat boys, makes clear that Gysin had a weakness for the music's homoerotic folkways. But the avant-gardist in Gysin also treasured its arcane musicology: Muslim healers, Sufi circular breathing, Andalusian court songs, and yes, the Lupercalia, where Pan's pipes were played. In fact, he told Davis, "One could trace the various folkloric dances and characters all the way back to the ritual processions of the Dionysian Mysteries, if one were so inclined." And many have been, not least Robert Palmer, whose *Rock & Roll: An Unruly History* unapologetically conflates three horned gods—Pan, Shiva, Dionysus—and goes on: "Rock and roll challenged the dominant norms and values with a *genuinely* Dionysian fervor." Italics in original. Writer overboard.

The fact is, nobody has much idea what genuine Dionysian fervor felt like, and as for genuine Dionysian music—well, it's a mystery. The most vivid references come from the Greek tragedians, who made their living civilizing the impulse to revel, and who were probably working from hearsay anyway. An aulos that resembled a rhaita more than the idealized flutes of Victorian Hellenophilia was certainly involved, and the dancing got pretty funky by Athenian standards, which were contained indeed. There was wine, and no doubt sex (less, I bet, than Athenian intellectuals believed). There was also blood sacrifice—for a time there, human sacrifice. Civilization does have its contents, doesn't it? Reading *Jajouka Rolling Stone,* I was reminded why I was no Dionysian when "a young outsider" who got in Bou Jeloud's way was thrown over a cliff by "a howling mob" as music and narrative proceeded apace. And pondering Gysin's theories, I couldn't understand how any ancient music wouldn't change utterly as it passed through Iraqi mysticism and Moorish high culture and the centuries that transform the most secluded societies.

In fact, I credit the Master Musicians' pull on my fellow psychic weaklings more to their capacity for corruption than their devotion to purity. Although much is made of the favor they once found with the king of Morocco, it's never noted that, throughout history, nothing has smoothed a rural artist's edges faster than a court gig. Similarly, there is no report of any shift in the Jajoukans' sense of audience when Gysin began presenting them in a Tangiers club he owned, which is either because no one will admit it or because no one was clear-eyed enough to notice it happening— which I guarantee it did. After Brian Jones, the Master Musicians began writing new songs ("Jajouka Rolling Stone/Jajouka really stoned," one violin-and-voice number goes), and young Bachir Attar conceived the dream of taking his hereditary music out into the world. Bachir ended up leading an East Village band called Hamduoillah. He also cut one of Laswell's better-integrated world-fusion experiments: CMP's *The Next Dream,* featuring Aiyb Dieng and Maceo Parker. And after a bitter split with the Brian Jones generation, he first seized the Master Musicians' name and then reconciled with the old guard, who capitulated for one reason above all: Bachir was getting paid. There was a time when local farmers tithed so the Masters could sit around smoking kif and playing with their gimbris. In recent years, however, the sons would commonly get jobs in Europe or sign up for a twenty-year army hitch, leaving their singular musical heritage to the boys and the old men.

The second set at Town Hall began with a long flute air by Bachir, who returned to earth after the drums reentered with their short, simply interrelated phrases. Then there was a lineup that went: pepper-grinder-looking hand drum/tambourine/pepper grinder/big two-headed drum/fiddle/Bachir's oudlike, strummed and plucked gimbri/somebody else's gimbri/little blue hand kettledrum/tom/little drum. The little drum was played by a short, stocky, barefoot old gent who'd pranced/danced jesterlike across the stage to close the first set and never mounted the rug-strewn platforms where the rest perched. Then violin call, gimbri response, with the call maintaining as the response faded—no real melody, except for the vocal. Then a hand drum called and gimbri-gimbri-violin responded. All, to be honest, fascinating but not compelling—familiar, somehow. Finally Bou Jeloud leaped out, eventually joined by the jester, who jutted his hips and stepped mincingly in what seemed almost comic relief. It was definitely pretty amazing—and definitely only the representation of a ritual, if that. I'd see them again in a minute, and understand more the second time around. But since music is my passion, what I really want is to hear those rhaitas again.

1995

A Goat-God in Exile: (Cheb) Khaled

Rai's web of influences—Moroccan, Gnawi, Spanish, French, and most specifically Bedouin—came together after World War I in Oran, Algeria. Its vanguard was a cohort of female entertainers—the best remembered a "wild and wayward" singer named Cheikha Rimitti Rilizania, every one a wanton by definition in the culture of chador. Like tango in Buenos Aires, fado in Lisbon, rebetika in Athens, kroncong in Jakarta, rai was sinners' music, performed in tawdry nightclubs, glorified whorehouses, lower-class bars, and dockside dives for a tough, hard-drinking audience whose big men were criminals more often than not. In the fifties and sixties, modernizing male musicians replaced the Bedouin flutes and lutes with accordions, horns, and electric guitars, and in the early eighties a whole subculture of singing studs who called themselves Cheb, which translates loosely as Kid, emerged from the slums. Significantly, some claim that once again the groundbreaker wasn't a cheb but a chaba—Chaba Fadela, whose 1979 "Ana Ma H'lali Ennoum" ("I Don't Care About Sleep Anymore") marked the beginning of the music's rockish "pop-rai" heyday, and who in 1985 joined her conservatory-trained husband, Cheb Sahraoui, on a duet that stands as the most universal rai song ever recorded. "N'Sel Fik," it's called, "You Are Mine"—an avowal of conjugal obsession that keynotes both Fadela's *You Are Mine* album on Mango and Earthworks's *Rai Rebels* compilation. Tumid with longing, spurred to an eternal cycle of overstimulated carnality by the Arab-funk percussion and oudlike guitar (or guitarlike oud) of multitracking superproducer Rachid, this one goes on the wedding tape no matter what language you speak. Look at another woman, it says in spirit if not so many words, and your helpmate will suck out your eyes; let another man touch you and your sweet daddy will chew your tits to bits.

In general, rai singers don't give a damn about politics. Their only demand is to rai all night long. But in the context of Algerian Islam—which pits staid state socialists against the reactionary fundamentalists whose latest bid to make their 1991 election victory stick involves killing veilless women in the streets—rai is the embodiment of rock and roll pleasure theory, that convenient and far from untrue formulation in which any pop music with ecstatic tendencies is subversive merely because it articulates needs no repressive society can fulfill. Never mind that the Oran bubble has burst, that the big chebs and chabas have long since relocated to France. After all, when Cheb Khaled, the unchallenged King of Rai, returned to Algeria to arrange a tour, the government—the so-called socialists, not the Shiite bad guys—threw him in jail just to prove how easily it could be done. He's no emigré—he's an exile, his rebel credentials intact for the foreseeable future.

For most curious Americans, unfortunately, there's a drawback to this fascinating story: the music doesn't connect. Even among the world-beat faithful, rai means almost nothing—not compared to Irish jigs or Bulgarian chorales or any number of sub-Saharan genres, and not compared to the way it's caught on in Europe. It has no demographic base. Just as the recent Avery Fisher concert of Sufi master Nusrat Fateh Ali Khan, the only Islamic musician to inspire any kind of devoted U.S. following, was suitably top-heavy with young Pakistani-Americans out on a quest, the high concentration of Algerians and other North Africans in Europe makes rai feel organic there, with Paris an even more indispensable epicenter than it is for soukous. Here, though, it's exotic-unfamiliar rather than exotic-beguiling. Having listened faithfully to something over a dozen U.S. releases since 1988, I could testify for Rachid's belly-dancing bass and give-my-regards-to-Cairo synth timbres, salt away Cheb Kader's hot violin while chucking Cheb Mami's warmed-over tuxedo, and fully enjoy a grand total of two albums: *You Are Mine,* and Cheb Khaled and Safy Boutella's

Kutché. But until Khaled's just-released *N'ssi N'ssi,* pinning these distinctions down felt very much like work.

Whatever it owes Chaba Fadela or Cheikha Rimitti Rilizania, modern rai is a fervently male domain, and Hadj-Brahim Khaled isn't just its king, he's its goat-god. The original Cheb, he cut an attack on high school called "Trig Lycee" at age sixteen in 1976, and royalties or no royalties he ran with it. Writing in *Antaeus,* Brian Cullman estimates that during the halcyon eighties Khaled never made much more than two thousand per off records that sold in the millions, including *Kutché,* cut with the assistance of a music-loving army colonel who threw in the passport that clinched the deal. Even today, he lives by gigging. Nevertheless, he's easily the most pop-wise and studio-savvy of the chebs and chabas. His classic singles—collected on two Blue Silver imports called *Le Meilleur de Cheb Khaled*—are basically logocentric. Riding propulsive, adventurous settings as likely to run six or nine minutes as three or four, their aesthetic suits rai's performance history as earthy, blueslike improvised songpoetry of little use to Anglophones not yet mesmerized by Khaled's voice.

Among Arabic speakers, however, hypnosis comes naturally. Just as rai lyrics reject the high-flown romanticism of Arabic poetry—Cullman tells of the singer who, when informed that "I will fuck you on the floor of the dirtiest hotel in town" would never do, came back with "I will fuck you on the floor of the most expensive hotel in town"—rai voices rarely truck with the transcendent high range of singers like Khan and his group, and Khaled's hypermasculine muscle is the model. He knows, however, that his timbre, power, and precise intonation won't take him to the top of the mountain anywhere else. That's one reason he recorded *Kutché* with Safy Boutella, a highborn Algerian from Germany and Berkeley with something of a classical rep.

Despite the André Previn look of Boutella's soundtrack-heavy resume, he did a job on *Kutché.* Not only is the music *arranged*—melodically enhanced, jumped up with a sharp ear for the thrill—but its colors and scales sound consistently North African. This is essential—while pop-rai wouldn't exist without rock attitude, it dies when it angles for fusion. Yet once I'd broken its code, *Kutché* always struck me as a little too raw—and also, I suppose, too macho. When Khaled played Summerstage in 1991, the crowd greeted his unmistakable force, coherence, and integrity with a polite enthusiasm they soon exceeded for the fusioneering Mory Kante and Gipsy Kings. In 1992, he resurfaced with a collaborator even more promising than Boutella—Don Was, who has made a specialty of helping genre artists find a contemporary voice that doesn't compromise their personal or stylistic commitments. Was did what he was supposed to and Canadian Enophile Michael Brook proved a creditable Boutella surrogate on the other six songs. Yet the album fell just slightly flat.

That's how a "world music" artist, even a major innovator with a broadly legible musical imagination, can slip between the cracks. *Khaled*—at thirty-two, he reckoned it was time to drop the Cheb—never found effective U.S. distribution. And when *N'ssi N'ssi* showed up on Mango with the same production strategy—four Was tracks instead of five, soundtrack art-rocker Philippe Eidel filling Brook's shoes on another five, and Richard Evans and Laurent Guéneau (who they?) producing one apiece—there was no reason to expect progress. Yet my far-flung quality controls all love it, the one exception being Cullman, who as Khaled's Boswell may know too much about him to judge—the objection that several tracks are remakes in disguise suggests to me that Khaled is relying on tested melodies, and while Cullman's feeling that the singing surrenders a soupçon of richness and resonance on these sessions no doubt has its objective correlative, I'm not enough of an adept to hear it. Anyway, I've played *N'ssi N'ssi* up against *Khaled* enough times to know the difference.

The most obvious improvement is the addition of Cairo strings to four of Eidel's tracks. By poaching the signature of the pan-Middle Eastern ughniyah style to which rai is a rebel-rock response, Khaled performs the usual pomo double whammy—it is his, he is its. But the main thing is they sound fabulous, an aural novelty and dramatic device more engaging and sonically appropriate than, for instance, the Fela-gone-L.A. brass filigrees that occasionally distract from both albums. Was seems more assured the second time around—the jazzy sax obbligatos, brightly idiomatic rhythm parts, and (just once) uncanny pedal steel are the kind of touches that transform something you enjoy hearing into something you want to hear again. Eidel et al.'s tracks are less American, not less universal. And don't forget, the songs are better too. Here in the land of the Great Satan, there's still nothing like a tune.

For me, *N'ssi N'ssi* establishes a context not just for *Les Meilleurs* and *Kutché* and *Khaled,* but for albums like Kader's *From Oran to Paris* and Earthworks's *Pop-Rai and Rachid Style,* filed away in hopes of a brighter day that now has come, and for Rachid's Moroccan rai comp, *Oujda-Casablanca Introspections Vol. 1.* It's also the most confidently, thoughtlessly, exuberantly, unremittingly masculine masterstroke of a year whose bounty has been long on testosterone. In fact, I'm sorry to say that its translated verses make me think of the supposedly cockamamy Alan Lomax theory in which all the fundamentals of musical production reflect or struggle against the sexual repressiveness of the surrounding culture. The goat-god's struggle has clearly been less sublimated than that of Mr. Worldbeat, the supernal Youssou N'Dour, who's about to release *The Guide,* the latest of his well-mannered rapprochements with a Euro-American market that might well prefer the dance music of his youth if pleasure was as universal as it's supposed to be. That Khaled's musical growth seems more graceful, if less visionary, may just mean he isn't trying as hard. It could even be why he isn't succeeding as well—one good record doesn't do all that much for your aura on the concert circuit where worldbeat luminaries great and small must make their dollars and their marks. But for sure it means that good manners are rarely the best way to show the world a good time.

1994

The Iron Curtain at Midnight: Pulnoc

No matter what you think of their music—assuming you've ever heard it, of course—the Plastic People of the Universe are world-historic, and I would no more have missed them than I would have missed the Sex Pistols in 1978. Their six-city U.S. tour was an event two decades in the making—so long overdue that by the time it happened they weren't even the Plastic People anymore. In 1988 this most persecuted of all rock bands had finally given it up, as three old-timers recombined with four young admirers to create a new seven-piece called Pulnoc, which is Czech for Midnight. On April 24, 1989, the day of their New York premiere, artistic advisor Ivan Jirous lost a parole appeal in Prague, and will do another ten months for reading the wrong poems in public. How could I skip this gig? There was no reason to expect another.

Arriving early to beat a crush that never materialized—P.S. 122's gym-turned-"space" was full but not jammed—I had time to absorb some good vibes. This was a gathering of the committed bohemians who never turn out in force at Maxwell's or CBGB anymore, and with the requisite quirks: a brown-suited man in his sixties who I imagined to be a local Ukrainian nationalist standing against a post with a bouquet, for instance. Me, I sat on the floor dismayed by the warmup record, Lou Reed's *Rock n Roll Animal*. How could I have been suckered by the arena-rock baloney of Steve Hunter's over-and-out solo on "Rock and Roll"? Little did I know that I was about to find out.

Oh how politically correct, I can hear cynics clucking as I describe my pilgrimage, and I do try, but not so's I can't handicap a good time—all I felt sure of was that the show would be interesting, as we world-historic fans put it. On the spotty recorded evidence (some half dozen albums, three of which I'd heard), oppression hadn't done much for the Plastic People's sense of humor. Where the circa-1974 *Egon Bondy's Happy Hearts Club Banned* came through sardonically rambunctious, *Passion Play,* recorded 1978, and *Leading Horses,* recorded 1981, seemed pretentious and funereal. Both articulated a staunchly unwimpy modernist variation on European art-rock—very much the group's own, and not stupid, but rock and roll only by association and fun only by comparison (with prison, say). Like lots of otherwise dissimilar Eurorock, they reminded me that Frank Zappa has never been kicked out of the pantheon over there. In 1984 I'd given *Leading Horses* an A minus, "upped a notch for existing at all," but when I played it to get in the mood for the show, my mood did not improve. I figured I was in for an evening of "composition," probably with "theater" and "improvisation" included—an evening of "art" more or less transfigured by the real-life heroism of the artists.

Pleasures so pallid no longer seemed inevitable—far from it. Maybe urban Africa was the crucible, but there was no reason to believe Europe couldn't cast off its classical shackles and contribute mightily to rock and roll renewal. Eastern Europe especially— because consonant-heavy non-Latinate languages suit rock's aggressive four-four, because the disconcerting minor keys and old modes of Slavic tradition constitute an underexploited musical resource, and because the Communist bloc suffers its own strain of cultural underdevelopment, with all the painful spiritual benefits that entails. America's magic—freedom of expression, consumer goods, blue notes—is still fresh for Eastern Europeans. But they're hardly naifs—they identify with the European avant-garde and their own self-conscious national traditions, and all but a few mystagogic reactionaries share collectivist assumptions that remain subversive here.

All of which produces no more good music than any other theory. The best I could vouch for would be the cute Polish punk of Lady Pank and maybe the furious Polish hardcore of Dezerter. The four Russian bands on Big Time's 1986 *Red Wave* compilation play tame art-rock, tame pop, tame boogie, and jumpy ska respectively, with a few acerbic harmonies poking through. Yugoslavia's Laibach are dangerous ironists who wear thin out of context. Even when I hied off to Europe last fall, efforts to ferret out the continent's indigenous future got me nowhere. Albums by Finnish new wavers and GDR balladeers and Slovenian punks, shows by Russians who dressed like Kraftwerk and moved like Devo in Hamburg and ridiculous Doorsy Germans sporting a CCCP logo in Amsterdam, the legal-bootleg *Glasnotes* cassette and its sickening succession of keyb ostinatos—all had their moments, and all were patently derivative, at best merely interesting, interesting, interesting. My one transcendent moment came on a lazy Sunday in East Berlin when I happened upon a fraulein singing "Mack the Knife" and phonetic blues in a tiny youth club. You had to be there. About fifteen of us were.

Since I'm working with a sampling error of plus or minus 90 percent, I'm sure there's better available. But let me state unequivocally that on music alone the Plastic People at their most avantly suspect have always been in their own class—maybe not the best Eastern Europe has to offer, but easily the best to come our way. So the thrill wasn't all history when the band took the stage. With few marketing ploys at their disposal, they were billed as the Plastic People, but they announced themselves as Midnight: three musicians in their late thirties who looked older, four in their late twenties who didn't. And though some claim Pulnoc is a new band in name only, it was clear inside of sixteen bars that neither *Leading Horses* nor the song-filled circa-1986 *Midnight Mouse,* which I tracked down later, would have prepared Nostradamus himself for their generational synthesis.

The root source is Frank Zappa's obverse, the good old Velvet Underground. The spur is veteran Milan Hlavsa, a Bill Haley fan whose nagging bass always gave the Plastics a compulsive edge. But the signature and energy belong to the new guys: Michaela Nemcova, an apple-cheeked, six-months-pregnant contra-Nico who sang three quarters of the material; Petr Kumamdzas, whose loud diddleybeats yelled "You Really Got Me" until I recognized the motor that drove "I'm Waiting for the Man"; Tomas Schilla, who turns his cello into a hands-on synthesizer; and Karel Jancak, who admires Hendrix and Page and Adrian Belew and Buck Dharma and I bet Steve Hunter. Sure it evoked the great ones: late

Sonic Youth in its momentum and discomfiting Slavic changes, early and late Ubu in its art-industrial postanomie. But it was also a little vulgar, and naive—arena-rock not as a defiant return to the AOR twentysomethings loved before they discovered punk, but as American magic. Nemcova's sweet gravity, Kumamdzas's fervidly efficient beat, Hlavsa's return to his roots, and Jancak's unshow-boating hard-rock virtuosity were all free of the ironic admixture of pose that signals safe distance to the tastiest art-rock crowd—by which I mean early Ramones fans, not early Genesis fans. Pulnoc assumed—incorrectly, I think, but isn't that what Harold Bloom calls misprision?—that they could just get up and play this music straight to anybody. Faith can move mountains.

And so, having carefully balanced my bones on the seat of my pants, I spent the next two hours on my feet. I wasn't quite up to the posthippie boogie gallumphed through by a barefoot post-girl and a Thurston Moore wannabe, to name just two, but as I bopped around the room or stood squeezing my date, I tried to remember the last time live music had been such serious fun. After 1980, when punk finally dissipated, I counted Flash at the Ritz '81, Hüsker Dü at Gildersleeves '83, Peter Stampfel at the Speak Easy '86. Maybe Franco at Manhattan Center '84. Not quite Gang of Four at the Pier '82 or Springsteen at the Meadowlands '84 or Sunny Ade at the Ritz '85. The difference has made all the difference throughout this anomie-ridden decade—in their antihegemonic way, the Gang of 4 and Springsteen and Adé had already been hegemonized. They weren't unlikely enough, enjoyed no surprise factor, and I'm probably robbing Pulnoc of theirs by raving on. But why not take the chance? As they gave their solid all to a well-rehearsed set—only two songs not in Czech (Blake's "The Tyger" and Reed's "All Tomorrow's Parties," since you're curious), with no mime or costumery in the way—Pulnoc made me feel for the first time in years that there might be a future for "rock" as it was reconceived by deluded white kids in the sixties, as the capital-A Art of a popular subculture.

Next afternoon, back at P.S. 122 to offer my thanks and make sure I spelled their names right, I latched onto some stray facts. Leader Hlavsa is retired on disability and fabricates plastic bags at piece rates in his home; frontwoman Nemcova gave up a music-teaching gig to tour; Schilla is an X-ray technician. The others work what we'd call menial jobs—window cleaner, orderly, driver, gofer.

The younger members are churchgoing Catholics. Everyone concurred when Hlavsa asserted that Pulnoc had "got rid of the pessimism" in Plastic People's music—Pulnoc was "faster," "sharper," "purified," "more rock." This wasn't a matter of will, but of external conditions—even in a satellite at war with decadent Moscow liberalization, the mood of their audience was up. Several Czech poets contributed lyrics, I was told. Talking about the music and then again about the words, Hlavsa, the only one who could formulate an English sentence unaided, twice told me Pulnoc addressed "the place of man in this world and the world to come." Since I wasn't there to get deep, I assumed without asking that this was a religious reference. Which was fine—especially under a dictatorship, you don't have to be a mystagogue to seek succor in church. Thinking about it, though, I realized that political and for that matter artistic prophets spoke in exactly the same terms. Isn't that what we prize most in our music? Intimations of a world to come?

1989

Culture Hero: Mzwakhe Mbuli

Although the music business lives off symbolic heroes, it generates no more of the real-life variety than any other institution, especially if you think heroes have better things to do than suffer for their art. Mzwakhe Mbuli is a real-life hero. A black man from South Africa, the one place in the world where everyone knows politics matter, he has been jailed eight times for reciting the poems he now sets to music. Usually he was just "detained," but once he found himself in solitary for six months. No pencil, no paper, so he wrote the 1989 album *Unbroken Spirit* in his head. He was "the people's poet," the most prominent policymaker on the United Democratic Front's cultural desk, the embodiment of cultural struggle. For a long time his m.o. was hit-and-run—he'd show up unannounced at some public gathering, perform, and disappear before the police moved in. Arrest never stopped him long, and eventually he inspired a legion of stand-ins—proud young Mzwakhe wannabes who'd deliver versions of his poems at every rally.

Music was an afterthought for Mbuli, but an inevitable one. He was born in 1959 in Sophiatown, the teeming Johannesburg neighborhood that was the center of black South African culture from the twenties until it was razed to make way for a white settlement called Triomf, and grew up with his seven brothers and sisters in a part of Soweto picturesquely nicknamed Sub A. His father was a Zulu who worked as a long-distance driver and met his Xhosa mother on the Cape. As his father's favorite, Mzwakhe was treated to an especially strict Zulu upbringing, denied shoes to build character and immersed in the tribe's choral tradition at the all-night mbube competitions his father loved. Politics was never discussed, radio listening limited to mbube, yet the young man's "questioning" spirit was spurred by a pass arrest when he was thirteen, and by the time of the Soweto uprising in 1976, his father was dead and politics were unavoidable. For two years Soweto's schools were on strike, and after Mbuli returned to complete his matric he also participated in a cultural group that continued the semiformal Afrocentric education of the strike period. There he was encouraged to write poetry. In 1981 he got up to recite at a funeral, and soon he was performing his poems of praise, pride, and defiance at weddings, cultural days, union meetings, May Day rallies, and funerals, many more funerals.

Mbuli's charisma came naturally. He's tall—almost seven feet according to some stunned reports, about six-five by my five-ten. His voice is distinct, resonant, wise, shaped by timbres and cadences that tinge moral zest with bitter irony whether you understand the language or not. Even unaccompanied, his mobile face, strong hands, and hunched shoulders pour on the body English, and his words cut deep. In his cultural guerrilla days, of course, voice, body, and words were all he had. As a poet rather than an orator he could exploit Pretoria's putative tolerance for art, a sop abrogated by the 1986 state of emergency. His unrhymed, rhythm-charged verse was rife with historical analysis, humanistic exhortation, and racial pride—with politics. But like all poetry it was concrete, structured, given to reverie and drama and lyric celebration. The names of the living and the dead—martyrs of apartheid, African rulers, ANC exiles, deportees—recapitulated Zulu praise-poem tradition, and the Latinate diction recalled the fellowship and inspiration of the classroom and the Marxist study group rather than their pretensions:

> Let my mind interpret my dreams of Mount Kilimanjaro
> Let my brain-power interpret the last struggle in Africa
> Unless human rights are embarked in the statute books
> Loyalty shall mean vengeance
> Obedience shall mean rebellion
> Conformity a bluff

And happiness a sign of danger
And Africa shall know no peace
Until we in the south are free

In 1986, South Africa's bravest independent label—called Shifty because it recorded on the run, in a sound truck—matched Mbuli with an integrated backup group featuring Kenyan guitarist Simba Morri. The banned tape became a literal underground hit in South Africa, where Shifty sold it as unmarked contraband, and surfaced here on Rounder as *Change Is Pain*. Much of the music, a rough avant-trad potpourri that owed dub and Philip Tabane's black-consciousness band Malombo, had to be created in Mbuli's absence, though he joined the final sessions. The collectively conceived music on *Unbroken Spirit* seems more whole, with touches of sax jive and mbube-style female chorus, and though for the most part Mbuli once again intones over backup, occasionally he sings as if he's been doing it all his life, which of course he has. It went gold with no help from the South African Broadcasting Corporation.

This was after de Klerk's thaw, which made life somewhat easier for troublemakers like Mbuli, but no simpler. Mbuli accused Shifty of failing to pay proper royalties. It took the efforts of thirteen embassies to get him a visa to play Europe with a newly formed band, the Equals. A weapons charge wasn't dismissed until 1991. And he became controversial on the typically fractious and exceptionally puritanical South African left, where some charged that he was a rogue, a self-promoter, and—based on his work with the UDF cultural desk and the South African Musicians Alliance—a "cultural commissar." It's difficult to judge such squabbles at a distance. But remember that the charismatic are often accused of roguishness and self-promotion, which even if it's true says next to nothing about their courage or their creative juice, and that the South African struggle has been complicated by the return of exiled heroes who expect and deserve their power back. Mbuli was probably too hard on Shifty. I'd guess that he overreached himself administratively—at one point he opposed an Abdullah Ibrahim appearance because the exiled pianist hadn't gone through channels. But the sad doubts about his creative juice expressed to me by several South African observers prove only what we already knew—that the winds of fashion blow no more reliably on the left than they do anywhere else. Artistically, he's still on it.

Shortly after Mzwakhe exited his UDF post, he embarked upon a career as a pop star—"poet-musician" is his term. He developed a live act, with intros and codas that free him to play congas or dance with a high-stepping muscularity that's pure Zulu and a self-deprecating postmacho that's all his own; his *Resistance Is Defence* is an atypical a&r venture for South African expatriate Trevor Herman, whose Earthworks label made its name with compilations. Although Mbuli has international ambitions—he sees his themes as "universal," "not confined to the South African situation"—his new album is less Euro than its predecessors. As before, most of the lyrics are in his richly accented, almost tonal English, but there's a lot of Zulu and Xhosa and Venda, and the Equals hit a township groove that rounds off blocky mbaqanga beats with the jazzier swing of the older, more urbane marabi style. I know why some hear *Resistance Is Defence* as mbaqanga *Sarafina!*-style, and there's probably a sense in which the edgy awkwardness of the Shifty albums better evokes South African bifurcation. But this is a gorgeous piece of music. Keyed to Tswana guitarist Floyd Manana, the multitribal Equals can play with any South African band from Mahlathini's Makgona Tsohle to Ray Phiri's Stimela. The poems have not just arrangements but tunes, often created from remembered snatches of mbube. Mbuli sings their intros and choruses with conviction, affection, and skillful ease. And he recites better than ever.

After all, there was nothing wrong with *Sarafina!*'s music that a little focus couldn't cure, and rarely has the black South African genius for jubilation under dire circumstances been put in sharper relief. "Lusaka," a shaggy dog song about political certainty as a function of political privilege, and "Land Deal," a quietly sarcastic skewering of apartheid doublespeak, achieve a head-scratching universality few universalists would think worthy of their grand designs. And while some South Africans suggest that the praise-poem tactic has outlived its usefulness, I find "Stalwarts" as gripping as Yeats's "Easter 1916," which also names a bunch of people I know nothing about, and fail to see how "Tshipfinga" will date: "When you govern the country/Think of those who died/When you are welcome in big city airports/Think of those who died."

For Mbuli, the fact that victory is inevitable doesn't mean it's imminent, and unlike most of the South Africans I spoke to, he's feeling no relief. The thaw hasn't melted the habitual contempt of police, politicians, and talking heads. The Inkatha violence is as horrific as any other. Homelessness is epidemic. And the vigilance of the people has by most accounts diminished, putting protest culture in decline. Barely noticed as an import, *Resistance Is Defence* will be released by South African EMI this month. But though he remains a draw at stadiums and universities from Cape Town to the Transvaal, there's no knowing whether the phenomenal success of "Papa Stop the War," a 1991 collaboration ordered up by township-disco hitmaker Chicco, means Mbuli has pop legs of his own. And whatever jealous South Africans imagine, he's not getting rich overseas. Watching him, his band, and his two amazing female singer-dancers rouse a half-filled weeknight S.O.B.'s or wolf down dinner from a hot dog cart before a late sound check at Fort Greene Park, he looked to me like one more struggling world-beat hero—the symbolic kind, this time.

Symbolic heroes who are political at all specialize in struggle once removed. They do more comforting and fortifying—and maybe, if they're as good as Mbuli, clarifying—than inciting to revolution. And though Mbuli is right to say his relevance transcends South Africa—he talks about the Irish mother who came up to thank him for helping her mourn lost loved ones—it's certainly rooted there. So I couldn't help asking whether he'd go into exile if the boot came down again.

"This time, yes—once bitten twice shy. Unless I'm experimenting with my life, I can't wait for death—just to be a sitting target. So I will be the one leaving."

I was a little sorry to hear it. But I can't say I was surprised.

1992

8

Careers in Iconicity

Madonnathinking Madonnabout Madonnamusic

Lest I get off on the wrong foot, let me emphasize up top that there's never been a celebrity like Madonna. And though it doesn't suit my thesis, let me add that a movie, *Truth or Dare,* is what put her over the top. Formally, I mean. Because there can no longer be much doubt that Madonna now regards celebrity itself as her art, or that she plies it with such gut instinct and manipulative savvy that all past and present practitioners—all those Swedish nightingales and sultans of swat and little tramps and blond bomb-shells and rebels without a cause and king pelvises and fab fours and billion-dollar thrillers and, though here one pauses, Teflon presidents—seem like stumbling naifs by comparison. In early 1990 the disappointing sales of *Like a Prayer* (still a mere triple platinum, well behind *Like a Virgin* and *True Blue*) made some wonder whether she'd played out her string. Now her capacity for self-renewal seems virtually infinite, and even if the bubble bursts, this century will not see her like again. I'm being ironic, sure—she deserves nothing less. But only a little, because I'm a convert. Madonna has rendered me a postmodernist in spite of myself, one of the burgeoning claque of marginal, left-leaning intellectuals for whom she has come to embody nothing less than mass culture itself.

For cultural conservatives, Madonna's invasion of discourse is a not altogether unexpected outrage—the dire future José Ortega y Gasset warned their forebears about. And consider this:

even they know who she is. What once would have been undifferentiated ignorance and hostility is now inescapable familiarity—the rare highbrow who's never heard Madonna sing or seen her perform or read her talk or mused about her multimedia mastery has almost certainly expended gray matter on her anyway. Her prestige is so pervasive that sometimes it irritates the middlebrow peons on the star beat who function as Madonnathink's worker bees. Most of them know her oeuvre better than your average highbrow, natch, but few are at home with it, and their punditry has been of radically mixed quality. Journalists become so cynical about the media that all but the most fawning or fair-minded flatter their own acumen by assuming the worst. So pro, con, or neither, a lot of what they write about her is pretentious, shallow, or both. And to step right into it, I'll note that many of the exceptions have been rock critics: thank you Barry Walters, Joyce Millman, James Hunter, Gina Arnold, Dishmaster Don Shewey, and poor Steve Anderson, who was hit by a class action suit from this newspaper's sexual liberation posse for suggesting that there was more gym than boudoir in the way she pumped her crotch.

The most fascinating exegeses, however, originate in the outlying districts of academia, where a network of younger acolytes trade bibliographical references and videotape while hep elders publish and teach. Although adepts snicker about Harvard's Madonna course, a *Boston Globe* tie-in by the prof, clinical psychologist and women's studies lecturer Lynne Layton, seemed fairly sane to me. Granted, Layton isn't altogether rah-rah—"role reversals don't seem to me to be what feminists have fought for these last 20 years," and so forth. But I say such homely points are legitimate, because I still think Madonna—along with the rest of this universe of signs we call the world—is subject to criticism, not just in the cultural theory sense nor even the *explication de texte* sense, but in the if-you-can't-say-something-bad-about-a-person-don't-say-anything-at-all sense. Really, star fans—dissing Madonna isn't square by definition. She's great, not perfect, and as tendentious as it may be to speculate about how her mixed messages affect her multifarious audience, it's nevertheless empowering, so to speak, to resist the gravitational pull of her thereness and adjudge this bit fabulous and that bit lame and the one over there provocative yet problematic. Credible though its notion of choice may be, "Papa Don't Preach" remains an antiabortion song for most who hear it—preferable as such to Graham Parker's "You've Got To Be Strong," but not to the Sex Pistols' "Bodies."

Such distinctions are foreign to most Madonna scholars, who despite their purported oppositionality are forever slipping over the borderline between postmodernist meta-analysis and positivist passivity. Reflecting the not unhealthy rise of sociology and perceptual psychology in the formerly "humanistic" arena of left aesthetics, their Madonnathink tends to be about mass culture itself—usually not mass culture as it is experienced, though that is the noble aim, but mass culture as a site of theory. Much of it feels translated—only the younger acolytes convey anything approaching the intimacy that comes naturally to millions of fans—and sometimes you get the feeling that their subject's incomparable fame relieves interpreters of the need to truck with lesser cynosures. In short, Madonna is honored less as an artist than as a cultural force. And this has to make you wonder. It's true enough that such concepts as "artist," "author," and "genius" carry the ideological baggage of bourgeois meritocracy. But though her scribes may downplay her agency with the most democratic of motives, as intellectuals they hold onto their own, no matter 'ow 'umbly they strive to serve the people. Madonna gains their approbation not on her terms, which most certainly include "art" and "power," but on theirs. One might even suspect that they love her not for all the things she is, but because it's fun to stick a bleached blond in your thesis advisor's face.

John Fiske's terms are those of an audience/consumer advocate—he believes receptors make their own popular culture, defined as "the culture of the subordinate who resent their subordination." So in *Reading the Popular,* he charters Madonna's wannabes—and also, yes, Madonna—as groundbreaking bricoleurs. E. Ann Kaplan's special interest is the construction of the subject. So in *Rocking Around the Clock* she dissects the "Material Girl" video like a surgeon, albeit one who doesn't know the difference between a car and a pickup truck or a producer and a director. There's definitely an ivory-tower taint to such analyses and other more journal-bound arcana. It's not as if ordinary folks who'd thought a little about the most famous person in the world didn't already have a grip on some of this stuff—ideas do exist before they're put into writing by Ph.D.'s. But there's also a more fundamental problem: the unremittingly visual focus. What is mass culture as academic postmodernism conceives it? Mass culture isn't something you read, and it certainly isn't something you hear. It's something you see. Basically, it's television.

I don't mean to suggest that Madonna isn't a creature of MTV, or that the tube isn't as mass as culture gets. But it isn't TV per se that generates our icons. What television personality is as omnipresent as Madonna, or even Michael Jackson? Bill Cosby, maybe? Oprah? Walter Cronkite? Bart Simpson? And though rock gods aren't as bankable as their Hollywood counterparts, that's economics—is, I don't know, Arnold or Goldie a full-fledged idol like Marilyn, in whose reflected glory Madonna was long assumed to bask? Instead, superstardom has become conspicuously coextensive with rock and roll. I'm not sure why this is, but rather than privileging music's mythic magic, I'm inclined to suspect it's because icons are a special if far from exclusive domain of the young, with time on their hands and identity problems wracking their very souls. Nevertheless, you have to figure that the specifics of Madonna's music contribute in no small part to her total triumph, and therefore merit exegetical scrutiny. Popular culture theorist Fiske demurs, however: "The pleasures of music are remarkably resistant to analysis," he notes preemptively, and anyway, "critics are disparaging" about her music (which they aren't, and as if that would stop him). And Kaplan, a film scholar who turned MTV expert doing the couch potato with her teenage daughter, relies on Nik Cohn's wonderful but notoriously inaccurate *Rock From the Beginning* and an obscure 1973 survey by the dreadful, long-departed *Times* stringer Mike Jahn to lead her to the foreordained conclusion that "rock music" is, er, postmodern. Or is that dead?

Well, surprise—either it's neither or it's plenty else besides. As polymorphously absorptive as the universe of signs may be, it doesn't obviate the usages of art and craft, be they narrative thrills or good beats you can hum along to—it coexists with them, another layer of available symbolic experience. If Fiske has every right to juxtapose chapters on malls, videogames, and TV news to one on Madonna, she's nevertheless not *merely* a phenomenon, an all-purpose "text"—she's also a *producer* of musical texts, texts that reconfigure her thereness as they reward and confound traditional modes of aesthetic reception. By comparing Madonna to other women singers, breaking down pop's collaborative processes, and arguing that MTV is good for rock and roll, multiculturalist Lisa Lewis's eye-oriented *Gender Politics and MTV* respects this inconvenient complication. But even Lewis says she "found very little in the way of useful models" for integrating "musical analysis" into "textual analyses of videos," betraying the critical limitations of a feminist fan who can't believe it isn't sexist to hate Pat Benatar—and who can't conceive why Madonna's music might be not just, er, valid, but better than Pat Benatar's.

In *Feminine Endings,* rogue musicologist Susan McClary chides Fiske and Kaplan, both of whom she dwarfs as stylist and critic. Then she sets about righting their omissions with a lengthy musical analysis (for slower students, video illustrations are provided) of "Live To Tell," "Open Your Heart," and "Like a Prayer"— the climactic exhibit in McClary's argument that tonal music's compulsive return to home key fuels a powerfully subliminal male supremacist narrative. This is audacious work, both in itself and in its challenge to the blindered snobbishness of academic musicology, which ignores pop as a matter of scholarly principle; that Madonna professes to have no idea what McClary is talking about doesn't diminish its truth value. But because McClary comes out of academic musicology, she too ignores crucial stuff. Having established that Madonna refuses the sort of melodic resolutions that define "masculine cadential control" in the two Whitesnake songs she parses, she gives no indication that she's examined less macho pop—I'd suggest Paula Abdul before Pat Benatar—for similar structures. And those "musical affiliations . . . with African-American music" must stand out more when Monteverdi and Tchaikovsky are your daily bread. On the bell curve of a music that owes r&b bigtime all the way to Whitesnake, Madonna is fiftieth percentile—a trailblazer in a raceless dance music with discernible roots in postpunk and Eurodisco who's also on flirting terms with such whitebread subgenres as Vegas schlock, show tune, and housewife ballad. The real racial provocations she reserves for live shows—and also, of course, videos.

Among intellectuals whose interest in rock and roll shriveled up with hippie and/or punk, Madonna's music is pigeonholed as disposable when its virtues are acknowledged at all. This meshes neatly with Fiske: "Madonna is only the intertextual circulation of her meanings and pleasures; she is neither a text nor a person, but a set of meanings in process." It's completely just in a culture so late to recognize the contingency of art and the creativity of the audience. And it's fair enough treatment for a celebrity-first whose specialty is the single—who designs music to get played on the radio/TV and then disappear. In this market system, the album is how pop music attains relative permanence—still contingent, but stable in itself, which celebrity can never be—and except for the debut, Madonna's best-selling albums have been patchy. But her compilations—the 1987 *You Can Dance* remixes and, especially, 1990's *Immaculate Collection*—are stunning, and as likely to remain stunning as *Blonde on Blonde* or *"Live" at the Apollo*. Their corny cool, postfeminist confidence, pleasure-centered electronic pulse, and knowing tightrope dance along the cusp of the acceptable capture a sensibility as well as an age.

But they're music, not just "culture." Listen to the singles collection, which dips to mortal only two or three cuts in seventeen, then watch the impressive but less consistent video comp of the same name, and notice how differently Madonna approaches the two forms, achieving the open-endedness postmodernists crave with diametrically opposite tactics. Except for the surreally wondrous "Cherish," which comes by its ambiguity subtly (and which nobody writes about), her videos are baroque, cluttered, multileveled riots of overdetermination. Even the kitchen-sink "Like a Prayer" single, on the other hand, is schlock done clean, and the minimalist discipline of most of her hits reflects a tour in Soho frequently elided by those who celebrate her Detroit roots. (It was actually "metro" Detroit, in a family her claque started IDing as "Italian" after "working-class" wouldn't cut it anymore.) I could be wrong—after a decade of junk expressionism, her garish videos have their own aesthetic pedigree—but I suspect that the music, with its spaces that cry out to be filled, will endure longer, if the test of time still turns you on. I don't want to make too much of how arty she is, or in any way deny her radical interpretability, especially since the artist in her aims for pan-schlock universality and deserves credit for getting there. But it's worth emphasizing that Madonna's songs give up "vulgar" and rarefied pleasure simultaneously—and that Fiske to the contrary, it's cynical, condescending, inaccurate, and perversely philistine to declare the rarefied an exclusively "bourgeois" realm.

Among its numerous aesthetic coups, *Truth or Dare* confounds candor as a category for public people. Instead of waiting for her own Memphis Mafia to spill the beans, Madonna commissioned Alek Keshishian to act as her authorized Albert Goldman, and at times she's alarmingly cruel, phony, and manipulative. At some level she clearly *wanted* to humanize and perhaps even debunk herself, yet as the most self-aware celebrity in history, she knew it was impossible—that every self-revelation would only reinforce a myth she spends half her career shaping and the other half hanging onto for dear life. It would be dumb to feel sorry for her, but equally dumb not to recognize that her power masks pain and carries burdens. If celebrity itself is her true art, music—and, yes, video too—is her refuge. For both her and many of the fans who adore her, it will remain, nostalgia for some and continuing revelation for others, long after her celebrity has become a bore, escaped her control, or both.

1991

Garth Brooks, Michael Bolton, Barney, and You: Garth Brooks

Garth Brooks has done nothing wrong. In fact, for a country singer who has sold twice as many albums as any other musician in any genre in the nineties, who with the help of the megaselling best-of *The Hits* and a few McDonald's tie-ins trails only the Beatles in the RIAA's all-time sales list, he's a paragon—humane, modest, progressive, even philanthropic, doing big-time benefit work for the safe Feed the Children and the demographically inappropriate South Central. Brooks's success is so phenomenal that almost everyone has some inkling of it. Yet among the hip and the self-consciously cultured the awareness often stops at an inkling—the overlap between elite aesthetes and Garth's masses is considerably smaller than the raw probabilities would indicate. So here in Hipville Garth finds himself a nonentity among casual music-lovers and a symbol of spiritual bankruptcy for tastemakers smart enough to know better and dumb enough to consider Dwight Yoakam the real thing. What said tastemakers forget is that artists rarely go quite this far through the roof just because people have bad taste. Even if you buy the lie that honky tonk is the one true country music, or the paranoid claim that the boom for Billy Ray Cyrus, Vince Gill, Wynonna Judd, and Reba McEntire reflects a cynical manipulation of antirap racism, the question remains: why do benighted record buyers give Brooks more bucks than they do Billy Ray Cyrus or Vince Gill?

Brooks's low cachet connects to two other peculiarities of

his achievement: his relatively puny singles sales and his failure to hit overseas in an increasingly multinational entertainment age. But these can be attributed to Brooks's chosen genre. The singles market for country music, which is now a largely suburban phenomenon, is delimited by country radio, a thriving yet defiantly insular segment of an industry whose growth sector these days is talk. And country has never aroused much interest in Europe, although the mythic status of fifties-sixties country-pop crooner Jim Reeves among an earlier generation of English-speaking black Africans is a quiddity worth bearing in mind.

So country music isn't considered classy, and country fans know it. One reason country radio looks askance at crossover, often to the point of dropping artists who attract pop airplay, is that its audience feels embattled in its very commonness. Yet the strange transfiguration of Jim Reeves—praised by one Nigerian informant of ethnomusicologist Charles Keil for "his cool sentimentality, his heart-awakening compositions, the voice and the instruments which make you feel the angels around"—proves it needn't be this way. Hear country songs with an open mind and some of them will touch you no matter who you are—including the pop stuff, I swear. And no matter who it is—Nirvana, Whitney Houston, the Bee Gees, Barney—any pop musician who makes this major a splash didn't do it by imitating somebody else. He or she has a trademark going, which means you may just like the music more than you expect.

Formally, Garth Brooks is even more country-pop than Jim Reeves. As an Oklahoman, he comes by his country naturally. But he's obviously no purist or neotraditionalist, and his voracious musical appetite is legendary. Growing up on album-rock radio in an era when James Taylor was considered as "rock" as Bob Seger, he preferred Dan Fogelberg and "Dust in the Wind" to George Jones and "Ladies Love Outlaws." Yet though he remains a softy as both singer and songwriter, Brooks's sentimentality isn't much like Jim Reeves's, because Brooks is anything but cool—he emotes as forcefully as his band rocks, and on ballads he's without shame. Indeed, his weakness for schlock emotion recalls both Elton John and Billy Joel, whose well-named "Shameless" he effortlessly claimed for Nashville on *Ropin' the Wind*. In fact, the nakedness of his emotionality recalls no current singer more than Michael Bolton. Fortunately, Brooks's country loyalties rein him in. His albums do run a little longer than the average Nashville product, but because he respects the tight conventions of the genre, he gets away with wearing his heart on his sleeve. It also helps that, unlike Bolton, he doesn't appear to be an egomaniac—having mastered the nice-guy aura that has escaped pop superstars since Como and Cole, he can get away with being a liberal. And unlike most of his new-Nashville competitors, a hunk he's not.

Basically, Brooks is what the biz calls a women's artist. Where most male country singers are content to wallow in their guilt, he actively identifies with female complaints and concerns. Presumably, guys can relate to his ex-jock's paunch, his good old good-timing energy. But the one time I saw him live, at Philadelphia's Spectrum in 1993, there was no discernible male bonding and plenty of out-with-the-girls. The biggest and highest-pitched cheer of the night came on the video-only final verse of "The Thunder Rolls," in which a wife murders her errant husband. Most of the female groups seemed to be better halves (or divorcees) on a spree, but unless fashions are different in Philadelphia, I also spied a few lesbian couples. Garth's bass-playing big sister, Betsy Smittle, a major presence in his band that night, had been outed by the *National Enquirer* in March, and he'd happily affirmed that his recent single "We Shall Be Free," introduced as "our first and only attempt at a righteous or a gospel song," attacks any notion of family values that excludes same-sex relationships.

In context, Brooks's musical fusions signify a comparable creative courage, and it helps that he can write. An advertising major who hit Nashville in 1986 with mucho solo-acoustic time under his belt, he's one of these guys you can tell just loves a great song. Sometimes he rolls his own—the Midwestern swing of the debut-opening "Not Counting You," or the cheerful live-and-let-die of *Ropin' the Wind*'s "Papa Loved Mama" ("Mama loved men/Mama's in the graveyard/Papa's in the pen"), or *The Chase*'s purple pastorale "Somewhere Other Than the Night," or *Fresh Horses*'s unselfconsciously self-referential "The Old Stuff." But like any self-respecting Nashville pro, he smokes o.p.'s—the rowdy Dennis Robbins domestic-bliss fantasy "Two of a Kind, Workin' on a Full House," or "Learning To Live Again," Stephanie Davis and Don Schlitz's wry heart song about a divorced man's blind date, or the show-stopping "Friends in Low Places," in which Dewayne

Blackwell and Bud Lee concoct the kind of chorus that convinced God to create Music Row—because Garth's not big on social graces, he thinks he'll slip on down to the Oasis, thank you very much.

There are worse models than Elton John and Billy Joel, both of whom have loads of great songs behind them. If Sonic Youth can make something out of Kim Fowley, Brooks has the right to try with Dan Fogelberg. And it's about time a man in a less fantasy-driven subgenre than pure escape-pop spoke directly to women. But Brooks's pop-eclectic reach isn't the plastic pandering you might guess. He really is country, and if you can imagine John and Joel kept in check by a form that insists an album comprise ten tuneful, well-constructed songs, with no indulgent solos or over-wrought apostrophes—a form less tolerant of conceptual flab than the pop/rock they embrace so juicily—you can glimpse why he might be worth your attention. Granted, sometimes he strays too far from the conventions that impart an almost sonnetlike min-imalism to Nashville product—where most country albums founder on filler, his overreach. And although on *Ropin' the Wind* and the somewhat moister *The Chase* the songcraft compensates, he could do with fewer forces-of-nature metaphors and rodeo songs—lots of times hot sex is more like gobbling lobster than hearing thunder, and if you're going to get nostalgic about a coun-try folkway, better it be blood on the barroom floor. But with as-surances that my opinion in no way represents that of Mr. Brooks or his umpteen million fans, let me put it this way—I don't give a fuck how Hank woulda done it. Hank died way too young to suit me.

As Brooks's juggernaut lost a little steam, his albums got even gaudier, and "Standing in the Fire," from 1994's *In Pieces,* can stand as his manifesto. Like "We Shall Be Free," it eschews country spec-ificity for philosophical generalization, devoting a stanza apiece to the self-possessed "cool" and "strong," a stanza to the self-indulgent "fools" and "weak." The switch that ensues should come as no surprise, because Brooks thinks the strong ones wear their hearts on their sleeves: "But you got to be tough when con-sumed by desire/'Cause it's not just enough to stand outside the fire." The metaphor functions first of all as an aesthetic manifesto. But at the same time it says something about the millions of sub-urban escapists who buy his records. It says they don't regard themselves as escapists at all—that they prefer to see their own lives as romantic sagas, as theaters of heroic feeling. It says they don't equate security and material well-being with passivity and complacency.

I don't want to make grandiose claims for this impulse. Heroic feelings aren't necessarily useful, much less progressive, and anyway, this is art, not life—and also fandom, not life. Without doubt many of Garth's admirers let their man do their standing in the fire for them, just as rock fans let Aerosmith, of all people, do their living on the edge for them. So it would be easy to readjust one's distanced disdain for Garth's masses to take such second-hand romanticism into account. But that isn't the only possibility, and the response that works for me is different. When I hear this song I remember again that the emotion Brooks puts into his singing—an emotion that compounds Hank Williams and George Jones not just with Dan Fogelberg and Gregg Allman but with Julio Iglesias and Michael Bolton—is rooted not just in his accomplishments as a performer, but in his faith that 5 million purchasers of this album are singing along. Those who believe a democratic culture has no room for his kind of miracle are standing outside the fire, that's all.

Since according to official Garthmyth, the singer's life changed in 1989 when Sandy Brooks phoned to say her bags were packed because he'd been messing around—"Women are so cool and as different as snowflakes," explains the now-reformed Garth, described by Sandy as "a very sexual person"—and he'd been talking about quitting the road for the sake of his marriage, I would have felt insincere seeing him in Philly without my wife and daughter. And I wasn't surprised that my little girl wasn't the only under-twelve in the 99 percent full Spectrum. But I didn't anticipate that kids would outnumber teenagers. It was date night only for marrieds, and white marrieds at that—not counting security, the one black person we saw appeared to be Nigerian. In short, this was the suburban horde Garth-haters believe has stolen the soul of country music. I never would have guessed how they'd stoke the show.

Based on common sense, word of mouth, and his relatively engaging stab at that tiredest of genres, the concert video, I figured Garth's live strategy would be to dazzle folks with rock moves, and from smoke machines and flash pots to ladder-climbing and cable-swinging, the moves were there. But they were icing. It was a given that the best-of format would accentuate both the consistency and variety of his material, and that his band would sound just as casually expert cranking it up as slowing it down. I expected too that Brooks's fundamentally ordinary voice—the kind of strong, flexible instrument journeymen die believing deserved better—would crest again and again on enthusiasm and emotion (although not that I'd be suckered by the solo acoustic "Unanswered Prayers," about how glad he is he didn't land that high school honey). But more even than with most arena acts, his audience was there not just for music but for each other—for the hell-raising camaraderie this society normally relegates to teens and singles. These ordinary Americans were there to be worked and served.

What's most appealing about Brooks is that he's simultaneously self-deprecating and voracious. His megastardom took him by surprise, and though he craves the world's love, he doesn't whine about it like Dan Fogelberg. The linchpin of the evening, and proof of the thing ladies still have for this monogamous, balding javelin thrower gone to pudge, was the gifts. As with Barry or Julio, flowers predominated, dozens of dozens of them, but the traditional nighties and house keys were nowhere to be seen; instead there were cowboy hats, a Garth statuette, stuffed animals, and, proudly displayed against the drum kit, baby clothes for the infant Taylor Mayne Brooks. A gofer-percussionist reduced the accumulation periodically, but left a little more than Garth could comfortably carry off at the end, leaving him literally staggering under the weight of his fans' largess.

I treasure honky tonk's rebellious irreverence and bitter grit, and so does anybody who signs his set with "Friends in Low Places." But often those virtues are suspended somewhere between memory and metaphor for me. I care about country because country is this century's most credible music of domestic life. Early pop was pretty much coextensive with the Victorian parlor, but as Tin Pan Alley evolved, it became either too sophisticated to care or too escapist to bear. At its worst, suburban country is as icky as Michael Bolton. But at its best, which is Garth Brooks, it cuts "Oh! Susanna" with "Home Sweet Home" and mixes in some sex and suffering so you know where you are. It doesn't capture the meaning of existence any more than "Home Sweet Home" or "Oh! Susanna" did. But it might just be good for what ails you.

1993–1994–1996

Bette Midler Sings . . . Everything

Bette Midler is a gay icon and a Hollywood fixture, and not even in that order. The star of more halfway decent movies than you could remember with cue cards, she barely records anymore—her major musical achievement of the past decade was moistly emoting the theme song of our attack on Iraq, "From a Distance." Yet that dubious achievement was enough to make manifest if not clear what a complex musical presence she can be. Ordinarily, I scoff at talk of guilty pleasure in rock and roll, which teaches us to take our pleasures where we find them, from "Bridge Over Troubled Water" to "Me So Horny." But Bette's Grammy-winning million-seller left me feeling I-just-don't-know—furtive, compromised, bathetic. There were times when it brought tears to my eyes.

In the quieter Nanci Griffith original, the distance that concealed all wounds remained somewhere between necessary evil and existential condition—she knew she was deceiving herself, and she wasn't boasting about it. In Bette's version, that hint of self-criticism was transmuted into a halo of self-pity—as if the distance had been *inflicted on her,* as if she could experience *even bigger feelings* if only she could get closer, and be *an even better person* in the bargain. Offensive enough in the abstract, this was infinitely worse in context, as Bette's nation convinced itself that innocent human beings had to die because ... because ... because life was unfair, because the alternative was worse, because Saddam would kill 'em all anyway, because—although no one would say it in so many words—they weren't the same as us. But it captured something. Rarely has the codependency of well-meaning self-involvement and high-grade schlock been so fully exploited or so richly explored. Julie Gold's songwriting—a lyric that captures a difficult idea everyone subconsciously understands in precise images that are simultaneously simple and grand, a chorus that subsumes the images' contradictions in a reassuring melodic surge—was essential. But it was Bette's no-stops vocal that turned the song into a catharsis that could first sop up the tortuous tension of the troop movements and then absorb the shock of the war. As a longtime fan of Griffith's version, I find that it has receded into Bette's, which now stands somewhere between great bad record and fact of history.

Of course, the context has changed yet again. No longer a proximate accessory to imperialist slaughter, the song can also be heard at a distance. Having gotten its start on 1990's *Some People's Lives,* her only true new album since 1983, it's now a star exhibit on both *Experience the Divine: Bette Midler: Greatest Hits* and the long-awaited tour the compilation is named after—a tour now settled in for a record-breaking thirty sellout shows at Radio City Music Hall. The tour is primary because Bette is a performer first, long-awaited because performing is a grind. Grammy or no Grammy, it makes perfect sense that her deal with Atlantic Records, the only label she's ever recorded for, should have long since proven little more than a bridge from the Continental Baths to Sunset Boulevard, and it also makes sense that in 1983, with her film career floundering after diva-quality feuds with working-class hunk Ken Wahl on the set of the well-named *Jinxed,* she should have sworn off the road anyway. Hollywood has always been Bette Midler's destiny—the stardom she set her sights on was the kind she'd read about in magazines. She didn't want to be Mick Jagger or Bob Dylan, both of whom she's since duetted with, because she didn't want to be Janis Joplin, whose doom she would eventually win an Oscar nomination for enacting. She knew without thinking twice that rock and roll was a lousy place for a woman. In Hollywood, a prima donna could get some respect. Ms. Davis, meet your namesake.

Young people may be surprised to encounter Bette Midler in the same sentence as rock and roll. If you want to find her records at Tower, you climb up to the third floor, where she shares space with Streisand and Sinatra in a section designated Vocals. Yet when she started putting together her take on cabaret for the gay orgiasts of the Baths, "rock" defined and dominated her act. The surprising part was that she made no apparent distinction between classy post-Beatles stuff—which came down mostly to what we would now classify as folk-rock: Bob Dylan's "I Shall Be Released," John Prine's "Hello in There," Tracy Nelson's "Delta Dawn," Buzzy Linhart's "Friends"—and such supposedly ignoble trash as "Do You Want To Dance?" "Chapel of Love," and "Leader of the Pack." In retrospect it's obvious that she knew more about how rock history would be written than your average hippie-come-lately; for a long time now, girl groups and fifties one-shots have enjoyed at least as much artistic cachet as, oh, Jackson Browne, not to mention Quicksilver Messenger Service. In 1972, however, this exercise of taste was prophetic and liberating. Ultimately, she was claiming the entirety of American popular music, which is why she also covered Glenn Miller, the Andrews Sisters, Bessie Smith. But across the room from the New York Dolls—who were also gay-identified, of course—Bette Midler was helping to rearticulate the rock canon.

Unfortunately, the inspiration didn't last. Without ever abandoning the teenage folkie in her—the one who formed the Pieridine Three with two girlfriends in Honolulu and couldn't resist "From a Distance" three decades later—Bette didn't just go Hollywood, she went El Lay. It's true that Allee Willis and Billy Steinberg and the odious Diane Warren have manufactured songs far more banal than those on *Some People's Lives*. But as the Marxists used to say, it is no accident that the only selections from that album on *Experience the Divine* are "From a Distance" and a "Miss Otis Regrets" so perilously overswung it's hard to believe she isn't just name-checking. Opening night at Radio City, she gave the album's newer stuff more slack—the Janis Ian-Rhonda Fleming title number started off like a trite "Hello in There" rip and then redeemed itself on the chorus, and "Spring Can Really Hang You Up the Most" was uncommonly subtle, as it is on record. But she also included a felicitous "Friends" and a friendly "Do You Want To Dance?," an unflagging "Delta Dawn" and an overembellished "Hello in There" and an automatic "Boogie Woogie Bugle Boy"— five 1972 songs in all, exactly as many as the compilation. If

Springsteen were to pay similar tribute to *Greetings From Asbury Park* or *Born To Run,* we'd say he was throwing in the towel. With Bette, though, it's different. Debut album or no debut album, *The Divine Miss M* still sounds not just fresh but of the essence. The 1977 *Live at Last* ain't so shabby either.

Live at Last—as well as the concert video *Art or Bust*—also might convey to truth-seekers who can't afford scalpers how Bette managed to sell two hundred thousand tickets to Radio City off a best-of that never got over fifty in *Billboard.* It isn't just the yucks—1986's *Mud* Will *Be Flung Tonight* is pretty funny for a comedy album and still doesn't capture half her pizzazz. So put it this way. You know how certain very acerbic comedians try to compensate with revolting shows of sincerity, whether it's a jerk like Don Rickles insisting that he loves all peoples or a genius like Richard Pryor grinning fondly at the poetic paramour he snuck onto *Saturday Night Live?* Bette's art lives off the emotional sources of that ploy. Her comedy isn't as mean and crude as Rickles's or as wild and fucked up as Pryor's, but it evokes both; at Radio City, the "politically correct" cracks died fast, but the Joey Buttafuoco routine ("Can you believe that *two* women wanted to have sex with Joey?") hurt just enough, the pedally deprived Delores de Lago and her politically dubious wheelchair was as crazy a trip as ever, and the inevitable Soph and tit jokes testified to her enduring self-respect. And like a talisman on the other side of the yucks was the line that defined her return to the footlights: "Have I done the ballad yet?"

She said it about as often as she invoked succor from her other running gag, Dr. Jack Kevorkian, making clear that she knew her oldest and truest fans—I've never seen such a turnout of middle-aged gay couples, and I doubt many gays have either—were really there for dish and hubba-hubba. But she must also suspect that they'd feel cheated without "Delta Dawn," and she has not the slightest doubt that the straight couples whose Saturday nights at the movies have made her a Disney heroine since the surprise boffo of *Down and Out in Beverly Hills* require healing dollops of sentiment after laughing at poor Mrs. Buttafuoco. Though back when she was redefining rock and roll I heard it differently, I can agree now that the hallmark of her ballad style is its imprecision. She doesn't massage a song, she loves it to death; when she's on, her emotions aren't overstated, they're all over the place, like her tits sans brassiere. It's because her movie audience craves this effect uncut that she's taken to putting in purchase orders with the El Lay mafia, whose specialty is sentiment that can't be mistaken for camp.

At Radio City, though, the change seemed justified. The endless closing sequence of *Art or Bust* features Bette in a vaguely Greek-looking gown ruining good songs and giving her all to terrible ones. Imagine "Everyone Gone to the Moon" with cubist props and balletic backup—I've never seen or heard her worse. The only selection to survive the intervening years was the climactic "Stay With Me"—lightened in both versions with a spoken interlude, followed at Radio City by "Wind Beneath My Wings," top-drawer El Lay generally interpreted as a love letter to her investment banker/performance artist husband, and a gratifyingly matter-of-fact version of "The Glory of Love," originally a hit for Helen Ward and Benny Goodman in 1936. This finale wasn't gangbusters, but it held its own, striking an unexpected balance between Hollywood and the Baths—and reminding those who were there for such revelations what a complex musical presence she can be.

Some People's Lives is double-platinum, her biggest-selling album ever. So you can figure she'll get back to the studio eventually—and that she won't mess with the formula, either. Too bad, I agree. But don't bet Bette's music is behind her quite yet. And when she tours again, which despite the never-again murmurs she will, try and beat the scalpers uptown.

1993

Lou Reed, Average Guy

Not counting art trendies who were "bored" by most rock anyway, even admirers of the Velvet Underground didn't suspect how seminal they would be back when they were actually a band. And just as the Velvets invented avant-punk without giving much thought to such humdrum precedents as the dirty raveups of the Kinks and the Yardbirds and the garage mechanics who ended up on Lenny Kaye's *Nuggets* anthology, so the Stooges and the MC-5 and the New York Dolls (although not, we know, Jonathan Richman's Modern Lovers) probably didn't think much about the Velvets. They were all geniuses of sorts. And they were all kind of inevitable.

Gather young, relatively unskilled white electric guitarists in a gritty city, grant them aesthetic acuteness by nature or nurture, and eventually it's bound to happen: rock and roll that differentiates itself from its (black, rural) sources by confronting the crude, ugly, perhaps brutal facts of the (white, urban) culture rather than hiding behind its bland facade. The underlying idea will be to harness late industrial capitalism in a love-hate relationship whose difficulties are acknowledged, and sometimes disarmed, by ironic aesthetic strategies: back-to-basics formalism, role-playing, humor. In fact, irony will pervade if not define this project: lyrics will mean more than listeners can possibly figure out, pain-threshold feedback will stimulate the body while it deadens the ears, and lock-step drumming will make liberation compulsory.

The Velvet Underground began life as the Warlocks, a sixties band like any other. The din they ground out at Andy Warhol's Exploding Plastic Inevitable was as anarchic a claim on individual freedom as anything jammed loose by the cornier West Coast groups. If their untried drummer and classically trained bassist shared an ignorance of rock commonplaces that helped determine a prophetic new sound, so did the rhythm section of another bunch of ex-Warlocks: the Grateful Dead. So beyond the New York coterie that also considered whip-dancer Gerard Malanga a poet to reckon with, they attracted admirers who regarded them as a bracing option rather than the one true way. Immersed in putative psychedelia, we, well, *dug* the singular sound of *The Velvet Underground and Nico,* admiring "Venus in Furs" for how imperturbably it rose out of a "decadent" lyric that seemed phony even if every word was true. We were sophisticated enough to forgive *White Light/White Heat* the literally sophomoric survival "The Gift" even if we weren't astute enough to hear that "Sister Ray" portended more than the Stones' "Goin' Home" as well as Iron Butterfly's "In-a-Gadda-Da-Vida." We quickly and gratefully succumbed to *The Velvet Underground*'s sweet/soft/slow indomitability. And we never bothered hating the Yule brothers because we thought *Loaded* was cool.

That makes four terrific studio albums. Add an excellent live double and at least one exemplary outtake collection (which sold far better in 1985 than anything released during a lifespan that ended in 1970), and you have a far-ranging oeuvre that gets more conventional as it matures. This is an old sad story, one John Cale was still moaning about when the group broke up again in 1993— unlike Lou, that conniving sellout, he wanted to write more material as profound as "Venus in Furs." But the musical revolution in the first two records owes less to the incongruent avant influences of Andy Warhol and LaMonte Young than to what Lou Reed brought to the avant-punk breeding ground. His dispassionate eye, verbal discipline, immersion in an r&b he felt no obligation to respect, attraction to a free jazz he respected too much, and long bar-band and pop-factory duty didn't just distinguish him from the folk-rock hippies who were among the many social subsets he couldn't stand, but from his bandmates. For intellectual ballast, add Cale's commitment to aggressive repetition; for reliable humanity, Moe Tucker's humbly prophetic beat. Punk is on its way.

But not until Reed expelled Cale did the Velvets reach their mountaintop and their peak.

The Velvet Underground has nothing to do with punk and everything to do with what had to come after—just ask the Feelies, the Buzzcocks, R.E.M. It isn't the only 1969 milestone to seek redemption amid ruin—cf. Neil Young's *Everybody Knows This Is Nowhere,* the Flying Burrito Brothers' *Gilded Palace of Sin.* But it took more guts. Rather than distilling countercultural disillusion, Reed was risking emotional breakthrough—he was a negative force flirting with positive energy, not a stoned optimist coming down. Love songs were such a big deal for him that they became religious visions, and his palpable warmth, quizzical sweetness, playful obscurity, and modest hopes for the future constitute an inspired preliminary probe of the familiar emotions his music has seesawed toward ever since he declared himself an "Average Guy" after getting through the seventies. Unimaginable without Moe Tucker or even Doug Yule, this is in essence the debut album of a solo career that has never abandoned its roller coaster for the rut.

Perversely unreliable, perversely professional, that career is marked by random peaks that rarely rise to and never sustain the ear-popping altitude of whatever VU opus fulfills your desires. Yet somehow Reed has gained focus and consistency instead of petering, burning, or checking out. *Set the Twilight Reeling* is his eighteenth solo studio album, and like most of those after *The Blue Mask,* 1982's Robert Quine-catalyzed, Sylvia Reed-stabilized benchmark, it's superior to most of those before. Straying only slightly from Reed's post-Quine guitar-bass-and-drums formalism, it's certain to be remembered as a love offering to quintessential New York pop avant-gardist Laurie Anderson, with whom he's been linked since around the time his marriage to Sylvia fell apart in 1993; at least five and perhaps seven or eight of the eleven songs invoke the first romantic coequal he's ever gone public with. But such speculations only take us so far. The lead track, which kicks more ass than any solo music he's recorded since joining Warners in 1988, is a nostalgic paean to that New York Jewish elixir, the egg cream. Anderson is a goy from Illinois.

Reed may be a great artist, but treating him like one has never done much for his faithful. Where patently wrong-headed biographers Victor Bockris *(Transformer: The Lou Reed Story)* and Peter Doggett *(Lou Reed: Growing Up in Public)* distort his music through art-world and lit-class prisms, impassioned critics Lester Bangs and Ellen Willis end up making him their mirror, obsessing on themes of transgression and redemption that compel them more deeply than they do their antihero. The saner option (one Bangs tried but was too big-hearted to stick with) is not to take Lou so goddamn seriously. Follow his explicit warnings—as on *Take No Prisoners,* a 1978 comedy album interrupted by dumb-to-excruciating music (schlock-rock "Pale Blue Eyes," what a moron): "Anyway, I will run for office next week—and I wouldn't vote for me on a prayer. I am not trustworthy"—and come to him ironically, skeptically, even cynically. Only then can you safely indulge in the identification his hyperactive image manipulation, confessional singer-songwriter usages, and, for all we know, genuine shows of emotion will sooner or later induce in anyone who can hear him at all.

Reed's late embrace of the liberal-het norm outrages and befuddles devotees of Warhol's hanger-on freak show, who were more comfortable with the mercurial genderfucks and death-defying substance abuse of Reed's spell as a struggling seventies rock star. But though it would be nice if the cynic who wrote love songs to a transvestite before maturing into an extremely married spirit of pure poetry could find it in himself to comprehend his own sexual contradictions, it would be silly to elevate this item on a wish list into an artistic imperative. Reed's contribution to world culture has virtually nothing to do with content. It's about language—verbal language, musical language, and how they mesh.

What's most instructive about Bockris's bio, which in the absence of available dish actually researches Reed's youth (hey, *I* wanted to know that "Pale Blue Eyes" is about a last fling with a college flame), is its account of his early career—not just his brief stint in a song factory concocting cheapjack dance crazes and musical Beatle wigs, redolent though that image is of *Mistrial* (weak record) and *Sally Can't Dance* (pretty good one), but his long bar-band experience. Like Doggett, you can valorize his undergraduate worship of Delmore Schwartz (whose artistic achievement, unlike Warhol's, Reed has long since surpassed) and the stray 1979 quote where he set his sights on Shakespeare and Dostoyevsky. Or like Bockris, you can attribute half the Velvets' edge to John Cale and assume Reed has lost it because he's worked to humanize an aggressively forbidding music. Me, I just figure his life was saved by rock and roll.

The core of Reed's sensibility is his visceral aversion to corn. This isn't to deny his goopy side—part of him really does wish ladies still rolled their eyes, and "spirit of pure poetry" is his phrase, not mine. But over and above his New York sarcasm and the all he's seen, Reed seems possessed by aesthetic distance. He's never more powerful than when his rock and roll heart transcends his dispassion without rejecting it—in cruel yet compassionate touchstones like "Street Hassle" or "The Kids." Usually, however, he settles for something homelier. Whether the topic at hand is joysticks or jealousy or nuclear holocaust or dirty boulevards or ouija boards or s&m or l-u-v, his pointedly flat plainspeech is more meaningful and evocative than his forays into imagery. And what he took away from his apprenticeship with the El Dorados and Pickwick International is just as conversational—an intimate knowledge of the vernacular chords of r&b, adjusted to a deadpan sprechgesang that disdained the soulful expressionism toward which every other white band of the era aspired. Formally, there's an acceptance and a reflexively democratic respect built into this approach that more than counteracts Reed's pretensions and his equally reflexive (if diminishing) mean-spiritedness—ideal for songs about s&m and l-u-v, transgression and redemption and just getting by.

Because its substratum is so sturdy, Reed's music has rarely sunk below an acceptable level—even his hopelessly inappropriate seventies soul girls survive as amusing distractions, although some of his musicians and stentorian vocal affectations from that period have met unhappier ends. This is one reason his good intentions (assuming he can be trusted to tell us—or know—what they are) don't guarantee exceptional music; his pretensions are another. *Berlin* (which never got near the conceptual grandeur claimed for it) and *Street Hassle* (magnificent title song, outrageous "I Wanna Be Black," unfun "Real Good Time Together," substandard filler) are no solider than the cynical *Sally Can't Dance* or the expedient *Coney Island Baby.* On his triumphant Quine-and-Sylvia triptych, the throwaways say more than the statements, and the album where he mixed Quine down *(Legendary Hearts)* and the one where he fired him altogether *(New Sensations)* are as satisfying as the one where Quine reintroduced him to his guitar if not his entire musical conception. The Warner period has been all good intentions, with the Cale collaboration *Songs for Drella* what it claimed to be, the sharp guitars of the socially conscious *New York* cutting through the banality of its generalizations, and the purely poetic mortality meditation *Magic and Loss* his dullest effort since *Mistrial* if not *Lou Reed Live*. Which is why the unkempt air of *Set the Twilight Reeling* is oddly encouraging.

The tenor here is reflective rather than descriptive, not Reed's long suit, and he gives every sign that he finds loving an artist who deserves as much attention as he does even tougher to write about than to do. So as often happens with Reed, casuals like "Egg Cream" and "HookyWooky" and "Sex With Your Parents" are the instant winners. But once they're absorbed the record doesn't quit. Longtime collaborator Fernando Saunders squeezes sublime noises out of his bass, and Reed plays the farthest-reaching guitar of his solo career, most spectacularly on the eight-minute "Riptide" and the climactic title track right after. And eventually, "Trade In," whose "woman with a thousand faces" is presumably Anderson, and "Hang On to Your Emotions," which could have been inspired by true love or a catty review or a shrink, risk soul without falling into corn. More than once, in fact, Reed declares himself reborn. I'll believe that when the placenta comes back from the pathologist. But I'm impressed enough to wonder how his thirty-sixth solo studio job might sound, long about 2021.

1977–1995–1996

What Are Realities of Prince Deal?
Hell, What Is Reality?

You may have noticed a brief flap a few months ago about the size of Prince's . . . well, his contract. That it wasn't about something as important as his you-know-what is probably why you remember it so dimly. This money stuff gets tired as fast as anything else—faster. Janet Jackson's ridiculous 40 million from Virgin was soon inundated by her bro's totally chimerical *billion* from Sony, now downscaled by biz reporters to a mere 60 mill, which is also the estimated value of Madonna's Time-Warner deal. But how much do you know or care about Barbra's new pact? Or RCA's ZZ Top signing? Legally, as we used to say before agents transformed renegotiation into natural law, Prince still owed his label five albums. On September 4, however, he came out of nowhere to vanquish the competition. "A King's Ransom for Prince / Artist Signs Record $100-Million Contract With Warner," shouted the Los Angeles *Times*. Only by the next day Warner execs were professing themselves "dismayed" that Prince's people were throwing such numbers around—after all, what would Madonna think? Under the headline, "What Are Realities of Prince Deal? Attorneys See Safeguards for Warner," *Billboard* quickly estimated that in order to break even on the announced 10 million dollars for each new album, the company would have to sell 5 million copies worldwide, something Prince has managed precisely three times. Duly constituted authorities postulated cross-collateralization, revolving advances, and other avant-garde techniques.

So it seems that whatever the exact details, Prince's reputed record breaker was at bottom a publicity stunt, one of whose functions was to improve his profit profile—to up his sales and thus his take from the company, which probably has less to lose than he does. But the ploy hasn't worked. Two months after its October 20 release, his new album—since its "title" is a supposedly androgynous graphic rune (I just see a female sex symbol, a cross, and a hautboy myself), we'll call it *Prince XV*—was plummeting down the charts even as Neil Young's *Harvest Moon,* out two weeks later, rebounded upwards. Unlike 1991's *Diamonds and Pearls,* the post–1984 5 million-seller that enabled Prince to get whatever he got out of Warner, it simply hasn't produced hit singles on the order of "Cream" and "Gett Off." Admittedly, this obituary could be premature. I'm working off U.S. charts even though Prince sells better overseas—certified double-platinum here, *Diamonds and Pearls* moved 3.3 million in the rest of the world. And I'm assuming that the buzz over the forgettable ballad "Damn U" will take it no further than the buzz over the funk bombs "Sexy M.F." and "My Name Is Prince" even though I'm a lousy judge of forgettable ballads. Sales patterns tend to be precipitous in this age of computerized retailer-to-compiler SoundScan charts. But labels promote catalogue product forever, and at this point Prince is quintessentially bankable—the wunderkind as commercial fixture.

Since Warner got only one extra album out of the deal, it was presumably to enhance and exploit his catalogue that the company renegotiated, but of course there was an obverse, its shape determined by the huge if far from record-breaking proportions of the little man's ego. As his attempted news management made clear, Prince believed the contract placed him on the same summit of celebrity as Michael Jackson and Madonna—or rather, given the proportions of his ego, affirmed a suzerainty over these pretenders that some had been foolish enough to doubt and most had been blind enough not to see in the first place. On the most obvious level, this means he's seriously delusional. Ever since he threw *Purple Rain* up against *Thriller,* his numbers haven't gotten near those of Michael Jackson, whose supposed flop *Dangerous* has passed 14 million internationally, and while his record sales vie with those of the blond authoress, his fame just doesn't match up—as a media manipulator, he's a standard-issue weirdo recluse. But in a sense these distinctions are too subtle. Prince may not be as big as he thinks he is—"Why settle 4 a star when u can have the sun?" he asks more unambiguously than modesty requires on *Prince XV*'s "The Continental"—but he's big enough to turn his delusions into a reality his admirers must contend with. And on the basis of *Prince XV* I remain an admirer.

Neither Michael Jackson nor Madonna has ever been conceived as rock and roll liberator rather than masscult signifier. Prince has. Burying the new album in the *L.A. Weekly,* Howard Hampton bewailed Prince's abandonment of his "heretical, utopian promise": "the sense that here division (between man and woman, black and white, straight and gay) could be trashed, and a new pop world would be born in its place." Celebrating it in the *New York Times,* Ann Powers extolled "one of the most complex artistic expressions known to pop." But while both writers invoke "pop," they're describing what used to be called a rock hero, and by now it should be obvious that this approach gets us less than nowhere with Prince. Even when he was writing songs that betokened some engagement with the outside world, he trashed division only because he had no head for differentiation—he wasn't complex, he was a mess. But only with *Prince XV* did I figure this out—did I learn to ignore his message altogether.

This was partly self-defense. The "plot" of the thing, which Prince has the nerve (and wit) to call a "rock soap opera," is the stupidest of Prince's inexhaustible store of stupid plots—*Under the Cherry Moon, Graffiti Bridge, Parade,* let us not forget *Batman,* and let us not forget *Purple Rain* either. You either skip Kirstie Alley, note Carmen Electra in passing, pity the supposedly royal / Egyptian / sixteen-year-old sex object Mayte, keep your distance from the "Bohemian Rhapsody" sendup "3 Chains of Gold," and let the lyrics come to you, or you'll never want to play the record again. Which would be a loss. Because *Prince XV* is the first serious proof since *Sign 'O' the Times,* which shoulda sold 10 million and never got to 3, of something else that distinguishes Prince from Michael Jackson and Madonna: he's a musician to the bone. This is in no way to belittle Jackson's musical genius or Madonna's musical savvy. But Prince is more gifted than either, and he's also obsessed—the most prolific superstar of our era, his album-a-year average subsuming countless B-sides as well as four double LPs (counting the seventy-four-minute *Prince XV*), he reportedly has four hundred fifty unreleased songs in the can. No wonder he's a weirdo recluse. Between fucking and the studio, what else does he have time for?

One reason Prince was a rock hero was that he rocked—far more supple than Springsteen or the Stones, he still inhabited a groove that was flat and heavy by the standards of the black pop world he came up in. But as a compulsive musician he could never leave it at that. He was always conflicted, always a mess, and as it turned out, *Sign 'O' the Times* proved a benchmark in more ways than one—ever since, he's been struggling more and more visibly with something else. Call it funk or rap, James or George; call it blackness, as in *The Black Album*. Sometimes he denies it, withdrawing *The Black Album* for *Lovesexy,* schlocking up *Diamonds and Pearls* and making it pay; in the movie version of *Graffiti Bridge,* he even demonizes it. But at the same time he surrounds himself with it: signing George Clinton to Paisley Park, enlisting gangsta-ish rapper Tony M. in the hopefully behandled New Power Generation, packing the soundtrack version of *Graffiti Bridge* with other people's funk. And on *Prince XV* he does it right.

Though you may think it's a little late to make a great-if-flawed funk album, face it—Prince was never ahead of his time. He was just an anomaly, a law unto himself. It was the rappers who were the vanguard, and for the moment Prince has them where he wants them. In 1992, only Eric B. & Rakim—sampled along with N.W.A on a track that doesn't booty-boom anywhere near as deep as Prince's own "My Name Is Prince" or "Sexy M.F." or "Love 2 the 9's" or "The Max" or "The Continental" or "The Flow"—put out better beats. If I were so inclined maybe I could extract a vision or at least a cultural meaning from these songs, but I know the lyrics well enough to leave their deeper meanings to his sexual partners and business associates, and I'm neither smart nor stupid enough to parse his racial struggle. So I'll just mention the "hornz," played by living human beings whose names I don't recognize—not up to Rakim's on "Relax With Pep," but a def, deft tribute to Uncle Jam nevertheless. And the messy and hence inevitable exceptions to the funky rule: "Blue Light," which until several reviewers dissed its skank didn't hit me as a reggae at all, just another seamless funk-lite ripoff (and the sharpest, least ambitious lyric on the record); an enigmatic little rock ballad called "The Morning Papers"; the catchily retrograde "And God Created Woman." None of which adds up to much more than "U

Got the Look" or "Raspberry Beret" or "Cream"—except maybe the kind of endless virtuosity that made James Brown the greatest rock and roller of all time.

Please, I know all time has now ended. I know Prince is a synthesizer rather than a creator, too. So if you want to make this the year you got permanently bored with him, I won't argue. Only do me a favor and don't pretend your boredom means anything either. Prince hasn't broken any promises worth keeping. He's just put in his time as a weirdo recluse. And whatever his delusions, however obscene or illusory his compensation, the evidence indicates that something in his synthetic, over-sheltered soul remains miraculously whole. May he put four hundred fifty more songs in the can before the money runs out.

1992

Making a Spectacle of Herself: Janet Jackson

I took my daughter to see Mariah Carey at the Garden December 10 with the most benign of critical intentions. At eight-and-a-half, Nina has attended more than her share of concerts, but never at the Garden and never without her mom, who was happy to take in *The Piano* instead. Since Nina had enjoyed a brief video romance with Carey's perky girl-group homage "Dreamlover," a song I kind of liked on an album I didn't hate, I hoped I could learn to hear a phenom and play sugar daddy simultaneously. And despite a late, skimpy opening act and a fifty-minute intermission that had the crowd chewing its chains, Nina enjoyed herself thoroughly, although by ten thirty she was so tired she asked to skip the finale. Me, I thought Carey stunk. Her PG uptempo and three-octave emotions evoked not the Bette Midler who plays to Long Island but the Long Island Bette Midler plays to. Coming from the wife of a record-company president, the believe-in-your-dream lies seemed in especially dubious taste.

As Nina couldn't help but notice—it was up there in lights six feet high—Carey was soon to be upstaged at the same venue by another MTV hero, Janet Jackson. Although she wanted to go, and I thought there might be a column for me in the parlay, I had my doubts, and the reason was s-e-x. My wife and I aren't shy, Nina's been told as much as she wants to hear about how penises and vaginas work, but when we saw MC Lyte with Kris Kross last year, I thought the male dancers' pelvic push-ups were a little over her head, and I assumed the show would be at least as steamy as *janet.* and its promotional accoutrements. This is tricky territory for any parent—you have to negotiate between stifling (and fear-inducing) overprotectiveness and bewildering (and fear-inducing) overexposure, with "expert" guidelines useless if your sexual mores and your instinct for your child's developmental needs are as particular as they ought to be. So you cogitate and improvise, compensating for mishaps as they come up. Relatively speaking, the Janet decision was a no-brainer. But I didn't make up my mind until it was too late to try for three tickets, so once again Nina and I were alone together in the pop marketplace.

By this time a column seemed unlikely—the L.A. DA's investigation into Michael Jackson's alleged child abuse had seen to that. How was I going to write Janet up with Michael so much on my and everyone else's mind—especially since I was positive she'd duck the subject? The show would have to be pretty spectacular, and even then I'd cringe. Only first of all she didn't duck the subject. Three songs in, still wearing that elaborately fringed white Vegasy thing that's in all the photos, she asked us to "bow our heads and say a silent prayer for my brother Michael." Pretty shrewd and pretty sweet—if so inclined you could ask for him to get out of trouble, but if you wanted God to forgive his sins (or punish his wickedness) you could do that instead. The interval must have lasted close to a minute, with many heads bowed, cheers minimal, and boos altogether absent; Janet appeared to be moving her lips and crying a little, although maybe that was just sweat from the dance numbers, and I confess that despite my hardshell atheism I very nearly sent up some sort of inchoate entreaty myself. Then she did her first slow one, "Let's Wait Awhile," a plea for sexual caution and romantic forbearance recorded when she was nineteen: "When we get to know each other/And we're both feeling much stronger/Then let's try to talk it over/Let's wait a while longer."

By this time I knew the show was going to be plenty spectacular—that had seemed a good bet even before Janet materialized, when Tony Toni Toné came out blazing at eight o'clock sharp and kept it up for forty minutes. The intermission was no shorter than Carey's, but despite a few "Ja-net"'s toward the end, the edge had been taken off our collective hunger. This was very much a big-ticket event—seats were fifty and thirty-five dollars where Carey's went for thirty-seven fifty and twenty-eight fifty, with capacity upped from fourteen to sixteen thousand besides—but starting with the sensationally assured and dynamic openers, splurgers got what is called their money's worth. From harlequin masquerade to brightly hued zoot suits to Timberland chic, subsequent costumes were gorgeous as well as lavish; the giant video monitors switched with thrill-a-minute savvy from promo-clip snippets to live close-ups to made-for-arena images; and the direction was more astute than the videos had harbingered. Not counting the matched drum solos and some token cock-rock guitar, the band and the three backup singers stayed out of the way, and where Mariah split her troupe into separate-but-equal platoons—five gospel-style matriarchs, four of them fat, and five lithe male dancers, four of them jheri-dreaded—Janet's two male dancers were noticeably outnumbered by the six women who helped her dominate the stage. On *janet.,* "If" is among other things a promise of head: "Your smooth and shiny feels good against my lips, sugar" ain't about his cranium. When the song opened the show, however, it was the guys who were kneeling and the girls who were getting serviced—only not so's the eight-year-olds in the crowd noticed. You'd best believe I didn't ask mine, but I'm sure she thought it was just dancing, same as the video. Because it was.

I've never concerned myself with Janet's artistic identity because ever since the preemptively entitled *Control* I've pegged her as a creature of Jimmy Jam & Terry Lewis—the very producer-composers whose signature song, the S.O.S. Band's "Just Be Good to Me," Carey had covered as a declaration of roots a week before. No stickler for chops, I nevertheless thought Janet was lucky not to lose track of her diminutive voice in the deep angles of the attendant beats. Now I'm less sure. With the help of who knows or cares what choral and electronic enhancements, she sounded stronger live than on record, and the half dozen *janet.* songs (in a set divvied up evenly among her three Jam & Lewis releases) converted me to a record I'd enjoyed too skeptically. The thing does throb, though how sexy one finds the slow songs is personal, as sex usually is—foolish though it may be to correlate erotic sweetness and savor with literary sense and sensibility, I'll never find out different now, and Jackson's tastes in poetry are way soft by me.

Janet. remains a formidable sex album. But where its three videos fleck a gender equality that's almost progressive by video's pitiful male-chauvinist standards with moments of what we'll call heavy petting ("If" 's choreography, hand-down-jeans in "Again," toe work in "That's the Way Love Goes"), the show soft-pedals the softcore and unbalances the gender symbolism. In Janet's arena-world, women rule. The two male dancers compete for the seven women's attention even though it could easily be vice versa. When the women doff their outer garments, the men carry them off. The audience member (or plant) called up for lap duty during "Miss You Much" looks as if his head is about to explode. And in the almost shocking encore version of "This Time," Janet, dressed like a green goddess, watches horrified as a female dancer discovers her man in bed with another woman. The guy brutalizes the dancer just as Janet's father and brothers are said to have beaten their wives, till she packs her bags and makes her getaway, only to return with a coven of black-garbed sisters to *execute him* with a ritual dagger, as Janet the green goddess looks on, benign yet powerless. The clear parallel and influence in all this razzle-dazzle is Madonna, but Jackson is far less schematic, bloodless, and kinky. Whether one finds that a good thing is personal, as sex usually is. I did.

In fact, I've never seen an arena spectacle to match it. The Pet Shop Boys' extravaganza at Radio City was patchier, Michael's *Bad* tour mere showbiz by comparison. Complaints that it's video-driven seem cranky to me, complaints that it lacks spontaneity irrelevant. Certainly the videos constitute one of the information pools from which the spectacle is constructed, as they damn well should, but this version of Janet is conceived on this social and audiovisual scale. I wonder whether anyone who found it too canned ever goes to the movies, which are literally canned—they come in cans, identical every time you see them. I generally prefer music that captures a moment as it flies by, and I generally prefer my venues smaller. But I'm no prig, and this megaconcert connected and signified. By eleven thirty, the third song of the encore, Nina had spent fifteen minutes alternating clapping and cheering with unconscious strokes of my hair, a sure sign that she needs to sleep, and so I took her home, delighted that she had spent two hours in an entertainment environment that put a womanist spin on this video-driven music. I was also delighted that I'd taken her to such a great show.

In the cab, I asked Nina about her favorite costume. She chose the sexy jeans of "That's the Way Love Goes." When I told her I'd liked "What'll I Do" 's zoot suits, she asked what a zoot suit was, and after my brief lecture on Latino gang culture observed, "Janet's youngest brother wears a suit like that in 'Smooth Criminal.' " This odd locution wasn't designed to avoid uttering the disgraced one's name—she just likes to show off her knowledge of pop history, gleaned from close attention to MTV and VH1 infotainment programming (where li'l Randy rarely comes up, I guess). My daughter has been a fan of many rock and rollers, from Elvis and the 4 Seasons to the B-52's and the Go-Betweens, but Michael has inspired her most enduring affection. Her friends care about him too—a multiracial bunch, they don't think it matters if you're black or white, but it made them feel good for Michael to put it that way. When my wife tried to explain what MTV's latest spate of Michael reports was about, Nina cut her off before she could get specific. She just didn't want to know.

Even before the allegations and the save-the-children blitz that preceded them, Michael's kiddie affinities were one reason adults had stopped thinking about his music, which hasn't diminished appreciably since *Thriller*—while his balladry has turned in on itself some, the sweet vulnerability is still there, and *Dangerous*'s "Jam" is harder-core than *janet.*'s "Throb," the most muscular funk track Jam & Lewis have ever constructed. It's also one reason the story is always played as the downfall of a celebrity rather than an artist—for most of the press, Michael isn't a great musician, just a successful version of La Toya. And I suppose it's why, amid all the lawyerly rhetoric and moral panic and vacuous reportage and lip-smacking gossip and media coverage of media coverage, no one ever mentions his fans except to wonder whether the silly sheep will still buy his product. So far they have. But their inevitable loss is worthy of our deepest respect and regret.

Obviously this loss isn't in the same league with the loss of a kid who has sex with an adult, which no matter how gentle and consensual robs the child of his or her precious, fragile purchase on erotic volition. And I'm not inclined to withhold judgment until

Michael has his day wherever he ends up having it, either. The available evidence is a mess, but even if you don't buy the credible but unproven and perhaps fabricated story of the thirteen-year-old who claims he was seduced by Michael, or the multiplying but much vaguer tales of earlier liaisons with other barely or not even pubescent males, his own (now discharged) investigator has said that Michael has often invited boys to sleep with him—clothed, in a huge bed. This isn't a crime, and it shouldn't be. But it is inappropriate behavior, period—behavior inexcusable in any adult, whatever the extenuations of genius or celebrity or disease or drug dependency or childhood abuse or arrested development. Stardom is almost always painful and disorienting, but that doesn't absolve stars of personal responsibility—if anything, the powerful have a special obligation to understand the ramifications of their power. No matter what his psychological problems, an astute-to-ruthless businessman who's committed to the young should know better than to burden any kid—which means any future adult—with such a confusing memory.

And nevertheless, the artist is one thing and the art is another. So I'm still often awed by his music. And I still wonder and worry about how Nina will remember Michael, whom she's never met and never will meet but who touches her imagination anyway. She responds to his beats and his hooks, to his supernatural agility and his tremendous fame, to his love of children and his childlike aura, to his weirdness itself. She dances to his music and ponders his videos. An only child for whom the large family is almost a mythic fantasy, she thinks about his siblings. And at some point in the next year or so she'll most likely get the idea that her pleasure in all this is tainted. A wellspring of delight will turn into a lesson in mistrust. Michael giveth, and Michael— with a big ugly push from the infotainment cynics who've been transmogrifying him into Wacko Jacko since long before the story got so lurid—taketh away.

One of the memories she'll be left with then will be Janet Jackson at the Garden. Not much in the way of compensation, you may think—even unpriggish types will tell you that Janet is not only a fabricated singer but a fabricated sex object, a creature of rhinoplasty and suicide diets. But I'm grateful her memory will be there. Whether you approve of the particulars or not, self-made sex objects generally have some sort of purchase on erotic volition, as Janet has been demonstrating all year. Really, not all MTV heroes are the same. And as Mariah Carey herself puts it in the song she has conveniently entitled "Heroes": "If you look inside your heart/You don't have to be afraid/Of what you are."

1993

9

Careers in Semipopularity

Selling the Dirt to Pay the Band:
Freedy Johnston

Freedy Johnston's *Can You Fly* is an impossible record. Out a year and still airborne, with sales accelerating laboriously to around thirty thousand, it's a throwback to a formal strategy cool people want nothing to do with right now. What I mean is, *Can You Fly* is a perfect album. Not a world-historical album or a ground-breaking album or even a concept album; not an album that'll grab you by the neck and change your life. Just a perfect album—thirteen songs, thirteen discrete, discreet little moments that connect lyrically and stick musically. Though it's so perfectly arranged and sequenced it's sure to strike some as too tailored, it can't be accused of sounding like money—it only cost twenty-two grand. Yet its tradition is the money tradition—the Peter Asher-style well-made album. Casting about for records with a similar feel, I found Elvis Costello's *Trust* too cheesy (sonically, *King of America* came closer), but beloved early-seventies oldies like Randy Newman's *12 Songs* and Paul Simon's *Paul Simon* and Steely Dan's *Pretzel Logic* fit right in. Rather than full-fledged money records, these were the kind of carefully produced gems that convinced bizzers they could buy quality—a faith they proved by creating a market that preferred *Aja* to *Pretzel Logic*. And they were also great albums. I may be wrong—these things take time—but I doubt *Can You Fly* is a great album. In 1993, perfect albums can't be great. That's one reason cool people want nothing to do with them—

although the coolest people of all want nothing to do with great albums either.

This uneasiness with perfection is a symptom of a high-level cultural anxiety that's hardly specific to rock and roll. Insofar as it's part fad and part hypochondria you can just call it fear of closure. There's a generation of cheap ironists out there who hope they don't ever have to mean anything again, and I guarantee that sooner or later—a few years after everybody else, probably—they'll see the error of their ways. But as usual with new habits of thought, this one makes some sense. There really is a crisis of meaning in this culture, especially for white males who regret at whatever level of conscious intellection their complicity in an ideology of domination they're at least half ashamed of. And from the simplest resolved tension to every loose end of content ever tied up in a square knot of form, perfect works of art owe that ideology just by being so sure of themselves. In the end, they bespeak command, and in the end that command is a lie. Everything put together sooner or later falls apart.

Perfection is problematic for rock and roll anyway. The music's most passionate sectarians are hooked on the sound of becoming—the excitement of hearing the unschooled make up their own rules as the unskilled learn on the job. And so they've always thrown the Stooges up against *Sgt. Pepper, Tonight's the Night* up against (the Peter Asher palimpsest) *Heart Like a Wheel.* It was along this fault line that the punk schism developed. But punk also preferred pop tune to rock pretension, and was destined to evolve every which way, until no wave, hardcore, and their unkempt-to-avant offshoots coexisted (and occasionally coalesced) with styles traceable to power pop, roots rock, and the neater, craftier musics that inspired them. Hence, Freedy Johnston, born and raised in a Kansas town equidistant from New York and San Francisco and now the star exhibit at Bar/None, a label traceable to Hoboken power pop legends the Individuals. Johnston is a singer-songwriter—there's still no apter term. For vocal reasons he's often compared to Neil Young, who's respectable in Alternative Nation, but in fact he grew up on country and AOR and still identifies with Hank, Zep, and, yes, Steely Dan. His 1990 debut, *The Trouble Tree,* gathered buzz on standout songs like "Innocent" and "No Violins," producer Chris Butler's ever-ready grooves, and an understandable measure of local-talent boosterism. But though it was craftsmanlike by alternative standards, it was too simple, or crude, to prepare anyone outside the Hoboken Kiwanis for *Can You Fly.*

Because a taste for singer-songwriters usually builds off a craving for well-turned vignettes, Johnston's critical admirers sometimes downplay the album's uptempo opening cuts. Indeed, there's a sense in which he pretends to throw them away, but that's appropriate, because they're also where he fends off the crisis of meaning. As evocative as musical short stories like "Responsible" and "Tearing Down This Place" may be, his greatest song is also his most process-conscious: the opener, "Trying To Tell You I Don't Know," which starts off, "Well I sold the dirt to feed the band." The title is a paradox that sums up his aesthetic dilemma—tempering romantic will with existential humility, it puts meaning and crisis in a nutshell. And the first line is an indie-rock joke that sums up his professional dilemma—while real rock stars enforce their Dom Perignon riders, this Hank-Zep-Dan fan will settle for dirt. All Freedy Johnston wants is to "wake up in your head"—"Trying to sing what I can't say/Trying to throw my head away/Trying to cry with a red light on"—but first he's got to find fifty bucks for the van. "In the New Sunshine" develops the metaphor, and the joke: "Now I will burn before I sing," he declares, apparently in the throes of a romantic-religious trope, only this cheerful-sounding fantasy isn't about creative passion or Promethean torment—it's about playing a rock festival without benefit of ozone layer.

But if both songs suggest that "this skinny white singer with no more time" knows he got here late, the biographical details make clear that he has no choice. Merely as joke and metaphor, that first line deserves a nod from the most casual listener. But in fact it's literal as well—Johnston did feed his band by selling some dirt, raising the last ten grand of his production budget by divesting himself of the family farm he'd inherited from his grandfather, which was also his first home. For him, obviously, this perfect throwback meant damn near everything. Yet it's not as if his music per se gives off much sense of formal compulsion. It's accomplished but only marginally unique, applying a subtle postpunk spareness to the country/folk-tinged studio-rock tradition. For better or worse, he's a true *song*writer, and so it's his historical mission to write tunes people want to hear. Give the album three or four plays and every chorus will draw you in. If that makes him some kind of cornball, so be it.

What I like most about this boho who traded his birthright in on art is that he's a Kansan despite it all—here in his chosen milieu, the honor he does the ordinary renders him almost esoteric. It isn't so much that his topics and characters are middle American, though many are, from the farmer and the angel in "Can You Fly" to the teenager who loves "The Mortician's Daughter" to the bumbling husband of "We Will Shine" to the happily deluded Vegas sucker of "The Lucky One" to the lost-or-found wanderers of "Wheels" and "Sincere" and "Remember Me." It's his total sensibility, which remains as matter-of-fact as circumstances permit. Johnston shows little interest in the one-dimensional Nashville approach, now as always the locus of many telling moments in middle American music as well as vast quantities of cottony dreck. None of his surfaces reads as clearly as, for instance, Billy Joel's or Bruce Springsteen's. But he's never as obscure as Steely Dan or as convoluted as Elvis Costello or as distanced as Randy Newman or as kooky as Neil Young; the sincere feeling and real life are embedded, sure, but not too deep, a little below Paul Simon and more or less even with the Go-Betweens, probably the finest semi-pop songwriters of the eighties.

I'm most taken with "Tearing Down This Place," an extended metaphor about the labor of ending a relationship. Like so many of Johnston's metaphors, it's palpable. You can see him doing day work on a demolition crew, and wondering who lived there, and finally projecting his own dead memories into the space: "Here's the room where they lay awake through a complicated night/He was staring at the wall/And she cried and cried and cried." Equally impressive is "Responsible," which evokes the finality and deep peril of parental love with an evenhanded compassion I can barely comprehend after eight years of thinking about my own kid. This is "She's Leaving Home" without sarcasm or schmaltz, recognizing the parent's pain and the kid's cruelty without ever denying that the pain might be self-pity and the cruelty absolutely necessary. Songs as knowledgeable as these remind me that Johnston came late to the game in more ways than one. At thirty-two, he's older than the newly solo Paul Simon and has more than five years on the Randy Newman of *12 Songs* or the Fagen and Becker of *Pretzel Logic*. If he's going to spend his life waking up in people's heads, he'd best get started.

Most likely *Can You Fly* is his shot—not many artists come up with two albums this good in a lifetime. So he's touring hard as the buzz on this one turns into a low roar. No folkie on record, Johnston rocks with surprising intensity live, and the groove laid down by Hoboken everydrummer Alan Bezozi and Human Switchboard bassist Jared Nickerson is tougher and funkier than Randy Newman's or Paul Simon's or even the swinging Steely Dan's. Freedy Johnston has put his all into a perfect record, and no matter how world-historical cool people think it isn't, he wants the world to know about it. Maybe its perfection is a function of a false aura of command. Maybe the times will deny it greatness. But it's asking a lot of a guy who has trouble coming up with van money to worry about throwing his weight around. And it's ceding history to the devil to ask the world to do without the guy's tunes.

1993

Are We Not Girls? We Are L7!

The women of L7 are so wary of the pigeonhole that they refuse to cooperate with stories about what are best just called all-female bands. This isn't just a women's thing, or an oppressed thing—all artists hate categories, which impinge on their precious individuality and serve analytic purposes they have no use for. But it's tough on the hapless music scribe. One can understand why the girls in the band resent comparison to the howling Hole or the archly childish Shonen Knife, with whom they share gender and little else. And as admirers of the Runaways and Girlschool who prefer the Ramones and Motorhead, they may not like being lumped in with Babes in Toyland or Scrawl or even their buddies the Lunachicks, all of whom do less with a roughly similar hardpop aesthetic. Nevertheless, L7 are women, a rare thing among rock musicians, and feminists, a rarer thing. Both categories make them special whether they like it or not. Maybe they'd be special anyway—definitely they'd be special anyway. But not in quite the same way.

Bassist-vocalist Jennifer Finch, guitarist-vocalist Donita Sparks, and guitarist-vocalist Suzi Gardner have been touring L.A. since 1987; Dee Plakas solved their drummer problem in 1990. Having recorded a negligible LP for Bad Religion's Epitaph label early on, they weighed in with Sub Pop's 1990 *Smell the Magic* EP, which in its nine-song, thirty-minute CD version should belie any suspicions that producer Butch Vig (multiplatinum Nirvana, new

Sonic Youth) was the making of Slash's current *Bricks Are Heavy.* From "Wargasm" to "This Ain't Pleasure," *Bricks Are Heavy* is one of those wondrous records where the old tricks—surefire chords, simple tunes, rocking beats—get off their asses and work. But I've come to prefer the raw real of *Smell the Magic,* where L7's theme song "Shove"—"Get out of my way or I might shove/Get out of my way or I'm gonna shove"—and sex rant "'Till the Wheels Fall Off"—"You and me we just fit/I'm addicted I just can't quit," and also, if I'm not mistaken, "People say you want to control/I don't care let's go go go"—generate a fierce momentum nothing on *Bricks Are Heavy* can keep up with. Together the two records sum up a hard rock damn near as potent, if you'll pardon my metaphor, as "Territorial Pissings" if not "Smells Like Teen Spirit." If they ever manage to mate the fierce with the surefire, these women will be scary.

L7 breathe life into what I've inadequately pigeonholed as "hard pop": the brief, clear, fast, tough song expounded, in ascending order of sweet impurity, by the Sex Pistols, the Heartbreakers, the Clash, the Ramones, the Buzzcocks—the concept/sensibility that for one shining punk moment seemed to encompass an inexhaustible formula. Really, that was what it was like—for a couple of months there, every forty-five Bleecker Bob put on sounded great, and for the next year or so bands you'd never heard of came up with another one. Then, phffft, it wore out. Wire and the Feelies arted it up, the Undertones and the Go-Go's popped it up, X and the Replacements and Hüsker Dü complexed it up, Jesus and Mary Chain fuzzed it up, Black Flag and Minor Threat and a thousand unremembered Stridex burnouts speeded it up. In the eighties, the prime exemplars were flukes—high points by the Descendents, the Rattlers, and Dag Nasty sound dandy to this day, but all were inconsequential one-shots no matter how long the bands stuck at it. And though the names may be different, chances are your faves were a bunch of fannish boys as well.

Oh yes, boys. Especially in England, punk's amateur ethos and hostility to natural macho were girl-friendly like rock had never been before. Yet despite godmother Patti Smith and a roll call of significant exceptions—especially the great Deborah Harry, Liliput nee Kleenex, and Poly Styrene's X-Ray Spex, whose songs remained uncompromisingly brief, clear, fast, and tough while

Lora Logic's sax dug a hole for guitar orthodoxy—the concept/sensibility started male and stayed that way. The Slits were quintessential can't-play-a-lick bashers when they surfaced at the Roxy in early '77, but by the time they cut their album with reggae pro Dennis Bovell two years later, their self-schooled skank went a long way toward defining postpunk possibility, with the uncertainly folky Raincoats and the wanly funky Au Pairs not far behind. Independently, these women found out that punk's square corners didn't suit them—they wanted a music with more give in it even if they had to learn to play their axes to get it. A lot of men resented punk's limitations too. Soon the formula was left to the permanent teen rebels of hardcore, which for all its DIY democracy and freeform radicalism was boy to the bone.

But not all aggro is testosterone-fueled, and for some women, the flailing garage-rock mosh pit that coalesced around hardcore felt like reality. In San Francisco, Frightwig joined the fray with obvious satire that was never as bitchy-witchy as they thought, but when Suzi Gardner urged Henry Rollins to slip it in on Black Flag's 1984 album of the same name, she found a tone while performing the minor miracle of making hardcore sexy—her mock cock-hunger celebrated bad girls as it made fun of them. (It made fun of bad boys too, as Black Flag knew—their bassist by then was a woman, Kira, who later took Gardner's part on the live *Who's Got the 10½?*, where she was also credited with possessing the donkey dong of the title.) L7 consists entirely of bad girls, but Gardner, a chain-smoking dyed blond who sings like she looks, seems to relish the role. *Smell the Magic* is her record, defined by the four songs she had a hand in writing: in addition to "Shove" and "'Till the Wheels Fall Off," the biker anthem "Fast and Frightening" ("Got so much clit she don't need no balls") and the self-starting "Broomstick" she's ready to shove up her snatch.

As befits the new album's more orderly riffs, its lyrics deal with more mature themes, mentioning masturbation only in relation to the war in Iraq. Significantly, all its most memorable songs—"Wargasm," "Pretend We're Dead," "Diet Pill," "Mr. Integrity," and "Shitlist"—were written solely by Donita Sparks, and except for "Diet Pill," a metal fantasy about a housewife's revenge, all are what you might call generally pissed off. Whether railing at war or conformity or punk ideologues or every asshole she's ever met, Sparks's sardonic growl is less gender-specific than Gardner's street shriek, often positing not a woman, but a human being who happens to be a woman. When the band played the Marquee, she carried the show with a charisma that subsumed sexuality, drawing back proudly and flashing a mad, sarcastic grin worthy of Candice Bergen or Katharine Hepburn every time some stage-diving lunk threatened to kick her in the chest in a fit of death-defying male bonding. Sparks is the band's *femme moyenne furieuse,* mediating between Gardner's motorcycle mama and Jennifer Finch's middle-class rebel. Finch may perform in a bimbo's halter and swear she'll kill the next mosher who steps on Donita's equipment, but her voice has been known to approach sweet reason, and her interviews touch on "the community" and "biological destiny." Sparks is more politically equivocal: "I pretty much lay off the feminist rap, even though I'm a feminist, you know?" she told a newspaperman who seemed pleased to hear it. "I don't want to sound like a traitor or anything, but we've gotten a lot of fans just by doing what we do."

One good thing about indie—other musicians will build on L7's lead whatever their political content or gross sales. And of course I'm talking all-female bands, or at least female-identified. (Because music makes strange bandmates, Hole's guitarist is male, and L7 discovered that drummers are a subspecies unto themselves while going through misfits of both sexes.) You don't have to be a feminist to root for them, either. In a supposedly prosex music whose two greatest abortion songs are the Sex Pistols' scabrous "Bodies" and Graham Parker's hateful "You Can't Be Too Strong," it took the women of L7 to found the scandalously belated Rock for Choice, but at this point, woman power can do more for rock and roll than rock and roll can do for woman power. Anyone with an appetite for brief, clear, fast, tough songs soon figures out that what makes them go is basically inexplicable—the commitment and enthusiasm that can turn a well-turned punk single into a great one. Because empowerment hones commitment and enthusiasm, I've been awaiting L7's arrival for fifteen years. And I want to know what comes next.

So one Sunday in May I went down to Wetlands to check out a *Sassy* showcase featuring Olympia, Washington's Bikini Kill, a quartet whose male guitarist is said to dance in a cage as part of the act. Expecting nothing, I was rewarded with a dose of magic. Dressed in an off-the-shoulder top that suggested cycle tramp and basic black simultaneously, frontwoman Kathleen Hanna had the suburban accent of a Valley girl who thought all "girls" were "totally cool"—only this one had utopian politics and punk attitude. She got my attention with "Fucked Up": "I am a racist bitch/ I'm no better than you." But she won my heart when a woman in the crowd heckled or admonished, "Can the girl shit, you're a woman." As a believer in sisterhood, Hanna tried to explain instead of coming back with a putdown: "I like youth culture because I think youth are also oppressed. So I like the word girl. If you find it offensive I won't call you that. But that's what I call myself."

Due to the flat Wetlands sightlines, the final encore, an acoustic thing called "Girlfriends Don't Keep," was performed below my eye level. There was mild hubbub up front. I kept wondering who was making out down on the floor.

1992

Lucinda Williams's Reasonable Demands

I loved the title, *Happy Woman Blues,* and the open-faced look of the cover photo. So without wondering how a 1980 Folkways album had shown up on my doorstep in late 1981, I found out what Lucinda-with-no-last-name sounded like, and got a whiff of every critic's secret vice, the thrill of being first. It wasn't the songs themselves, I wrote, so much as the off-key generosity with which this "guileless throwback to the days of the acoustic blues mamas" put them across. The words rueful but never down-hearted, the music bluegrass blues, the voice an amazement, it became one of those out-of-the-way records I'd play to cheer visitors bemoaning the dearth of female rock and rollers. With apocalypse-now as inane a pop move as the happy ending, a real-ist who knows she has it good anyway is a treasure to share.

As so often happens, Lucinda Williams was cannier than I'd figured. The daughter of a poet/critic and a bunch of Southern college towns, she's always maintained a sizable and well-informed support network, one of whom advised her to mail me her product. I was notified by postcard when she moved from Austin to L.A. in 1984, and if I'd known we had so many mutual friends, I could have tracked her travails. Instead, 1988's *Lucinda Williams* seemed to come from nowhere. Although her own politics are embedded in the personal, Williams is certain to remain the only artist ever to proceed from the staunch old-left indie Folkways (now Smithsonian Folkways, which has remastered and rereleased *Happy Woman Blues* and an earlier acoustic blues session called *Ramblin'*) to the staunch new-left indie Rough Trade (which has now sold *Lucinda Williams* and the *Passionate Kisses* EP to ex-indie Chameleon). Just as she was the only new artist of any consequence to appear on Folkways for a good twenty years, she was—with the arguable exception of Louisiana eccentric Victoria Williams, no relation—the only traditionalist ever to breach Rough Trade's proggish postpunk palisade. Yet in the end the album was the U.S. branch's all-time bestseller at something over thirty thousand; the label even entertained heroic fantasies of breaking her in the country market.

Lucinda Williams is one of the best-reviewed records of all time. Produced by Williams and guitarist Gurf Morlix, it steadies her warm, edgy contralto without smothering it in pitch-conscious propriety, and moves her loosely folkish arrangements toward a hooky yet far from mechanical country-rock; the opener, "I Just Wanted To See You So Bad," bowls you over on avidity alone. But the clincher is the writing, as the merely clear-eyed lyricist of *Happy Woman Blues* pulls you into her language. The accrued detail of the bar-girl profile "The Night's Too Long" and the lover's manifesto "Passionate Kisses" recalls Newman, Prine, Springsteen; Dave Alvin is the only other under-forty who's savored the literal so enthusiastically. The astonishing "Changed the Locks" starts literal before it spirals into bereft, suprarational defiance. Other lyrics turn on situation: she knows the man she wants to see so bad mainly by telephone, and if "Am I Too Blue" got the attention it deserves from every woman unjustly accused of indulging her emotions, it would be the most widely sung song since "Rockabye Baby." Journalists who bemoaned the dearth of female rock and rollers and secretly believed the tradition wasn't played out yet could hardly let *Lucinda Williams* pass.

Though great press is never more than a beginning, it can mean plenty to an artist not set on instant superstardom, like the woman who concocted the reasonable demands of "Passionate Kisses"—food and clothing, a comfortable bed, a pen that works, time to think, those kisses, and "a full house/And a rock and roll band." It had been eight years between records, years of working in restaurants and bookstores and living off gig fees and label advances, of labor-intensive demos with big-time producers that convinced her to settle for Rough Trade, where she could do it her way. After all that struggle she finally seemed ready to put her music out there, and though she was a mite stiff live, that would certainly come. So in 1989 she toured with some regularity—if her bassist and drummer of choice couldn't yet join her rock and roll band, the houses were often full anyway. And then she dropped from sight again, just like that.

Those who knew the old stories nodded wearily at the report that she had departed acrimoniously from Rough Trade to sign with RCA, where new prexy Bob Buziak was the latest bizzer to tell her he loved her. Sequels in which Buziak got canned and Williams hated her RCA demos also seemed hauntingly familiar. But fortunately, so does the just-released *Sweet Old World*, cut with her Rough Trade band for Chameleon, an indie with a new prexy named Buziak. Strange though it may seem, Williams was right about her demos: on the dub I've heard the drum sound and such do indeed get in the way, while here the production is only marginally fuller and tighter, the kind of professionalization that authenticity nuts grouse about while everyone else notices that the songs sound better than ever. "Something About What Happens When We Talk" compliments someone she wishes she'd kissed; "Lines Around Your Eyes" celebrates someone she can't resist kissing again. "Sweet Old World" and "Pineola" take death so hard that it's hard to believe the Shakespeare-reading, r&b-loving drunk whose song comes in between is still among us. Even the relationship-driven commonplaces of "Prove My Love" and "Which Will" are touched with grace, and when she turns sentimental it's always with a difference—the verses of "Sidewalks of the City" won't teach you much about the homeless, but the chorus that implores her baby to keep her safe will teach you plenty about Lucinda.

Most of all, *Sweet Old World* proves how much she loves this sweet old world by immersing in the literal. In an effort to pay attention to the singer-songwriter who opened her Bottom Line gig, I started jotting down anything that could pass for a concrete noun. The best he did was *field;* the likes of *gambler, road, race,* and *black-and-white movie* were metaphors. On *Sweet Old World* we get *shoelace, donut shop, chess pieces, cross on a wall, music books, paperbacks, dresses that zip up the side, the lines around your eyes,* a bunch of proper nouns, and many more. In my favorite, "Hot Blood," Williams praises her love-from-afar by naming objects he's touched: his dirty clothes, his tire iron, his casserole. The honor she does this writing-class staple is another reason critics go for her, and though she's never taken a writing class, it's in her nurture if not her nature. Her father, Miller Williams, is no celebrity—poets rarely are. But neither is he some tenured unknown—he's far more prominent in his little world than his daughter is in hers. As one critic puts it, his determinedly collo-quial verse is "fascinated with the names of things specific to this world"; his compilation volume is called *Living on the Surface.* And while John Ciardi, with whom he wrote an influential if now outmoded handbook called *How Does a Poem Mean?,* was a vocif-erous Dylan-basher, Miller Williams's tastes are more ecumeni-cal—he's buddies with Tom T. Hall, who provided a blurb for *Happy Woman Blues.* Though his daughter cites Dylan, Flannery O'Connor, and Robert Johnson as influences, she can also quote her dad: "I write poetry dogs and cats can understand."

Maybe fathers are less threatened by their daughters than their sons, and maybe female musicians set on being themselves need a leg up to get anywhere at all. Or maybe it's pure coinci-dence that, unlike any male rocker you'd care to listen to, Bonnie Raitt and Rosanne Cash also have famous fathers. Because if Wil-liams has any artistic sisters out there, it's Raitt and Cash, roots-conscious songstresses much closer generationally to this late bloomer than PJ Harvey or L7. But despite the protofeminism of "Am I Too Blue" and "Something About What Happens When We Talk," the main thing that unites their line on men is that none of them expects too much. Raitt is sensual, Cash psychological, but both seek wisdom in relationships, whereas Williams still goes for divine madness; my brilliant wife calls her "a cowboy in matters of the heart—confused, naive, riled up." She's now put in four years with the same guy, a musician who'll tour with Steve Forbert while she spends two months fronting for Graham Parker. But it's hard not to suspect that her taste for the quest connects to the eternal dissatisfactions of her career.

When you think about it, Lucinda Williams's reasonable demands turn out to be more than almost anyone gets—food-clothes-shelter OK, but passionate kisses and a rock and roll band translate to endless love and fulfilling work, and to expect time to think in the bargain is to ask for heaven. Nevertheless, all these things are precisely what we socialists believe everybody deserves, and since Williams was visionary enough to sing about them and stubborn enough to persevere, I say she deserves to get there early. Though I've spoken to several people who might reasonably believe that her quest had done them dirt—somebody else told me she had "betrayed" Robin Hurley of Rough Trade, which seems like a balanced interpretation to me—I detected not the slightest hypocrisy and only the merest self-interest when every one of them hoped her time had finally come. She is clearly one of God's elect, and just by making us think that maybe life is fair after all, her success could enlarge us all. Anybody out there who knows Bonnie Raitt should talk up Lucinda's catalogue. And anybody who knows Graham Parker should tell him she always gets a sound check.

1992

The Ballad of Polly Jean Harvey: PJ Harvey

In February, 1995, I spent three hours interviewing twenty-five-year-old singer, songwriter, and quondam guitarist Polly Jean Harvey in New Orleans and Los Angeles, where she was rehearsing the professional quintet that had replaced her rough-hewn trio for convention gigs unveiling, celebrating, and promoting *To Bring You My Love,* which would eventually win every critics' poll in the country. Although her 1992 debut, *Dry,* had quickly and astonishingly established her as the first female rocker of any vision to play guitar better than she sang, as a vocalist she'd been no slouch either, with the guts and smarts to correct for thin timbre by cultivating her physical and dramatic range—you never knew what would happen when she opened her capacious mouth. Three years and three albums later, singing was her focus, and once again she astonished: rather than imposing a deathly decorum, more opera lessons had bulked up a strapping, skillfully controlled instrument.

Harvey had been in something like seclusion since the late-1993 *4-Track Demos.* Not even the image-hawking young media-suckers who are a fixture of British pop enter the maw of the publicity machine with much grasp of how disorienting it is to have your picture in the papers all the time. But for Harvey it was a special shock. She was never exactly the fresh-faced country hippie you could read all about in 1991 and 1992, when she conquered Britain's pop press with the indie singles "Dress" and

"Sheela-Na-Gig." But since the bohemian-expressionist artistic tradition she comes out of honors the work of art and the true self it theoretically embodies, disdaining all attendant fooforaw, and since most beginners make the same mistake, she was truly surprised to learn that once the music went public it wasn't hers anymore—that people would make of it, and by extension her, damn near anything they wanted. At first, however, the young expressionist just assumed that sincerity was her only option—that her mission was to be as naked in the media as she was in her music. What's harder to accept as a spontaneous gesture is her literal interpretation of this quaint notion—on the back cover of *Dry* and the front cover of *NME* she actually removed her clothes. Raise a fuss? Little old Polly? How could anyone think such a thing?

Nevertheless, I was inclined to trust her need to keep herself to herself. So what if she was capable of provocation? If the simple fact that she's a performer didn't tell you that, a single listen to *4-Track Demos*'s "Reeling"—you know, "Robert De Niro sit on my face"—should have done the trick. It's not a ruse or an inconsistency that she can be both, as she put it, shameless and introverted—it's a tremendously fruitful contradiction. Since not even fifteen-minutes-of-famers like it when sex creeps and crazies ejaculate fan mail, when they can't buy a bottle of water without strangers bothering them, when valued friends and starstruck acquaintances expect time they just don't have anymore, it was only fair for this far more traditional artist to put maximum distance between her work and her private life. So my chief aim was to deepen my understanding of music that's more forbidding than eager young ecstatics assume. But I also hoped to dig a little deeper into the oft-told tale in which Polly, the unassuming daughter of two rustic hippies—a blues concert-producing Dorsetshire sculptress and her less prominently featured quarryman husband—emerges full-blown from the heads of Howlin' Wolf and Captain Beefheart to forge a punk(ish) rock of uniquely raw and/or female sexual power.

I call this standard biography, based mostly on a sheaf of early clips, "The Ballad of PJ Harvey." It's a useful myth, but there's stuff it doesn't account for. Bohemian affinities are always damnably complicated. "I think my dad would protest to being a hippie," Harvey told me, at the same time praising his draftsmanship and noting that there is considerable art to cutting stone. And her mom, who's given up promoting except for an annual do with a bar band she knows, finds much of her paying work doing gravestones and datestones, an exacting and honorable craft that isn't what most people think of as sculpture. Most important, the Harveys weren't as isolated in their tiny village as is usually assumed—they were part of an extensive network of art-loving, music-loving, nature-loving local artists, photographers, and sculptors, many of whom Harvey counts among her dearest friends, and many of whose children are now successful artists themselves. These are political people mostly as regards the hot topic at the pub, and if some are on the left, many aren't. "For instance, my mom and dad are Conservative and loads of other people I know are too. Conservative artists, there you go. A lot of country people are; a lot of farmers are."

Her parents did impart their passion for r&b, and she did learn from the famous blues musicians who stayed at her house. But while it's been said that her chief countervailing musical influence was *Top of the Pops,* nearby Yeovil, a sizable market town of about twenty-five thousand, provided a more significant alternative: the Electric Broom Cupboard, where hard-working student Polly and her teenage friends would hang out and listen to music—"every other week, it was a regular thing, there was really nothing else to do." The bands were mostly U.K. indies, even more purist and insular than their U.S. counterparts, and young Polly joined two of them: John Parish's percussion-oriented quintet Automatic Dlamini, in a two-year hitch that included sleep-on-the-floor tours of Poland, East Germany, and Spain, and Andrew Dickson's Bologna, a Portsmouth Sinfonia-style subprofessional orchestra that included her saxophone, the only instrument she's studied (she now finds its sound "quite nauseating"). She also wrote lots and lots of songs, exactly one of which was featured by each band. And so she started her own—a duo with bassist Steve Vaughan. Drummer Robert Ellis would come soon enough. And so would the cover of *NME.*

Harvey had already set her sights on becoming an artist one way or another, perhaps a sculptor like her mom, except that she would study at a proper art school up in London. (A close-knit family, this—her brother's a quarryman like his dad.) But even as a four-year-old acting out "The Three Bears" she'd had a thing for performing—usually theater, which now that she's a celebrity she'll likely try again. It was only natural that watching the bands at the Electric Broom Cupboard she would repeat to herself the mantra that has animated hundreds of thousands of rock and rollers: "I could do that, I could do that, I could do that." Only because Harvey grew up immersed in music and the very concept of the aesthetic, her ambitions were less idle—and more competitive. "Often I thought the music that you'd go and hear was shallow, was silly. There was no soul to it, there was no feeling to it, and it just made me want to go up to people and shake them."

There was nothing punk about the Electric Broom Cupboard or *Top of the Pops* or her parents' record collection, and only for a change of pace was PJ Harvey the power trio ever all that fast or basic. Its trademark device was the dramatic dynamics of Led Zeppelin's lingua franca, and as Harvey points out, its first singles were well-made *pop* songs, successful ventures in a craft she no longer worries about. On the other hand, the trio's unpolished musicianship and unregenerate ugliness owe indie's DIY ethos big-time. If Harvey snuck in the eccentric harmonies and extra beats you read about occasionally, she was no more aware of it than the country bluesmen who inspire the same kind of loose talk in ethnomusicologists—less, to hear her tell it. Sure she recognizes a chord when she hits on one, but that doesn't mean she knows its name. She insists that what makes her music go is emotion.

It goes without saying that women as strong as Polly Jean Harvey serve as role models whether they like it or not. But it's not just avoidance for her to tell anyone who'll listen that she doesn't conceive the emotion in her music as gender-linked, or to maintain that when she changes the register of her voice it's instinctual: "I like singing low—it can change a song very much, can make things more demanding or more vulnerable or more something. Other songs I want to distort it, and sometimes I want to make it sound thin and tiny." Harvey understands that because she's a woman people will always hear gender in her voice, and acknowledges that at some subconscious level they could be right. But she claims that in the act of creation she's often not even aware of what sex she is. This stubborn denial drives feminists nuts, and since she's equally stubborn about not saying what her lyrics mean, they're sane to feel that way. You don't have to be a riot grrrl to agree that if "Man-Size" ("Let it all, let it all hang out") and "50ft Queenie" ("Bend over Casanova") aren't calculated genderfucks, nothing is.

Of course, her smarter feminist admirers would point out that Harvey's very unawareness is a historical triumph—the ultimate goal, prematurely achieved in a society that's pretty much as sexist as ever. They'd just appreciate some small show of solidarity. But it's not likely they'll get it. Harvey's basic artistic impulses have little room for the social or the collective: "Music is a very spiritual thing. I let it happen and it happens. I can't always make it happen—sometimes it does just come and it kind of dictates how it should be, so I'm not consciously steering it in one way or another."

That the trio Polly Jean called PJ Harvey was no punk band didn't stop Steve Albini from recording it like one, leaving Polly's voice be and milking her guitar for a cold, harsh, galvanized flatness. Yet 1993's *Rid of Me* is certainly her most striking album—every song has an edge that Albini couldn't have dulled if he'd wanted to, which for all his famous perversity he probably didn't. The songs were written after she'd fled London. She'd come up to the city not as an art student, as originally planned, but as a shy, hugely ambitious young rock and roller who thought at first that fame couldn't come "as fast as I wanted." But not only was she hopelessly stressed out by fame itself, she never took to London. Except for her roommate from back home she had few friends, and she still can't quite verbalize why: "I did have one boyfriend that grew up in the city and I just felt that we were so different in our approach to life." The people she met didn't need space the way she did. "They're tougher, they're tougher people. I'm not a very tough person anyway. I *am,* but not in that kind of . . . they're quite mentally strong, tough people." The aggression level made her close up—"that fight or fly thing." She ended up with a near-breakdown and a therapist she still goes up to consult when things get bad—a drastic step (and admission) for any Briton.

So although *Rid of Me* was written in a modest Dorsetshire flat and recorded in a dismal Minneapolis studio, London is what it's about. Somebody else might have done more for the tenderness you can peek glinting through the barbed wire. But spiritually, Albini is perfect for its graphic lust, pain, and hostility. No record I've ever heard, blues included, is so in touch with the carnal details that saturate our experience and memory of erotic love. And don't kid yourself—these songs are never just about sex. The love is unusually desperate, and maybe unusually young as well, although Harvey doesn't seem likely to thicken her skin appreciably anytime soon. But it's definitely what's at stake.

"Do you associate sex with love?" I asked her.

"Yes. Absolutely."

"Always?"

"Always."

From almost anyone else, *To Bring You My Love* would seem erotically charged. "I've lain with the devil," "We lay in it for days," "Blue-eyed girl become blue-eyed whore," "You want to hear my long snake moan," "What a monster/What a night/What a lover/What a fight," "Let me ride/Let me ride/Let me ride"—these are sexual tropes. But up against *Rid of Me* they're mere abstractions, as Harvey acknowledges. "I was just growing up and suddenly this was all new. I'm a bit more old and jaded now—been there, done that—and I'm interested in other things as well, in overviewing life with a capital L."

So two years after her London album, Harvey has generated her Dorsetshire album—the meditations of a febrile recluse who devotes her human energy to "hanging on for grim life to a couple of friends that I care about and worry about losing," whose idea of a good time is to tend the garden at the house she bought for cash (and which she'd like to sell so she can move closer to her parents, now all of half an hour away). But if for almost anybody else life with a capital L is a synonym for pomposity, this is a woman who's taken opera lessons and lived to sing about it. On its own terms—established formally by the voice-dominated *4-Track Demos*—*To Bring You My Love* is a triumph. Say it's about love with a capital L multiplied by sex—or is that spirit?—with a capital S.

These days Harvey looks back on the trio's music and finds its ugliness irrelevant. Like *4-Track Demos, To Bring You My Love* was originally laid down by Harvey alone at home, but most of it was arranged on keyboards, a certain sign of encroaching gentility, and after it was brought into a real studio for production that amounted to many weeks of overdubbing, seven of the ten main guitar parts were ceded to her old pal John Parish or eggheaded *Guitar Player* editor Joe Gore, both future employees, both her superiors in sheer sonic command. It was mixed and coproduced by Flood, who comes via a management company Harvey shares with U2, although she prefers his work with Nick Cave and Nine Inch Nails. Not only did he get her the rich feel and myriad effects suitable to a voice of vastly increased power and emotional detail—a voice now capable of lyricism and kindness and hope as well as new shades of desire and need, sarcasm and vulnerability, indignation and terror—but he saw her through the process. "Flood knows when you have to leave something and try again later, when you need to be shouted at or when you need to be consoled, comforted. He'd be a good therapist."

Let's hope Albini or the Edge or somebody convinces her to return to her unschooled guitar—in the great tradition of John Lennon and Neil Young, she's a player. But although *To Bring You My Love* is as much of a cleanup job as the Replacements' *Tim* or Sonic Youth's *Goo,* in Harvey's case the aural shift matches a shift in vision. And of the three records only *To Bring You My Love* seems likely to stand equal to the earlier work—or to prove its fulfillment.

The title song is definitely for the audience—a metaphorical catalogue of how she suffers for her art that I take at its word. Two or three others deal with the biological consequences of sex—no, not disease, conception, with the mysterious "Down by the Water" legible as a guilty dream about abortion or birth control. But for the most part these are songs of erotic transfiguration that generalize the sometimes lewd, sometimes fantastic physical facts of *Rid of Me* into images of ravishment and rapture. Although the divine manifests itself explicitly only in the climactic "Send His Love to Me" ("I'm begging Jesus please") and "The Dancer" ("Touch the face of the true God"), the pervasive mood is religious. Harvey, who was not brought up in the church, professes herself ignorant of the (always female) medieval mystics whose passions hers so vividly recall. But she reports that she reads the Bible a lot, and cops to "rapture" if not "ravishment" as a key to what she's after. It's almost as if she's crying, "Take me away from all this—from my fear, my insecurity, my discomfort, my body like a stranger, the prisonhouse of my self."

To Bring You My Love is a benchmark work. By demonstrating Harvey's ability to mature, a killer for most young rock and rollers, it marks her graduation from the College of Brilliant Newcomers. She's now a major artist. Where her enduring fondness for Beefheart, Cave, and Tom Waits has been said to reflect a tomboy's attraction to bad-boy attitude, something far more telling distinguishes these bad boys from legions of other guitar-associated male chauvinists—their simultaneous commitment to blues materials and avant-garde ambition. This has consequences not just in sound but in mythic scope—none of them are embarrassed about indulging their romanticism and acting like artists with a capital A. Harvey likewise yokes free-radical bravado to rooted confidence with an equanimity that's startling and irresistible in the age of pomo self-consciousness.

Needless to say, her increased listenability is hardly guaranteed to render her a free and equal salesmate of U2. And even if it does, there's no guarantee she'll stick around to build off her status. She's strong and strong-willed, but in a pop world teeming with sensitive souls, she's also an exceptionally fragile figure—a shameless boho and country girl who's overwhelmed by the attention her shamelessness brings her. So early on I asked what motivated her, finally. Why did she feel compelled to perform?

"It's a need I have to do it. It's the nearest I get to fulfillment, though it's still not enough. That's why you keep chipping away at it a bit more, trying a little bit harder."

"Fulfillment means what?" I asked.

"You know—the hole that's empty—fulfillment means trying to fill it up a little bit."

And although I'm not fragile or unfulfilled, I did know. Anybody who's thought hard about what happens when we make love knows about that hole. As great as it is to come, coming is only a means to an end. Maybe we need God, maybe our mommies. Whatever. So as our conversation came to a close I tried to link fulfillment to rapture. Harvey was talking about her fear of losing control.

"Isn't it true," I asked, "that in certain kinds of good sex that feeling of being in control just becomes irrelevant?"

"That's what I'm led to believe, yes. That's what people say."

"I said irrelevant—I didn't say you lose control. It's like control doesn't mean exactly the same thing anymore. But not for you?"

"No."

"Then would you lose control in that rapture? I do get the feeling that there's a discomfort with the self and that that discomfort is connected to this hole you talk about. Can you see why I think they're connected?"

"Yeah. No, I was about to say . . . you've hit the nail right on the head. But I don't feel I can talk about it any more than that."

1995

Two Backsliders: Iris DeMent / Sam Phillips

It has become suspiciously axiomatic that rock and roll, like so much American popular culture—including a countercultural tradition of communes and charismatics traceable to the Great Awakening—is rooted in evangelical Christianity. The plausible exaggeration that all its rhythms come out of the black church connects neatly to the guilt complexes of such sometime secularists as Little Richard, Sam Cooke, and Al Green. And if for some dumb reason the black church isn't what you mean by evangelical Christianity, white fundamentalism has left its own anguished testament, epitomized by the fierce argument Jerry Lee Lewis had with Sam Phillips before they cut "Great Balls of Fire." Otis Blackwell's title, in case you didn't know, is a Southern expletive that makes light of Pentecostalism's defining moment, when the Holy Ghost manifested himself in "cloven tongues as of fire." But while the argument (which can actually be heard on Jerry Lee's Sun box, where it stands as vivid confirmation of how much rock and roll meant to its creators) was touched off by this blasphemy, Jerry Lee's dread of "worldly music," as he calls it, is more general: "Man, I got the Devil in me! If I didn't have, I'd be a Christian." And there in a nutshell is a psychodrama exploited by play-acting Mr. D.'s from Mick Jagger to Glenn Danzig, a metaphor mined by every rock and roller who's ever reveled in sin or longed for redemption.

Romantics are attracted to this schema for its primal passion, which supposedly suits both fundamentalism and rock and roll. It's red-blooded, it's rip-roaring, it's got a big dick—or a fat, juicy cunt, like one of Polly Harvey's sheela-na-gigs. And I wouldn't deny it its portion of truth. But as someone who spent his youth in an evangelical church, as well as someone whose life was shaped but not saved by rock and roll, I've always felt it was tendentious and condescending. There's nothing remotely monolithic about a born-again Christianity that sheltered urban liberals equate with the right-wing bad guy of the moment. Conceived in populist individualism, it remains radically schismatic, and people move in and out of their faiths all the time, rarely with as much sturm and drang as Jerry Lee Lewis or Al Green. Usually the break is difficult, as is only to be expected, but painless drift is at least as common as chronic torture. And unless you believe music has to be primal and rip-roaring to mean something, these homely facts suit rock and roll just fine.

I started thinking about these things in connection with two artists many would say aren't rock and roll at all—Iris DeMent, who played the Supper Club July 14, and (the other) Sam Phillips, who hit the Bottom Line five nights later. Although the singer-songwriter niche these women share is normally associated with folk music nowadays, that's ridiculous for Phillips and not as sensible as might appear for DeMent, whose artistic affinities are plainly with such Nashville-progressive supporters as Emmylou Harris, Nanci Griffith, and John Prine, and who is nevertheless not marketed as a country artist. It would be silly to make too much of how uncategorizable she is—"folk" is reasonable shorthand. But her work signifies under rock's umbrella, and although the music of the white Pentecostal church remains her deepest inspiration, it's unlikely she'd have ended up where she did without the likes of such childhood favorites as Aretha Franklin and Bob Dylan (both of whom, I can't resist pointing out, are or have been born-again Christians).

I went to see DeMent in the hope that she would exceed my expectations, just as she had when she topped 1992's understandably overrated *Infamous Angel* with a follow-up as consistent as everyone wished the first one was. But I expected nothing. I knew she had no jokes, no line of patter, that she just sat there strumming her guitar and singing her songs, slowly, and one reason I'm not a folkie is that I think this low-rent approach is a misguided way of overcoming what some call alienation—the distance people inevitably feel in a world where everyone's self-expression is out there for everyone else's empathetic delectation. Then she started to perform—I don't know what, it was five songs before I gathered the wit to take notes—and I forgot all that. DeMent is a small, demure woman, but her supposedly "angelic" voice—memorable enough on record, where it resonates with the unaffected twang of country's lost past—is huge live; I wasn't surprised to learn that when she first tried out her songs in her adopted hometown, Kansas City, the open mike was turned down as soon as she let out a note. What's more, she inhabits her material with a concentration that also seems unaffected—she doesn't make with the heart-be-still intensity, just focuses on the details of songs so simple, so literal, so free of irony and metaphor that it's hard to believe they were written in postmodern times. No wonder Harris, Prine, and Griffith are in awe of her—they need something like literature to approximate the directness this high school dropout with a G.E.D. seems to achieve, well, naturally. Authentically. You know.

Of course, art never comes naturally. Attend to DeMent's soft speaking voice and you understand that her penetrating vocals are a miracle of post-Appalachian convention; think about "Sweet Is the Melody" and you realize that she's led off an album called *My Life* with a song about the conscious discipline of sitting around waiting for the song to come. Some of her strongest lyrics are imagined fictions—"Our Town" is nowhere she's ever lived, and the trapped housewife of "Easy's Getting Harder Every Day" doesn't have a husband who quit his job in the fire department to become her road manager. But she is a *relative* natural. One reason her work seems unforced is that she's so new at it; now thirty-three, she didn't start writing till she was twenty-five or tour till she was thirty-one. And another is the particulars of where she comes from, with the Pentecostal faith she grew up with second only to the family that instilled it in her.

Despite talk of DeMent's "hardscrabble" rural roots, she's a California girl—her family emigrated to Orange County from Arkansas when she was three, and the father she adored worked not as a farmer but as a janitor-gardener in a movie museum. But there were plenty of other displaced Southerners around, many of them at a church where worshipers spoke in tongues every Sunday, where celebrants danced with the Holy Spirit, where musical get-togethers with other Pentecostal congregations (some-times even Assemblies of God) were a social staple. Yet though her now deceased dad had put away his fiddle for the Lord, the family was so musical that what they too called "worldly music" was always tolerated, and early on Iris absorbed the albums her older siblings brought home. Some of her thirteen brothers and sisters remained devout, even formed gospel groups; others retained their beliefs but stopped going to church; others left the faith, as she eventually did. For Iris the crux was that she didn't believe all non-Christians were going to hell; she just didn't believe it, that's all. Her falling away was not without conflict, but her parents never rejected her, and she still loves and respects them keenly. She misses her religion sometimes, especially the music. But she doesn't feel any guilt or uncertainty about her decision. Her large and unique talent isn't merely a function of her circum-stances. Nevertheless, it's no conceit to suggest that the spiritual tenor of her kind, humble, clear-sighted songs derives from the fellowship of the church. Her music is her way of maintaining a link to an upbringing she's thankful for.

Sam Phillips is also a California girl—grew up in Glendale, never left L.A. But even among born-again Christians, there are many kinds of California girl. The daughter of an accountant, Phil-lips was raised secular upper-middle class in a rocky marriage that held in the end. The music in her house was Broadway shows and especially jazz; Randy Newman and Joan Armatrading she took out of the library. She came to Jesus via her older brother, who discovered fundamentalism as a boy and stuck with it, which Sam hasn't. Sure she started out as Christian singer-songwriter Leslie Phillips and married countercultural rock Christian T Bone Bur-nett. But she's so sick of disavowing Jerry Falwell that these days she calls herself a "Christian atheist," praises Catholic mystic Thomas Merton, and dedicates "Baby I Can't Please You" to Rush Limbaugh. Struggled for rather than breathed like air, Phillips's Christianity never evinces the bedrock cultural assurance of, say, the Maybelle Carter songs DeMent covers—she's a permanent seeker, and even when she moralizes she does so with a puzzle or a question mark. Nor is she arrogant enough to nail the fine sar-castic dudgeon T Bone could muster at will back when he was hungry. In fact, for all her political dread and literary talk, this Walker Percy fan has written only one indisputably superb lyric—

"Lying," which kicks off 1991's *Cruel Inventions* by warning how hard the truth comes to her.

Since Phillips is billed as a singer-songwriter, this confused many of us. So did her strong, strange vocal attack—Tanya Tucker as detached new waver, say, with Lennonesque pretension where the sexy cornpone used to be. And in my case, so did her admirers' frequent allusions to the Beatles. Maybe I would have gotten the idea sooner if *Cruel Inventions* were half as catchy as the new *Martinis and Bikinis,* but it was only after I heard her roll out the nifty if predictable hooks at the Bottom Line that *Martinis and Bikinis* fell into place for me—as a sharp, solid pop record that fills the same kind of need as Matthew Sweet's *Girlfriend,* which also doesn't get across on words. If Phillips's (and producer Burnett's) *Revolver* extrapolation is less arresting than Sweet's Voidoids homage, it's still fun to sing along with her titles, and Sweet's girl problems merit less sympathy than Phillips's metaphysical riddles. Nevertheless, she does take ordinary tropes very seriously—in the titles of the new album alone I count one rain, one sky, one road, one wheel, one circle (plus the "circle of changes" that hooks "Same Changes"), and two fires (plus the "fire burning underneath" in "Signposts").

Phillips worries about the media, the ecology, the money changers in the temple, her real feelings. At some level she's still combating a spiritually desiccated suburban affluence I've never believed was as uniformly arid as concerned rock and rollers claim it is. Where DeMent's cover from nowhere is Harlan Howard and Bobby Braddock's secularly Christ-centered "God May Forgive You"—"God may forgive you but I won't/Jesus may love you but I don't"—Phillips kicks off her encore with Cole Porter's flirtatiously sinful "My Heart Belongs to Daddy," complete with smoky glances at T Bone, who favored a cheerfully unreadable "Diamonds Are a Girl's Best Friend" himself. And for all that, her troubled faith pervades her music as deeply as DeMent's abandoned faith does hers. A lot of things in this country come out of evangelical Christianity. And if you want an axiom that applies across the board, say they're all as different as they are the same. Just like rock and roll.

1994

On the Real Side: Warren G/Coolio

All hardcore rappers are scared of seeming, not to mention being, soft. So whenever they feel themselves selling out, they prove their manhood by waving a gat or treating some bitch like a ho. The concept behind this posturing is "reality." In the 'hood, we are told, dealing and drive-bys are what's real, with all attempts to transcend or escape doomed—except rapping, that is. Although it helps to meet a few of the hard-working heads of household whose statistically typical lives belie this dogma, a myth beloved of young black losers and the white powermongers who feast on their defeat, you don't have to be from the 'hood to figure out that it's standard rock and roll ideology—young males fending off existential insecurity by declaring their experience the only truth.

Throughout the middle nineties, the big news in hip hop remained that ominous emanation pundits called gangsta rap. Yet what that meant kept getting vaguer as a "movement" whose diversity surpassed all punditry incorporated bootstrap economics, identity politics, the cliquish localism of dozens of music scenes, and the formal hair-splitting endemic to all arcane arts into a fervent but malleable ethos of purity. In the land where rap began, the gangsta menace was perceived primarily as a threat that New York was over—regional first, musical second, philosophical maybe. Nas's austere 1994 *Illmatic* could have come from heaven as far as worried locals were concerned—immersed in hard, uninviting East Coast beats, its grimly articulate lyrics devoid of shoot-'em-up sensationalism. Soon, however, it was supplanted by Staten Island's Wu-Tang Clan, where the dark trip-hop of demon soundscape designer RZA suffused spinoffs by Raekwon *(Only Built for Cuban Linx . . .)* and Genius *(Liquid Swords)*. This was music almost as willful about beats as about the true-crime thrillas it camouflaged so postmodernistically: smart, strong, violent, yet rendered in an aural and verbal code so subcultural no outsider would bother criticizing it—or censoring it.

But in all this music you could discern a post- if not anti-gangsta mood that, although part marketing ploy and part formal inevitability, toned up the credibility, conviction, and beats the gangsta faith imparted. And at the same time, its commercial viability suggested that we'd yet to reach the point where the average adolescent male, ghetto-bound or not, would just as soon smoke your ass as look at you. It became less and less accurate to charge that the records in question advocated violence, although whether they glorified it remained a closer question. The typical hardcore MC depicted street life with cartoonish exaggeration, narrative relish, and a cold eye, only to warn that it led to no good. The pessimism wasn't merely pro forma—criminal-minded rappers evolved from hedonistic egomaniacs into thin-skinned, self-contained, death-obsessed neurotics. Genocidal though the mortality statistics of young black males are, the social usefulness of this development was dubious—if metal and its progeny have taught us anything, it's the limitations of Romantic morbidity. Nevertheless, it was a welcome change.

Local scenes tried to be street, yet the likes of Atlanta's Goodie Mob and Cleveland's Bone-Thugs-n-Harmony figured out ways to downplay the tough talk. In Northern California, good little crews like the Coup and Capital Tax countered Too Short's pimp ethos. And while the industrialists down south made big bucks off the self-righteous sex criminal Tupac and the pent-up yap of the Dogg Pound, they didn't limit their product line to sexual boasts, hedonistic fantasies, and pleasurable grooves for a short-term general audience that liked its young black males funky and nothing else. In fact, two of their greatest successes of the mid nineties were postgangsta with a will, hold the vengeance.

Supposedly discovered along with his partner Snoop Doggy Dogg when his much older half-brother Dr. Dre needed music for a party, Warren G fit right into the strange new stereotype of the cooled-out gatslinger riding phat beats to flavor-of-the-monthdom: calling card on the *Poetic Justice* soundtrack, major move on *Above the Rim*'s cross-promotional device, debut a chart-topper out of the box. By an odd coincidence, the lead cut of *Regulate . . . G Funk Era* told pretty much the same story as the genius opener on *Ahmad,* a conventionally "commercial" SoCal rap album that went nowhere: rapper gets jacked, gets away, gets laid. But in "Freak," Ahmad skedaddles, disappearing down an alley where he finds the very party he's been unable to locate all night, while in "Regulate," Warren is in much deeper trouble until his homeboy Nate Dogg tracks him down, pulls a pistol, and makes "some bodies turn cold." In other words, Ahmad plays a self-sufficient teenager running from trouble, Warren a tough guy backed up by an even tougher subculture. And it's Warren fans believe in.

Warren's credibility comes out in his beats. Ahmad's virtuosic "Freak" was too frantic, too densely joyous, too African in its layered vocal polyrhythms and too American in its breathless forward motion—too pop. Warren, on the other hand, had learned his deep cool from an acknowledged master, even if he's not acknowledged by me. There's no point arguing with *The Chronic,* which established the parameters of an engaging groove more gifted humans are now free to fill out. Although I'm not the only one who thinks the thing builds its myth off a few jeepbeats and a worldwide stupidity epidemic, we're definitely a minority among those who care at all. Still, I must report *Regulate . . . G Funk Era* a more satisfying album in every category except rap style itself. The content-free (when we're lucky) Snoop has no serious competition on either record. But that's not to grant parity to the principals—Dr. Dre's clumsy arrogance is manifest every time he opens his mouth, whereas his half-brother has his own languid, tentative voice, which is completed by Nate Dogg's chilly singsong. With Nate's minitunes backing him up, Warren G's music is catchier, and this may be why I find his grooves more redolent as well. It could also be the unlooped basslines he favors. Or maybe it's just the lifestyle that's projected onto them. *The Chronic*'s brutality is both generalized and unrationalized, boiling down to a collection of empty threats. *Regulate* is more specific—and also more defensive.

In the title tune, Nate Dogg only goes ballistic when Warren's life is in danger, and the next song, "Do You See," explains the choices they've made. "You don't see what I see/Every day as Warren G/You don't hear what I hear," goes the chorus, while the verses describe a scary-warm world: "Another sunny day another bright blue sky/Another day another motherfucker die." Take him at his word and it's not hard to see why he pumps gangsta rap as an improvement over gangsta period—the dopeslinging and gang-banging he says he left behind. The progress is barely incremental—guns show up in five of the twelve songs, not always as defensive weapons, and bitches-and-hoes get verbally smacked on the usual continual basis, with yeast and halitosis added to the ever-lengthening list of their crimes against humanity. But its insinuating music and verbal detail render this world more seductive and more frightening than competing gangsta fantasylands.

Warren G likes to call himself the G-Child, spiritual heir to George Clinton's StarChild, and though the "child" probably just exploits his kid-brother relationship to Dre, the association is eerie. Warren Griffin would have been a very young Clinton fan, just the right age to have gotten the funk as a geepie, which is what the P-Funk mob used to call the subteenaged target market of Bootsy's Rubber Band. The geepies seemed a visionary concept at the time, and they were, but nobody envisioned a world in which these young fun-seekers, although imbued with Bootsy's childlike hope and properly and humorously warned off booze and dope, would have reason to regard Warren G as normal. Puritans and neoconservatives would claim that this was at least partly the fault of the art—that musicians like Clinton allowed these gullible children far too much latitude, seduced them into growing up too soon. I'd counter that their younger siblings' fate proves how quickly artistic hopes get bulldozed under by material realities.

It would be absurd to ask Coolio to lead hip hop out of this wasteland. Not only is he less original and ambitious than such lapsed visionaries as Chuck D and Posdnuos, he's considerably less brilliant than the Long Beach or Staten Island posses. In fact, subbrilliance is one thing the over-thirty with the goofy dreads is selling, probably on the theory that it beats stolen hair dryers. The young Artis Ivey actually did time—for passing a money order he says he didn't take, only that's OK because he was boosting plenty else at the time. MCs like to portray themselves as ex-dealers who haven't so much reformed as landed a better job, but Coolio didn't sell drugs. He bought them—he was a crackhead. In gangsta-inflected hip hop, this is the definition of weak, while work in the crack trade is seen as regrettable but honorable: a man's gotta do what a man's gotta do, and it might as well be a player, a black father, or whatever getting those chumps their merchandise. Coolio is down with the chumps.

From its title on down, 1994's *It Takes a Thief* made a point of Coolio's criminal authenticity. Stix were smoked, suckers dissed, hoes fucked, gats waved, cops shot. But several such moments seemed like sops to his boys, and at its best and best-selling the album also made a point of the hopes and vulnerabilities he was no longer young enough to feel embarrassed about. *Gangsta's Paradise* takes off from there. The irresistible title hit, by Stevie Wonder out of *Dangerous Minds,* is explicitly fictional—"I'm twenty-three now but will I live to see twenty-four?"—and explicitly cautionary. Except for two pro forma guest-G boastfests and an unfortunate skit called "Recoup This"—in which a double platinum rapper murders not only his (black, as it happens) label owner, which isn't funny, but the owner's secretary, which is sadistic—this isn't the music of Everygangsta. It belongs to ordinary "ghetto" dwellers like the scuffling hustler and striving student whose dialogue kicks things off. Having made his fortune reinterpreting Lakeside's "Fantastic Voyage," Coolio boosts more pop-funk hooks than anybody since decaplatinum Hammer—from Stevie, Sly, Smokey, Kool, the Isleys, Billy Paul. And his themes are equally universal.

There's a softly nostalgic song about pitching woo and a sneakily scary song (with a sensationally scary video) about AIDS. There are credibly wacky songs about partying and getting fucked up, credibly sweet songs about parenting and black womanhood. With a major assist from the aforementioned Mr. Paul, there's even a guilty song about adultery. And then there are all the songs about life in the 'hood, which is genially referred to as "this motherfucker." Every one is violent, and not one comes close to glorifying violence. These citizens will tell anybody naive enough to think they're cool how they wish they could escape the trap of the street. They fight the law and the law wins. They fight each other and nobody wins. Their basic advice is to punk out when you're called out. They're totally unheroic. And in this they're far more typical of their homies than the real-siders who populate the self-generated cartoons, monster movies, fantasies, and ambitions of hip hop fans in and out of the inner city and its suburban simulacra.

Coolio isn't a great rapper, although his articulation from within what's almost a slight speech defect does sum up his everyday smarts. Nor is he an original thinker—community leaders and plainer folks have been making these points for years. Purists will label him a sellout, and among too many listeners who I wish knew better, they'll prevail. But they can't destroy his realness, or the deep-not-soft satisfaction he offers fans with an aversion to nonsense. He does an honest job of evoking the streets without romanticizing their excitement or their danger. Next time somebody starts palavering about the gangsta scourge, mention this convicted felon you know. Hum a few bars and you might even shut the fool up for a while.

1993–1994–1995–1996

Art-Rock You Can Dance To: DJ Shadow

Although *Endtroducing . . . DJ Shadow* surfaced as a long-awaited debut album in Great Britain, it's misleading to classify it as U.K. dance music. This isn't because the vinyl junkie formerly known as Josh Davis hails from a college town off I-80 near Sacramento. Nor is it because he so disdains the term "trip hop," which was devised to account for his 1994 single "In/Flux," that he is said to visit record stores and sneak his virtually rap-free product over into the hip hop section. And it isn't to deny that you *can* dance to the thing—people free-form to some strange shit in the post-dance world, and Shadow's funky sound-collages do generate a pulse. You can also trance to it, I guess—it's quiet and midtempo and crucially cushy. But this record wasn't put on earth to work your body or chill your brain. It was designed to reward consciousness. Lured by its smarts and sonic authority, or merely by its rep, the curious listener must follow the musical story line or fall away bewildered. So if you want a tag, and why shouldn't you, bite the bullet and call it art-rock.

Sensing that I admire Shadow, one might expect me immediately to dispel any prog taint by drawing some avant-garde comparison, perhaps to a cut-up specialist like Christian Marclay. Since Shadow concocts all his music from his record collection, his art-rock can't very well involve Wakemanesque shows of manual dexterity, can it? But in fact the lead cut is a dazzlingly virtuosic forty-nine seconds on the wheels of steel that reduces more rap records than I can count into a pronunciamento that Shadow is "your favorite DJ savior." And although he's a noise-friendly postmodernist in good standing, he shares with many postdance artistes a fondness for symphonic gravity and grace. In fact, he deploys several of the compositional tactics that enabled Yes and King Crimson to make such terrible rock and roll—the multipartite structures, the rhythm shifts, the themes and variations. And it isn't just his hipper taste in materials that makes these effects so damned effective.

The up-to-date materials do their part, however. The thirteen tracks, which range from under thirty seconds to over nine minutes, draw on four major sound groups. Most essential are the beats, built from drum phrases and bass lines looped and layered with incomprehensible attention to detail. While the bare melody is generally carried by a naturalistic organ or piano riff, horn or horns, guitar, even sometimes a bass line, at decisive junctures it will turn symphonic—in aura if not fact, since I bet the strings and such come mostly from soundtracks and garage-sale obscurities. For seasoning we get cello, triangle, tympani, backup choruses, a wealth of good old-fashioned scratching, and the miscellaneous audibles DJs love. For purposes of this CD, these avoid machine and nature references to focus on the dregs of recorded sound itself, celebrating and exploiting and joking around with the work of music in the age of electronic reproduction—scratchy surfaces, distorted transmissions, groaning turntables, digital malfunctions. Finally there are the words, which given the lack of lyrics per se are surprisingly prominent. Sometimes unrecognizable raps or songs make brief appearances—is that Kevin Coyne moaning about rain in the middle background of "Changeling" (and does his lawyer pay finder's fees)? But a much bigger role is played by spoken-word swatches from the vinyl beyond, appropriated with a cockeyed assurance that is at once definitive and impossible to pin down.

If the music that tells Shadow's stories seems to belong here, the voices remind us that this is an illusion—although they're good American voices, most of them are clearly from another era and cultural place. A drummer introduces cut two with words that could be Shadow's own: "From listening to records I just knew what to do; I mainly taught myself." Only he's impossibly straight- and slick-sounding, and Shadow caricatures the chuckle at the end of his little speech with a loop. And what about the calmly lascivious hayseed who provides the voice-over on the untitled funk fragment that goes in its entirety: "Maureen's got five sisters. They all got ass. One of 'em has eyes as big as Jolly Ranchers. Beautiful girl, she's a beautiful girl"? What the hell is *that,* you wonder. What does "eyes as big as Jolly Ranchers" even mean? For that matter, what does the whole track mean? Why is it here? Yet the guy and his trope are both so paradigmatic, so weirdly normal, that after three or four plays you find yourself greeting it as warmly as the hook of "It Takes Two."

But since one of the things that makes *Endtroducing* an art-rock record is its attention to placement, there's no knowing whether the same bit would be as beguiling somewhere else. Its organic absurdism follows a selection from Shadow's famous "What Does Your Soul Look Like?," and right afterwards comes the lyrical first theme of the very multipartite "Stem / Long Stem," picked reflectively on a guitar or a keyb in drag. Heightened by the contrast, the theme's yearning for the good and the beautiful is then accented with a triangle—only to be bombarded a minute later by a drum-machine chain explosion, orchestrated some, left to coexist with more drum chaos, interrupted by a sub-Lenny Bruce monologue about getting locked up in Long Beach (I now smack my lips over the strange phrase "while I'm awaiting to be heard on my traffic offenses"), then developed yet again. At 7:44, a nine-second pause precedes a piano coda that you keep waiting to evolve into the theme and never does. And I'm leaving stuff out. And that's just one track.

What I'm describing is a highly potent species of musical structure. If *In the Court of the Crimson King,* let us say, exploited a similar stratagem, its materials were too broad or pretentious for me to get that far—because for me, these effects and the feelings they produce, while now permanently available, didn't kick in until I first acclimated myself and then sat there and listened. Nor do Shadow's art-rock affinities stop there, because his structures work to place the musical weight on the least funky, most symphonic elements—the very melodies and textures that sound so ostentatious when emulated by progs and so schlocky when embraced by fellow romantics in the postdance jungle. The beats stir up ferment, the words bear meanings glimpsed but not grasped, and then the melodic actors—not just strings, but lush fake-orchestral synth chords, classical piano ostinatos, rock guitar hooks, soul riffs, fuzak tunelets, a vamp I could swear was lifted from Pharoah Sanders or John Coltrane—proffer the same home-sweet-home reassurance that the return to the tonic is supposed to provide in sonata-allegro procedure. All that's missing, and it's everything, is that dead-certain pall of nineteenth-century closure.

What's most impressive, perhaps, is that Shadow didn't compose these melodies, and that to call them "found" would be too easy—"discovered," maybe, although it's more accurate to say they've been accessed and reimagined. Because they're so anonymous, they carry none of the wink-nudge intertextual referentiality of quoted bricolage, and though they're nothing special to start with most of the time, they now give off the kind of direct aesthetic emotion that's so hard to come by in this hyperconscious cultural era—an emotion you'd hardly expect to arise in such a formally pomo context. It's plain enough that Shadow loves the disconcerting beats and impolite sounds of hip hop and is no stranger to other ways of coping with musical alienation. But it's just as plain that in his encyclopedic store of obscurities he recognized dreams and aspirations from another cultural place, dreams that want nothing to do with alienation except to vanquish it. I have no idea whether his ability to realize these dreams is a promise of cultural health or a mark of individual genius. But if it doesn't make Rick Wakeman jealous as hell, he's even dumber than I think he is.

1996

Honk if You Love Honking: James Carter

When all else fails, there is always jazz.

When guitar bands grind down ruts they call four-lanes, when black pop runs on concept, when dance music melds functionalism and obscurantism into "dance" music, when bohemians play trivial pursuit, when Sweden falls as flat as Polynesia falls as flat as Benin, when the rock and roll pickings are too damn thin, America's other great vernacular music is waiting over in the next bin. So even if you suspect jazz greatness of upscale postvernacularity, make that slight adjustment and sink your ears into some unplumbed genius—Monk or Coltrane or Armstrong or Parker if you're a novice, one of the hundreds of superb lesser voices if you've mastered the basics. Me, I spin lots more jazz than I have the chops to write about, and spent my formative live music years around jazz clubs. Eric Dolphy blew me into one of the transcendent experiences of my life when he joined Coltrane at the Village Gate on Labor Day of 1962. Yet I'd never heard most of the stuff on Prestige's nine-CD Dolphy box—Oliver Nelson albums, are you kidding? So let me tell ya—it's smokin'.

But it's also stuck in a noble past inextricable from the nagging sense that the jazz tradition is as closed as that of Europe's self-appointed classics. To us outsiders, it sounds like both sides in the Lincoln Center controversy are wronger than right—the neoclassicists incorrigibly straitlaced, the avant-gardists eminently full of shit. And though I'm aware of the major-label reinvestment and thriving clubs, the proof hasn't jumped out at us record addicts. After getting the word on Joshua Redman, for instance, I started playing his poll-topping 1993 *Wish* at jazz moments, which in my house means dinner and bedtime. But it proved way too polite to impose its solid enjoyability on my leisure, or lure me out to see him live. Since I am reliably informed that the Harvard summa's plummy tone and peachy technique serve an abiding soulfulness, I regret this. I wouldn't have thought about it twice, however, if all four of James Carter's albums hadn't jumped me good.

Like Redman, Carter is twenty-seven, and like Redman he's beyond feuds—as is often noted, he's a protege of both Lester Bowie and Wynton Marsalis, which is like studying with Cage and Karajan, or DJing for P.M. Dawn and KRS-One. Unlike Dewey's son Joshua, however, Carter—the unretiring, adored-I-bet youngest of five kids, with one brother who clocked dollars with P-Funk and another who sang r&b, a mom who played piano and violin and a dad who played radio—never went to college. Having acquired his first horn at eleven (he knows the date) and toured with Wynton while still in high school, the prodigy decided to forget Berklee at a 1988 New York cutting session where he couldn't tell when one schooled young saxman stopped and the next began without looking. This is a grave charge. Collective creation would be everything in jazz if only radical individualism weren't also everything, and countless players have literally made their names by forging a personal sound any fan can recognize before the chorus is over. No doubt adepts can ID Joshua Redman this way. But since I'm not an adept, I'm impressed that I'd know Carter's voice anywhere.

The man has recorded on six different horns. He wouldn't be his protean self if he just played tenor. But tenor is where he lives, and I can't recall a single major jazzman whose natural tone on Ben Webster's and Coleman Hawkins's and Lester Young's and John Coltrane's axe is so brash, harsh, impolite—even the sexy ballads of 1995's *The Real Quietstorm* are tough as alligator hide. This sound is nasty plus. Free jazz rebels Pharoah Sanders and Archie Shepp come near it, but the true source is their half-acknowledged forebears, low-class r&b honkers like Willis Jackson and Red Prysock. Carter loves to honk. Only he can honk *anything*—any rhythm, any phrase, any change, any noise, any era. A child of tha noize, he exploits feedback and has a trick of audibly snapping off a phrase by snatching the horn from his mouth. He can even soften his edge for a bar or a chorus or a tune or, who knows, a phase of his career. But for now nasty sound plus unbounded stylistic range are enough to put his brand on DIW's *JC on the Set* and *Jurassic Classics* and Atlantic's *The Real Quietstorm* and *Conversin' With the Elders*.

The signature carries the DIW albums, the first comprising three originals and five covers, the follow-up seven tradition-respecting homages to Monk, Rollins, and comparable titans. Both feature Carter's regular quartet—homeboys Jaribu Shahid on bass and Tani Tabbal on drums, Detroiter and Berklee grad Craig Taborn on piano. But the Atlantics' conceptual smarts beef up what I pray will prove his crossover legibility. *Quietstorm*'s cock-sure boudoirisms reveal Grover Washington Jr. to be almost as big a liar as Dave Koz. And the nine new *hommages* on *Conversin'* are duets that define Carter's own tradition rather than bowing to anybody else's. In addition to two features for eighty-one-year-old Kansas City monarch Buddy Tate, who inspired the project, these include a poky march by the infamously unswinging Anthony Braxton and an opener and closer from Lester Bowie of the challenged chops—an infectiously ragtag reggae that sounds like somebody's been listening to the Skatalites and an equally tuneful and hilarious waltz that breaks into fractured bebop soon enough. Like Bowie except he plays better, Carter has a big sense of humor—his unending virtuosity is so delighted with itself it makes you laugh out loud. The main reason he doesn't laugh himself is that his mouth is full.

In short, for all his love of history and worries that jazz's brothel roots demean its innate spirituality, Carter is an upstart with pop instincts and avant-garde leanings, genuinely respectful yet also genuinely arrogant. Inevitably, his facility is resented. He's been accused both of faking it, as if the way he occasionally welds changes to noize is a defeat rather than an embrace, and of lacking soul, which with players this amazing is usually code for showing off—and showing up your elders. But while he hasn't recorded enough originals or made a convincing case for his homeboy rhythm section, he's certain to outlast the backbiting. Since he comes by his ecumenicism more organically than an earlier gen-eration of all-embracers that encompasses Arthur Blythe, Henry Threadgill, and crucial predecessor David Murray—since he makes music rather than statements—it's even conceivable he could change the tradition permanently while teaching ignoramuses to like it. When Steve Miller compares himself to Picasso, you want to pin the asshole's ears to his asshole. When Carter compares himself to Mozart, you want to tell him not so loud.

Joining the world-saxophone-sextet-plus-drummer of Qwest's fine eponymous *SaxEmble* album at Sweet Basil, Carter blasted away my fears of one-for-all musical democracy instantaneously. This guy was the S*T*A*R, nobody in the room thought different. Power suit and all, he was also the most shameless showboat in a notably ebullient ensemble, and he wrecked his reeds spectacularly for major minutes. Last Tuesday's opening set at the Vanguard began when SaxEmble's wild, solid Alex Harding, guesting on baritone, boosted Carter toward a tremendous solo that morphed from bebop change-running into pure honk, with a brief return to the "I've Got You Under My Skin" theme that merely opened the gates to yet another guttural flag-waving session. But the set peaked there: a comical double-baritone workout on the Braxton march could have been ten minutes shorter, and much as I love speed I was disappointed when Tate's "Blue Creek" didn't end up a ballad.

By early Friday, with Harding relegated to late shows, the extended parallel solo was less awesome, yet he played the set of my dreams—only as a speed lover, I hadn't dreamed it. I loved the way Carter snuck up alongside a staccato modal head and flattened each note against an imaginary wall, the way the tender clarinet of this "Blue Creek" changed into something more saxlike and out. And I was transported when he topped himself with another long ballad, the tone of his tenor achingly mellow for once, only occasionally he'd spit on it or rough it up. Was he mining the changes throughout? Probably, but who cared? This was the enthralling modulation of mood and incident that jazz storytelling is supposed to be about. Maybe he cheated, maybe he didn't. Either way he won, and so did everyone with the soul to hear him. I know jazz clubs are a little upscale. But for this guy you can dig into your wallet and swallow your pride.

1996

Unlikely Samba: Arto Lindsay

I knew Arto Lindsay years before he started DNA—as a gawky, high-foreheaded gofer from the *Voice* display department with nerd glasses and a beatnik name. Arto was a wonderfully eager kid, always up in edit talking art with anyone who'd listen, and I was disappointed the first time I saw him wring the neck of an untuned guitar, gurgling garbled wordbursts while fledgling drummer Ikue Mori banged a funereal quick-step and demented organist Robin Crutchfield added something like music. To me it was obvious that what was instantly dubbed no wave took DIY way too far, ignoring punk's crucial pop component in kneejerk embrace of arty edgism. But in DNA's case I was wrong.

It was my wife who pointed out how funny Arto was, how individual, how rhythmic—how much life he had compared to Mars, Lydia Lunch, or even James Chance, the other postpunk extremists on Brian Eno's 1978 *No New York* showcase. His depressive compatriots' psychological compulsion was Arto's formal imperative—the next punk step, downtown style. When DNA demolished rock's sonic boundaries, they left bricks, not rubble, and today their twenty-minute recorded legacy sounds like anchovy buttah as painterly bassist Tim Wright replaces Crutchfield and Arto learns to articulate the apparently aleatory atonalities of his ten-dollar ax. By 1979 he was also shredding the Lounge Lizards' "fake jazz" with impishly timed skronk bombs. And then, in the early eighties, as shyly and startlingly as a frog kissed by a sex therapist, the avant-garde supernerd emerged at occasional downtown gigs as a soft, sensuous, endearingly hesitant samba crooner—the weirdo as seducer, every bohemian's secret fantasy.

Although it is often noted that Lindsay was raised by missionaries in Brazil, his background is more liberal and cosmopolitan than that implies. His Southern Presbyterian father—a humanitarian teacher, not a soul-scarfing preacher—sent Arto to high school in the big port city of Recife, where he sang in a rock band while absorbing Hendrix and the Velvets, liberation theology and LSD; the Florida church school he settled for after Harvard and Swarthmore spurned his SATs was a permissive, core-curriculum kind of place where he met Mars. So at 44, he's been on his boho course for three decades. And although it was a jolt when the geek who invented horrible noise turned to tropical kitsch, his samba tendency runs just as deep. Unlike so many CBGBites, he and his friends listened omnivorously, and he started making me Caetano Veloso tapes around 1980. So as the other no wavers sank into nothingness or tripped over their own two badfeet, Lindsay explored a funky option that came naturally. A Recife hippie when Brazil's military government began the musical crackdown that would force Veloso and Gilberto Gil into exile, he had enjoyed a rich rhythmic education, and because he was fully bilingual, he could directly apprehend what has long been the world's most aestheticized pop tradition.

For such a nerd, Lindsay is good with people—not some conniving eye-contact specialist, just an amiably relentless guy whose quick-witted enthusiasms invite cooperation. He's never lost his interest in weirdness, even ran the Kitchen for a year, and in the eighties his unschooled guitar was in demand all over downtown as he radiated out from the overlapping John Lurie, Anton Fier, John Zorn, and Kip Hanrahan circles to enterprising jazz and funk guys as well as Cuban drummers who dug his shit and Brazilian drummers whose shit he dug. All these sounds fed directly or indirectly into the prescient 1984 *Envy* (long out of print on Editions EG), credited to Arto Lindsay/Ambitious Lovers and introducing keyb genie Peter Scherer, who wrote most of the music and would coauthor 1988's glorious *Greed* and 1991's lackluster *Lust* (both on Virgin). Droll, lyrical, jumped up with extravagant electronic and Brazilian percussion and noise effects, *Greed* is the pop-funk triumph, but there's an even rarer delight in the way the disjunct *Envy* demands and rewards the on-site user assembly of its clashing parts—tribalized no wave ululation, skronk refracting into rhythm, percussion from a rain-forest junkyard, Jesus-he's-singing-in-Portuguese, eighties funk lite like the thematic "Let's Be Adult," protoloungecore, protojungle. Rather than effecting a smooth fusion that could only deracinate all these things he loves, Lindsay simply unites them under the rubric of his unlikely self.

By the nineties, he wasn't merely an art star in Europe and Japan, where he tours annually—he was a player in Brazil, where he has produced records for Veloso, Marisa Monte, David Byrne, and many others. When Ryuichi Sakamoto made his proposition, however, Lindsay felt a little reticent. Although he long ago vowed to guard his virginity by never actually learning guitar—"to let it grow on its own and not weed it"—his singing he nurtures. He even took classes with Laurie Anderson's voice teacher, intense hours "like nothing you've ever experienced outside of fucking or being on stage." But if only because he believes that the road to good singing leads straight through embarrassment, in the end he consented to meet his heroes on their own turf by recording an album of original bossa novas, in English and Portuguese, for Sakamoto's Japanese label, ultimately picked up by Bar/None.

Shot through with the delicate picking and chromatic chords of Brazilian guitarist Vinicius Cantuária, *O Corpo Sutil/The Subtle Body* is quiet and traditional-sounding—a formal translation of what samba means to Lusophones like Lindsay, for whom it's a music not just of entrancing groove but of world-class poetry. Without question Brazilian pop is as savory as its vast coterie claims, but those who don't understand the words have no reason to envy the patina of sophistication to which it too readily reduces without them. Songs as literate as *O Corpo Sutil*'s "Child Prodigy," in which Lindsay spins off verbal riffs on the inner life of a two-year-old to a Veloso melody so gorgeously conceived and orchestrated that many a general would bring him up on charges of divine ambition, add supple backbone to bossa nova's romanticism—its aura of cultivated magic and delicate eroticism, sunstruck regret and grateful repose.

Typically, however, Lindsay wasn't content with an *hom-mage,* and having gotten up his nerve, he edged further out. On *Mundo Civilizado,* no English translation required, he decided, "Let's put some beats on this shit"—electro from Mutamassik and DJ Spooky, and surdo, caixas, bacurinha, djembe, timbau, and other Bahia caboodle from some kids he borrowed off Carlinhos Brown. He also risked a couple of covers all too close to his safe American home, by singers a truly gawky fellow might find over-awing: Al Green's "Simply Beautiful" and Prince's "Erotic City." These could be clumsy travesties, pallid failures, or "ironic" self-deceptions, but they're not. They're simply beautiful, cures for skepticism—the Green as straight as downtown gets, Worrell-Ribot-Gibbs-Bowne-surdo paying organ-quintet respects to a warmly desperate Arto, the Prince bedizened with a hothouse of drum breaks as Arto states his cool control. Throughout the album, culture-as-nature coexists with techno-as-nature, creating an atmosphere that enhances Lindsay's sometimes erotic, some-times metaphysical imagery. Maybe you can do without verse like "Terrifying face of pleasure in the painting/Red palms and soles stand out against blue skin," or "To lay claim to/Declare a twin-ship with/By declaring to assume/And donning to become/(Dis-appear like bubbles on a tongue.)" But the intricately unassuming lyricism of Lindsay's vocals and music makes you want to slip into those words like a lover's kimono. This must be what my Luso-phone friends are always raving about.

Lindsay keeps busy. He's working on a studio in Bahia that can capture the long soundwaves of the enormous new percussion ensembles springing up there, one of the many world subsets he says is now reconfiguring drum 'n' bass live. Gramavision has just released a surprisingly useful remix comp in which his New York illbient buddies turn *Mundo Civilizado* into *Hyper Civilizado.* A third samba album is in the can, more percussive and more sophisticated all at once if the rough mixes hold. And in the fall he'll tour not just Europe and Japan but Brazil and, for Bar/None, the U.S. of A.—bicoastally, anyway. For practice he and Cantuária and *Mundo* coproducer Andrés Levin visited the Fez's citadel of avant-gentility June 6, starting with that twinship song, a lovely samba entitled "Titled." Just before the last verse he grabbed his unused guitar and skronked us good. This set the tone. Mostly he stuck to poetry—no Prince or Al, sad to say. But every once in a while he'd unloose some horrible noise—noise as strum, noise as slide, noise as Jimmy Nolen scratch. And for a finale he launched a full-bore version of "Egomaniac's Kiss," which he'd first gurgled with DNA so many years ago.

1997

Stereolad: Pavement

With Nirvana a skyrocket and Sonic Youth decade-bridging fore-bears like Neil Young before them, Pavement stands as the finest rock band of the nineties—by critical acclamation. And if you think the codicil turns superlative to faint praise, note that it's been a while since Pavement's art project was the province of a coterie. Internet-advertised shows at NYU, CBGB, and Westbeth last week sold out post-haste, and although the student-discount crowd elicited a certain uncertainty the first night, the band engaged nevertheless, then revved into loud, friendly, focused spontaneity for the CB's faithful one night later. While New York is a stronghold, these faithful are everywhere Matador records are sold. Let's suppose half the two hundred thousand or so consumers who purchased 1994's *Crooked Rain, Crooked Rain* were converted by its hoarse whines, calculated shows of feeling, jokes without punch lines, ramshackle structures, purloined riffs, exploding minimelodies, and tangy shreds of guitar. That's zip by the standards of *Seinfeld* or Smashing Pumpkins. But it's a great many by the standards of mandarin surrealist John Ashbery, who supposedly inspired the lyrics of the new *Brighten the Corners,* or of archminimalist Richard Tuttle, who supposedly gave heart to Whitney guard and Pavement main man Stephen Malkmus: "When we saw pieces of string on the ground, we knew we could do *something.*"

Instigated circa 1989 by Malkmus and second banana Scott

Kannberg in a Stockton, California, that could have been any American upper-middle-class nowhere, Pavement surfaced as the archetypal four-track-in-the-bedroom band, although in fact they began recording in the garage studio of a mad, since-discarded older drummer. Epitomizing Amerindie's closet-/pseudo-/semi-/student-intellectual collector strain the way Nirvana did its rowdy, unkempt, street-poet, "grungy" garage / bar ethos, they had a bead on their unpopulist mission well before anyone suspected that Nirvana was destined to make all such concepts seem elitist. Since Malkmus plainly has as much talent if not genius as Kurt Cobain, with whom he shares the essential pomo gift for cramming pleasurable music with punishing, liberating quantities of dissonance and dissatisfaction, he's lived in the shadow of Nirvana-sized comparisons ever since. Would he accomplish fate? Change the world? Make Gerard Cosloy a million bucks? Malkmus is of two or more minds about these questions, as he is about most things—pretty firm about disliking "rock stars," he's even firmer about wanting his creative output remembered. But hell, so is John Ashbery.

I've never seen stardom in Malkmus's horoscope myself. Granted, I once felt the same about David Byrne, but those doubts looked naively cynical as of *Remain in Light,* after four albums and five years. With Pavement even further down the road, I stand firm. *Brighten the Corners* will probably correct the sales swoon of 1995's perversely eclectic *Wowee Zowee,* and I'd be gratified if it sailed past *Crooked Rain* on the strength of steady roadwork, pre-production rehearsal, and live recording—the kind of homely miracle that's never come naturally to a far-flung unit whose replacement wildman, drummer-keybist Bob Nastanovich, is a Kentuckian who now owns his own racehorse. But the historical moment for a pop breakthrough has passed them by. They could certainly become a much bigger cult rumor than they already are if they put their backs into it, although it's hard to imagine them slogging to mythos in a tour van the way Sonic Youth did in the late eighties. This is not a band with a metaphorical affinity for broad backs, or broad mythos either. Given the makeup of the American Academy of Arts and Sciences, the John Ashbery route is beyond their means as well. They're smarty-pants and there's nothing they can do about it.

As they continue to map their alternative course, I discern steadier progress than most of the band's critic-fans, who adored the first two albums but had their collective doubts about *Wowee Zowee.* For me it's the 1992 debut *Slanted and Enchanted* that's worn worst—sonically thin, caught up in the lo-fi that they're sometimes credited with or blamed for and that Malkmus now reports he's outgrown, pretty great anyway. *Crooked Rain* smooths out and beefs up its postpunk tunecraft, giving the guys who once said they wanted to popularize noise the way Stocktonite Dave Brubeck had popularized jazz a chance to camouflage their precious detritus in artful song and songful flow. In contrast, *Wowee Zowee*'s eighteen-cut assortment was both slowed down and abruptly segued, and while Pavement was never as speed-driven as all that abrasiveness led some to believe, a quarter-tab of acid (you know, just enough to make you sit there and watch the streetlight refract) wasn't most people's idea of a good time. I demurred: although I like an organic whole as much as the next fellow, I found *Wowee Zowee*'s disoriented lyricism uncommonly beautiful. And just like *Crooked Rain,* the shorter, clearer, tighter *Brighten the Corners* fashions a convenient carrying case for its predecessor's unruly attractions.

Because *Brighten the Corners* is markedly less woozy than *Wowee Zowee,* its rockin' moments—especially the indelible choruses of "Stereo," "Embassy Row," and Kannberg's two otherwise low-profile originals—stand out. But although I too once looked to Pavement for rock and roll future, I'm now convinced that Malkmus's poetic soul is better suited to quasipsychedelic weirdness than what-goes-on raveup—that he's better off undergirding melody with noize than helping the cacophony go down. *Brighten the Corners* is hardly a ballad record; when Malkmus waxes lyrical, he doesn't serenade—he singsongs, converses, muses, talks in the shower. But if what Pavement's name signifies, as Matador's Cosloy put it back when they were on Drag City, is "full of rock," these pebbles and gems and shale and scree and phenocrysts are porous as pumice. Mark Ibold's bass is basically McCartneyesque, though damned if I can find that "Type Slowly" hook on *Abbey Road,* and for all I know Malkmus, as dedicated a recycler of found materials as fellow I-5'er DJ Shadow, has been trolling for tunelets on Three Dog Night LPs. Sure there's ugly guitar; sure lines of sound criss-cross at crazy angles. But from the artificial woodwinds to the bicycle bell, this music is not hard—which from the artificial woodwinds to the bicycle bell doesn't make it commercial either.

Malkmus has warmed up his detached, weedy vocal affect, and were he to fall in love with sex like Byrne before him it's possible to imagine him as another winning soul nerd. Even while he indulges the romantic skittishness he shares with so many lesser fanboys, the tentative sweetness of his vocals undercuts his famous irony with a kindness lesser fanboys pretend isn't there. But the four-track-in-the-bedroom aesthetic has always democratized singing too sweepingly for the populace, and Malkmus will never get airplay until he settles for stupider jokes or can imagine performing, as he once put it with a slight shudder, "a heartbreakingly personal song over and over a hundred times on the road." The new album begins with an art boast that reminded me of "Overnight Sensation (Hit Record)" on the Raspberries' *Starting Over*, cut back in 1974, before Amerindie even existed. Eric Carmen wanted not money, not fame, just, well, communication: "a big hit record / One that everybody's got to know." What has Malkmus excited is significantly less public: "Oh! Listen to me! I'm on the stereo! Stereo!"

That's one of many suggestive tropes proffered by lyrics that are certainly less thought through than good John Ashbery (who for his part has never been able to keep a band together), but add incidental diversion, enveloping atmosphere, decisive color, and crucial identifying detail. Skeptics may cite this typically alt-indie disregard for the verbal as crippling, but in a time when dance music and black pop are even more impatient with lyrical craft, it's willful to pigeonhole it as collegiate artiness. Anyway, the words skillfully convey what the group is driving at. As Malkmus pushes thirty, his muso references are subsumed by images of domesticity and maturity that from perfect roasts to colonized wrath are wryly affectionate, not satiric—perfect for a skittish guy who's watched his supporting cast put their royalties into houses, horses, and, most threateningly, matrimony. He's only an upper-middle-class smarty-pants, an elitist by temperament who's enlightened enough to resist it. But he's well on his way to the cooperative construction of a body of work—an oeuvre, as they say in the academy—that means to endure in a previously uncharted cultural space somewhere this side of coterie. If he succeeds, that will be world-changing enough.

1997

Grrrowing Grrrls: Sleater-Kinney

As a media event, riot grrrl was a classic skyrocket, hooked on a brand name so catchy it could have sold bikinis to Eskimos. First no one but its tiny constituency and a very few interested observers knew it existed. Then, whoosh, there were grrrls everywhere, even to the top TV show in the land. And now the movement is missing and presumed passé.

To a limited extent, this reflects the reluctance of the trademark originators to distinguish between righteous rhetoric and righteous music—to admit how often the useful theory that anyone can make great rock and roll reduces in practice to automatic hardcore, inept pop, and posturing to the converted. You'd never have known to read the supportive accounts of likable efforts by, to choose (relatively) well-known bands I've put time into, Slant 6 or Tribe 8 or Team Dresch or Bratmobile or Huggy Bear, how incomplete their albums were in the end, and when boosterism masquerades as criticism, outside credibility fades fast. But as with feminism itself, most of riot grrrl's rapid disregard was a simple function of male chauvinist piggery, with a dollop of unsisterly factionalism thrown in—a fear of antimale confrontation masquerading as the canard that ideology is incompatible with formal impact or expressive truth. Which is why it's so encouraging that no fewer than four of the key riot grrrl bands have ignored their supposed spiritual demise and put out new records this spring—and that not one betrays complacency, stasis, or bad nerves.

Queercore stalwarts Tribe 8 and Team Dresch may never deliver musically, but second time out Lynn Breedlove is aiming her vocals and Donna Dresch's mates are deploying their guitars like a team. As for Kathleen Hanna's revolutionary cell, Bikini Kill has followed the trajectory of so much good punk before it and gone pop, a little.

The holy quest for good punk is finally why any rock and roller should cheer riot grrrl on. What makes punk so quintessential isn't just its formal strictures and saturation guitar. By definition, it's a music of becoming—simple enough to encourage half-formed human beings to create themselves, accessible enough to allow bystanders to witness the miracle, which has been a rock and roll thrill since young Elvis P. sang "That's All Right" for his mama. And no riot grrrl has generated this thrill with anything approaching the musical instincts or emotional breadth of Corin Tucker. Now twenty-three, Tucker first surfaced in Heavens to Betsy, a duo with drummer-bassist Tracy Sawyer that put out the usual singles and compilation cuts and an enduring Kill Rock Stars album called *Calculated.* Her current and I hope future band is Sleater-Kinney, a trio named for an intersection near Olympia's Evergreen College, where Tucker graduated with one of those vague TV-film-media degrees and twenty-one-year-old bandmate Carrie Brownstein hopes to get her B.A. in sociolinguistics in 1997.

Structurally, Brownstein is an equal partner. Like Tucker, she sings, plays guitar, and collaborates on the songs; on Chainsaw's ten-song 1995 *Sleater-Kinney,* her lyrics are if anything more wrenching than Tucker's. And without question Sleater-Kinney is the richer band—on both of their excellent collections, especially the inexorably catchy new *Call the Doctor,* the second guitar guarantees that there's more going on. Nevertheless, Sleater-Kinney sounds very much like Heavens to Betsy and not much like Excuse 17, where Brownstein and Becca Albee started off plashing in childish Tiger Trap clatter before revving up to a yell on Kill Rock Stars's 1995 *Such Friends Are Dangerous.*

The obvious reason Tucker dominates the band is her voice. Neither riot grrrl proper nor its Hole/L7 correlative is devoid of commanding singers (Hanna, for one), but the sensibility doesn't attract belters or thrushes, and instruments as individual as Tucker's are rare anywhere. Its high, almost girlish register doesn't diminish its strength, and its slight natural vibrato deepens the penetration of an attack that's at once meditative and abandoned—you can just see Tucker closing her eyes and throwing back her head as she gets into the lyric, although that's not what she actually does on stage, where she's playful and self-possessed.

Since the most insuperable barrier between what we'll call postalternative and what we'll call the mass audience is said audience's weakness for big voices and the big emotions they share with poor stunted us, Tucker's physical gift could constitute a major professional advantage if she chose to channel it properly. But of course she doesn't. Instead she limns her alienation, she complains bitterly about socialization and compromise, she equates stardom with sexual victimization, she declares herself unmoved or worse by several penises, she screams, she goes off. Although she's never stupid she's rarely deep—in a contrary mood I might nominate *Calculated*'s "Waitress Hell" as her most incisive moment. But ideas aren't the point. In a music of becoming, Tucker's albums enact a coming-of-age-in-progress that's conveyed by the conviction in her singing rather than the acuteness of an analysis millions of young women have already stumbled toward. From a parental perspective like mine the effect is intense, touching, an up. For her fans and peers I bet it feels like life itself.

Yet when Brownstein—who makes a virtue of her milder pipes on relationship songs that close the two Sleater-Kinney CDs vulnerably, humanly, specifically—is at the mike, nobody's going to think she's rejoined Excuse 17, because Sleater-Kinney's music, like Heavens to Betsy's before it, is also its own. You know how riffs are—some got 'em, most don't. Tucker and Brownstein got 'em; like the good rock and rollers they are, they're in it for the guitars, which take over in virtual call-and-response with verses and sometimes lines. The aesthetic isn't quite elegant, but it's close enough—formally canny, minimalist in its own way, original without self-indulgence, often fairly fast but never speedy, a punk-informed variant sure enough of where it's headed that it can take its time getting there. Once it builds a little live, it surges and calms itself and surges again, the way sex does sometimes when it's fighting an undertow of insecurity or fatigue. This is music that waits confidently for you to come back to it. It's also music with growing room.

As we drove down to Bryn Mawr last Saturday to check out

the band before their first New York appearances, photographer Bob Berg asked casually whether Sleater-Kinney was a lesbian band, as their publicist had indicated, and I realized I'd never thought to wonder myself—not because I'm too sophisticated to suffer curiosity about women's private affairs, but because the songs rendered the question irrelevant. Both Tucker and Brownstein sing songs about bad sex with guys and bad relationships with anyone—boys, parents, lovers, friends, many of them apply across the board. There's no reason in theory why hitting on transvestites or using the wrong bathroom, to choose two topics from Tribe 8's *Snarkism,* might not come to seem as universal as sniffing glue or taking the bus to the beach once did, but Tucker especially has the pop gift for generalization—for lyrics that bear upon a range of recognizable emotional experiences rather than pinning one down. When I arrived I discovered that they'd sanely decided to replace pen-pal-turned-drummer Lori Macfarlane, whose Australian address made practicing extremely inconvenient. The new member was the decidedly butch and out powerhouse Toni Gogin, and from the way Tucker held her hand and blew in her ear I wondered whether they were an item. But musically, the question remained irrelevant.

The Bryn Mawr gig, one of thirty-plus shows on a whirlwind u-drive-it tour, was free, but it was poorly publicized, attracting fewer than fifty fans—three quarters female, most not from Bryn Mawr, some still in high school. The opening act had gotten lost, so when Sleater-Kinney went on as scheduled at nine-thirty the crowd had been waiting over an hour, and the band was slightly bummed. Brownstein's cold kept her from yelling the vocal overlays, which can get pretty loud, and despite her splay-footed young Elvis C. moves, the stagecraft was more offhand than it had to be. At times during the nine nevertheless terrific songs—all they ever do, they're wise enough to know that at their level of competence even your favorite band can get boring after forty-five minutes—their concentration flagged. But at other times watching these young women ride the surge was enough to make me shout out loud. The truth is that most people can't make great rock and roll, or create themselves in public either. But the more people get the chance to try, the better off we are.

1996

Blown Away: Nirvana

With Christmas upon us, the marketing of the late great Kurt Cobain has begun in earnest. From the Geffen group there's the inevitable CD / audiocassette version of Nirvana's December 1993 *MTV Unplugged* appearance, already broadcast dozens of times on the channel to which it owes its existence, as well as *Nirvana Live! Tonight! Sold Out!!,* an eighty-three-minute videocassette utilizing scattered MTV snippets but no *Unplugged* material. And from MTV's print counterpart, *Rolling Stone,* there's a lovingly designed book, beautiful down to the woody fragrance of its heavy, unslick pages, that consists almost entirely of previously published *Stone* articles and is simply called *Cobain.*

A painful aura of regret hangs over all this retrospect, which proves yet again that recycling and capitalism go hand in hand. After all, once you shred the soda bottles you can make a picnic table out of them, but these reclamations are stuck permanently in the past. There's more future in Hole's *Live Through This* or R.E.M.'s *Monster*—or, hell, the Offspring's *Smash* or the Notorious B.I.G.'s *Ready To Die*—than in these or any other conceivable Nirvana products. Nirvana is blown away forever, and all a record or video or book or feature film or marble bust in the National Gallery can do about that is make us feel it more acutely. As it happens, however, all three of these consumer objects grab our coats with intelligence, discretion, and even, occasionally, originality—so much so that perhaps they might serve a social function after all, convincing a few more know-nothings that the yowling din of three undereducated, self-indulgent stoners is of enduring artistic value.

Unfortunately, or maybe just ironically, one of the many infuriating things Kurt Cobain accomplished with his suicide was to make it even harder for us to extricate the art he lived for from the fame he failed so utterly to comprehend. Not, please, the fame that killed him—the only credible suspect in this crime against nature is Kurt Cobain, although if you wanted to be nice you could say he was murdered by his own life. But no matter who done it, the bottom line is that his passing packs unprecedented mythic force. Where his Stupid Club colleagues Janis and Jimi and Brian and Jim all OD'd one way or another, succumbing to what Greil Marcus has designated "the common cold of rock deaths," this heroin user did not go comatose into that value-free night. He took his death into his own hands. With the oddly forgotten half-exception of Joy Division's Ian Curtis, he's the only major rock star ever to go out like that. So far.

This was a heinous act. Cobain's exit broke faith with the fans he meant most to—all the young losers who took his sloppy triumph over loserdom personally. It was a surrender of artistic control that subjected him to a sanctification he would certainly have kicked against had he remained alive. As Donna Gaines writes in one of the sharpest of *Cobain*'s inspired essays and field reports, it also "negated an unspoken contract among members of a generation who depended on one another to reverse the parental generation's legacy of neglect, confusion and frustration"; there were at least three apparently related suicides, one by a twenty-eight-year-old who shot himself directly after attending Cobain's vigil in Seattle. And in a classic cycle-of-neglect pattern for a divorce victim who believed his happy childhood ended when his parents split up, it demonstrated the limits of his love for his now abandoned daughter Frances Bean.

Yet it was also a sad, pitiable act, and a powerful negation. After Cobain's March 3 tranquilizer "accident" in Rome, anyone with decent antennae had to be aware that his pain wasn't just the latest superstar soap opera. But that was very late in a saga already rife with the band dissension, media feuds, marital sturm und drang, drug rumors, and foolish public pronouncements of a rock and roll ego out of control—knocked for a loop by the wealth and attention that makes fools even of those who spend their lives scheming for it (which, all stray fantasies granted, Cobain didn't). We didn't have to indulge in the sexist priggery of the Courtney-bashers or the guitar envy of the grunge-sucks contingent to find this bullshit somewhat tiresome, to assume that sooner or later Cobain would emerge on the other side of his nay-saying psychodrama, probably with his music sapped but we could dream. Well, he showed us, didn't he? Is there a louder way to say no in thunder than with a shotgun? However weak and irresponsible his final act, it was clearly the culmination of more misery than ordinary humans can imagine. Cobain reported all manner of agonies during his run, and I now believe every whine. The smug bastards who smirk at his claim that smack relieved the chronic burning in his stomach should eat ground glass so I can kick them in the gut.

It's impossible to hear deep into Nirvana's music unless you take Cobain's suffering seriously, and this, as much as their inchoate-sounding punk-metal-pop noise, is why the band quickly became a generational marker. Most parents feel life just isn't that bad. But their kids are convinced otherwise—starting with what they (supposedly) deserved and didn't get from said parents themselves. Cobain obviously wasn't the first rock hero to find power in his vulnerability—male fantasy figures from Elvis to Michael to Eddie Vedder have invited mothering as part of their natural shtick, and that's not to mention wimps as out-front and various as Pat Boone, James Taylor, Luther Vandross, and Morrissey. But no pure rock and roller at this level of talent and recognition has ever cried out for a hug as palpably as Kurt Cobain. Where the music on Nirvana's other albums was structured to transcend this need—guitar-bass-drums agon resolved in melody, subdued verse run over by cranked chorus—*MTV Unplugged in New York* accentuates it. Don't prejudge the CD by the concert you've seen, which is wooden visually and lacks decisive aural detail (as well as two excellent songs). But by no means forget how skinny and self-effacing Kurt looks on that tape, because the memory will intensify the plaintive frailty that is this music's greatest strength.

Recorded without retakes on November 18, 1993, in the comparative calm preceding the European tour that led to the suicide, the album comprises eight originals and six covers—three from the Meat Puppets, one each from David Bowie and Cobain's beloved Vaselines, and the haunted Leadbelly finale "Where Did

You Sleep Last Night." By deliberately avoiding the anthemic, it showcases the songcraft of one of the few guitarist-bandleaders ever to honestly massify the indie-rock aesthetic—although he was unhappy with how the trick worked out, which is one reason he took this opportunity to scale down. You'll hear Krist Novoselic's accordion, Dave Grohl's brushes, Lori Goldston's cello, ex-Germ Pat Smear's guitar, and the Kirkwood brothers sitting in on the *Meat Puppets II* selections. But mainly you'll hear Kurt Cobain's naked, nicotine-cured voice—sad, lyrical, weary, young; part lounge croon, part hillbilly drawl, part shy murmur, part stressed croak—pronouncing or sometimes slurring his leaping, depressive, half-fathomed words. The snatches that jump out sound eerie now. "I'm so tired I can't sleep." "Love myself better than you." "Well I swear that I don't have a gun." It's as if this were a concept album about how much he could blow away.

It isn't, of course. Cobain could just as well have chosen "Scentless Apprentice" ("You can't fire me because I quit"), or "Breed" ("I don't mind if I don't have a mind"), or why not "Milk It" ("Look on the bright side is suicide"). The difference is the musical form, which highlights verbal content never noted for its joie de vivre. What made Nirvana such a wildly popular band was how thoroughly its shoutable tunes, glorious cacophony, and ecstatic whomp subsumed the lived angst from which the music sprung. We're lucky that Kurt stamped his foot and insisted that Steve Albini replace Butch Vig between *Nevermind* and *In Utero,* because it leaves us with two sonically distinct, qualitatively equal versions of their verse-chorus-verse; Vig's, so digitalized Michael Azerrad calls it "a jagged stone encased in Lucite," emphasizes the slightly superior tunes, while Albini's is raw and harsh and galvanic. And we're lucky again that Cobain did *Unplugged* his way. For one thing, the acoustic arrangements show off the verse in his verse-chorus-verse—when Nirvana rocks, the choruses rool as you'd expect, but here both of the wee melodies that go into each song coexist as singalong partners, which often resets the lyrics as well. Simultaneously, the arrangements realize his emotional commitment to the homemade music he liked to talk about, with the Meat Puppets a gratifyingly adolescent replacement for the willful childishness of K Records' Calvin Johnson, whom Cobain admired as loyally and foolishly as he did the bozo art-metal of the Melvins.

Fundamentally, though, *Unplugged* is a memorial; it wouldn't exist if Cobain weren't dead, and his death determines its meaning. So right now, with the live-and-loud disc scheduled to complement it postponed (till next Christmas?), *Nirvana Live! Tonight! Sold Out!!* is the alternate image that might have been. Originally conceived by Cobain himself, it segues footage from several years of gigs, sometimes within a single song, and intersperses the music with offstage hijinks, dumb newscasts and major domos, and other marginalia. Visually, it's no *Stop Making Sense* or *Sign 'O' the Times,* but for a concert video it's smashing. The prize is a perverse solution to the "Smells Like Teen Spirit" perplex that enunciates every word, with anthems like "Lithium," "Breed," and "Territorial Pissings" also provided. No doubt a more musically undeniable live tape will come along sooner or later, but I'll be surprised if it says as much about the band. Because what's compelling about the interviews and horseplay here is that they're not compelling at all. Cobain is a good deal more insightful and charismatic than his bandmates, but he altogether lacks the knack for the media parry that's been a specialty of rock antiheroes since Lennon and Dylan. No less than his high school bassist and his D.C. drummer, he's a goof—an intelligent goof, with the love to back up his political impulses, but a goof nevertheless. So maybe he was right—maybe he didn't have what it takes to triumph, however sloppily, over loserdom.

What am I talking about? He settled that question forever on April 7. But damn it, it still kills me that I'll never have a more detailed answer. Because we need the goofs—we need them bad.

1994

Modern Maturity

The Goduncle: George Clinton

It's a tribute to George Clinton's genius that it took him forty years in the music business—the Parliaments got together in 1955, when Clinton was fifteen, twelve years before "I Wanna Testify" became the first of his four-count-'em-four top-forty hits—to get into the Rock and Roll Hall of Fame. To be honest, I'm still a little surprised he made it at all. He can't sing, he can't play, and he's not truly a songwriter, because his songs (not to mention his "songs") rarely make sense out of context, although as hip hop testifies, his jams sure do. Equally discomfiting for would-be canonizers, he's more than a nonrelic. Nonrelics you can deal with, and there are loads of them; Uncle Mick's 1993 *Wandering Spirit* is arguably a better record than Uncle Jam's 1993 *Hey Man . . . Smell My Finger,* not to mention his 1996 *T.A.P.A.F.A.O.M.,* credited in the wake of Parliament-Funkadelic's belated canonization to not just George Clinton but George Clinton and the P-Funk Allstars.

The difference is that Clinton never matured. Evolved, yes; became an elder, definitely; matured, no. Although it's odd to picture in the author of "No Head No Backstage Pass," and silly to make too much of, he seems to have remained with the same woman throughout the P-Funk period, and several of the kids he fathered by his first (and different) wife eventually helped him take it to the stage. But that cuts both ways—a fat lot of stability his domesticity signified back when he was gobbling LSD and dedicating his art to the Process Church of the Final Judgment. He remains a loose cannon—an outrageous, eccentric, visionary crank. Check the interview in *Seconds* where he forswore hip hop solidarity by dissing the world's most famous rapist—"Tyson had that Bronx 'Yo, bitch' mentality"—and then went on (for quite a while) about Charlie Manson being down with the Mafia. At the end, he summed up his own contribution to humanity: "I'm a lazy motherfucker. In fact, I'm looking for a place to lay down right now. You know, I know how to get away with shit. I'm the type of mother-fucker who'll go to your house, smoke your pot, eat your chicken, borrow twenty dollars from ya—I do that shit a lot of the time on purpose just to get all that wide-eyed awe out of the way."

In other words, canonizers have Clinton's go-ahead to dismiss him as a con man—a self-promoting svengali with a good band under his thumb. He himself told *Seconds* that the reason P-Funk albums wear so well is that they have Eddie Hazel and Bernie Worrell and the rest soloing all over them. But that's just George, greasing the wheels as usual. Spinoffs from Hazel's *Games, Dames and Guitar Thangs* to Worrell's *Blacktronic Science* go to show that Dr. Funkenstein—with essential conceptual help only from Bootsy Collins—is the artist, the others his material. Wheeler-dealing entrepreneur, harmonizer turned ace producer-arranger, r&b interlocutor as first rapper in the known universe—if any entertainer ever crossed the American huckster with the African trickster, it's George Clinton.

As this job description suggests, Clinton hasn't devoted much energy to smoothing out his resume. In 1979–1980, for instance, a band that might as well have been called P-Funk released seven albums on Warner Bros., Casablanca, and Atlantic under the names Parliament, Funkadelic, Bootsy's Rubber Band, Bootsy, Parlet, and the Brides of Funkenstein. Beset by fatigue, jealousy, and fiscal discontent, the Mothership was going the way of all communes by then, and while Clinton had produced definitive music in disco's teeth—*Mothership Connection* (1976), *Hardcore Jollies* (1976), *Funkentelechy vs. the Placebo Syndrome* (1977), *One Nation Under a Groove* (1978), and *Motor-Booty Affair* (1978), to stick to the prime stuff—he was having trouble positioning himself commercially, so most of these records are far from great. But as with Westbound-era Funkadelic, which takes some six albums to get its shit together, all of them are vehicles for memorable music, just like every other record he's ever put in gear.

It's another mark of his genius that his output doesn't compile comfortably past its own inconsistencies. PolyGram, always the most effective of his labels in the basic matter of keeping his oeuvre out there, naturally chose to make a two-CD set called *Tear the Roof Off 1974-1980* the flagship of its Funk Essentials series in 1993, and I played it with pleasure that entire summer. Because it isn't confined to radio edits and lasts two-and-a-half hours, it's less hyper than 1984's superb but disorienting serial orgasm, *Parliament's Greatest Hits.* And since Parliament was conceived as the pop band, two CDs worth of catchy riffs and chants are there for the sequencing. But when I go back to the originals, I find myself loving the playlets, the slow stuff, the jive—like *Funkentelechy's* "Sir Nose D'Voidoffunk" and "Wizard of Finance," or "Rumpofsteelskin," which fills out the endlessly entertaining first side of *Motor-Booty Affair.* It's the same with *Go fer Your Funk* and *"P" Is the Funk,* the two often ear-opening, always ex post facto outtakes collections Clinton put out himself on AEM from P-F HQ in Eastpointe, Michigan. And it applies as well to *Music for Your Mother,* two CDs of completist triumph comprising the A and B sides of every Westbound forty-five Funkadelic ever released. The fifteen nonalbum tracks, including even the filler instrumentals, are far from d'void. But the albums are full of funk, full of meaning, full of shit.

Just because Funkadelic and Parliament were the same doesn't mean they weren't different. The standard analysis distinguishes Funkadelic's heavy rock from Parliament's light funk, but from here it sounds to me like Funkadelic was the ghetto band. Forget "Papa Was a Rolling Stone" and Isaac Hayes and the rest of that velour. No music better evokes the bombed-out hopes of the black-power young in the early seventies—the druggy utopian fantasies that fuel the despair of *Sweet Sweetback's Baadasssss Song* and John Edgar Wideman's Homewood novels—than the Westbound albums. The most consistent are *Standing on the Verge of Getting It On* and *Let's Take It to the Stage,* but listening now, it's not hard to hear why *Free Your Mind and Your Ass Will Follow*— the first time Clinton was given the run of a studio, twenty-four acid-demented hours as thirty acid-demented minutes—is a cult fave in slackerland. Not only is the shit weird, the weirdness signifies. From the educational "Jimmy's Got a Little Bit of Bitch in Him" to the devotional "Cosmic Slop," *Music for Your Mother* is merely the cream.

Whether the secret is musical development, changing patterns of substance absorption, or enough money to go around, the Warners Funkadelic albums are sunnier, more rousing and communal—especially if you choose to view "The Doo Doo Chasers" as a jolly Jim Jones parody and the manically depressive *Electric Spanking of War Babies* as some combination of label kissoff and *There's a Riot Goin' On* (with Sly pitching in). And immediately following that came *Computer Games,* his first "solo" album for Capitol and without question the most spiritually complete record he's ever made. It's got jams—"Get Dressed" vies with the now obviously definitive "Atomic Dog" itself. It's got intimations of romantic responsibility from an old dog unlikely to be remembered for his love advice. But what's most noticeable in retrospect is how easily Clinton relates to the twin teen cultures of the time, rap and videogames. He's not just indulgent, he makes them his own, in an avuncular but far from uncritical way. No other nonrelic can make such a claim.

All that said, it must be added that in the years since *Computer Games*—which followed the first Funkadelic albums by only twelve years, after all—Clinton has slowed down. The first half (formerly side) of the *Computer Games* follow-up *You Shouldn't-Nuf Bit Fish* is so much fun it could change your philosophy, and don't think for a minute that 1989's *Cinderella Theory* or 1993's *Hey Man* . . . are more mortal than such B jams from the seventies as *Trombipulation* and *Uncle Jam Wants You.* But note that the man who was once an ever-flowing fountain of funk has released only four new albums since 1986. In later years his major source of currency, both historical and monetary, has been sampling, which he was Dutch uncle enough to find cool long before it was worth two cents a record and 50 percent of the publishing. As of 1993, which due to his popularity with the West Coast gin-and-juice set was a kind of heyday for him, he'd already cut some three hundred such deals, more than JB himself. Moreover, he was unlike JB in one crucial respect: hip hoppers always respected his moral vision as well as his beats. And in typical get-away-with-shit fashion, Clinton happily exploited this well-earned honor for meaning and profit.

Behind JB in the godfather sweepstakes when he cut *The Cinderella Theory* in 1989, he extracted cameos from Flav and Chuck while adjusting his Paisley Park debut to the electro style of his label head, one of the few pretenders he never accused of faking the funk—where race men unsure of their manhood assumed the supposed worst about the flamboyant little Twin Cities mulatto, the benevolent Uncle Jam didn't care how much bitch Prince had in him as long as his beats warped and woofed. On *Hey Man . . . Smell My Finger,* horn charts and nonsense syllables were primed for rental while guest shots from Chuck, Flav, Ice Cube, Dr. Dre, Humpty Hump, Yo Yo, Kam, and MC Breed evoked straight-up hip hop. And speaking of moral vision, the youngbloods' gratuitously tough talk and wishfully literal protests pointed up whose mind was free and whose wasn't—even if Clinton couldn't resist the self-praise that was funny when Trick James posed a threat, but seemed like rap cliches after hip hop had proved him as large as he thought he was. Then, changing labels yet again just as black music was rediscovering the comforts of r&b proper, he declared it exactly the moment to construct his most luxurious groove album ever. So on *T.A.P.A.F.A.O.M.,* smooth high-register choruses male and female body-surfed along on buoyant booty-bump bass lines as Clinton and associates rapped and sang about the beach and the Cherokee trunk without disrespecting the mirrored boudoir or the overstuffed layaway couch.

None of the late records certifies his nonrelic status or fully reinforces our longing for Clinton's impact to remain cultural as well as musical. Only a hit could do that, preferably a monster untainted by novelty, which seems a cruel demand to place on the man who lit up the phones with "Flashlight" and made a star of Mr. Wiggles the Worm. No "My Ding-a-Ling" for this name brand—he needs his own "Rockin' in the Free World," which I hereby nominate as P-Funk's first cover version ever (b/w Sun Ra's "Rocket 9"). Nevertheless, the evolution of these barely diminished albums bespeaks not commercial expediency but a responsiveness that can only make one wonder what George Clinton thinks of Tricky and the Chemical Brothers. And if one wonders hard enough, one may conclude that one has a couple of clues.

Hardcore Jollies's scandalously scatalogical "Promentalshit-backwashpsychosis Enema Squad (The Doo Doo Chasers)" isn't actually a Jim Jones parody, I don't think, although it was sure timed right and does ape true believers in the throes of the call-and-response so oft extolled in utopian accounts of the African-American tradition Jones perverted. "The world is a toll-free toilet," Clinton intones, and the band comes right back at him with a ragtag "The world is a toll-free toilet." "Our mouths neurological assholes," Clinton continues, and once again the congregation recites. And so it goes, through Tidy Bowls and music to get your shit together and meburgers and lunch meat and holy shit, half shock comedy and half postcountercultural ridicule of the ego and the intellect and the decay of the word. The humor lends a depth thus far unknown to Tricky's morbid maunderings, and the message conveys its own wildly burlesqued hope of redemption, but the darkness of the historical analysis is ahead of its time, and so, significantly, is the murkiness of the textures, in which falsetto doowop harmonizers obscure phrases like "in a state of constipated notion" and Peter Lorre can be overheard asking, "Which one is George Clinton?" That's easy—he's the one with the stinky diaper. And if anybody ever hires him for a trip hop record, "The Doo Doo Chasers" is ripe for remix—as squishy as old Limburger.

As for chemical brotherhood, refer to Capitol's *Greatest Funkin' Hits,* a 1996 remix album that avoids the promotional overkill and commercial double jeopardy of its half-assed demigenre. The live track, the previously unreleased, the woofing bookends, the recycled P-Funk show-stoppers, the remakes from George C.'s unnoteworthy 1986 *R&B Skeletons in the Closet* and Jimmy G.'s unnoticed 1985 *Federation of Tackheads* (featuring, one is told, Clinton's wayward kid brother)—all are conceived as atomically mongrel antidotes to what the funkateering annotator-illustrator Pedro Bell labels "the flunkmare of wooferless pop musik." Commercially it's a slightly dated hip hop exploitation, with new interpolations from Coolio, Ice Cube, and Humpty Hump, and musically it's sex-various but also heartbeat-deep, which Clinton has always told us is the way any good sex must be. In short, it's not uncorny. The oldest mix on the record, however, is the previously uncollected twelve-inch of "Atomic Dog," which I hadn't heard as such since the middle eighties. And in the sonics of its hyped-up synth-bass I could easily discern arena-techno's block-rockin' beats. One can only look forward to Clinton's excursions into drum 'n' bass, conning who knows what skinny London boy with digital smarts.

The best of all possible worlds, at least in this dystopian century, will have the heart to give it up to the goduncle for as long as he shall slam. Maybe we don't need him, but for sure we can use him. Fried ice cream remains a reality, and somebody has to stand up and shout about it.

1993–1997

Pop Songs to God: Al Green

All aesthetic judgments are open to perpetual debate, but try these on for size. Al Green isn't just the last soul man; except for James Brown, he's the greatest. And except for Aretha Franklin, he's also the most gifted singer ever to work the turf. In fact, he may conceivably be the finest vocalist rock and roll has ever known—even though he supposedly retired from secular music many years ago.

As with most popular singers, Green's vocal style transmutes and resynthesizes his speech. The complication is that when Green is on—which means anytime this intensely self-alienated man can be observed in what feels to him like a role, in performance or offstage or at business—his talk is even more stylized than his singing. It combines three major elements. The *downhome* is rooted in the migrations of Green's upbringing on an Arkansas dirt farm and in the black downtown of Grand Rapids, Michigan. The *ersatz-formal,* common among undereducated successes, usually takes a preacherly tone in its black variant; Green conjures the professorial as well. And the *cute* is his own innovation. The man crinkles up his voice as if he's trying out for *Sesame Street;* he drawls like someone affecting a drawl; he hesitates and giggles and murmurs and swallows his words.

When he sings, Green melts these mannerisms down until they flow and shores them up, rhythmically, against their own nervousness. This style then becomes the vehicle for a persona that is modest, even fragile, yet undeniably compelling, a term that in Green's case can mean only one thing: sexy. One wants to go to bed with a person who is downhome, ersatz formal, and cute because these qualities have their conventionally attractive counterparts—earthy, self-possessed, vulnerable—and yet are also idiosyncratic. Combined with Green's physical charms—lean body, winsome face, warm vocal timbre—they make for a fantasy that is both sweet and original. And not just for women. Green's sexiness is so pervasive that no male who responds to his singing can do so without feeling a jolt that transcends identification.

Of course, we turn on not to a real person, but to a fantasy of a real person that compounds several roles. Moreover, the chemistry is not our own. Green manufactures his persona, in a process as calculated as a Gatorade assembly line and as natural as the production of sugar in photosynthesis, for the same reason all stars do—to inspire admiration while retaining control of his ego base. It can be disturbing to realize this, but it is rarely decisive. In October 1974, a woman who had gotten close enough to Al Green to learn that he was nowhere near as self-possessed, earthy, or vulnerable as a fan might hope persisted in her dreams of matrimony anyway. Green rejected her. In retaliation, she attempted to disfigure him with a scalding pot of grits and then killed herself. I don't know why the woman continued to love Green: maybe she was still ensnared by the fantasy, or maybe there was something in the reality that continued to satisfy her. Maybe both. For those of us who bask in Green's ability to create fantasies of character amid billowy air-castles of pitch and timbre and rhythm, that's just the way it is.

Green was a major star in his brief heyday, putting six consecutive singles in *Billboard*'s top ten between the winter of 1972 and the summer of 1973. But his artistry has often been undervalued by people who should know better. He gets barely a sentence in Gerri Hirshey's *Nowhere to Run,* the only history of soul to grant equal weight to the Stax-Volt and Motown sensibilities he synthesized and transcended, and a mere three pages in Peter Guralnick's *Sweet Soul Music,* based in the Memphis where he's lived and worked as a recording artist and preacher for a quarter of a century. This neglect is partly an accident of timing—because he concocted his style just as black pop's visionary youngbloods were figuring out funk and arriving at disco, he had few advocates and, in the secular realm, no heirs. And partly it's due to his singular musical ideas. Soul goes nowhere without a bottom, and especially when he worked with his greatest producer, Willie Mitchell, Green's records boasted an exceptionally fat and propulsive low range. He could and can belt off that bottom—that's why we treasure *Al Green Gets Next to You,* cut before his style was finalized. But his genius breaks free at—and over the top of—a register that darts and floats and soars into falsetto with startling frequency and beguiling ease. Green's brashly feminine and seductively woman-friendly signature sound was his ticket to stardom. Among soul traditionalists, however, his implicit disdain for old studs like Wilson Pickett's man-and-a-half and new studs like chesty Teddy Pendergrass cost him credibility.

The main reason Green's music outlasted these cavils so spectacularly is that it's beautiful—so physically attractive that denying its pleasures proved a deprivation few who loved any kind of rock and roll were willing to live with. But Green's acute musical intelligence also helped. He's a structurally unconventional composer whose lyrics veer savvily between stone-simple romantic vows and tormented reveries on the heaven-and-earth split that haunts all soul music. And his best-remembered performances aren't just lovely pop songs—they showcase an almost jazzlike filigree work that only Marvin Gaye and Aretha herself have ever approached. Although it's reported that Green can spend hundreds of hours perfecting one vocal, often his music sounds off the cuff if not out of left field. The miracle is that once you're aware of this contradiction it disappears. Fabricated or improvised? You can't tell, and it doesn't matter—he seems to inhabit a state of late-night hyperconsciousness where obsessive calculation and unmoored inspiration meet on the other side of the moon.

Green got his professional start as a young teenager, singing lead in a family gospel group, a stint that ended when he was thrown out of the group and the house for listening to Jackie Wilson. His father, perceiving all that baby-workout as devil's music, couldn't understand that his son had a different kind of religion. "Music engulfs one's soul to exert himself beyond imagination," Green has said. "That music just tripped me out." Later, in 1967, when Green was twenty, he and another Grand Rapids musician made a record called "Back Up Train" that eventually hit forty-one in *Billboard.* He never got a cent for it. Soon he headed south, where a 1969 encounter with Willie Mitchell in Midland, Texas, induced him to seek his fortune in Memphis. There was chart action by early 1970, but not until late that year, when a cover of the Temptations' "I Can't Get Next to You" was a major r&b hit, did Green and Mitchell feel they were on their way. And not until almost a year later, with "Tired of Being Alone" and its number-one follow-up "Let's Stay Together," did they perfect their pop formula—a shifting amalgam of cream and grit, fluff and guts, feathery strings and power-packed beats, wayward promises and passionate truths.

Although Green remained a supernatural cover artist—eventually, the Doors, the Bee Gees, Hank Williams, Willie Nelson, Roy Orbison, Kris Kristofferson, and "Unchained Melody" would all get the treatment—by this time he was writing most of his own material, often with Mitchell and sometimes with drummer Al Jackson, Jr. or guitarist Teenie Hodges. Although both music and persona were in a conservative black tradition, both were romantic enough, at least in theory, to pass as white pop—and this is what Green intended. Yet although he was always marketed as a singles artist, his groove as well as his song sense insured that all eleven albums he cut between 1970 and 1979 would sustain start to finish. His greatest-hits collections make surefire gifts and his four-CD set preserves an unusually worthy level of collectible as it cherry-picks, with the long live "How Can You Mend a Broken Heart" a revelation. But lovers should just collect the whole set—starting, I suppose, with *Call Me* (1973), *Livin' for You* (1973), *I'm Still in Love With You* (1972), *Al Green Gets Next to You* (1970), and *The Belle Album* (1978).

Because Green's records are so enduring, and because he's worked the gospel circuit since 1980, even admirers astonished by the television appearances preserved on Robert Mugge's 1984 *The Gospel According to Al Green,* where his expressive face makes a startling impression, often fail to factor in his live performances. But the stage is where he overwhelms his own good taste, providing a subtlety and oomph not so easily available in your living room—until Green has been seen live just once. Not only are his clothes tailored to show off the lithe eloquence of his body; they also humanize that body. In the early days he would even appear carrying a shoulder bag and looking slightly rumpled, as if he'd just gotten off a Greyhound, and he likes to perform with a layer of fuzz on his face, making it impossible to tell whether he's growing a beard or just forgot to shave. Every time he draws back from the microphone so his high moans can waft unamplified over the arena, he works his savvy, diffident style of sexual confidence on all of us who strain toward the stage to hear. Every time he laughs mischievously at the passion elicited by his boyish come-on, he shares a joke about the pleasures of the tease. His interplay with the band is a model of generous authority, his interplay with the crowd a dream of self-possessed appeal. And as the climactic riff sets in, he strides and belts manfully enough to get the house off.

Needless to say, all this became more complicated once Green abandoned pop. It was *The Belle Album,* his first self-production, that signaled the departure. Going for an airier sound on songs that implied religious themes, it negotiated a decisive turn for the star who was by then the pastor-proprietor of Memphis's Full Gospel Tabernacle—a spiritual balancing act captured in all its precarious brilliance by the likes of "Jesus Is Waiting" and his acknowledged masterpiece, "Take Me to the River." Most of Green's Christian albums aren't as readily accessible as his secular work, or as musically inspired. But for unbelievers with ears to hear, they have their own peaks, more individuated than in traditional gospel—peaks that share as much conceptually with Green's own pop songs to God as with the Swan Silvertones canon they derive from. Among the album highlights were 1981's all-sacred *Higher Plane,* the 1986 Willie Mitchell reunion *Soul Survivor,* and 1987's *I Get Joy,* where Green's covers of "He Ain't Heavy, He's My Brother" and "You've Got a Friend" effortlessly transported his Jesus fixation into the realm of universalist-humanist schlock. As Green broadened his interpretation of what might constitute musical service to the Lord, especially after he was elected to the Rock and Roll Hall of Fame in 1995, his show evolved into a wacky, magical amalgam of soul and pop in a gospel framework.

More than anyone else in soul—even nightclub preacher Solomon Burke, plainly a less tortured artist—Green embodies the contradictions of the style. Back when it looked as if he might achieve conventional superstardom, the riff that climaxed his live show went with "Love and Happiness," a playful euphemism for good sex and all the good things that go with it. But when he settled temporarily for the pop second-string, the show stopper became "Take Me to the River." You get the feeling with many soul singers that the spiritual root of their music (call it God) and its emotional referent (by which I mean sex) coexist at the center of their vision. Green apotheosized this confusion at its most extreme in a lyric that was unclear in a mystical rather than euphemistic way. Rambling past an apparent referent to his musical past (the phrase "sweet sixteen" is a title from *Livin' for You*), he seems to beg for a sexual deliverance that is identical to a country baptism. He demands to have his feet on the ground and walk on the water at the same time. All of soul's creators have longed to do just that. None of them have come closer than Al Green.

As Green passed fifty, his voice began to show a few rough spots, as voices will. Yet it remains surpassingly youthful even so, still hinting at the access to eternity that has been the goal of his art in all its guises. After all, defying mortality is what rock and rollers have been doing since the first rush wore off around 1958 or so. We know we're not going to get away with it forever. But we intend to put in our time trying.

1975–1991–1995

Wasted on the Young: Neil Young

What makes Neil Young our favorite rock and roll survivor isn't his famous changeability—folkie to rocker, choirboy to grunge daddy, earth-firster to technophile, dove to hawk to dove. It's how stubbornly he sticks at what he does best. His true chameleon moves—the sci-fi voices of *Trans,* the rockabilly joke, the little country record that wasn't—came during his lost Reagan-Geffen years, and even then his music was all the same. Loud or soft, raw or cooked, impassioned or half-assed, smart or stupid, Young is always simple harmonically and melodically—classic when he's on, dull when he's off. The lyrics invariably mix literal clarity and obscure fancy. His soulful quaver has remained unmistakable as its eerie high end ages. Rick James and Booker T. connections notwithstanding, he's as d'void of funk as any ex-folkie working. And although he's renowned for his protogrunge guitar, most of his major albums, including *After the Gold Rush* (1970), *Rust Never Sleeps* (1979), and *Freedom* (1989), give equal time to his quiet/acoustic side.

Toting up his canon, most would fill out that short list with the demented *Tonight's the Night* (recorded 1973, including "four or five songs on the first side all in a row" one drunken Crazy Horse night; released 1975) and then add a few favorites from among *Everybody Knows This Is Nowhere* (1969), *Zuma* (1975), *Comes a Time* (1978), *Ragged Glory* (1991), and *Mirror Ball* (1995). Except for *Comes a Time,* these are all guitar showcases, rockinger than anything on the short list, which some would claim should feature *Ragged Glory* rather than *Freedom* anyway. They're all fine records, too. Yet although I recognize Neil Young as the principal font of Thurston Moore/Kurt Cobain industrial avant-primitivism and thus of the Roar—the loud, rhythmic, bone-drenching electric-guitar drone that was grunge's gift to our brains, our ear-holes, and our bodies themselves—and although I live for out-of-body experiences like the tidal wave that was "Like a Hurricane" at the Palladium in 1976 or the twenty-minute serial explosion that was "Down by the River" at the Pier in 1985, I take my recorded fix from the finale of *Live Rust* (1979) or perhaps the two-CD *Weld* (1991). Canonwise, I prefer *Comes a Time*—or better still, nothing, since with Neil Young even more than most rock and rollers the notion of a canon is a kind of desecration, an insult to a lifetime of principled mess. If there's anything wrong with *Freedom* and the nineties albums that followed, it's their consistency, even their quality. They're not *weird* enough, and they suggest the possibility that weirdness is now beyond him.

Or maybe it's just that weird isn't weird anymore. Emerging from the swamps of Reaganism just as Bush the Yalie replaced Ron the cowboy, Young was hailed as a respected elder in Alternative Nation, where eccentricity wasn't just tolerated but expected. Thus his chance of crossing the line into formal un-acceptability dipped radically—even 1991's *Arc,* a precise equiv-alent to Lou Reed's scandalous *Metal Machine Music,* barely raised an eyebrow. Political unacceptability might come easier—it would be surprising if in some part of himself Young *wasn't* sympathetic to survivalist compounds, Internet revolutionaries, and bank robbers on a mission, although his shock at the Gulf War makes clear that he could never hack terrorist bombings. But in the musical environment of Alternative Nation, where pop is a bad word and the blues-based basics Young championed against seventies progressivism are finally showing stretch marks, an environment that respects out-and-out crazies like Hasil Adkins and Daniel Johnston and professional neurotics like Lydia Lunch and Genesis P-Orridge and avant-gardists in good standing like Derek Bailey and Sonny Sharrock, an environment where provo-cateurs like Primus and Nine Inch Nails are mainstream while the incorrigibly self-involved Stephen Malkmus and Polly Jean Harvey reign as critics' darlings, an environment that has supported Neilkins from J Mascis to Howe Gelb to Ira Kaplan, Young is hard put to wig out.

Although I'm down with all the albums on the short list, I love my very favorite for sentimental reasons. That would be the folky and/or country-rock *After the Gold Rush,* which was where I first fell for Neil and which will always remind me of a year of stoned solitude in L.A., the morning sunshine warming my melancholy without dispersing it. After that, *Rust Never Sleeps*—for the survivalist "Powderfinger" and the lumpen-lovin' "Welfare Mothers" above all—and then *Tonight's the Night,* as influential and definitive as it was unconventional, and well behind that *Freedom,* a triumphant return that will always mean more to young alternarockers who'd never fallen for a new Neil Young album than to the oldsters whose life and lives it validated. But well ahead of *Freedom,* maybe ahead of everything but *After the Gold Rush,* the Neil Young records I reaccess with the sharpest pleasure are all out-of-print vinyl obscurities, although the first three will assuredly be reissued just as soon as the master remasters them, conceivably in this millennium: *Time Fades Away* (1973) and *On the Beach* (1974), *Hawks and Doves* (1980) and *Trans* (1982). The first pair—released between the heroin deaths that inspired *Tonight's the Night* and the cult enthusiasm that greeted it, thus setting Young gallumphing toward his *Comes a Time-Rust Never Sleeps-Live Rust* trifecta—address existential failure. And in the wake of that trifecta, the second pair sidestep artistic success, instead musing on the miasmas of American politics and groping primitive computer technology, greasing Young's slide into a confusion they render tuneful along the way. The first pair transcend mess, the second neatness; the first pair inspire passionate advocates, the second sane defenders. But none of the four are canonical—at least not yet. And without question that adds to their charm.

Time Fades Away rejected the slickness of the L.A. seventies as forcefully as *Tonight's the Night,* only no one took it seriously. Young wasn't the first to package selected concert recordings of new songs in a world where live albums are supposed to exploit catalogue—compare the MC-5's *Kick Out the Jams.* But the tactic was widely regarded as cynical and lazy until Young translated it to the "studio," where the rough bar-band aesthetic of the home-recorded *Tonight's the Night* proved so compelling that in retrospect Crazy Horse sound solid, even pretty—especially up against the wiry caterwaul of *Time Fades Away*'s Stray Gators, a defter bunch whose country tinge was, as usual with Young, considerably less Nashville than L.A. believed. For Crazy Horse's irreplaceable wild-ass conviction it substitutes the ragged glory of crack musicians who sense they're in on something but aren't sure it's worth the pain. Their prize is a display of the same postcounter-cultural drug-casualty despair that fuels *Tonight's the Night,* explicitly compounded by the addled anxieties of a stone loner—with visions of stardom he acknowledges and disparages in so many words—who's somehow reached a mass audience via "Heart of Gold," *Harvest,* and Crosby, Stills & Nash.

Sardonic and harrowing when it invokes the cultural moment and the woes ordained to follow, *Time Fades Away* is fond and clear-eyed when it turns to the lost past and love's solace. It peaks with the wavery pitches and obsessive repetitions of "Don't Be Denied," a warmly inspirational piece of chin-upsmanship that runs aground on the cultural moment, and then "Last Dance," which exploits and exposes the deep, useless relief of getting lost in rhythm—even, or especially, a whomp as crude as that of Turtle-turned-Gator Johnny Barbata and the kindly sasquatch in the patched jeans. Both songs address the fans all live albums assume on an uncommonly direct, one-to-one level—not as cheering section cum power supply or commodifying threat to artistic freedom, but as kids whose dreams of success Young knows well enough to worry about. If those dreams come true, if "a pauper in a naked disguise" becomes "a millionaire through a business-man's eyes," love and friendship will get wasted. But if they're dashed, it's even worse, because instead of "Working on your own time/Laid back and laughing," you get stuck on a freeway treadmill of job and home, job and home. In case anyone's missed the point, the final track ends with Neil and occasional Gators repeating the word "no" sixty-eight times, in groups of three with one quintuplet for variety. When he's done he hollers "Last dance"—the title's first and only appearance.

Succumbing to this despair, the private, nakedly self-indulgent *On the Beach* shrank from the kids *Times Fades Away* reached out to. Basted together by drop-ins from Crazy Horse, the Gators, the Band, even CSNY, its homemade rock invited comparison to Bob Dylan's *Planet Waves,* a David Geffen kissoff that preceded Young's weirdnesses by nearly a decade, and also Skip Spence's

Oar, in which the Moby Grape acid casualty got so casual he fell off the edge of the record. And though loyalists bought it anyway—it was the only one of the five standard issues between *Harvest* and *Comes a Time* to make top twenty—it seemed ominously disoriented and forlorn. But now that Young has demonstrated that his season of rue didn't signal a descent into autism, we can hear it as one of those rare instances when a slop bucket holds a mess of pottage. Back then I admired the self-knowledge of two lines: "Though my problems are meaningless that don't make them go away" (from the whiny "On the Beach") and "It's hard to say the meaning of this song" (from the wacked-out "Ambulance Blues"). Now I'm impressed that even in his despondency Young never lost his grip, because *On the Beach* lets us empathize with the depths he'd sunk to, with clear and specific attention to his fame.

"I need a crowd of people," the loner admits, "but I can't face them every day." So in "For the Turnstiles" he compares himself to a bush-leaguer hung out to dry, an explorer going to his granite reward, a sailor serenading his seasick mama as a pimp charges ten at the door. How does such pain measure up against the nine-to-five drag of "Last Dance"? Like heaven. But Young is still the one who has to get up and fill that laid-back time when he doesn't have a thing to laugh about, obliged to unloose some power within that will help a prisoner of the freeway get home. He has a right to mewl about the "good old days"—"Then the money was not so good/But we still did the best we could." And his means to that power is his El Lay buddies, who fashion their homemades with such ingrained skill and traditionalism that *On the Beach* sounds in retrospect like a found picking session from some psychedelic Appalachian-Sierra outback—miles, eras, eons from the alt meanderings of Palace, early Sebadoh, even Howe Gelb's Giant Sand, beholden to and adoring of Neil Young though all may be.

Over the next few years, Young made up with Steve Stills, birthed the recognizable *Zuma* and *American Stars 'n Bars*, and compiled the three-LP *Decade*, with its famous annotation favoring the ditch over "Heart of Gold"'s middle of the road—a musical testament for the kids who would soon found Alternative Nation. In the wake of these accommodations, *Comes a Time* seems like the record he wishes *Harvest* had been: the most assured folk music anyone save fellow Canadians Kate & Anna McGarrigle managed after *Blood on the Tracks* ended Bob Dylan's commitment to quality in 1975. And just as Dylan had in 1965, Young immediately trumped himself by honoring the most radical rock and roll in the air without compromising his sense of the fundamentals—except that where Dylan risked lynching when he went electric, *Rust Never Sleeps*'s rhetorical rapprochement with punk only strengthened his hold on fans who by then cheered his iconoclasm. And having defeated fame's great bogey, the fear that a public identity will induce you to do the thing that is not-yourself, he started feeling around for how far he could go.

So inspired by whatever—Central America? Iran? Ron the cowboy?—Young proceeded to muck about with war and peace. Defined by Ben Keith's laconic dobro and Rufus Thibodeaux's sawing fiddle, *Hawks and Doves* is as guarded and slight as any concept album ever. The supposed "doves" side takes off unsteadily on "Little Wing," creaks into gear with a mind-bender starring a naked rider, a telephone booth, and some prehistoric birds, squeezes a bridge by an electronically treated "munchkin" into another nutty song, and climaxes with a modern sea chantey about, it just may be, a yachtsman who as of "1971" (the year is named in full) still hasn't gotten over a skirmish with "the Germans"—and "a young mariner" who hopes he can "kill good." All pretty unsettled for peace. In fact, disregard the nuclear incident left playfully unspecified in "Comin' Apart at Every Nail" and the uneventfulness of the five brief songs on the thirteen-minute "hawks" side comes as a relief—not Nashville, just straight praise of true love, the job-and-home life, and the American Federation of Musicians ("Live music is better bumper stickers should be issued"!). With its unambiguous parting words—"If you hate us, you just don't know what you're sayin' "—*Hawks and Doves* is either a defense of the ordinary Americans outside Young's audience or a realistic appraisal of the ordinary Americans in it. It's no last word, but as with *On the Beach,* its fragile music and incomplete analysis have gained a cockeyed lyricism with the years, and the simple songs on side two are very strong. It was politically incorrect before there was any cachet in it. It normalizes the weird and vice versa. It's probably Young's most underappreciated album.

We know now what inspired *Trans* two years later—not Devo or Kraftwerk, as was conjectured at the time, so much as a private struggle no one could call self-indulgent. Young's second son was severely afflicted with cerebral palsy, requiring not only hours of exhausting work from his parents, but an intimacy with the computers *Trans* is still mindlessly believed to satirize. Although it's remembered for masking Young's all-too-human voice behind Vocoders and octave dividers, *Trans* is typically bifurcated, balancing three naturalistic Crazy Horse songs that include the decidedly unfuturist "Like an Inca" against the computerized material. His most hummable album of the eighties, it flaunts a fictional science that came naturally to a guy who was calling spaceships "Mother Nature's silver seed" back on *After the Gold Rush.* And while the likes of "Sample and Hold" and "Computer Cowboy" are certainly humorous, to call them satirical is to miss the benignly utopian goofiness with which they accept a digitalization whose limits they plainly perceive. Given what Young was going through, *Trans* is heroically lighthearted, a spiritual if not aesthetic achievement on a par with *Tonight's the Night* itself. It's probably Young's most misunderstood album.

No one understood it worse than David Geffen, who didn't steal Young from Warners so he could turn into some Chipmunks joke, and the businessman's nay, rather than Young's turn to jingoism, may be why the oddball records leading back to Warner Bros. and *Freedom* leave so little taste in the mouth. But those days seem gone forever. From standards like "Rockin' in the Free World" and "I'm the Ocean" and "Harvest Moon" and "Wrecking Ball" to personal favorites like "Safeway Cart" and "Piece of Crap" and "Downtown" and "Music Arcade" and the import-only-so-far "Cocaine Eyes," the inductee who serenaded Rock and Roll Hall of Fame fat cats with "F*!#in' Up" and a song no one I asked had ever heard before is classic-not-dull as a matter of habit. You might even wonder whether he hasn't grown so confident in his aversion to complacency that he could play out his career as solidly and unmomentously as, say, Muddy Waters—never dismissed, but taken for granted. Who can say? No previous rock and roller has reached this place. And while taken for granted is never enough, and no pitch of permanent vitality will answer the artist's eternal question of what to do for an encore, Young at fifty seems certain to keep unfurling rock and roll's vastest major body of work.

Yet awesome though it is in its way, this work is also definitively modest. "They all sound the same," shouts an audience dissident to introduce 1997's *Year of the Horse,* inspiring the affable artist to explain, "It's all one song." Low on intellectual content if not verbal stimulation, it could be said to be about nothing but itself—a pure affirmation like gospel music, only with no room for the divine, a peculiar and telling absence in such a dreamy if not spiritual guy. Like the Rolling Stones, Young celebrates rock and roll as form. But because he has no use for the Stones' meanness or professional precision, he makes that form seem incorrigibly democratic as they never do. Weirdness is his trademark in part because he's pretty weird. But in part it's his version of the Ramones' gabba-gabba-hey. He accepts you he accepts you because you accept him you accept him, and round and round it goes, self-affirming and self-negating, a perfectly and completely inexplicit demonstration of why rock and roll means as much as Shakespearian tragedy or the contents of the Louvre to people who are supposed to know better—as well as a lot of equally worthy people who aren't.

1997

CREDITS

Except as noted below, all the essays in this book other than the introduction originally appeared in *The Village Voice,* and are copyright © V.V. Publishing Corporation, reprinted by permission of *The Village Voice.* All have been edited slightly, and a few combine different essays on the same subject.

The essays on Chuck Berry and the Rolling Stones are slightly revised versions of essays that first appeared in *The Rolling Stone Illustrated History of Rock & Roll.*

The essay on John Lennon is a condensed version of an essay that first appeared in *The Ballad of John and Yoko,* by the editors of *Rolling Stone,* edited by Jonathan Cott and Christine Doudna.

The paragraph on the Beatles originally appeared in *Request,* and is copyright ©1996 Request Media, Inc. The article originally appeared in the Beatles Limited Collectors' Edition of *Request* magazine.

The essay on the New York Dolls is a slightly revised version of my essay, "New York Dolls," in *Stranded: Rock and Roll for a Desert Island,* edited by Greil Marcus. Copyright © 1979 by Alfred A. Knopf Inc. Reprinted by permission of the publisher.

The essay on Public Enemy interpolates material from a piece that first appeared in *L.A. Weekly* into a piece that first appeared in *The Village Voice.*

The essay on Lou Reed combines essays written for *The Village Voice* with a review that first appeared in *Spin* in 1996.

The essays on PJ Harvey and Pere Ubu are revised versions of pieces that first appeared in *Spin* in 1995 and 1997.

The essay on Al Green combines essays written for *The*

INDEX

Dolphy, Eric, 95, 430
Domino, Fats, 17, 126
Donato, Chris, 297
Donegan, Lonnie, 105
Doobie Brothers, 81, 230
Doors, 340, 465
Dors, Diana, 197
Dorsey, Jimmy, 40
Dorsey, Tommy, 40
Dostoyevsky, Fyodor, 126
Douglas, Alan, 95
Douglas, Jack, 205, 206
Dowd, Tom, 102
Dresch, Donna, 444
Duncan, Tommy, 40
Dunlap, Slim, 302, 303
Dunn, Duck, 98
Durant, Will, 276
Dust Brothers, 267
Dylan, Bob, 11, 32, 45, 51, 72, 77, 93, 99, 110, 113, 127, 140, 141, 143, 154, 194, 195, 196, 201, 204, 248, 257, 366, 367, 404, 416, 451, 471, 473

Eagles, 179, 180
Eare, Joseph, 281
Earth, Wind & Fire, 143, 252
Easter, Mitch, 298
Eckstine, Billy, 18
Eddy, Duane, 190
Eddy, Nelson, 32
Edge, 412
Edison, Sweets, 21
Edsels, 196
Edson, Richard, 309
Eek-a-Mouse, 266
Eidel, Philippe, 336
El Dorados, 374
Electra, Carmen, 378
Ellington, Duke, 18, 38–39, 127
Ellis, Pee Wee, 128, 129, 130
Ellis, Robert, 408
Ellison, Lorraine, 239
Emerson, Lake & Palmer (ELP), 227
Eno, Brian, 140, 153, 434
Epstein, Brian, 104, 117
Equals, 345
Erasers, 219
Esposito, Joe, 54, 55–56, 58

Essential Logic, 293
Ethridge, Chris, 239
Etting, Ruth, 39
Evans, Richard, 336
Everly Brothers, 110
Excuse 17, 444, 445

Fabulous Poodles, 216
Faces, 180
Fadela, Chaba, 333, 334
Fagen, Donald, 175, 394–395
Fairport Convention, 163, 167
Fairweather, 179
Falwell, Jerry, 418
Farafina, 330
Fat Boys, 278
Faulkner, William, 126
Feelies, 372, 397
Felker, Clay, 5
Fiedler, Leslie, 46
Fier, Anton, 226, 435
Finch, Jennifer, 396, 399
Findlay, Seaton, 62
Fine Young Cannibals, 24
Finnigan, Mike, 95
Finster, Howard, 53
Fiske, John, 353, 354, 355, 356
Fitch troupe, 40
Fitzgerald, Ella, 26
Flavor Flav, 268, 273, 459
Fleming, Rhonda, 367
Flipper, 246
Flock of Seagulls, 261
Flood, 412
Fluffy, 229, 231
Flying Burrito Brothers, 11, 372
Fogelberg, Dan, 180, 359, 361, 363
Foghat, 81
Forbert, Steve, 404
Ford, Henry, 269
Fouratt, Jim, 291
Four Lads, 17, 18
Fowler, Pete, 177–178, 182, 183
Fowley, Kim, 308, 361
Foxxx, Freddie, 284
Frampton, Peter, 180, 207
Franco, Luamba, 11, 341
Franklin, Aretha, 32, 35, 56, 100–103, 136, 416, 462, 464